To:

Mr. Virgil Pettaway.

From

Miss Allison Uhl

# Phoenix Suns

## *Rising to the Top with the "Team of Oddities"*

by Lee Shappell

Sagamore Publishing
Champaign, Illinois

Production Manager: Susan M. McKinney
Cover and photo insert design: Michelle R. Dressen
Editors: Russ Lake, David Hamburg

Library of Congress Catalog Card Number: 93-84954
ISBN: 0-915611-84-8

Printed in the United States.

*To Patty, for her support, encouragement, and back rubs while she was working on a pretty significant project of her own—our first baby.*

———————————————————

# Contents

# *Acknowledgments*

---

Let's just say that I came into this a bit naive. For all you aspiring first-time authors out there, take it from me: it's twice as big a project as you might envision.

So you need help, lots of it.

First, it would have been impossible to do this book without the cooperation of Jerry Colangelo, his front office staff, and the coaches and players of the Phoenix Suns, who more than likely would have preferred to spend their summer vacations doing something other than talking to me. Their contributions are greatly appreciated.

Thanks to Tom Ambrose, Suns vice president of public relations, and Jim Brewer, the team's publications director, for the use of their photographs which appear on the cover and inside the book.

Also, the support, encouragement — and permission — of the management of *The Arizona Republic* allowed it to happen. Special thanks to John Oppedahl, Bob Franken and Jeff Dozbaba.

And finally, I want to thank all of my loyal readers who have been with me during my 17 years at *The Republic*, the past seven covering the Suns. It's been an unbelievable ride bringing Suns fans their daily coverage from the depths of a drug investigation in 1987 to the heights of a celebration parade in 1993. I hope you enjoy the book, because it's for you.

# Introduction

This was going to be a year like none before it for the Phoenix Suns.

They were moving into a new arena. They had a new coach. Even their logo and uniforms were redesigned for their silver anniversary season.

And, they added Charles Barkley and Danny Ainge, two of the game's biggest characters.

The Suns seemed destined to be not only meaner and nastier, but funnier. As a member of the Dream Team in the Barcelona Olympics, Barkley had set himself apart as an international sports celebrity and one of the game's best players. Ainge already was a well-established imp.

On those rare nights when they didn't win, they'd at least be entertaining.

As it turned out, they were winners on more nights than any team in the league.

What a run it was!

In June of 1992, the $89 million America West Arena opened in downtown Phoenix as Suns President Jerry Colangelo presided over festivities like a proud papa, which in a way he was. He fought with the city council to have it built, pressing ahead when public opinion was not entirely in his favor. It's now hard to find anyone who admits thinking the arena, as a joint venture between the city and the Suns, was a bad idea.

It was not uncommon to see Colangelo, in hard hat, on the construction site each day supervising every detail during the gestation of his baby.

Having weathered that storm, two weeks after the dedication ceremony Colangelo created another by trading one of the franchise's most popular players, Jeff Hornacek, for Barkley, who seemed to be a little wild for this conservative neck of the woods.

And yet another week later, the Suns used their first-round draft pick on Oliver Miller, a center who was so overweight at an

NBA pre-draft camp in Chicago that one league scout said Miller ought to wear a bra. He did bounce a little.

The first of July, free-agent Ainge agreed to his contract, bailing on the Portland Trail Blazers, who called his bluff and lost. A fierce competitor, Ainge once was kicked out of a game for biting an opponent.

Of course, Barkley had been kicked out of a few himself.

They brought a different personality to a plain vanilla franchise that was rolling along with its 55, 54, 55, 53 wins every year, going nowhere in post-season action.

But they were awfully nice guys.

So that would change a bit. Barkley, for example, was kicked out of his first game in a Suns uniform.

The changes meant adjustments for those who'd been with the club for some time, most notably for point guard Kevin Johnson. No longer the star of the show, he would have to find new ways to make his mark, and he did. He also found new ways to get hurt. KJ opened the season on the injured list, because he tried to lift Miller during an exhibition game celebration and became the victim of an abdominal strain at first thought to be a hernia. KJ also ended the season on the injured list after straining a knee at Portland in celebration of the wackiest finish of the season: Barkley grabbing an inbound pass that Miller ricocheted off the backboard with less than a second to go and making the game-winning basket.

That's the kind of season it was.

KJ would miss more than one-third of it with various injuries, yet the Suns pulled ever farther away from the pack.

They often took it to the limit, rallying for a last-second win in some unorthodox fashion, or losing a big lead and creating a photo finish. They were adept at walking the ledge.

It worked.

The fans quickly were captivated by them. In December, at a practice that was opened to the public, 21,000 people showed up. Only 18,000 of them got in.

The Suns roared through December undefeated, 14-0, a club-record victory streak.

The streak ended in wild fashion in San Antonio in January in an overtime game the Suns protested because the Spurs had six men on the floor. Protest denied.

Also along the way, Barkley had his first well-publicized misadventure as a Sun when he hopped the scorer's table after a loss in New York and chased referee Jimmy Clark. Cost him a game and a lot of money.

The Suns, and their rookie coach, walked the ledge with two highly talented but suspect rookies, Miller and Richard Dumas.

Dumas returned in December from a 13-month suspension for violating the league's anti-drug agreement with the players' association.

Miller was so heavy that his knees and feet couldn't take it. He had tendinitis and a stress reaction, just short of a stress fracture. He went on the injured list and into an out-patient monitored weight-reduction program that required him to spend his nights at a Phoenix hospital. He returned six weeks later more than 40 pounds lighter and unmasked the talented player that was hidden beneath the fat.

Earlier, the Suns said good-bye to another of their most popular players, Kurt Rambis. They waived him and ate his $1.1 million contract, and then tried late in the season to get him back for the playoffs after he signed with Sacramento. But the Kings wouldn't accommodate the Suns by waiving him, even though he wasn't playing much and he was going to become a free agent at season's end.

There were so many other bizarre twists.

In March, the NBA handed out record fines and suspensions following a bench-clearing brawl with the Knicks. KJ was judged by the league to be the instigator and was hit hardest by the penalties.

In April, Dan Majerle, taking an inbound pass with less than two seconds to go, swished a 33-foot three-point basket to beat the Los Angeles Lakers, who had rallied from 20 points down with 11 minutes remaining.

Later in the month at Portland, Barkley, just off the injured list because of a shoulder injury, completed the ricochet-pass play from Miller.

Westphal, after the Suns clinched the best record, termed the final week "exhibition season." He was criticized for creating an atmosphere in which the Suns could lose momentum. The top-seeded Suns did fall behind the last-seeded Lakers, the only team in the playoffs with a losing record, 2-0, at home, but rallied to save the series after Westphal boldly predicted they would.

Barkley, in rapid succession, was chosen the league's most valuable player, was named to All-NBA first teams in separate awards from writers and fellow players, and was named to the all-interview team because of his quick wit.

But falling behind 0-2 at home to the two-time champion Chicago Bulls in the NBA Finals finally was a hole too deep for even these zanies — although they came back stronger than anyone ever expected. It took a three-point shot with less than four seconds left in the sixth game to bury them, and even at that the series ended dead even, 640-640. The difference was that the Bulls had a trophy to show for it.

More than 300,000 fans, hooked on the team and refusing to let go of a captivating season, turned out on the hottest day of the year in downtown Phoenix along A 2.5-mile route to honor them in a runners-up parade!

The Suns had been four seconds away from playing Game 7 of the NBA Finals on their homecourt.

What an ending for a team that preferred to pull up and shoot a three-pointer on a fast break, a team that rarely practiced, a team of oddities.

They were just getting warmed up.

Successful and crazy as the Suns were in Barkley's first season, they are likely to be that and perhaps more this season.

This book is an attempt to capture some of the color, excitement and craziness of this unusual team's quest to be the best in pro basketball.

## Chapter One

# VOLUNTARY COOPERATION

The door swung open at the top of the stairway, and a beacon shone through.

Of course, when you have a shaved head like Charles Barkley's, a beacon is with you wherever there is overhead lighting.

This was symbolic, though. And dramatic. It was as if he had been sent from on high.

Down the steps he came into the Suns' brand new practice gym at America West Arena, for the first time wearing the word "Phoenix" across his practice jersey.

Wednesday, October 7, 1992. The day the Phoenix Suns became Charles Barkley's team.

Not that he views it as "Charles Barkley's team." There still are a few tiny hairs on his head, and calling the Suns his team will make them bristle.

"I don't really concern myself with whose team it is," Barkley said. "I've played on teams with Doc, Moses, Andrew Toney, the greatest players to ever play the game. It isn't an ego thing. You just want to win. I don't care who I play with. I could play with Michael Jordan.

"Pat Riley has an expression called 'voluntary cooperation.' That's what it takes to win. Voluntary cooperation, that's all basketball is."

Down on the court, an informal game was in progress among Barkley's new teammates. Training camp wouldn't open for another couple of days, but most of the Suns— even those whose idea of off-season conditioning is wrestling to pull on their jersey as they dash onto the floor at camp— had been in town working out most of the summer.

Would YOU want to be the first to be ripped by Barkley for being out of shape? You know what he does to Angolans and Godzilla — to say nothing of Armon Gilliam and Charles Shackleford.

The Suns thought they were ready, but it didn't take Barkley long after he got into the game to test them. There had been quite a bit of bickering over foul calls, and finally Barkley stopped the game.

"Wait a minute!"

It got quiet in a hurry. He had the floor. Even the Suns' army of vice presidents and marketing geniuses, who'd come to the pit for this occasion in full suspended regalia, snapped to attention.

"From now on," Barkley instructed, "let the defense call the fouls. We're going to play the honor system. Now, let's go!"

Nobody said a word. But for the rest of the morning, the defense called the fouls and the honor system was observed. The Suns had bowed and given him their first collective "Yessir, Mr. Barkley." The tone was set.

Cotton Fitzsimmons, the former Suns coach and now their senior executive vice-president, sat with reporters in the balcony, taking it all in with a smile.

"Well," said Fitzsimmons, who had befriended Barkley at Nike social functions, "that takes care of that crap. That's what I like about Charles."

Even Paul Westphal, the Suns' young new coach, was amused.

"It was funny," Westphal said. "I thought our players were a little nervous when Charles got here. I think our players have anticipated this day just like everyone else. They didn't know quite what to expect. I think they're a little in awe of him. They wanted to show Charles what they can do, but they ended up standing around and watching him."

Barkley's impact touched the Suns long before he arrived for that first workout.

Kevin Johnson spent the summer strengthening the legs that brought the Suns great joy with his lightning-quick first step to the basket, as well as great disappointment with injury after injury, often during the playoffs.

Mark West, the Suns' bulky, cymbal-handed center, worked hard to correct an experiment that failed. During the previous season he was asked to bulk up. At 6-10, he often gives away two to six inches in the post. His extra weight the previous season had made him slow to the ball. He lost the explosiveness of his jump, and he lost his starting job. But suddenly he was back in the picture, because Andrew Lang, who'd put him on the bench in 1991-92, had been traded to Philadelphia in the Barkley deal. So West "redistributed" his weight during the summer. Now he was sleek, like a track and field athlete. But he still couldn't catch.

And Tom Chambers, accustomed to spending the off-season on his ranch in Utah, was tired of hearing critics say that he always reported late and out of shape. At 33, and in the final guaranteed season of his contract, he could see the end was near. But Chambers was playing in informal workouts like the Suns' scoring recordsetter that he'd been in 1989 and 1990. Would he, or the other veterans, have been that far along that early if it weren't for the impending arrival of the cantankerous Barkley?

They were stung by recent early playoff departures — in the opening round in 1991 and in the second round in 1992. Those shortcomings were made more bitter after the Suns created high expectations with successive trips to the conference finals in 1989 and 1990.

Never had the Suns worked so hard during the off-season, come back so early, or played so competitively in informal workouts.

They were all there, huffing, puffing, sweating as they'd done almost every day since Labor Day when Barkley bounded down those steps for the first time into the gray block-walled, subterranean torture pit.

In their four seasons under Fitzsimmons, the Suns had won 55, 54, 55, and 53 games. But they had deficiencies.

After they lost that second-round series to the Trail Blazers in 1992, Jeff Hornacek, the Suns' leading scorer and one of their few consistent players, said, "Obviously, we need to make some changes." Little did he know that he, Lang, and starting forward Tim Perry soon would be on their way to the Philadelphia 76ers.

Hollins hadn't been quoted often during his four seasons as an assistant coach of the Suns, but after his players trudged off the Portland Memorial Coliseum floor, losers in five games, Hollins uttered prophetic words that have become the most quoted in the rebirth of the franchise:

"We've got to go get us a Charles Barkley."

Sometimes, legend exceeds the truth. Not in this case, Hollins said.

"I did say it. We were in the anteroom across from the locker room, and Jerry Colangelo and myself and Paul were sitting there," Hollins said. "We were rehashing all the games, and what happened. In each of those games in that series we were there, we were close, but we couldn't close it out because we couldn't score.

"I said, 'Well, what we need is a Charles Barkley, a guy who can get us the big rebound at the end of the game,' because in two of those games, that's what was needed. We also needed somebody who could score or get fouled down the stretch.

"I really did say it, though."

The Suns knew they had no halfcourt offense. They knew they needed help on the boards. They knew they needed a dynamo who could lead them through a physical series against the likes of Portland. They knew that their loose, running-gunning style that brought them loads of victories during the regular season wouldn't necessarily be successful in the postseason. It was as obvious to anyone who'd watched the Suns as it was to Hollins.

Why settle for "a Charles Barkley," if you can get the real thing? The living, breathing, foot-stomping, pouting, hilarious, outrageous, vulgar, compassionate, hard-working original?

Colangelo, who has gotten what he has wanted since he bought the Suns in October of 1987, actually had pursued Barkley for more than a year. In June of 1991, 76ers owner Harold Katz told Colangelo that the price would be three starters, one of whom had to be KJ, an All-Star guard. Colangelo wasn't ready to pay the price.

Clearly, the 76ers were going nowhere, and Barkley was ripping them at every opportunity by the end of the 1992 season. He called Katz a money-grubber who didn't care whether the product on the floor was competent as long as the dollars flowed in. He called his teammates heartless. He had little bad to say about Jimmy Lynam, the Sixers' coach, until Lynam moved upstairs to general manager and fired trainer Tony Harris, one of Barkley's closest friends.

Barkley's best rip was directed at Gene Shue, who later would be removed as Sixers' GM. Barkley called Shue a "clown whose only ambition is to caddy for Harold Katz."

New 76ers coach Doug Moe, meanwhile, watched videotapes of Philadelphia games and came away saying Barkley had to go. Moe didn't think Barkley's sore, aging body could withstand the rigors of Moe's motion offense. He wasn't convinced Barkley would exert the effort necessary to make it work. The Sixers also could see that their supply of marketable players had dwindled.

Barkley had the most trade value, but it was dwindling.

"The year before, we had tried to get Charles and tried to get Hakeem Olajuwon," Hollins said. "We had dialogue with both of those teams because there were rumblings that both of them were on the market. Then we started talking to them, and it was always, 'No.' In Philadelphia's case it was people asking astronomical return for their player. When we went to Chicago for the predraft camp, Freddy Carter, the Sixers' assistant coach, came up to me and wanted to talk, and all he wanted to talk about was our players. He proceeded to tell us about Charles, how he did this, and he did that. We knew about Charles. Freddie asked about Andrew and Tim. They just wanted to get a feel. It was kind of an 'unofficial official' conversation. I told Jerry and Cotton about it later over dinner. Then it just kept building and building until it happened.

"It's like the Dennis Rodman situation: eventually he's going to stay in Detroit, or he's going to be traded somewhere that he wants to go. The reason I say that is because expectations of what you can get keep diminishing over time when you find that nobody's willing to give you the moon for your player. But even if Charles or Dennis hadn't said anything, nobody's going to give half their team for one player unless it's David Robinson, Shaquille O'Neal, or Hakeem, centers who dominate in every phase of the game basically."

The scene was set. The phone rang in Hornacek's north Phoenix home early in the afternoon on a scorching June day. A friend from Chicago was calling to tell him he'd heard on the radio that Hornacek had been traded for Barkley.

"I thought it was a joke," Hornacek said. "I mean, my name hadn't really been in trade rumors. Nobody from the team called me."

There'd been a leak in the NBA office. The news was on radio stations from coast to coast before the Suns and Sixers could inform the players and arrange simultaneous press conferences to announce the blockbuster deal.

A few minutes after Hornacek's friend called, Westphal got through to make it official. Hornacek was in shock.

Barkley was elated. He had emotional attachments in Philadelphia, as Hornacek did in Phoenix. But unlike Hornacek, Barkley was surrounded by incompetence. His remaining years were growing short, and he could see that Philadelphia couldn't be rebuilt into a championship contender before he retired. Barkley had a list of teams he'd consider: Phoenix, Portland, Seattle, San Antonio.

"Wherever I went, I was going someplace where it's warm and where they have a chance to win it all," he said.

In Barkley, the Suns snared one of the game's greatest players and one of its greatest characters — one who two months later would become an international hero/villain during his gold-medal run with the U.S. "Dream Team" at the Olympics in Barcelona.

But in Phoenix, the league's most quotable player was joining players who are perfectly capable of expressing themselves well, but more often than not choose to speak the company line.

It seemed an odd marriage: Charles Barkley in Phoenix, a sleepy desert city; playing for the Suns, as vanilla a team as there is; in Arizona, a state that at that point had no paid holiday honoring Dr. Martin Luther King, Jr., one of Barkley's few heroes. Many outsiders viewed Arizona as racist because voters rejected the King holiday in the 1990 general election, a decision that prompted the National Football League to quickly yank the 1993 Super Bowl out of Tempe. It was the latest in a series of blows on the issue. Two years earlier, the NBA moved its annual meetings out of Scottsdale after former Arizona Governor Evan Mecham rescinded the King holiday, which was created by his predecessor, Bruce Babbitt, now U.S. Secretary of the Interior.

"Well," Barkley said, when asked about it during his introductory news conference, "the Klan never marched outside our hotel when I was here with the 76ers, and it did march in Birmingham, which is near my hometown. So it must not be too bad here."

He was off and running.

One year later, when reflecting on his first season in the Valley of the Suns, Barkley said the place gets a bum rap.

"You know, I really didn't know that much about Phoenix, and one of the first things I wanted to do was not stereotype it with preconceived notions about the Martin Luther King Holiday, the state being racist, the city being racist," he said. "I just didn't want to prejudge Phoenix at all. I think it is a tremendous city. Obviously, the best thing about it is the weather. The hospitality is one of the things I've been amazed about more than anything.

"It's unfortunate, but I don't think racism is getting better in America because people need an excuse to be unsuccessful. I think the media does not do a fair job of portraying both races. I think they portray black people badly, and I think they portray white people badly. I don't think most white people are racists, and I don't think most black people are thugs, either, contrary to the media's perception.

"It's like, look at the news. I would think all black people are thugs, too. Then you've got all these shows about cops. All the people they arrest are black. I don't think every white person in this world is in the Ku Klux Klan. As a black athlete, I have to keep standing up. That's one reason they didn't like me in Philadelphia very much. But I think all athletes should promote that. If you're an athlete people don't look at you the same way they do other people.

"I just hate when people stereotype people. That's why I never do that. That's why I had no preconceived view of Phoenix. I feel comfortable here, but I feel comfortable all the time because I accept that there are times when racism does exist. But I don't think you can blanket a community or a whole race of people."

Barkley is more sensitive to it than most. He chose to marry a white woman.

"You just get it from both sides that way," he said. "The only thing that does is a lot of black people give me a hard time. It is just flat-out wrong to dislike somebody because of the color of their skin."

# Chapter Two

# A JERRY-BUILT ORGANIZATION

The Suns flirted with success off and on during their first 24 seasons in operation. They made the playoffs in their second season, and actually had the Los Angeles Lakers of Jerry West, Elgin Baylor, and Wilt Chamberlain down, 3-1, in a best-of-seven series before losing.

During Fitzsimmons' first stint coaching the team, 1970-72, the Suns won 48 and 49 games but failed to make the playoffs because of the league's alignment and playoff format in those days.

Their run to the 1976 Finals was unexpected following a 42-40 regular season under Coach John MacLeod. From 1978 through 1983, MacLeod's Suns averaged 52 wins a season but never got beyond the conference finals. But from 1983 through 1988, the Suns averaged only 35 victories and suffered some of their darkest days.

The low point was 1987, a year to forget:

— In February, MacLeod was fired after a run of nearly 14 seasons.

— In April, three players were among those indicted by a Maricopa County Grand Jury on drug-related charges. The case generated a mountain of negative publicity nationally. It still is referred to as the "Suns drug scandal," even though most of those indicted didn't have a connection to the Suns, and none of those indicted was convicted of a drug-related felony. It proved to be much ado about nothing and cost the county attorney who initiated it his job.

— In June, Johnny High, a former Suns guard and a figure in the drug investigation, died in a mysterious early-morning auto crash. It was ruled an accident.

— In August, starting center Nick Vanos was killed in the crash of a Northwest Airlines jet in Detroit.

— In September, the Suns were put up for sale and speculation was that they would be moved — something that wouldn't have upset the league office. The NBA had had it with Arizona politicians and law-enforcement agencies.

It was one catastrophe after another, compounded by the Suns' inability to beat anybody on the court.

Negative publicity and five years of nonwinning basketball had worn thin on the three owners, Richard Bloch, Donald Pitt, and Donald Diamond. They were ready to take their profit and get out. Got $44.5 million? The Suns are yours.

Colangelo didn't have $44.5 million, but he already felt as if the Suns were his. Throughout the Suns' history, the common thread had been Colangelo's guiding hand. Colangelo came to Phoenix from Chicago in 1968 as the 28-year-old general manager of the expansion team. Twice, he stepped in and coached the Suns on an interim basis. He was always a hands-on manager. He is among only a handful of those who remain today from the small group of original Suns employees — the others are Ruth Dryjanski, his assistant; Joe Proski, the trainer; Paul Steingard, the physician emeritus, and Dick Van Arsdale, "The Original Sun" who now serves as player personnel director.

Colangelo had no ownership stake in the team all those years, but he always treated it as if it was his own. He had to get the permission of the owners for any major moves, but all of the day-to-day decisions bore Colangelo's imprint.

The owners always promised him they'd give him first crack at buying if they ever chose to sell, and they honored their word. Colangelo, meantime, was convinced that if he didn't buy them, the Suns would be sold to out-of-town interests and moved.

Finding that kind of money in a tight economy — the recession already had hit Arizona — wasn't easy. Colangelo hastily set out to assemble a group of local partners to go in with him.

John Teets, chairman of the board of Dial Corporation — it was known as "Greyhound" then — quickly convinced his board of directors to commit $6 million. Soon El Dorado, a subsidiary of Pinnacle West, was also in. There was a multitude of smaller, limited partnerships. It was a grassroots effort.

Even at that, two other potential corporate partners fell out of the deal on a Wednesday before Colangelo was facing a Friday deadline to present the plan to the league's board of governors. On Thursday, Colangelo got the then-Arizona Bank to commit to the necessary remaining funding.

It was done. He'd put the deal together in about 5 1/2 weeks. He signed on the dotted line on a sunny, warm October Friday afternoon, just as training camp was opening.

A drastic change in the Suns' fortunes was about to occur with Colangelo as their president and chief executive officer.

And it wasn't a moment too soon. On the following Monday, the stock market plummeted . If the deal had dragged on through the weekend before closing, it would not have been executed with the group Colangelo put together.

Colangelo is a private man, a shrewd man. He tells you exactly as much as he wants you to know. He comes across as stuffy to many people, but those who know him well dispute that.

He could have bought the franchise and moved it himself. Several other cities wanted an NBA franchise badly. He bought it to keep it in Phoenix, and he was committed to downtown Phoenix.

Two months after he took ownership, Colangelo was offered $60 million for the team by a Columbus, Ohio, group. He refused to accept this handsome, quickly turned profit at a time when many businessmen were bailing out of deals to avoid financial ruin following the stock market crisis.

Colangelo immediately made a series of bold moves. He needed to sell his product, and he had to repair its image. He essentially gutted the roster, save Hornacek. The biggest trade involved shipping Larry Nance, one of the most popular players, to Cleveland for Kevin Johnson, Mark West, and a draft pick that became Dan Majerle. At the conclusion of the 28-win 1987-88 season, Coach John Wetzel was released, and Colangelo slid Fitzsimmons back into the coaching chair he had occupied 16 years earlier.

The Suns' meteoric rise back to respectability had begun.

Their success spurned a number of other successful ventures tied to the club, the foremost being a new arena. Hardly a day went by that Colangelo wasn't on the construction site, overseeing every detail like a proud papa. The America West Arena has 88 luxury suites, a practice gym, full-service restaurant and catering service, a fast-food court, a merchandising outlet, a television editing and production studio, a health club, and two parking garages.

Before he could turn the first spadeful of dirt, Colangelo faced considerable opposition to the deal with the City of Phoenix. The city would own the $89 million building, the Suns would operate it, and sign a 40-year lease to play in it. Many citizens believed Colangelo was using taxpayer money to line his own pockets. The city chose to fund its share through hotel and rental-car taxes. The critics overlooked the role the building would have in generating revenue, however, in attracting conventions and events that would help other local businesses, particularly those a stone's-throw away downtown.

It wasn't until the building was up and running — and proving to be a success for both parties — that Colangelo and the city council really were off the hot seat. The Purple Palace is recognized as one of the finest basketball facilities in the world. With control of the building, the Suns now were in the entertainment business, serving as booking agents for everything from rock concerts to tractor pulls.

From the new facility was born a host of arena sports teams, owned by Colangelo and partners, to fill the summer dates — football, soccer, tennis.

An advertising agency was created. Next to open was a health club. The next big venture Colangelo is considering is the creation of a superstation. Years before, in fact, Colangelo had the foresight to bring the Suns' radio and TV packages in-house.

On the horizon may be major league baseball and a retractable-domed stadium adjacent to the arena.

Merchandising also has taken off, with the creation of Suns team shops throughout the Valley, including one in the lobby of the arena adjacent to a fast-food court where business is always brisk. In less than six years, Colangelo has built a burgeoning empire.

When he was general manager answering to absentee owners, Colangelo was bound by their wishes. Because they were reluctant to spend a buck or make a deal, the Suns were regarded as skinflints who doted on mediocrity. So the second generation of the Suns is also something of a second lifetime for Colangelo. He's now much more than some guy who owns a basketball team. Suddenly, the Suns were firing coaches, hiring unrestricted free agents, and clearing the roster with blockbuster trades.

Colangelo wasn't afraid to take a risk or pay the necessary price to bring success. He finally had his franchise right where he wanted it— on the cutting edge. In 1990, the Suns opened the season against Utah with two games in Tokyo, the first regular-season U.S. professional team sporting event to be played outside North America. In the meantime, Colangelo secured the 1995 All-Star game for the new arena, and he also got the Suns invited to the 1993 McDonald's Open in Munich. In June of 1993, he received his fourth NBA Executive of the Year Award. Nobody else has more than two.

"The thing that really helped me through even the down times is I've never been fearful of losing the job or fearful of failing," Colangelo said. "That's part of my upbringing. My attitude toward that is, as a human being, you're going to make mistakes. You don't belabor the point. You don't spend time looking back. If you make your mistake, cut the cord, cut your losses, and move forward. Roll up your sleeves, and do what has to be done.

"And you must be willing to put yourself in a position where you make another mistake. I really believe that in order to go from Point A to Point B, if you wait for the tide to come in and take you with it, you're going to wait forever. You've got to be willing to step out there. You've got to be willing to roll the dice."

But, Colangelo advised, do it with "calculated" risks, not "blind" risks. "That usually comes with experience and knowledge and doing your homework," he said. "And even with all that said, you're still likely to make a mistake.

"I'm in a different role today than I played for so many years. Most people in our business, in professional sports in my position, are afraid to make mistakes because they're afraid they're going to lose their jobs. I was never afraid of that, and I think that gave me a strength. I just took that a step further when the ownership change took place. Now there weren't any people to check with, weren't any votes to be taken on personnel changes or anything that was happening with the franchise. You just react instinctively.

"I'm a person who needs flexibility, needs autonomy, and needs to be in a position where I can make mistakes. I'm not afraid to make them. But I want to be in a position where I can."

Along the way, he's made and learned from enough mistakes to boost him to his present position. He also draws on his background as a source of the drive to his success. Colangelo classifies the "Hungry Hill" neighborhood where he grew up in Chicago Heights, Illinois, as "tough."

"People were very appreciative of what they had because they didn't have very much," he said. "And the ability to do something for the first time — to go see a major league game, or go see a college doubleheader — was always something you really appreciated. You might not get another chance to do it, so you took full advantage of that opportunity.

"When I saw people carrying a lunch pail every day and looked at the mills that were across the street from my home, that's where it could have been for me."

Sports, as it was for so many of those who play on his team today, was the out that changed his fortunes. It led to the scholarship that gave him a college education. It gave him a competitive drive that made him a successful businessman.

"I got an education that I probably never would have gotten without sports, because we couldn't afford for me to go to college under any circumstances," Colangelo said. "So I think you develop a mental toughness about life, not that there isn't a soft side of me. I think there is a very soft side of me."

Colangelo takes care of those who take care of him.

"Our organization is built around loyalty when you look at the people who have been here as long as they have and you look at the former players who are part of it, I think people recognize that in our community. I think players who are within the structure recognize that and feel better. They are more apt to produce for you, because they recognize that there is a family attitude that exists.

"And that's who I am. That's something that is very important to me. When our franchise is recognized, and in the past year we were voted by people in the league as the franchise that they'd most want to go to work for, that was a nice tribute to the Suns organization. And I took it that way."

Colangelo has become one of the most powerful men in Arizona. His consistent building blocks in all of his ventures: loyalty and family. His army of vice-presidents has been in place for years and they will have jobs for life as long as they produce and don't cross him.

Colangelo values his ties to the past. He brought back Connie Hawkins, the only Suns player enshrined in the Basketball Hall of Fame, as Community Relations Representative. He brought back Al Bianchi, whom he had fired as an assistant coach, as a scout after Bianchi was fired as president of the New York Knicks.

It's hard to look at Colangelo now and envision a stumblebum in the world of business, but that's exactly who he was 30 years ago. He was advised to change his surname because he was told no one with an Italian surname could be successful.

He was just out of the University of Illinois, and he and his wife, Joan, had two small children with a third on the way. He was involved in a small tuxedo rental and dry-cleaning business back in Chicago with a man who was "kind of a father, uncle, brother, good friend." They had a verbal partnership for a 50-50 split. The key word was "verbal." After three years, his friend shut down the business and Colangelo didn't get a cent out of it.

"After three years, it finally hit me between the eyes that I didn't have anything," he said. "And after three years of blood, sweat, and tears, and wasting a lot of time, I walked away from that relationship and learned some very valuable lessons, lessons that have stayed with me in terms of creating part of that toughness that I'm referring to. You'd better get everything in writing because that's reality.

"But, that led to an opportunity."

He was introduced to businessman Dick Klein, an acquaintance of his father-in-law's.

"After meeting with him and him offering me a job, his recall was 'Jerry Colangelo, the athlete who played basketball and baseball at the University of Illinois.' At least, in the Midwest there was some name recognition."

Klein offered Colangelo a job that was going to pay him twice what he had taken home previously.

"Then two weeks later, he advised me that he had an interest in acquiring an NBA franchise. So there I was, in a situation where there was excitement. Here we had a chance to get an NBA franchise in Chicago, and six months later, we did. So the whole world kind of opened up for me."

The failure of his tuxedo rental business also led him to much more. His confidence to handle adversity and personal challenges was shattered. He was down and out. He needed something more.

"There are going to be times when you're knocked down in life and you find you can't handle it yourself," he said. "That was the experience that led me to become a born-again Christian."

Colangelo's title with the Bulls at age 26 was Head Scout and Director of Merchandising. But, much the same as he does today, he had a hand in nearly every detail. He was involved in designing the Bulls' logo, which is essentially unchanged since the team came into the league in 1966. He distributed press releases to the Chicago newspapers. In fact, he had to brave a winter snowstorm, in which he managed to lock his keys in his car, to distribute the release announcing a news conference at which Klein would confirm that Chicago had been awarded an NBA franchise. During the Bulls' second season, Colangelo was promoted to executive assistant to Klein.

Klein is now working for Colangelo as a part-time scout during his retirement years in the south. Their relationship has come full-circle.

In 1968, Milwaukee and Phoenix were coming into the league. Both franchises offered Colangelo the job as their first general manager.

"I came to Phoenix, and after taking one look at the community and just meeting a few people, I decided this was it. I wanted Phoenix and not Milwaukee. I don't look back on that for a minute, and never did."

There wasn't much population base in Arizona. The biggest thing the state had going, in sports, was the dynasty of winning football created at Arizona State University by Coach Frank Kush (to whom Colangelo offered the job of coach of his arena football franchise). It seemed an unusual market for a pro sports franchise to crack.

The selection process wasn't sophisticated. Richard Bloch was an acquaintance of the new ownership team in Seattle. Things were going well there, so Bloch was interested in getting his own NBA team. Bloch met with NBA commissioner Walter Kennedy, who was not enthusiastic about expanding to Phoenix.

"As the story goes," Colangelo said, "the market research that was done was Walter Kennedy flew into Phoenix, took a cab over to the Westward Ho Hotel, spoke to the cab driver, asked him a few questions on the way there, got his shoes shined at the Westward Ho, asked some questions about whether Phoenix would be a good city for the NBA, got back on a plane and went back to New York. And that was the extent of it. Not very sophisticated. But let's put it this way: He had foresight, because it worked."

Let's put it this way: So did Colangelo, when he envisioned building the Suns into a consistent winner, and building an arena that would be the centerpiece of the revitalization of downtown Phoenix, a ghost town after 6 p.m..

"When I got involved in the NBA, it was a mom and pop league," Colangelo said. "The numbers were $100,000 for national television money. Today it's close to $10 million per team. Our first payroll was $180,000 for 12 players. Today the average salary is over a million and a half per player. We're a big business today.

"One of the things that we've attempted to do organizationally is stay ahead of the curve a little bit, recognize that we were in a growth industry and there are a lot of changes taking place. We wanted to be pioneers in many regards."

The Suns were among the first to bring their radio and television productions, and with them the packaging and selling of ads, in-house.

"We served as a model years ago," he said. "I'm talking about WAY back. That goes to show you that if you are fortunate to stick around long enough, you can have a couple of downs and come back and be considered a model franchise again. Not many people get that opportunity.

"We had tried to stay abreast, bring a lot of things in-house, recognize that there were a lot of great opportunities."

They were not among the early pioneers in merchandising, but now they have a strong product with wide appeal. As recently as 1986, the Suns were doing about $75,000 a year in novelty sales. Colangelo said they went over $4 million during their silver anniversary season.

Although in only the 19th-largest television market in the league, the Suns ranked No. 1 in the NBA in local television ratings.

"That's really something," Colangelo said. "When I hear a statistic like that, I think back 25 years when Phoenix was awarded the franchise and the Eastern experts were saying Phoenix would never make it as an NBA city because it has nothing there, no history, doesn't have the market, doesn't have any of those things.

"To be recognized as one of the outstanding franchises and enjoy the success we've had, and have everyone else recognize it, I'm proud for the city. I think that's a great accomplishment."

Colangelo admits the Suns were not on the leading edge in the new wave of arenas. Those began popping up around the league in the late 1980s while the Suns still were playing in Veterans Memorial Coliseum, their original home, built in the 1960s. It was one of the smallest in the NBA and it had few amenities. Worse, from the Suns' viewpoint, they had little opportunity for ancillary income from parking, concessions, and advertising signage. The "Madhouse on McDowell" had no luxury suites. It was representative of the Suns' blue-collar beginnings. But they were ready for something more reflective of their growth into yuppie-hood although Colangelo frowned on moving to the suburbs.

"We were trying to play catchup because there were a lot of people way ahead of us on that score, but we caught up, and then jumped ahead of them in terms of what we were able to develop, taking the latest technology and ideas and incorporating our own. With that, we recognized immediately that there were even more opportunities. Other teams have new arenas, but they haven't done anything further with it. I see a big world out there, and I see a lot of opportunities."

Colangelo, as a member of numerous civic organizations, has ample opportunity to sharpen his speech-making skills. "Opportunity" is one of his favorite topics.

"Opportunity walks right by most people and they don't recognize it," he said. "It's there. And when people complain about not getting a chance to do this or that, probably five or six times in their lifetimes there were opportunities, and they didn't see them."

Colangelo and staff immediately felt that the opening of the new arena was an opportunity of a lifetime to go from one level to another.

"So when you talk about the other arena sports teams, football, soccer, tennis, our own production company, our own advertising agency, our new health club, that's all excitement," he said. "I see us being a real factor in the local economy all of a sudden in terms of providing jobs and creating new businesses. And that's kind of neat."

Now, the Suns alone are worth $125 million, nearly triple what Colangelo paid for them six years ago. But Colangelo didn't pile up NBA Executive of the Year Awards for building a conglomeration of entities spun off the Suns. He keeps winning them because he makes the right moves to keep the Suns highly competitive.

"Most often, the thing that triggers winning that award is player personnel moves, and how that reflects in your team's performance," he said.

The Suns had a number of those. Barkley was the most obvious. The Suns moved three starters for a talented player who some thought was a malcontent, and it worked. It resulted in 62 wins, the conference title, and the best record in the league.

The Danny Ainge signing was recognized as a quick and decisive move to snare an unrestricted free agent. Having risky rookies Oliver Miller and Richard Dumas work out during the season, and finding veteran Frank Johnson in Italy and bringing him back to the NBA after three years away also were recognized.

All of those new faces had an impact on the Suns' run to the Finals.

"Also, my involvement in the league, as strong as it is, and serving on the committees I serve on (he chairs the expansion committee) put me in a position where I'm very much involved, and I think that's recognized by people around the league," Colangelo said.

"When all those things come together, it's a big year. And that's exactly what this was for our organization and for the city. And I couldn't be prouder."

*Chapter Three*

# THE NEXT GENERATION

Barkley's colorful arrival was the first of many changes for the Suns in 1992-93, their silver anniversary season, the start of the next generation.

The new arena.

New uniforms: The Suns' duds, which had been essentially unchanged from the day they came into the NBA in 1968, sported a dynamic new sunburst on the jersey, and the shade of purple was deeper. Black was introduced as one of their trim colors. Even the mesh air vents were horizontal instead of vertical.

New players: A goofy collection of personalities with loads of talent.

New attitude: Voters approved the King holiday when the issue went back on the ballot in November 1992. The NBA quickly awarded the 1995 All-Star Game to Phoenix. The NFL retraced its steps and agreed to bring the 1996 Super Bowl to Tempe. The state's battered image began to heal.

And with it all came new expectations for a team that averaged 54 wins under Fitzsimmons but could never seem to get the job done in the playoffs. Suns fans were tired of coming close. They saw Barkley as the man who would put the first championship banner in the rafters.

If there was any question about Barkley's mission, Colangelo set him straight while he gave Barkley a tour of his new workplace.

"He was telling me how great this was compared with the Spectrum in Philadelphia and I said to him, 'You know Charles, we had it sold out for the season even before we traded for you,' " Colangelo said. "He looked at me and said, 'You mean you don't need me to sell tickets, then?'

"I said, 'Not a one.'

"He said, 'You just got me to win?'

"'That's right.'

"'Then we're going to do that.'"

The Suns no longer were some enigma out in the desert running up scores that basketball fans living in Eastern time zones would read about only in two-day-old box scores. Now they were the team that Charles Barkley played for. No one would be satisfied with the Suns continuing to roll along to 54 wins with their wide-open playground game, and then blowing it in the playoffs.

The surprise was that the Suns could get Barkley without giving up KJ. It appeared to be too good to be true for the Suns, and a numbskull decision for the 76ers.

Harold Katz had struck again.

If Moe thought Barkley wasn't suited for motion offense, what must he have thought when he got his first look at Perry and Lang? Sure, they're athletic, but neither really has a feel for the game. They're passive, mechanical players.

Once, during a preseason game at El Paso, Texas, during Perry's rookie season, Fitzsimmons yelled at him to set up "down on the block." Perry looked at the coach quizzically.

"The block!" Fitzsimmons repeated.

Perry still didn't get it. Finally, Hornacek pointed to the area in the low post along the free-throw lane.

Even though Lang had deposed West in the Suns' lineup, West was the one the Suns thought they'd be giving up in the trade. West is tougher than Lang, more experienced, more suited to Eastern Conference basketball. But Moe didn't intend to play Eastern-style ball, and the Sixers thought West was too old. Lang is a well-intentioned young player who may yet develop into a serviceable center. But he's still feeling his way. Meanwhile, the Suns plugged West back into their starting unit, and he served them well playing alongside Barkley.

The loss of Hornacek was hardest for Suns fans to take. They identified with him. He was living proof that the bootstraps philosophy still works. Hornacek went from being the final player to make the roster as a rookie in 1986 to an NBA All-Star in 1992. He was the only player the Suns retained in a purge in 1988 following five straight nonwinning seasons. Fans watched Hornacek's game mature, while the franchise reversed its fortunes.

Hornacek has a nice way about him that the people of Phoenix took to. He is low key, often self-effacing. His personality was the antithesis of the modern pro sports athlete. The community liked his wife, Stacy, who was active in many civic service projects. Shipping Hornacek to Philadelphia was as big a blow to Suns fans as it was to the Hornaceks. But you have to give up something to get something, and the Suns had given up their emotional heart. Letters to the editor of

Phoenix's two daily newspapers, *The Arizona Republic* and *The Phoenix Gazette*, were as hot as the summer desert.

How could Jerry Colangelo move a solid citizen and great player like Jeff Hornacek for Charles Barkley, a man who learned he'd been traded to the Suns moments after successfully defending charges of battery and disorderly conduct in Milwaukee stemming from a late-night streetfight following a 76ers game during the season?

Barkley was stranded at the Milwaukee airport, riding out a tornado warning, when he got the news. Colangelo wouldn't pull the trigger on the trade until the jury came in with the acquittal.

And the Sixers? They picked up three starters in the trade, added their own draft-lottery pick to their roster, and still were considerably worse than they'd been in Barkley's final season.

On the Olympic "Dream Team", Barkley showed that he was a better player than anyone in Philadelphia realized — and better than most of the critics in Phoenix realized.

Had Katz waited until after the Olympics, he undoubtedly could have gotten far more for Barkley than Perry, Lang, and Hornacek. Katz might even have had second thoughts about trading Barkley at all. And as the season wore on and the Suns and Sixers took wildly divergent paths, everyone wondered: How could Katz have made such a bad deal for himself? The popular theory was that he wouldn't be Harold Katz if he hadn't.

Katz had built Nutri/System into a successful business empire, but don't forget that he is also the man who in one day traded the first pick in the draft to Cleveland for Roy Hinson, and then moved Moses Malone and Terry Catledge to Washington in exchange for Jeff Ruland and Cliff Robinson.

Yikes! That No. 1 pick he sent to the Cavaliers, by the way, became Brad Daugherty, now an All-Star center.

Six years and one day later, Katz made the Barkley trade.

The Suns could see Katz coming. Two years before, he gave the Suns a first-round pick for Jayson Williams! Katz is almost as revered in Phoenix as Colangelo.

In July of 1993, Katz gutted what was left of the Sixers to sign first-round pick Shawn Bradley, a 7-foot-6 center who hadn't played basketball in two years while a Mormon missionary in Australia. This will prove to be the deal that reverses Katz's fortunes, or forever cements him as one of the game's all-time saps.

Following Barkley's gold-medal performance in Barcelona, accolades poured in. It was as if Barkley was just being discovered.

"It's amazing what playing with better players does for you," Barkley said. "I'm the same player I've been for eight years. If you check my statistics, I've been on a pretty high level ever since I came into the

NBA, but people equate you with your team, and I was playing on a bad team.

"I'm not a better player now, I'm just better known because of the Dream Team."

Chuck Daly, who coached the "Dream Team", said he always had high regard for Barkley while coaching against him in Detroit.

"But after I was with him all summer, watching him practice every day, I could see that Charles is a much better player than I ever realized," Daly said. "He's one of the two best in the world."

The 76ers fired Moe early in March when his motion offense became motionless. Barkley took that as an act of vindication.

"I'm one of God's chosen children," Barkley said of the Moe firing. "Don't ever say bad things about me. Doug Moe won't ever say bad things about me again. He said I was too old and couldn't play anymore. God punished him."

And the Suns? They cruised through the regular season with the best record in the league, 62-20, and set the stage for a championship run with their new superstar and new coach.

Each spring, the eternal question had been raised: Would this be the final season for the veteran vagabond coach, Cotton Fitzsimmons? Each year, Fitzsimmons gave the same response: "When it's time, I'll know."

While Fitzsimmons richly deserves credit for bringing the Suns from one of the NBA's biggest losers to one of its biggest winners — in fact, in his first season, 1988-89, he took them from 28 wins to 55, one of the greatest turnarounds ever, and was named NBA Coach of the Year — it was obvious that his nonstop chatter had worn thin with his players. They were tuning him out.

Seldom did the players complain. At least not on the record. One former player said Fitzsimmons lives to play with the minds of those who speak out against him. Nobody did.

Fitzsimmons announced his retirement on the eve of the 1992 playoffs, effective when the Suns concluded their run. In fairness to Fitzsimmons, he never put in a low-post offense because he never had a reliable low-post player like Barkley. The Suns played the way they played, because the loose style fit the jump-shooting skills of the personnel.

The Suns who Fitzsimmons coached weren't regarded as tough people. They were overly sensitive. They had to be stroked generously. Perhaps that is why Fitzsimmons didn't want his players making negative public comments. He didn't make negative public comments about them, either.

It was a combination of people and circumstances that allowed the Suns to take a giant step out of the doldrums of the NBA's draft lottery in 1988-89. But when the Suns were bounced by the Blazers in the 1992 playoffs, it was just as obvious that it was time for the second phase of the rebuilding. It was time for a shakeup.

As he said he would, Fitzsimmons knew it was time, possibly because Jerry told him it was time.

"I had a feeling for a couple of things," Fitzsimmons said. "No. 1, I felt I had taken that particular group as far as it could go. I've been with other teams, I've done this for so long I have a feel that maybe someone else wouldn't have. I couldn't take Chambers, Hornacek, KJ, Dan Majerle, West, that group, any further. Fifty-five, 54, 55, 53, that's who they are. I can't get any more out of them. Over a period of four years, we got the most that was there. They did an outstanding job.

"We were working on the Barkley trade at the time, and also we had Danny Ainge targeted, but we hadn't been able to do anything yet. Yes, I felt in my mind maybe I'd go one more year if we got Barkley, because that makes it a totally different thing. I do have a very close relationship with him, but I said, 'No, this is the time.' We can do this now, and also it might help us in the playoffs. I, of course, denied that because I did not want that to be used as a ploy, but I WAS using that as a ploy.

"But that primarily was it," Fitzsimmons said. "It wasn't something that occurred on the playing court. It wasn't something that had built up to it. I truly enjoyed coaching them. As far as any difficulty, I really didn't have any difficulties. The toughest thing was coaching Tom Chambers as his minutes declined and as I thought his abilities declined as he got older. No player ever wants to admit that."

Kevin Johnson, regarded as Fitzsimmons's star pupil — his nickname is "Junior" — agreed.

"Cotton is better with younger teams," KJ said. "He was effective with us when we were a young team, but we're a more mature team now. I think that calls for a different voice."

That voice belongs to Westphal, whose demeanor couldn't be further removed from that of his predecessor.

Fitzsimmons never sat down. In fact, Phoenix beat writers had their seats moved toward center court along press row because Fitzsimmons constantly stood in front of them. Even at 5-foot-8, he blocked their view.

The beat writers are now back at the end of the table toward the Suns bench. Westphal rarely gets up to yell. Who says you have to be on your feet to work an official?

When news of the Barkley trade came down that June 17 afternoon, almost two months after Fitzsimmons announced his decision, he smiled and said, "I quit a year too soon."

"I knew they were going to be good, and every coach wants to take that big ride," Fitzsimmons said. "I was not surprised at the season the

Suns had. I think a lot of other people were. You add a Barkley, you add an Ainge, you get Richard Dumas back from rehab, who I felt would have started at small forward for us the year before. So you add all that in to the mix and throw Oliver Miller into that thing, there's no way the Suns weren't going to have a good team.

"But, if you remember, four years previous, the day that Jerry announced that I would be the head coach and Westphal would be the assistant, I did make a statement that I wanted to live by. I wanted to make sure I left Paul Westphal a better team than I was taking over, and I did."

The new coach generally is Mr. Calm. He's also young, 42, a first-time NBA head coach, and a former player who might better relate to his players than his 62-year-old predecessor.

Or so it seemed at first.

How much control would Westphal have to assert, be able to assert, to keep Barkley in line? Would a firmer, established coach with a "presence" like Fitzsimmons' be better suited for the job? Or would Westphal, who might be more inclined to stay out of the way as much as possible?

Westphal said that the best policy would be to let Charles be Charles, as long as he wasn't disruptive.

"I'm sure this will change the image of the Suns," Westphal said the afternoon he became Barkley's new coach. "Charles is a good guy, but he doesn't go anywhere without attracting attention.

"It's been said that only one person got to be Elvis. Well, only one gets to be Charles. But that's why we made the deal: he adds something special."

As it turned out, so did Westphal. He subscribes to the philosophy that "If it ain't broke, don't fix it," and he acts like a coach only when it is absolutely necessary. Unlike Fitzsimmons, a nice man but one who can become a little overbearing and sometimes come across as pomp-ous, Westphal is nondescript, which proved to be a valuable quality with this team.

The acquisition of Barkley, Danny Ainge, and Frank Johnson, coupled with on-board veterans such as KJ, Mark West, Dan Majerle, and Tom Chambers, changed the character and age of the Suns.

Suddenly, it was a players' team. These were veterans who knew the game, knew the league, and didn't need a heavy thumb on their every move like the younger Suns teams Fitzsimmons coached.

Initially, Barkley wasn't sure Westphal was strong enough.

"You can't be everybody's friend if you're the coach," he said after the Suns lost successive games early to the Los Angeles Clippers and Chicago Bulls.

Few would have mistaken this crew for world beaters, nor Westphal for NBA coach of the year. Some skeptics said the Suns would be lucky to win 45 games, that they'd given up way too much to get Barkley, and had added an aging Ainge and questionable Miller.

If that didn't bring out Westphal's competitive juices, nothing would.

Look at the juggling act of diverse playing skills and personalities that Westphal faced coaching the Suns' next generation. There was KJ, who more than any of the holdover Suns was stung by criticism. Many in the Valley of the Sun were angry because the Suns traded Hornacek instead of KJ in the Barkley deal. Johnson was viewed as too soft, too moody, too distracted. He does have numerous interests outside of basketball. Being "one of the jocks" has never been high on KJ's list of priorities. Johnson had missed the 1992 All-Star game after successive trips, he was the biggest star on the roster. How KJ would coexist with Barkley seemed a fair question.

Then there was Chambers. It was no secret that the Suns had tried unsuccessfully to trade Chambers for two summers. It was also no secret that Chambers, as much as anyone, put the Suns back on the basketball map and had plenty to do with the renewed fan interest that led to the building of America West Arena.

But here was a former All-Star whose play had deteriorated rapidly. This could be traced to injuries, which in turn might have been a by-product of his age. Westphal said early that Chambers would have to earn his playing time. It wouldn't be automatic just because he was Tom Chambers. Westphal would be the coach who would put Chambers on the bench and convert him into a role player. Chambers can be a cantankerous sort.

Majerle was now the rising young star with Hornacek gone. He had flourished as one of the NBA's top sixth men for three seasons. He seemed better suited to small forward than big guard, but Westphal plugged him into Hornacek's spot, and — Presto! — another All-Star season. Majerle, whose name was booed when he was drafted with the 14th pick in 1988, is now a crowd favorite. So is his new restaurant and bar located two blocks north of the arena.

Ainge is a fiery competitor who, like Westphal, owns a championship ring from the Boston Celtics. The Suns were really proud of themselves for snaring Ainge as an unrestricted free agent from Portland minutes after his contract expired in July of 1992. The Blazers were willing to offer him only two years, the Suns countered with three. Barkley and Chambers agreed to restructure their salaries to fit Ainge under the Suns' salary cap. Ainge was steamed at the Blazers for not taking care of him sooner, so it really wasn't a difficult decision for him. The Suns had visions of Ainge filling Hornacek's shoes.

Also, there was Negele Knight. The Suns received a number of tantalizing trade offers after Knight successfully filled in for KJ late in the 1991 season. Knight's numbers during a seven-game stint practically mirrored KJ's: 20-plus points, 10-plus assists. It was the popular theory that Knight could have started for many teams in the league. He thought so, too, and more than once said he'd be happy being KJ's caddy for a year or so, and then would like to go someplace where he could expand his game. But Knight was coming off a slow-healing hip and foot injury that ruined the final two months of his 1991-92 season. He was clobbered by Johnson in practice. The Suns weren't overjoyed with Knight's attitude during his recovery and were even more disgusted when he didn't play on a summer league team that they'd essentially set up for his benefit.

When Johnson suffered still more injuries during training camp in 1992, Knight got the call, but he was less than impressive.

Westphal initially had high hopes for Jerrod Mustaf, a forward the Suns acquired in 1991 from the New York Knicks in the Xavier McDaniel trade. Mustaf was young, out of Maryland following his sophomore season. He had seen some action with the Knicks as a rookie, but Fitzsimmons rarely used him. Westphal said he liked Mustaf's game and indicated that Mustaf would likely be in the starting lineup.

Of course, those plans were made before the Suns traded for Barkley. Barkley's arrival also had serious implications for Kurt Rambis and Ed Nealy, two aging role-playing forwards. Westphal's initial plan was to play Barkley at small forward while Mustaf, Rambis, and Nealy alternated at power forward.

That changed almost immediately at training camp, when Barkley showed that he could be taken by small forwards with a quick first step.

"Heck, Cedric Ceballos beat my butt every day in training camp," Barkley said.

Less than a week before the opener, Westphal made it official: he moved Barkley to power forward, and slid Ceballos in at small forward. That put Mustaf on the end of the bench and Rambis and Nealy on the waiver wire.

Westphal hinted all along that Ceballos was only warming his spot for Dumas, who was suspended on the eve of the 1991-92 season by the NBA because he failed the mandatory rookie random drug test. Nobody doubted that Dumas was a fantastic athlete, but hardly anyone was buying the superlatives Westphal was throwing around. Of course, not many people in Phoenix other than Westphal had seen Dumas play straight. When he finally was cleared to rejoin the Suns in mid-December, the straight and sober Dumas made his coach look like a genius.

Westphal had little choice but to put West back into the lineup at center, which wasn't as bad as it sounded. West's off-season work made him quicker to the ball, more explosive off the jump. Those qualities had served West well while dominating the Los Angeles Lakers in the 1990 Western Conference Semifinals. West taught Vlade Divac a lesson that he still hasn't forgotten. With Lang gone, Westphal's options were limited. Chambers could play center in some situations. He's nearly 7 feet tall and can take most centers outside and off the dribble. He can't guard them inside, though.

Then there was the rookie enigma, Miller.

Many thought the drafting of Miller low in the first round was as big a folly as Westphal's suggestion that they take a chance on Dumas in the second round of the previous draft. Few questioned Miller's skills. He'd had excellent seasons early in his career at Arkansas. His troubles began later when a series of personal problems caused him to eat obsessively: he was falsely accused of being involved in a sexual assault. He successfully sued the television station that first aired the report, but the harm was done.

At the predraft camp in Chicago in June 1992, Miller checked in at 323 pounds. That's pretty chunky over a frame that is barely 6-foot-9, and it's really shaky on feet and knees that had a history of buckling under the weight. A stress fracture in his foot had set him back in his senior season.

Miller and Ainge were the two players Westphal really wanted to add to the mix to offset the loss of Hornacek and Lang.

So there they were, the collection Westphal was supposed to mold into NBA champions.

## *Chapter Four*

# WALKING THE
# STRAIGHT AND NARROW

It was during the height of the Vietnam War that Paul Westphal grew up in Southern California. That also happened to be the height of UCLA's dominance in college basketball.

Westphal was the California player of the year at Aviation High in Redondo Beach. He could have gone to college anywhere; he had the opportunity to be a Bruin, and play for the Wizard of Westwood, John Wooden.

The whole UCLA scene didn't appeal to him, though; there were war protesters on that campus. Too radical. Too many hippies.

The University of Southern California, a private school, beckoned Westphal, an honest-to-goodness conservative at a time when many of his contemporaries were considerably left of the California coast line. And that's how Westphal viewed them: all wet.

"Absolutely," Westphal said. "I just wanted to go play basketball. I didn't know the answers to the world's problems. There was a lot more activism at UCLA on the side of 'this country stinks and we should turn on, tune in, drop out,' that type of stuff. I just never understood that. I thought that was a much bigger influence at UCLA and all the state schools than it was at the private schools like SC. I didn't think I needed to wear bell bottoms, wear my hair long, and start smoking dope. I just wanted to play basketball."

So USC it was. After all, it wasn't as if there was no life beyond the Rose Bowl in Trojans athletics.

"I have the utmost respect for Coach Wooden," Westphal said. "That was the biggest drawback of not going to UCLA. I happen to think Bob Boyd is a great coach, too. It wasn't like I was going someplace to play for some knucklehead. And I didn't get the feeling that John Wooden liked what was going on at UCLA much, either.

"I just didn't understand what all the fuss was about. There was a lot I didn't understand, but at least I *knew* I didn't understand. I didn't think all the leaders of the country were trying to wreck it. I was just a kid trying to do well enough in history to get a B and not work too hard at the same time, and just go play basketball. How am I going to tell the country how it ought to be run?

"I sure knew the drug culture was a dead end. I was smart enough to know that there were no answers there. I just wasn't interested in it and didn't want to get exposed to it to the point it would take away from what I wanted to do."

Westphal is the product of a Christian home where he was taught that the Bible is the word of God, that Jesus Christ is Lord and Saviour.

"I always have examined everything in the light of that, and never found it to be anything other than the truth," he said. "Rush Limbaugh has a great expression that I'm sure people hate. He calls young kids 'young skulls full of mush.' Until they get educated, that's all they are. They can be formed either way. I was just a young skull full of mush. I was different than a lot of kids because of my upbringing, but at the same time I was the same. I didn't know that much about why anything was the way it was, and didn't much care. I just rolled along.

"I really am thankful for that upbringing. It's the most important thing in life, to understand who God is, who you are, and how that makes everything fit together. I really think that a lot of the protests, and the searching through drugs that other people were going through, was because they didn't have that foundation in their lives. They didn't know which way to turn. True Christianity, in my opinion, is a very logical, intelligent, historically defensible belief system. The more I've studied and the more I've learned the basic teachings of the Bible, and the more I examine everything through that, the more it makes sense."

As he grew up, that became validated in him.

"I think that the more you ask, the more scrutiny you put God's word under, the more the answers come back that strengthen your faith because it's true," Westphal said. "It's true every time."

That is why you  see him as a calm, collected person on the sideline.

"That's not the reason to be Christian," he said. "There are a lot more important ones. Your eternal destination is a lot more important than helping you keep your perspective in a basketball game. But that's a byproduct of my beliefs because I know everything's going to be OK. But I also understand that winning or losing is not what validates or invalidates my life."

Westphal doesn't swear. That is where he and Barkley cross paths. Barkley spices many a practice with four-letter words that Westphal wouldn't dream of uttering.

After the Suns stumbled through an uninspired first half at Charlotte in early December, Westphal read them the riot act at halftime.

"Paul got mad at us — you could tell because he used profanity, and Paul never uses profanity," Barkley said.

Barkley's quote made it into print.

Even though the Suns rebounded to win and keep alive what became a five-game Eastern sweep, Westphal still was irked the following day. Why?

"I'm doing pretty good but my wife's mad at me," Westphal said. "She read in the paper where Charles said I used profanity. I didn't do that! I admit I was pretty upset, but I was under control."

He was kidding, right? He wasn't. It was a serious issue to him. He said his children were kidded at school because of the remark attributed to Barkley.

Don't forget that Westphal got his coaching career off the ground at tiny Southwestern Bible College near Phoenix. With little budget and uncompetitive facilities, he coached it to a 21-9 record in his first season.

From there, Westphal became coach at Grand Canyon College in Phoenix, a Southern Baptist school. In two seasons, he compiled a 63-18 mark and won the 1988 NAIA championship.

Westphal quickly had motivational passages from the Scripture made into posters that hang on the walls of the Suns' new clubhouse — it is too palatial to qualify simply as a "locker room."

Westphal works for a man, Colangelo, who is a born-again Christian, as are a number of front-office personnel with the Suns and America West Arena. Westphal won't hit you over the head with his beliefs, but if you ask, he'll talk.

"You can't force it on anybody else," he said. "I try not to push anything down anybody's throat. Everybody has to make up their own mind."

Yet from this structured, disciplined, principled man came a team that was loose, unorthodox, at times seemingly rudderless.

"Paul did a remarkable job this year in handling this team with its myriad of personalities," said Scotty Robertson, the aged traditionalist-style coach who was surprised when Westphal appointed him as an assistant. Robertson had been a head coach in New Orleans, Chicago, and Detroit.

"Paul himself is an interesting person in that he's very lenient, very loose if you want to use that term, in the handling and the organization of the team," Robertson said. "On the other hand, even though I don't know him that well personally because he's not the easiest guy to know, just from talking with him from time to time, from overhearing conversations with friends and acquaintances, hearing some of his comments about national current events, he gives me the feeling that he's a very conservative person. So it's interesting how you can have, you might say, two different personalities when it comes to your profession and then your family and everyday living."

Others in the organization view Westphal's approach as, well, different, also.

"He's like no other coach I've seen in this league," said Dick Van Arsdale, a teammate of Westphal's on the 1976 Suns, who made the Finals, and now their vice-president for player personnel. "He's a cool customer. He really operates under the philosophy that if you have a group of players who want to win, you've got to let them. That's the way he wanted it when he played. When you have as much talent as this team does, I think that's one reason he says, 'I'm going to let this team play basketball. I don't want to put the handcuffs on them and have everything go just by the books; they're smart enough and talented enough to know how to play by themselves.'"

"But I really always wanted to coach. I figured I'd get a coaching job right out of college, but then I was able to play in the league a pretty long time."

There was a time when Westphal was certain the last team he'd ever coach would be the Suns. As a player, he took them to arbitration — twice. Lost them both.

"There are disagreements in any family," Colangelo said. "That was a long time ago, and it's long forgotten."

While ever feisty, Westphal is smart enough to know that he has to temper his authority with good judgment. Having been a player seemed to serve him well in his dealings as a coach. For example, it was not uncommon for the Suns to receive days off.

"We know what Barkley can do. We know what KJ can do. I'd rather get it from them in a game than on the practice floor," Westphal said. "I mean, what's the point? I've played for coaches who wore their guys out for no particular reason with three-hour practices every day. Basketball is supposed to be fun, right?"

Right. One of those hard-line coaches to whom Westphal referred was John MacLeod, the Suns' winningest coach who guided the club to the 1976 Finals.

Leonard "Truck" Robinson, who was captain of the 1980-81 Suns team that won 57 games, the franchise record that stood for 12 seasons, said it's no coincidence that Westphal's team knocked MacLeod's out of the Suns' recordbook.

"Paul really understands that players are paid to play, so he lets them play," Robinson said. "That's why he has been so successful right away. John, for example, exerted much more control as a coach. Too much, for me. If Barkley misses three in a row, do you think he's coming out? Danny Ainge had a little slump late in the season, but Paul stuck with him and rode it out. It was different when I played."

Even the way the Suns travel is more geared toward the players' preferences. Of course, Westphal has the advantage of having a charter jet at his disposal, while the players in MacLeod's era flew commercially.

"But we'd always be on the first flight out no matter where we were going," Robinson said. "Just one example: Paul flew into Sacramento at 1 p.m. the day before a game. John would have had us on an 8 a.m. flight, and when we got there we wouldn't have checked into the hotel right away. We'd have gone straight to the practice gym, and he'd have run us like dogs for two hours the night after we'd played."

Nice praise from a former teammate, but Westphal is the kind of guy who'd stick with his plan even if he was being ripped instead of praised, as long as he thought his plan was right.

"When I was a kid," Westphal told *The Arizona Republic's* Bob Young just before the All-Star break, "my dad had me memorize the poem 'If' by Rudyard Kipling. There are several great pieces of advice in that poem. One of them has to do with public opinion.

"Once you know what is right, you cannot waiver in the face of unfair criticism. If you can meet with success and disaster and treat those two imposters just the same, then you're a man. I always took that to heart as something to shoot for, to not worry about what people think as much as about what is right. I've always been grateful to my dad for making me do that. But he had to bribe me. He paid me to memorize that."

Westphal is an intensely competitive man. In his initial training camp as coach, he turned everything, even the simplest drill, into a game. He kept score for everything, whether it was the number of times the defense correctly executed its rotations, or the proper movement in the new low-post offense. Losers had to run.

"I don't care how much money these guys make, they want to have fun," Westphal said. "They play better when they do. That's why they got into it in the first place. You can make it fun for them. It doesn't have to be drudgery."

That's his unmistakable imprint.

"When I was a player, there were times in practice when scores were kept," Westphal said. "I always enjoyed those times the most. These guys are competitors. If they weren't, we wouldn't want them. In these games, you find out who steps up when times get tough, and who wilts.

"It will never happen, but I'd like to work toward them deciding what's going to happen on the floor without me shouting out directions. I want them to be able to relate to each other on the floor and be creative."

So sometimes, Westphal even lets the players make up the rules. Fitzsimmons said that's not a surprise.

"If you go back to a lot of my quotes, and I know I say a lot of things that don't mean anything, he's everything that I said he was when Paul took over," Fitzsimmons said. "I think he's unique in his style of coaching. No. 1, he tries his very best not to show his emotions but he is emotional. Don't let him kid you. I watched him play against my teams, and I watched his emotions when he did good things, like go down the middle and stuff left-handed or something."

When Wesphal's Suns fell behind the Los Angeles Lakers in the opening playoff round in 1993, Fitzsimmons saw it again.

"The further we went in the series, the more emotion I saw from him on the sidelines," Fitzsimmons said. "So don't let anybody tell you he's mild, meek, laid back.

"He also is a very creative guy. He is an off-the-seat-of-his-pants type of coach. Yes, he is organized. I might tell somebody I'm organized to convince them I am. Westphal would like to tell them he's not organized so that they don't think he is. And then he'll get 'em. He is smart. As the old saying goes, he is dumb like a fox, and you can never read him on what move he's going to make next. A lot of my substitutions really were his substitutions, when I'd have odd-looking characters out on the court all at one time. That was one of the things that he taught me."

During the Finals, one Chicago writer described Westphal as a "concierge coach," the point being that Westphal is inclined to take a step back and get out of the players' way.

"I think I'm the kind of guy that has to maybe let people know I'm in charge," Fitzsimmons said. "Paul's the kind of guy that that doesn't bother him. But he is in charge. He stands back, lets them do their thing, and when they don't do it the way he feels they should, he tells them about it."

But taking days off without practice? Pulling up for three-pointers on a fast break? Those are Westphal's trademarks. He was told by more sage than one that his team is undisciplined.

"Yes, Paul is loose," said Fitzsimmons. "He runs a loose ship. But how else would you run this team if you had Charles Barkley out there? So if your No. 1 guy is loose, going to do what he wants to do, when he wants to do it, how he wants to do it, what do you expect the head coach to do? Are they going to knock heads? Are they going to go to war?

"Charles is not a rookie. He's a veteran All-Star, one of the best players in the world. So what's a coach to do? That's why you saw a team that was loose. But in the long run, it helped them."

That became apparent when the Suns lost the first two games at home to the Lakers and were one more loss away from a humiliating first-round exit from the playoffs.

"You've got to go to the Forum and play. Well, oh my, you've got to be scared," Fitzsimmons said. "But there was only one guy that was afraid, even though he made such a bold comment that they were going to win on such and such a night, then come back to Phoenix and win — Paul was concerned because he knew the situation. But the Phoenix Suns players weren't concerned because of the way he allowed them to be. They were loose, they did think they were going to win, and they did win."

There was more of the same in the Finals against the Chicago Bulls.

"How many people thought that same team, after getting beat both games on their home court, would go to Chicago and win two of three, and just about win all three?" Fitzsimmons said. "My point being, I can't criticize him for something that looks like it's loose, looks like it's out of control, looks like people do whatever they want to do.

"They come down on a four-on-one fast break, and back it up and shoot a three-pointer. A guy like me, I'd have had the biggie. I'd do a Fred Sanford. I'd say, 'Here it comes.' But that's the way Paul is. That's the way Paul allowed them to play. No, it wasn't the proper strategy. If you've got four-on-one, you give it to a guy and he stuffs it. You get two points. But that's the way they played, and like I used to say all the time, don't change faces on me when things are tight. That's the mark of a Charles Barkley, and a Paul Westphal. They do not change faces whether they're up by 20, or whether they're down by 20."

Colangelo, who has a lot of traditional coaching values in his blood, kind of wants to go along with it, too, but he's not so sure.

"I've shared with Paul my own opinions about this 'looseness' issue," Colangelo said. "But I'm a firm believer that when you hire a coach you've got to let that guy do what he wants to do unless it's totally off the wall. You may disagree with it at times but it's the coach's call. I really firmly believe that. I've always had the kind of communication with my coaches where we can share, we can talk, we can offer suggestions, offer anything in the way of constructive criticism, but then it's still the coach's call.

"The normal response when things are going bad is to tighten up. Paul's approach is not only unique, it was the kind of approach you don't often see in professional sports. How can one argue with the success we had? That was a truly amazing story in itself. The bottom line is we had a particular atmosphere that was created when we went to training camp, and it continued into the regular season. It served us well with the personnel we have and with the coaching staff we have. I think as we all look back, we'd have to say this team, on and off the court, was probably the most entertaining of any team we've ever had."

Colangelo and staff have roundtable discussions about the progress of the team.

"I might make a suggestion here and there about things I see, even about this 'looseness' question. You might want to tighten the ship a little bit. You may want to keep it as loose as it's been. That's the call that he has to make. It's what makes Paul comfortable and what he believes is the best kind of an atmosphere to get the most out of his team. So I accept it for what it is. I do respect Paul."

And vice versa.

"I have to say that I'm very fortunate to be working for people that know what they're doing," Westphal said. "That's not always the case in the NBA. Jerry Colangelo knows what's important, and you can't fool him, anyway. He certainly knows what it takes to be successful in the NBA. That's not like working for some owners I could name, or some general managers I could name."

Still, Westphal receives his fair share of second guessing, not only from the fans and media, but even in these top management "roundtable discussions."

"In one of the discussions one day, somebody said, 'Well, I don't agree with Paul. I think he could use this guy, this guy, that guy a little bit more,'" according to Fitzsimmons. "And I listened to everybody. And being a former coach, when they got done, I said, 'How could anybody in this room say we ought to use this guy more and that guy less when we won 62 games?'"

Fitzsimmons  has studied his successor, first as a player, then as a coach.

"I watched Paul's Grand Canyon teams, and he pretty much let them play," Fitzsimmons said. "The story I always tell that is characteristic of  Paul Westphal, and as a head coach in the NBA he has not changed, was when his son Michael came down to the huddle during the course of a timeout at Grand Canyon and asked for money to get a soda pop. Michael's like six  years old. Well, Paul reaches into his pocket, gets a dollar out, hands it to Michael, the horn blows, it's time for his team to go back on the court. I always say that if my son Gary had ever done that while I was coaching, Gary would be dead now.

"I didn't see Paul change, other than Michael is older and probably carries enough money.  But if it had happened in the Bulls series, Paul'd have reached in and pulled out the money for Michael and not missed a beat."

In the Western Conference Finals, Westphal used three different starting small forwards.

"And this was a crucial series to see who went to the Finals," said Hollins, who, among those in the Suns hierarchy, is most closely aligned with Westphal.  "Paul's ability to be flexible and his ability to downplay the importance of a situation is the thing that made the team realize it always had a chance. If we're down 20, don't get uptight and think he's going to run you 20 laps tomorrow."

For one thing, chances were good there wouldn't be a practice the next day, although following losses there generally was.

Loose? Before he got the Southwestern job, Westphal and his wife, Cindy, owned homes in Phoenix and Southern California. They weren't sure where they preferred to settle. They put both homes on the market and decided they'd live in the one that didn't sell first.

How different the Suns might be if the Phoenix home had sold first.

Even Westphal will acknowledge that he is a bit of an unorthodox coach.

"I do try to coach the way I wanted to be coached, but there are certain times that I treat certain guys not the way that I would have wanted to be treated," he said. "I do try to treat them like an adult until they prove they're not. And if they're not, I can come down on them. I try not to come down on somebody for something that doesn't matter."

If there's no film to watch, Westphal stays home. Some coaches are afraid to do that because of the perception that they are not out-working the other guy.

"I don't think anybody has their team more prepared than we have," he said. "I try to be honest with the team. I try to not waste their time by saying the same thing over and over again, or by just talking on. I try to tell them what's important, and why I think that's important. I try to tell them in a way that I think is the most effective way to communicate at that time. I yell at them sometimes, I joke with them sometimes. Sometimes I might let the assistants coach a little if I think the players are tired of hearing me."

That, he said, isn't much different from his approach in the beginning back at Southwestern — except he didn't have assistants.

"I don't think that this year has been some eye-opening experience," he said. "I felt ready for this. It wasn't like I hadn't coached and all of a sudden you dropped me here in the NBA, 'Gol-lee, it sure is a different world.' It just wasn't like that."

And just as he doesn't view himself as the center of the universe, he tries to give his players a similar perspective. Hence the signs on the wall containing Biblical passages. Westphal says they are not intended to proselytize.

"The signs are just to remind us that we didn't invent things, and that things are still going to be rolling along after we're gone," he said. "I think that anybody should be able to agree on that fundamental point but I think we all need to be reminded of that."

The players didn't protest.

"First of all, we don't have a player on our team I think would disagree with the sentiments that I put up" Westphal said. "Personally, I believe it's very important to define who is Jesus Christ, did he come out of the grave, and what did that mean to me? To me, it's the most important question. But because my job is to coach them in basketball, I don't feel I have the right to ask them that question. So there's no sign in the locker room that makes them deal with that, because it's not right for me to make them examine that.

"But I do think Biblical quotes talking about—the one where God asks Job, 'Where were you when I laid the foundations of the Earth?' well, there's not one guy in that room that could really say he doesn't believe in God. That's something they can at least acknowledge, that this was in the Old Testament. Mormons, Jews, Muslims, Christians, agnostics all accept the Old Testament as a historical document. At least in theory they say that. They can say, 'Well, this is a good question. Were we around when all this stuff started? Because if we weren't, how can we know? How can we make ourselves important?' That's not a theological bone of contention for anybody in that locker room. It's just something to remind them that they're not the center of it all.

"So that's how I justify putting up some of those things. It's trying to give them a little bit of wisdom to remind them that this isn't everything in the world, and to help them focus on basketball better because it takes a little of the pressure off. As a person, I care about everyone that I come into contact with, and hope that they have their lives in order. But as a basketball coach, I don't care. If they can play, it just doesn't matter."

There are a lot of guys in the NBA who can't even spell "Testament," but the Suns are, by and large, an intelligent, deep-thinking lot that takes strength from the messages.

Or, they're so independently strong, they simply ignore them.

"That is interesting in that it's a little bit away from the way some people see Paul," Robertson said. "Sometimes, you get the impression that Paul is very loose. He believes that as professional athletes that these guys should get themselves ready. He doesn't spend a lot of time motivating people. And yet, you look around, and you see these signs on the walls, which are, in my mind, motivational tools."

And then there is Westphal's fascination with Rush Limbaugh. Many in Arizona live for Limbaugh's nightly lampooning of bleeding-heart liberals. Westphal is among them. That, however, only further causes Westphal to be perceived by his detractors as aloof, elitist, smart-alecky, and condescending.

"I started listening to Rush and really got a kick out of him," Westphal said. "I'm really good friends with Mike Lupica of the *New York Daily News.* We go back to our early 20s in Boston when he was at Boston College and I was a rookie for the Celtics.

"Anyway, about a year ago Rush happened to go to a college football game that Mike was working. Rush was up in the press box. So Mike called me up and said, 'I've got somebody who wants to talk to you.' He puts Rush on the phone and we started talking. We had a nice conversation and decided we'd get together for dinner if we were ever in the same city. When we went back to play the Knicks, we got together and had dinner a couple of times, and kept in touch.

"I would think that people in the business would have to get a kick out of him. I just don't understand why the media doesn't like him. When you listen to what the guy says, first of all, the guy's hilarious. You can't get away from the fact that he's got a great sense of humor."

Limbaugh had been the Westphals' guest during the first two games of the Finals in Phoenix.

"It seems to me that most of the criticism he receives is from people who don't listen to what he says. I think it's pretty hard to argue with most of it. I'm not even that political. I don't think that politics can save the world. Even if you did everything Rush Limbaugh says, I don't think you could save the world. So it kind of shocks me that so many people wouldn't at least listen to what he's got to say because they've got to see the lunacy that's going on around them. And all Rush does is make fun of it."

Westphal admits that Limbaugh's TV program had him laughing out loud between the third and fourth games of the Finals at Chicago.

"Marv Albert (of NBC-TV) had made a comment about Rush being there during the telecast," Westphal said. "He said, 'It's a good thing Rush Limbaugh isn't in charge of the NBA. There'd probably be five years mandatory for traveling.'

"Rush picked up on that. He said, 'First of all, I don't think there should five years mandatory for traveling. I think they should just enforce the law. If a guy travels, give it to the other team. That's the law. Just enforce it. What would happen if Marv and his liberal buddies ran the NBA? If there was a foul, first you'd have to analyze the motivations of the fouler. Was he forced to do it? Did he have a bad childhood? And then, you'd have to diagnose the impact this would have on the self-esteem of the other players. If you punish this one guy, is that fair to his teammates or the fans who supported his team? What if it's a player of one race fouling a player of another race? Is there bias invovled?'

"He was just killing me. He said the liberals could never run the NBA."

Perhaps the greatest controversy surrounding Westphal, though, was his labeling the final 10 days "exhibition season" after the Suns locked up the best record in the league.

In fact, the closing games meant nothing other than a chance to rest tired and injured players. The Suns had a lengthy list of both. But when they lost five of their final eight games, including a home blowout to Houston, the natives, who thought they saw a championship slipping away, got restless.

In publicly labeling the games "exhibitions," Westphal set a tone with which many fans, and even some of the players, were uncomfortable.

The Suns were coming off an incredible high, having blown through an Eastern road trip unscathed, including wins in Barkley's emotional Philadelphia homecoming, over the Bulls in the Stadium, the Celtics in Boston Garden, and Indiana, which earlier had dealt Phoenix an embarrassing home loss. The Suns did seem to lose an edge during "exhibition season."

"Personally, I think it was a mistake, however in essence that's what it was," Robertson said. "But you don't have to say that. Paul is a very bright guy. He's his own man. But in my opinion, he opens himself up for criticism at times by making statements about things that he doesn't necessarily have to. And this is not any of my business, this is just my personal approach.

"He likes to comment about politics. He likes to comment about religion. It's his right to do that. If he feels because of who he is, with his position in the community and the fact that he is in the limelight, that he can further his beliefs in these areas, then he's doing the right thing by making these comments. However, sometimes he opens himself up for criticism that he doesn't need to."

Others among the Suns' basketball operation tend to agree with Robertson about the "exhibition season."

"I probably wouldn't have done it that way," Van Arsdale said. "You've got to be a man and admit that maybe it was a mistake to look at it that way because of the old theory about losing momentum at the end of the season and not being able to regain it. There's a lot of truth to that, and I thought maybe the Suns did lose some momentum. It wasn't a major blunder, though."

Nor was the pre-playoff mini-camp in Prescott, Arizona, Van Arsdale said, although Westphal took heat for that, too. The idea was to get the team some solitude and bring them together to rebuild that lost momentum. Instead, the Suns were mobbed everywhere they went in the tiny mountain community about a two hour's drive north of Phoenix.

The practices were closed, and as a result, Westphal said, he did accomplish everything on the court that he intended. Outside the locked gym, though, was a mob scene that disturbed the players. And with KJ injured, the Suns opened the playoffs poorly.

"You've got to look at Prescott and wonder, 'Did that hurt the team? Was that the reason we went down, 0-2, to the Lakers?'" Van Arsdale said. "I don't think so. I really don't. I thought the biggest reason we went down to the Lakers was because of the way they played. They played great basketball."

Colangelo said he knew exactly what Westphal was attempting to accomplish with his "exhibition season" proclamation and with the mini-camp.

"But I did feel, and I shared this with him, that we lost an edge at the end of the year," Colangelo said. "We were playing the very best basketball of the season coming off that last Eastern road trip. We clinched a little bit early. As a result, what Paul did was the right thing in terms of player personnel. We did have a player who got injured, Charles. Could he have come back a couple of games early? Probably. But what was there to gain? The net effect was we were not ready physically or mentally. We had a little bit of a breakdown in the last couple of weeks because of that.

"In retrospect, I would think you would handle that a little bit differently. The important thing is we survived it. Had we gone down in the first round, people would have been talking about the last few weeks of the regular season for the next six months. But, all the drama that took place, the fans would have missed out on. We had unbeliev-able games, memorable shots for game-winners that kept everybody right on the edge throughout the playoffs. So maybe that's exactly the way it was meant to be."

Even Fitzsimmons said that Westphal's terminology was a mis-take.

"But he didn't need everybody to tell him. He didn't need the owner to tell him, the senior executive vice- president of nothing to tell him, his assistant coaches. He knew he made that mistake," Fitzsimmons said. "He made that mistake to the fans because it's not exhibition season to them. Paul did the same thing we've all done: he tried to rest his players. Sometimes because of that, we're criticized. If that's his biggest sin, he's going to have a long career."

Westphal and Hollins, however, said they'd do it again.

"I know that a lot of people I respect think I made a mistake in saying that, and I have to take that into consideration, but I think it was exactly the right thing to do, and I can't imagine why anybody would think it was wrong," Westphal said.

"We were real banged up. The thing that made me maddest all year was Rick Barry saying that Charles Barkley wasn't hurt and didn't have to go on the injured list. He went on ESPN and said, for a fact, he knew Charles Barkley wasn't hurt.

"He was lying. Barkley was hurt. The doctor said he couldn't play for a week to 10 days, so we put him on the injured list.

"And KJ was in a fragile condition. I cared about the playoffs with him. I didn't care about meaningless regular-season games. Majerle needed rest. People forget he had knee surgery in the offseason. Tom Chambers suffered the quadricep injury. To me, trying to drive the team to win every regular-season game under those circumstances would have been suicide for the playoffs. By taking the pressure off the players and saying the games didn't mean anything, other than keeping our conditioning, enabled them to focus in on what our season really is all about, which is the playoffs.

"Even though I respect the criticism from people who said it cost us momentum and stuff like that, if I would have treated those games as life and death, we still would have lost a lot of them because we were so banged up. We would have been more banged up, and I don't think we would have gotten out of the first round. So I stand by it, and I'll do it again."

Hollins was in Westphal's corner.

"Everything that was done had a hand in getting us to the Finals — Kevin not playing back-to-back, cutting back on Majerle's minutes, taking the mental strain off the team," Hollins said. "We had accomplished everything we could have accomplished during the regular season. So taking a step back and throwing it into low gear for a couple of games certainly helped us to rev back up and get going into the playoffs. Calling them 'exhibition games' in my mind wasn't that bad. Fans took it the wrong way. Nobody said a word about what the games were called until we got blown out by Houston. If we had played all the guys we had for 48 minutes that night, Houston was going to beat us pretty bad because they were on a serious roll at that particular time.

"I have to say what we did worked out. I won't say it was totally like we planned it, but it worked out."

Westphal hand-picked Hollins and Robertson as his assistants because he respected and wanted their divergent points of view. Hollins had been an assistant with Westphal under Fitzsimmons for four seasons. Robertson had been the Suns' NBA scout during the Fitzsimmons regime, doing on-floor coaching when presenting scouting reports, and occasionally doing some individual coaching. Hollins, like Westphal, is a former player who owns a championship ring; Hollins got his in Portland.

Robertson never played in the NBA. He is a career coach. Westphal uses Robertson's years of experience to play the devil's advocate to Westphal's brainstorms.

"You've got the traditionalist who's come up through the ranks, high school coaching, college coaching, professional coaching, done the whole bit — and that's me," Robertson said. "And then you've got the ex-player in Lionel Hollins, whose thinking is pretty much like Paul's in most regards.

"So hopefully, there's a balance there, a situation that allows for input from both sides of the coin, so to speak. That's not to indicate that we don't ever agree because we certainly do, but at least we see things from two different perspectives. Then, we try to put it all together. "

It was like a dream come true for the 60-ish Robertson.

"I'm a coach. That's who I am," he said. "To have an opportunity to come back on the bench and actively coach, not only in practice, but in the games has been wonderful for me. This afforded an opportunity to be with a winner, one we all felt had a legitimate shot at the championship. Comparing that with the other seven NBA teams I've been with, this was a dream come true."

But Robertson wasn't so sure at first.

"When Paul approached me last year following the close of Cotton's last season and said, 'I'd like for you to be one of my assistant coaches,' I said, 'Quite frankly, that shocks me,' because I wasn't sure how comfortable Paul would be with me, since I'd been a head coach and since our backgrounds were so different. However, I said to him, 'The fact that you've asked me to do this causes me to respect you more than I ever have because I think it's the right decision on your part. Is this your decision?' He said, 'Yes, it's mine 100 percent.' I thought maybe some of the powers that be had told him that he needed an experienced person, but he assured me that it was his choice, so because of that, I said, 'I'm going to give you everything I have.'"

Hollins has discovered that while he may be a young coach at age 40, the league and its players have covered quite a bit of ground since his playing days.

"It's hard to tell somebody how tough the NBA is anymore," Hollins said. "We charter all our flights. There's no 5 o'clock wakeup calls anymore. Somebody does all the laundry. You come to the game at home, you don't have to bring anything. They've got razors and toothbrushes right in the locker room. When I played, we took both of our uniforms home. We washed all of our practice gear. We went on the road, we washed our own uniform. We pretty much were on our own. Nobody took care of us. The guys who didn't mature and take care of their responsibilities eventually went by the wayside. They just got lost, like being in a big city.

"So today it's really hard to say to young players, 'This is how we have to do it.' They say, 'Well, so-and-so, he made it and he didn't have to do it that way.' What you try to teach them is responsibility and the love of the game.

"I'm always trying to ask trivia questions and see how much these guys have studied the game, because the true lovers of the game, they know who were the contributors of the past. They know who did what. When they get close to something, some record or something, they know who they're passing, what it means. That's important to know, the tradition of the game. If you're just playing it for the money, you don't last long."

What a collection they had to work with!

Phil Jackson, coach of the Bulls, on the eve of the playoffs described the Suns as "a team of oddities."

"That's fair," Westphal responded.

Most players who are successful in the NBA have something about their game that creates a mismatch, something about their game that is unique that causes them to rise above the crowd and the Suns are loaded with such players.

"Whether it is extreme quickness like Kevin has, or great leaping like Richard Dumas has, I just think that the league is built on slight advantages," Westphal said.

The smart thing for a coach to do, then, is put players who can do something well into a situation where they can best do it.

"We have a couple of guys who are great three-point shooters, Ainge and Majerle. So I think you'd be silly not to spread the defense and use those advantages that they have," Westphal said. "If you're going to play those guys together, you're going to have a shorter team, and you must have a penetrator with them to take advantage of the spread floor. Well that's KJ, with Barkley as the post-up player.

"All those guys I think fit together because of their uniqueness. It does make us less than a classic team. We don't have a 6-10 power forward or a 7-foot center, all the stuff you think you need to make up the 'perfect' NBA team. Yet we do have guys who have strengths that complement each other.

"One of the things that makes us tough to guard is we have a lot of guys who can score. We do have weapons at each position, except Mark West. And he can score from right under the basket when people leave him. That's usually where he is, so they have to guard him."

But the young players, particularly Miller and Dumas, proved to be a challenge.

"I think that guys like Ainge, Majerle, KJ, Barkley, and West, you know who they are and what they're capable of doing. And to me, they're the easiest guys in the world to coach," Westphal said. "I think the younger guys who are trying to find out where they fit into the league, find out what the league's all about, find out who they are, those are the guys who are the hardest. There have been times where I've been tested by Richard, Oliver, Cedric, and to a lesser extent, Mustaf, and Negele.

The bad days make you appreciate the good days even more, if you ever get any good days. The problem is there are no guarantees of any good days to come."

But the Suns had their share of good ones.

"It was pretty nice when we beat Chicago in Chicago in the regular season," Westphal said. "Jerry Colangelo is from Chicago. After the game we went out to this restaurant. They held it open. The owner of the place was cooking for us and bring the food out. It was just a great calm.

"It's hard to top having the best record in the league and beating the world champions on their floor, and then going out and having a great meal with the people you helped accomplish that with."

But that high was balanced by Miller's weight battle.

The low point of the season for Westphal, he said, was when Oliver Miller was placed on a weight-loss program in which he spent his nights at a hospital, where everything he ate and drank was monitored.

"He volunteered to do it," Westphal said. "The frustration level was real high at that point, both with Oliver and with ourselves. You could see the talent and potential that guy has. We tried everything. He tried. He didn't know how. It was a real emotional, intense, tough time. I'm very proud of how he's responded. He still has a long way to go, but he's going in the right direction.

"We had to have that rock-bottom time in order to go back up. That's why I laugh when I read in the paper that I'm so mild and everything. If they could have heard me in the room with Oliver that day before he went into the hospital, they would never say that about me again. I think I said what he needed to hear, and it wasn't very nice. There are times when you have to get a little drastic.

"It was probably the turning point of the year because we would not be here without Oliver. He knew he was at the crossroads. He went the right direction."

Overall, so did Westphal as a rookie head coach.

"It's quite amazing what he's done," Barkley said. "He set the record for wins by a rookie coach. People say it was a good team already. Well, I don't think that's fair because we did give up three starters. To give up three starters and win nine more games and be without your second-best player for a period of games, I think it's really remarkable. But you know, people don't want to give him credit. You can't say anything bad about Paul, considering what we accomplished. He is just a fun person to play for."

In fact, Westphal had some support for coach of the year, although Riley won.

"The years that I was coach of the year I happened to get a clean shot, but this year, in my opinion, there could have been four," Fitzsimmons said. "My coach of the year, in all honesty, would have been Rudy Tomjanovich, and the reason I say that is he had a team that really did have troubles. The Suns at least liked each other. They didn't like each other in Houston. They didn't care about each other, and they didn't want to play with each other, so he was able to pull that thing together and make a nice run.

"Paul is right there with him. Riley is right there with him, and George Karl. Paul has said it before, and I truly believe Paul, that he would rather be like Riley was with the Lakers, never be voted coach of the year, and just win. And I feel the same way. You can have my coach of the year awards and every other award I've ever got if you can just give me a ring. I haven't had one."

## Chapter Five

# JUST PLAIN CHUCK

Living the life they lead, seeing the things they see, NBA players aren't fazed easily. But when Barkley arrived on the scene at that first informal workout, the Suns had no idea how to interact.

They've all got TV sets. They'd all seen the Olympics. How do you treat someone who is bigger than life? This was going to be a new experience.

Initially, the Suns approached him with the same reverence any fan would, as if the proper salutation was "Mr." Eventually, he became known to them as "Chuck." He'd been called a lot of things, but that was new.

"People seem to think that Charles is bigger than life, but that's why we call him 'Chuck'—just a regular guy," Hollins said. "He really is. He gets a lot of jokes put on him. He's the brunt of a lot of kidding. He takes it good-naturedly. He dishes a lot out, but he gets a lot. The only time you know Charles is different, other than his ability on the court, is when the media comes around."

At various times, Barkley had been known as "The Round Mound of Rebound," which he hated, and "Sir Charles." Interestingly enough, Barkley hadn't even been "Charles" until he got to Auburn.

"Everybody in my hometown to this day calls me 'Wade,' " Barkley said. "I was never called 'Charles.' My real name is Charles Wade Barkley. In the South, everybody goes by middle names. In college, they didn't know that."

Didn't matter. The Suns quickly settled on a new name for him, after they got to know him, and with Barkley's personality that didn't take long.

When "Chuck" screwed up, Ainge or Frank Johnson let him know.

"And he'd let them know when they screwed up," Hollins said. "It was give and take."

Barkley quickly took to the two veteran guards, who became his best friends on the team — especially Johnson, who like Barkley was alone in town. Barkley was separated from his wife, Maureen. Johnson's family remained in Minneapolis because of the suddenness of his landing the job and the uncertainty over how long he would have it. So the two of them socialized.

"I just respect guys like that who have tremendous heart and courage," Barkley said. "They're like me, they just go to work. I gravitate to players who go to war for you.

"Frankie and Mark West are probably the ultimate professionals."

Johnson said Westphal assigned him to keep Barkley out of trouble, a task he accepted with relish.

"He always gave me a hard time about everything, and I gave it back to him," Johnson said. "We did get along, did a lot off the court. He said I was his conscience, if that's possible.

"Imagine being Charles Barkley's conscience! It was like, 'Hey, Chuck, it's time to go home, what do you think?' Something like that. He'd say, 'Why don't you grab a beer?' because he knew I wasn't a drinker. I never acquired the taste, so I'd just drink the water. Finally I'd say, 'Alright Chuck, let's go.'

"Someone might come up to him who's pretty obnoxious, and it was, 'Alright Chuck, leave him alone. Don't worry about this guy.' And he'd walk away. I'd be there just in case maybe I'd have to help.

"Paul always told me, 'Frank, if there's any trouble, you jump in front of Charles and take the punch,' or, 'You throw the punch and you can get in trouble. Don't let Charles get in trouble.' That never happened. There was one instance where I said, 'Chuck, don't do it.' He just grabbed me like this, boom-boom, and moved me aside. From then on, I never stepped in front of him to stop him from doing anything."

Colangelo knew there was a potential for trouble with Barkley. Remember, he delayed completing the trade until he was certain Barkley had been acquitted of charges in Milwaukee.

Phoenix had not played host to many fast-living, gregarious sports personalities. Those who had passed through couldn't back it up on the court the way Barkley can. Bringing in a reputed troublemaker was contrary to the "plain vanilla" image of the Suns. But Colangelo knew more about Barkley than the public did. Besides, he was ready to shake things up. He was prepared for the backlash, but he didn't expect much, and he didn't get much.

"The thing about Jerry," Barkley said, "is he has big balls. Most owners wouldn't even try to win in his situation. Most of these owners are just trying to make money, and they're in the ultimate money-making situation. He's got it made. I mean, the arena is sold out every night, and he's going to make money on paraphernalia and things like that, and the TV money is too good to be true. So he doesn't have to make this team win.

"But Jerry does want this team to win, and the thing that impresses me most about him is he put it on the line and he did what it took to win. Not many owners would have done that, but he wants this team, this city to win so bad."

Colangelo said Phoenix was ready to welcome him with open arms.

"That's exactly what they did," Colangelo said. "They embraced him from the day he came to Phoenix. He was going to have to go way out of his way to turn the fans against him, and of course that didn't happen. The respect and adulation was building all year, and he had a fantastic season."

Many other things had to happen for the Suns to have the run they had. Even Barkley couldn't carry it by himself. He had to have the support. The Suns had to give him the personnel. Everything had to work together.

"It was interesting with all the ups and downs we had during the course of this year, with people hurt and injured and in and out, it was amazing to me that we had as much consistency as we did," Colangelo said. "Charles played through it all. He put some big numbers on the boards, and he made some strong, sound statements about his game."

It wasn't totally without incident. He chucked a beer at an obnoxious female at a Scottsdale bar. He'd spice up practices with his favorite twelve-letter expletive — whether the gym was empty or there happened to be a tour of schoolchildren passing through.

In the Western Conference Finals at Seattle, Barkley toyed with the crowd, calling on his colorful vocabulary and corresponding hand gestures. A rather large photo of him making a gesture that can best be described as "flippant" ran in a Seattle newspaper.

"Charles is a grown man," Colangelo said. "I think he's very bright. He's a very emotional guy. A person who is under that much pressure from the media and the fans kind of marches to a different drummer. There are a lot of pressures involved. And maybe that's too much to expect from any individual. Look at Michael Jordan's decision not to speak to the media. You can criticize it, but unless you've been there and recognize that this guy has no personal life or privacy any place he goes — I mean, he has to live like a hermit. That's not a real nice existence. That's a sad thing."

Barkley, on the other hand, likes to play the crowd.

"Once in a while, he has stepped over the line. But that's an opinion," Colangelo said. "Maybe in his mind he hasn't stepped over the line. When there's an incident or two that I find distasteful, I have to accept it. I may not like it, but I think he knows, himself, right after it happens that he wouldn't do it again. And maybe he would. I just think when you're dealing with grown men you have to accept the little bit of bad that goes with the good.

"I haven't called him on anything because my attitude with Charles Barkley is that I was going to treat him with respect, I would never demean him, I would never talk down to him. I would expect to be treated the same way by him. I think we have a great relationship because mutual respect is there. He knows how I feel about situations."

It has been suggested that Colangelo is taking a kind of grin-and-bear-it approach with a superstar who not only is helping the Suns win games but is bringing in dollars the Suns never envisioned through merchandising. People around the world now know who the Suns are because of Barkley.

While winning certainly is important, Colangelo has tempered his treatment of Barkley with the knowledge that the Suns also are in the entertainment industry. Show business.

"You look at many athletes who are so plain vanilla in terms of their approach to the job, to the game itself," Colangelo said. "When you have personalities, you have something very special. Charles is right at the top of the list in terms of personalities. When you think of personalities in the league, you think of Magic's charisma and smile, Isiah Thomas, Shaquille O'Neal, and Michael Jordan. But I don't think any conversation could take place without mentioning Charles Barkley in the same breath. He is so good for the NBA because he is a showman."

Watch Barkley. He plays the game, works the crowd. He's got the officials going, he's got his own teammates going. He's working his opponent. He's got all these little side things going on. That's quite a balancing act.

A fortunate thing happened for Barkley and the Suns shortly after the trade was made: the Olympics. What a merchandising and public relations bonanza, his elbowing of an Angolan notwithstanding.

"I saw it take place in living color in Barcelona," Colangelo said. "He became a pied piper internationally. I mean, he moved himself from one level to another.

"With all the great athletes who were there, the media swarmed around Charles Barkley, because he was the one who was going to give them the good interviews, give them the lines. And the fans just loved him. He was the most popular athlete there. He was a pied piper. When I saw that, it just reinforced everything I thought that was starting to build."

Back in Phoenix, the Suns began bracing for an onslaught. They were stepping into another league, too. This would be something they never before had experienced. A parade of national and international reporters found their way to the Purple Palace to chronicle Barkley's first year wearing the purple and orange.

They discovered some of the quirks of a man who appears to be complex but really lives by a simple philosophy: "Life is easy, people just make it hard."

For starters, Barkley is a neat freak. Two days before the season opener, Barkley, as usual, was the last one in the locker room. He moved slowly. First, a long soak in the Suns' mammoth Jacuzzi accompanied by Danny Ainge's rubber duckie and a newspaper.

Then, a rinse off. Then he made his way back to his locker, where there always are reporters — newspaper, radio, TV — waiting to capture his mood, his antics, his words. On this day, Barkley was irked. Somebody had helped himself to his deodorant — and failed to return it.

"I can't believe that," he said. "That's just inconsiderate. How can you do that to your own teammate?"

Then, taking a look around at used towels strewn about, and the big-screen television tuned to MTV that was left playing at extremely high volume, Barkley shook his head in disgust, walked over, turned it off, and said, "I'm living with animals."

His mother and grandmother were meticulous housekeepers. Young Wade took the cue.

"Oh yeah, I like everything clean," he said. "Keeping things clean was ingrained in me, but I took it to the extreme. I like everything in perfect order. I just think it's better to be clean than dirty.

Frank Johnson and Fitzsimmons can vouch for that.

"I wouldn't live with Charles. He's too much of a clean freak," Johnson said. "I like to have things clean, too, but this guy's waking up at 3 in the morning and cleaning his windows. I really wanted to hire him as my maid. That would have been great."

Fitzsimmons is the closest to Barkley among those in Suns management.

"I knew that as vice president of nothing that one of my jobs was to keep up with Charles Barkley, and I enjoy doing it," Fitzsimmons said. "Between my wife, JoAnn, and me we see to it that Charles is all right. Charles is a pretty independent guy. Like the mail in his mailbox might stay in there for three months. Somebody's got to take care of that.

"Charles is really something. You can go into his home anytime you want to and eat off the floor. He might have 20 pair of Nikes, but I promise you they'll all be on the shelves, they'll all be in order just the way he wants them. And that impresses me about him.

"I was over to his house the other day. You would think it was a model home that he was showing that day to sell, because there wasn't anything out of place. Even the dish towel was rolled up, folded perfect and in the right spot."

Fitzsimmons seems to have Barkley's ear. Fitzsimmons doesn't try to be Barkley's conscience. Like Johnson, he learned long ago that it's a futile endeavor. But he does advise. Usually, Barkley listens.

"Charles likes to talk and I like to talk," Fitzsimmons said. "During the course of our games all these years, we've had some pretty good conversations. He'd tell me how he's going to kill my team, and how he's going to stick it to me. Many times we've gone at it pretty good. Through the Nike things, we'd played golf together, we'd played cards together, we'd done a lot of things together and had a good time. So we had this relationship and I'd go at him pretty good, too: 'OK, Charles, get your 45, we're still going to win. I don't care what you get.' One of the reasons I was never concerned about Charles Barkley coming to Phoenix like some other people were was because I knew him."

First of all, he's a nice person who doesn't want anyone to know it, according to the Vice President of Nothing.

"He's a big fake, a big con, "Fitzsimmons said. "He tries to hide all those things about himself. But don't get me wrong. You cross him, and he'll tell you exactly what he thinks of you.

"But with kids, with people who reach out and want to touch somebody like that to get some inspiration, he's always there. See, a guy can be wild, get in a fight in Milwaukee because some guy challenges him because of who he is, and it doesn't make him a bad guy. He spent a night in jail. He isn't going to run from anybody. You can't challenge a guy like Charles Barkley because he's going to go to war."

Maybe that's why Colangelo chose not to call Barkley on anything.

"But anybody who respects his grandmother and his mother the way Charles does is a good person," Fitzsimmons said. "There's other players I've had to worry about because they didn't have that respect. They were wild and they did a lot of bad things. But not Charles."

Well, there was a table-hopping incident in Madison Square Garden in January when Barkley tore after the officials following a loss to the Knicks.

Barkley was suspended for the following game at Cleveland, and the Suns lost another close one there. Fitzsimmons had a chat with him about it.

"Charles is emotional," Fitzsimmons said. "Charles will never tell you 'I'm sorry I did it.' I told him very simply, 'The team needs you on the court,' and I let him know why we lost the Cleveland game, because he jumped over a table, went after an official and got suspended. That can't be. I said, 'Charles, your job is to win. Some way, somehow, you have to control your emotion.'

"The good thing for me is I don't have to coach him. We are friends and I don't have to walk on eggshells around him. I always tell him exactly what I think, and he always tells me, 'Go get a job.' And I'm still looking for one."

They do talk frequently. Fitzsimmons said that when you're older, you're supposed to be a little wiser because maybe you've learned from experiences.

"Don't preach to him," he said. "I told him what I thought about New York. I was only disappointed that his teammates and his coaches didn't see it happening and could have kept him from being suspended. I don't mind him getting upset but I would have rather seen them 'rassle' with him all the way back to the locker room, and him hollering all the way, than for him to get to the official, have his say, and then be suspended. He thought he got fouled. He was frustrated about the game. He just doesn't take things lying down."

Another example came years ago when Cotton and JoAnn were in St. Thomas at a Nike gathering with Barkley, who at that time was dating Maureen.

"He wanted to get Maureen this beautiful bracelet," Fitzsimmons said. "If you've been to St. Thomas and places of that nature, you've got to bargain a little bit. And luckily for Charles, he had some women with him, some of the college coaches' wives. My wife, who also was there, said, 'Charles, that's beautiful, but we've got to negotiate.' Women negotiate when it comes to jewelry. Men just buy. So they negotiated pretty good, had a pretty good deal, felt they'd be able to go back and buy it at a nice price.

"So now they start heading up the street, and after they'd gone up a little ways, they look around and Charles was gone. So what'd Charles do? He went back to the place and paid the full price. Why? 'It was beautiful, I wanted it.'

"That's a Charles Barkley story. That's the way he is."

Few can deny that Barkley is a man of extravagant deeds who is willing to pay the full price for them.

"He's an interesting person, a generous person, he's a good person," Fitzsimmons said. "Probably the thing that I admire most about him is that he comes to play every night. And the second thing is he doesn't necessarily say that he is the best player playing basketball, but he doesn't say that anybody else is.

"So if I've got Charles' ear, then I've got a good ear."

So does Frank Johnson. Barkley loves to go out, and his "conscience" usually went along for the ride.

"Charles enjoys the attention. One thing about him, he isn't going to let his position in the public eye stop him from doing the things he wants to do," Johnson said. "But every time we went out somewhere, he always had someone there to look after him.

"He always gave a lot of time to people. It's so funny. Charles would say, 'I'm not signing any more damn autographs,' to a group of people. He may go 10 steps, and, boom, he signs. I'd say, 'Charles, I thought you said you weren't going to sign any more.' He never responded. This happened all the time all year. I won't ask him that again. He enjoys seeing people happy, smiling. I think that's what keeps him going. Charles enjoys very much being around people. No matter where he goes, he's the man. He may be in a room with Michael or whomever, but I guarantee you Charles will get the most attention. It's his presence."

Van Arsdale had a similar story relayed to him by a friend a few weeks after the Suns' loss in the Finals.

"A friend of mine had just been to a function in Atlanta," Van Arsdale said. "They had like 300 of their corporate people there because they were going to sponsor the '96 Olympics. They had people like Rafer Johnson come in and some of the top Olympians in the last couple of Olympics. Charles was there. He said Charles was incredible. After the program was over, they didn't care about Edwin Moses or any of the swimmers. Two hundred of the 300 people were lined up to get Barkley's autograph. He does have a presence about him."

And Barkley knows it.

"I love making people happy," Barkley said. "I have a gift. I believe that. I do think God made me special to entertain people. I have a unique ability to make people laugh. I think I have what they call charisma. People say I'm a little like Muhammad Ali. That might be true as far as we both just have fun with what we do. I'm not the most religious person, but I pray every day, because I really believe that God made me special.

"I love to get the fans excited. I love to get people pumping and going. That's a great feeling when you get the crowd going. That makes me feel good. I think they make you play so much better, like when you get tired. It's just a great rush."

Barkley and the Suns had them going in Phoenix, without a doubt. Who else could draw 300,000 people to a runners-up parade in 100-plus-degree heat?

"I was successful in Philadelphia, too, but it just didn't have the same effect," Barkley said. "Obviously, it's a different situation here because they don't have as much to do as they do in Philadelphia, where they have all the professional franchises and all the colleges. But I think it's still pretty amazing how the community supports the Suns. It's great to be in a situation like that as a player."

He cultivates his following not only with his ferocious, all-out play but also with his quick wit.

Robertson recalled one exchange between Barkley and a referee.

"Charles didn't like a call and he was complaining about it," Robertson said. "The referee told him to keep quiet and not say another word about it. Well Charles said, 'Let me tell you something, man, we don't have to keep quiet anymore. In case you don't know it, Lincoln freed the slaves. We're free to say whatever we want. It's about time you kept up with the times.'

"Charles is a guy who just says what he thinks at any time, but generally it's correct, it's accurate. Sometimes it's stated crudely. He's very quick. Charles Barkley is an extremely intelligent and bright person. He's never at a loss for words."

Barkley once chided Arizona residents for driving the speed limit in the outside lane: "Don't they know that lane is for speeders?"

Once, after not receiving a call, he told the refs, "I know women who don't hold me that tight."

One reporter even made the mistake of asking Barkley where his tickets were for the Super Bowl: "They're at the 50-yard line. What do you think? I'm a star."

It is said that behind every funny man is a sad one. Is his comedy a defense mechanism to cover the pain of growing up poor and without his father? Of having to endure a rough existence in his childhood? Of having to endure the inconveniences of this crazy life he has made for himself because he can run and dunk — and quip — with the best of them?

It's hard to say. Barkley does say that those experiences have helped make him a successful, directed, hard-working person who hasn't forgotten who he is or where he came from.

His father, Frank, left the family when Charles was an infant and moved to California. It is only in the past five years that Barkley and his father have rebuilt much of a relationship. His mother, Charcey Glenn, cleaned houses, and his grandmother, Johnie Mae Gaither, worked as a meat packer to make ends meet while they all lived together in a small apartment   in Leeds, Alabama.

"I think I feel cheated that he wasn't there, but it probably helped me, too," Barkley said. "I think all kids feel cheated in a situation like that. It gave me more drive, more dedication, more determination.

"We have a great relationship now. But it was a learning process. I knew exactly where he was all the time. He'd been on the West Coast. I talked to him once in a while. He just wasn't there."

Barkley has had to endure harassing treatment not only from whites but also from black people because his wife, Maureen, is white. Blacks accused him of selling out his race. His separation from her during his first year in Phoenix also wore on him. His locker is filled with photos of their daughter, Christiana, 3, who made a few trips to Phoenix during the season to see her dad. He phones her nearly every day.

Barkley said he wants to get his life squared with Maureen, too.

"She's the greatest person in the world," he said. "She's been with me through a lot of stuff. I've got to get that situation together."

Away from the court, Barkley is, indeed, an interesting man.

He claims he hates the media, yet there isn't another player in the league as accommodating to reporters as Barkley. He'll give you his time. He claims he isn't a role model—he says that's a parent's job—yet he'll talk on about an athlete's responsibility to speak out on racism, education, family, children, and hunger.

On the court, obviously, he's a dynamo, too. He understands full well that is what makes everything else possible for him. That's why every time he slips in his mouthpiece and wipes his sweaty brow on the shoulder strap of his jersey, he digs in and gives it everything he has.

He doesn't feel that the world owes him a living. That has to be earned. In fact, Barkley gives the impression that he's some guy still making the league minimum, trying to convince someone he's worth the really big money.

He did impress Colangelo with that attitude, that work ethic, that competitiveness — and 25.6 points and 12.2 rebounds a game later, the Suns had a franchise-record 62 wins and were on their way to the Finals.

"We could all be a lot better," he said. "I could actually average another 10 points a game if I wanted to, but I'd rather wait for the double-team and make my teammates better. I've sacrificed some of my game scoring-wise to do that. Everybody has to sacrifice."

That meant adjustments from the likes of KJ and Chambers, who'd been the Suns' heroes for four seasons. Barkley referred to KJ as "the second-best player on the team," not out of conceit or any disrespect to KJ. That's just the way it is.

"If Kevin would have had a problem, then I would have said something," Barkley said. "You know, people are bad. People are bad. For people to assume that me, Kevin and Tom could not get along before we even met each other or played together is ludicrous. But that's the way people are. They want to assume the worst. I can honestly say I never had a problem with Tom Chambers or Kevin Johnson."

Coming, as it did, on the heels of his gold-medal ride with the Dream Team, Barkley's MVP season capped one of the greatest years anyone ever had in basketball. Every step of the way, he was consistent with Fitzsimmons' description: Charles was Charles, he didn't change face.

Of the Dream Team, Barkley said: "That was just to make money for USA Basketball and the Olympic Committee. That's what that was about. But it was the greatest basketball team ever, and it meant something to me to be part of that."

On hopping the scorer's table in New York to chase referee Jimmy Clark: "The wrong thing to do, but he pissed me off saying that stuff, saying that my complaining was going to cost me money. I don't play basketball for money. You can't threaten me with money. Money don't mean that much to me."

On his return to Philadelphia, where the Sixers were booed, the Suns cheered, and his old fans erupted into chants of 'MVP! MVP!': "A great, great  feeling for me. I didn't want them to boo the Sixers, but them welcoming me back was something I'll never forget. "

On gathering in an inbounds pass that had been deliberately ricocheted off the backboard and swishing a desperation shot at the buzzer to win at Portland: "It's just been an incredible year. You know, Majerle hit that three-pointer to beat the Lakers, too. That just shows how much we competed all year."

On taking over Game 7 of the conference finals against Seattle with 44 points and 24 rebounds — his playoff career  highs — to move his team into the Finals: "That was a great feeling for me. We'd come so far, we were so close. It was right there, we all felt we just had to reach back for that little bit extra."

On dividing up the Suns' playoff winnings: "Some of the people who don't make a lot, they cheat. I didn't have to worry about math in school, as long as I was getting points and rebounds. Now, I have an accountant and a financial advisor. I don't actually have to count money myself."

The Suns all said how much they gained from playing with Barkley. But he said they gave him something, too.

"They have tremendous heart and courage," he said. "There were so many times when we were written off,  but our guys did everything it took to win.

"Also, just hanging out with Majerle, looking at his leftovers. Majerle's running this city. I'm way down on the totem pole. Golf with Ainge. Hanging out with Frank Johnson. Kidding around with Oliver Miller. Just the guys. It's really a diverse group."

When it was all over and Barkley was about to head out for the summer and a succession of celebrity golf tournaments, some movie-making, and international travel to unwind and promote, Barkley finally admitted that the biggest burden he carried with him was living up to the expectations of Suns fans.

"I was really proud, just how I handled the whole pressure and the expectations put on me," he said. "You can't understand what enormous pressure that is. If we hadn't got to the Finals, everybody would have said that the trade was an enormous flop. I mean, that's enormous pressure on me."

That's why the thought of retirement crossed his mind, but not for long.

"I cannot. We haven't won the world championship yet, so I cannot," he said. "I've got to give it another shot. I've got to do a better job on my body. They're going to put me on a comprehensive weight-training program. I'm getting old now, I've got to do it. I'm going to really dedicate myself to the weight room because I need to make some changes.

"I need to get stronger, take better care, eat better. I think when I come to camp I'll have a different body. I'll be doing a lot of traveling, but I'm going to lift weights and get stronger and maybe I won't break down as much during the season.

"My body's sore right now. I'm hurting. It's such a struggle with the knees, the back, and the shoulders. It takes a lot for me to get physically ready to play. My hamstring is shredded something terrible. I think our strength coach, Robin Pound, wants to spend some time working on that.

"I'm a fast-food junkie. As you get older, you have to take better care of yourself, and I haven't done a good job of that. I think that's one of the reasons I am 30 but my body's a lot older. I would like to lose maybe 10 pounds and play at 240 next year, maybe get physically stronger, get more defined. My body won't be as sore and beat up during the season and I'll just hold up better."

Sure, Chuck, sure.

Much as he hated to, Barkley already was thinking about the next season. He knows that the Suns will be at the top of everybody's hit list.

"I understand because I'm a marked man and I was on a couple of marked teams in Philadelphia," he said. "I don't think nobody here other than Danny has any idea how hard we're going to have to play next year, or how difficult the season's going to be. I know it on an individual basis. Every game somebody's out there to get me. As hard as it is to get to the NBA Finals, it's even harder to come back as a marked team the next year. That's why you got to respect the Bulls."

Everyone does. And respect for Barkley runs just as deep, which is why the Suns went after Barkley before the season.

"Once we knew there was a chance, there was never any hesitancy on our part," Colangelo said. "What we were holding back was the name Hornacek in our conversations with Philadelphia. We thought through the pros and the cons — couldn't come up with many cons.

"When you consider that here was one of the most talented players in the world, disgruntled, and just begging for a change in scenery, what you probably would wind up with is a guy so happy to get out that he would have a tremendous year. He would feel liberated. When the deal was made and Charles first showed up in Phoenix, he hugged me and said, 'Thank you, thank you, thank you. You don't know what you did for me. You got me out of purgatory.' So to me, that was not a big risk. To me that was a slam dunk."

Robertson understands why everyone didn't see it that way, though.

"There were all the questions that you would naturally expect about whether it was the thing to do," Robertson said. "We had the 'good guys' assembled here in the Kevin Johnsons, the Jeff Hornaceks, the Andrew Langs — people who never made waves, outstanding character as well as basketball talent.

"And all of a sudden you talk about bringing the quote-unquote bad guy of the NBA — if you were to believe the stories coming out of Philadelphia from the players, the management, the news media — into Phoenix, Arizona. Now you've got the guy that gives you some toughness, some leadership, a guy that is volatile. We found out the third day of training camp when he just side-body-blocked and took out Cedric Ceballos on a play in practice, we found out in our opening game when he got a technical foul, we found out in New York City when he jumped across the table to go after the referees, we found out in practice when he and Oliver Miller had the very, very physical fight — and I might add that Charles kept trying to avoid it, but finally he was faced with it and had to go ahead and handle it. So I guess the point is he is an explosive-type personality, but that was something that we needed on this team. We needed to change the image of the Phoenix Suns."

Van Arsdale was surprised that Barkley did it so effectively.

"He is a better player than I thought he was before he came here," Van Arsdale said. "You have to see someone more than two times a year to fully appreciate them. You can talk about his demeanor, his attitude, his will to win, his ability to make big plays at the right time, and realize that only superstars can do the things he does. He makes plays that only a guy like Barkley could make. He's able to extend himself almost like a superhuman at times and pull off a big play. There are very few players who can do that.

"I guess I was amazed at his athletic ability. He explodes more than I remember. He'll come up with that big block or big steal at the right time. He's able to do things with his body that I've never seen anybody else do at that size.

"He demands the respect of those around him. That's a great trait to have. I don't think he'd be a lot of fun to be around every night if he were losing."

# Chapter Six

# A POINT GUARD REDEFINED

If there was a car stalled in the street, he'd get out and help the stranded motorist. If there was a family in the grocery line struggling to pay its bill, he'd cover it for them. If a group of underprivileged children needed a mentor, he would be their guiding light.

In fact, he spent more than a quarter-million dollars of his own money the day after he signed his first big-time pro basketball contract to buy land on which he would build the St. Hope Academy in Sacramento.

That's who Kevin Johnson is.

He was raised by his grandparents in Sacramento, who happened to be white. KJ's grandfather knew that his grandmother was pregnant by another man when he married her. The baby was black; that was KJ's mother. She became pregnant with Kevin when she was 16. KJ's parents never married, and his father was found floating in the Sacramento River when KJ was 3. His grandparents agreed to raise KJ.

KJ knew he was different, yet in a way he wasn't. Hardly any of the families in his neighborhood included two parents. Most of the neighborhood kids were raised in single-parent families, or by grand-parents, or in some situation that is not recognized as the norm.

In his case, it was slightly different, because there were different races in his family.

KJ once described his household as "a big mosaic" because his grandfather's best friend was an Asian and his grandmother's best friend was Hispanic.

His late grandparents gave him solid moral values that KJ always has carried with him, that he said kept him away from the drugs and crime that captured many of those with whom he grew up. She taught him the value of completing a task and doing it well. He taught KJ the importance of preparation before tackling a project. They both taught him the importance of family, of education, of helping others, and of taking the time to acknowledge a good deed when someone takes the time to do one for you.

Unbeknownst to them, they had also laid the foundation of the St. Hope Academy.

KJ wanted to create something similar to his home environment for at-risk children in his old neighborhood, where they can go to receive the same care, guidance, and protection from negative forces that KJ received in his home.

No longer a dream, it has been up and running for two years. He is considering building a St. Hope Academy in south Phoenix as well. His long-range dream is to establish them from coast to coast, like YMCAs.

KJ also founded a reading program in a Phoenix elementary school district. He has appeared in NBA public service ads to stay in school and to stay off drugs. He received a Point of Light Award from former President Bush. He was also named winner of the league's J. Walter Kennedy Citizenship Award in 1991.

KJ went out of his way to make those around him feel special, just as he'd been taught to do. He wasn't doing badly on the court, either.

In 1989, KJ joined only four players who had ever averaged 20 points and 10 assists in a season. And then he did it a second time. And then a third in 1991. An unprecedented feat, and still unmatched.

He was selected to start in the 1991 All-Star game in Charlotte, and he chose to wear the jersey number of a close friend who he says toils in obscurity: number 41, Mark West.

Being one of the guys never was very interesting to KJ. He'd rather stay home and read. He is fascinated by the machinations of the political system and government, although he says he has no political aspirations. He is also very interested in religion, and is a regular at pregame chapel services. He has not yet quenched the thirst for knowledge that led him to the University of California at Berkeley.

Those things set him apart from many of his teammates.

So here was this unusually nice young man who wasn't a regular in the card games at the back of the bus, but who was making quite a name for himself in basketball.

He seemed so good that many were beginning to view him with a suspicious eye. There was a growing feeling in Phoenix that he was phony, that many of his deeds were calculated to gain publicity.

In 1992, KJ's production tailed off slightly, and the critics of his on-court game piped up. His Herculean 20-10 outputs became the standard by which he was measured. In that sense, he had created a monster. It was like, "What's wrong with KJ?" if his scoring "plummeted" to 19.7 points. He missed the All-Star game for the first time in three years.

"People do expect a little too much from Kevin Johnson because of what a phenomenal thing he did here," Fitzsimmons said. "Here's a guy that nobody knew the day we made the deal with Cleveland. For him to step forward like he did, take the basketball, go with Tom Chambers — who stepped forward like he did — and put us where we are, unbelievable. It just doesn't happen."

But KJ was bypassed for selection to the 1992 U.S. Olympic team, the Dream Team. That was a once-in-a-lifetime opportunity to play on the best team ever assembled, and he felt he belonged.

KJ appeared to be stung by it all, especially by the criticism that he was too nice, too available, too Mr. Goody-two-shoes, too distracted, too soft — always too something. He was always injured, and he hadn't taken the Suns to the Finals. He couldn't put them on his shoulders and carry them the way other superstars carry their teams, the critics said.

KJ heard them. He seemed to wonder: Are they right? If he got nasty on the court, would the children he works with view him as a hypocrite? More importantly, if he changed to suit his critics, could he look in the mirror and not feel hypocritical himself? Everybody seemed to want him to be something that he wasn't.

Whether the Barkley trade had been made or not, it's a fair guess that KJ would have been on a mission in 1993.

KJ changed his game and, some say, his personality. Why? Everyone had a theory: He resented a heathen like Barkley being idolized; he resented having his role reduced by Barkley, having the spotlight taken by Barkley; or he had an inner struggle working between being the Christian and having to be mean on the court; or he was fed up with the demands on his personal life and was going to put an end to it and reclaim his privacy; or he was fed up being injured all the time.

Maybe it was a little of all of the above.

He was a little nastier on the court, a little less accommodating off of it. He developed a harder edge to his personality than he'd ever shown before. He cut back his charitable appearances. He reduced his media accessibility. After games, he often was out of the locker room like a shot.

Everyone wondered how he would adjust to Barkley, whose game and personality seemed to be the antithesis of KJ's. If KJ had been the Suns' "point," Barkley now would be their "counter-point."

Those were formidable challenges. Then came another string of injuries. KJ's fragmented season went like this: out six games to open the season, back for four; out 12, back five; out one, back 18; out seven, back 11; out two, back six; out one, back one; out one, back two; out one, back two; and out two to wrap it up. He missed the playoff opener against the Lakers and then played in 23 straight playoff games, his longest uninterrupted streak. Finally, he was playing like the old KJ — comfortable and confident.

"Kevin, as far as I'm concerned, was very uncommunicative this year," Van Arsdale said. "I don't think he spoke two words to me all year. That's partially my fault because I don't try to interact with the players very much."

But at the same time, Van Arsdale thought this was the best year KJ has had.

"At the end of the year, he was the best point guard in the league, if you don't consider Jordan to be a point guard," Van Arsdale said.

Hollins suspects KJ found conflict in being physical and aggressive on the court and still being who he said he was off the court.

"I think that's the thing that may have been eating at him," Hollins said. "I saw a guy who changed his attitude and became an aggressive, hard-nosed, do-whatever-it-takes type of player to win a game. That might have been a conflict for him morally. He may disagree with me, but I think Kevin being a Christian, and his wanting to be an example for the young people that he teaches and tutors, wanted to be all of that all the time. It's a conflict for him to be inconsistent."

Robertson thought the lack of recognition bugged KJ.

"I think Kevin, having the great character that he has, said, 'OK, what can I do to show people the kind of player I am?'" Robertson said. "I think, and I told Kevin this personally in our season-ending meeting, that he still is not the player he can be. I really feel that the upcoming season is going to be the greatest season Kevin ever had. I'm hopeful he'll be healthy. Mentally, he'll have made the adjustment to the cast of characters we have now. I think he's going to come out more mature and show everybody who he really is as far as a player in the NBA."

Barkley and KJ did not appear to be the other's kind of guy. Barkley is outgoing, sometimes crude and vulgar.

"That was an unknown," Colangelo said. "We didn't really know how things were going to play out. We were hopeful that all the personalities would really blend and mesh. Certain people had to give up certain things, too, in order for that to happen."

But Colangelo said he was convinced early that the players were going out of their way to make it work.

First, Barkley and Chambers agreed to restructure their contracts in order to clear room on the salary cap to sign Ainge. Then, on the eve of training camp, KJ did likewise to accommodate the signing of Miller.

"I think the restructuring of contracts in itself was a good sign," Colangelo said. "Those were positive signs that people were willing to do what was necessary to sacrifice for the betterment of the team."

KJ, no longer the go-to guy offensively, revved up his defense.

"I don't think he gave up his role, I just think he changed it," Westphal said. "He redefined himself, which was really smart on his part.

"When he was the focal point of the offense it took a real toll on his energy. He didn't get after a guy on defense all the time the way you would ideally like a guy to do. Kevin redirected his energy and he was every bit as big a factor as he'd ever been, just in different ways."

Being a former hard-nosed defensive player himself, Van Arsdale was impressed.

"I thought Kevin Johnson always was a player who could do more defensively," Van Arsdale said. "This year, for the first time that I've seen, his defense was incredible. He accepted his role very well. He really became a defensive force and was a bigger contributor than when he scored the 20 points a game."

Was KJ trying to prove his worthiness to Barkley, to the fans, to himself?

"There was a lot of pressure on Kevin to find his niche, and find it quick," Hollins said. "I think a lot of it came from Charles. That's not because he says anything, but he has that dominant personality, and the fact that he is a star. Kevin had been the star."

He knew that with the ball going inside now, it was unlikely that he'd be scoring 20 points and getting 10 assists. The solution, then, was to become more of a defensive menace. When he was healthy — and he played in only 49 games — KJ made it awfully difficult for the opponent to get the ball across midcourt most nights.

"You have to find a way to contribute, and Kevin did that," Westphal said. "For example, Charles saves his energy on defense just like Kevin used to. He doesn't break his neck every time down the floor by any means because he's only got so much. So he uses it on offense just like Kevin did when he was the focal point."

It wasn't as if KJ didn't know what it takes to win.

"But I think maybe he was hoping that he could do it his way," Hollins said." There are times out there when guys are holding and grabbing you, and the referees are not protecting you. Then you've got to take matters into your own hands.

"I think that was something Kevin internalized."

Barkley had a lot to do with KJ's redefining his game.

"Tom's role was defined for him when we got Charles: You're going to come off the bench, Charles is the star, you'll play center and forward, and you'll play some nights 30 minutes, some nights 15 minutes," Hollins said. "Whereas Kevin was starting and playing with Charles, and maybe wondering, 'Now what is my role? Do I keep penetrating and shooting? Do I back off and throw it inside to Charles every time?' That was a difficult adjustment. I think Kevin was out-standing. I just read in *The Sporting News* where some guy wrote that this year Kevin proved he was overrated. Well, I think that this year Kevin proved he is one of the top —if not THE top— point guards in the

NBA. I mean, defense, scoring, penetrating, assists, the whole all-around play which he always has had the ability to do."

There are three reasons for that: Barkley becoming a force in the low post meant that the ball had to be directed to him more; less emphasis on the two-man game that KJ and Chambers ran so well for so many years (Chambers' reduced minutes also affected KJ), and the coaching change.

"Kevin became feisty. Kevin became downright tough. At times he became overaggressive," Fitzsimmons said. "I think that was the biggest conflict Kevin Johnson had to overcome. That wasn't his nature."

True enough. KJ doesn't show that side to many people.

"But this year he showed that," Fitzsimmons said. "He might have thought that Charles had to see it. I think you see the admiration Charles had for him as he spoke up when the fans got on Kevin here in the Finals. Not many players do that, but that's Charles, and that's the respect that they have.

"But Kevin would do the same thing when Charles would have a bad game. He'd say, 'Hey, this guy carries us, give him a night off.' So I think it was certainly a big adjustment for Kevin, but I think he handled it."

"Here's this guy who is deeply religious, deep thinker, and now he's gonna become a warrior, he's gonna go out and kill.

"I think that was an inner conflict for Kevin that people misrepresented as a chip on his shoulder. But I think once he looked around and watched a guy like A.C. Green, who is also a deep thinker and very religious—when he sees A.C. take somebody's head off in a game, then Kevin can deal with it too. I think that was a little conflict he had to work through, and I think he satisfied himself."

Westphal isn't so sure that was it.

"I never talked to Kevin about it, but I don't think a Christian is prohibited from being feisty," Westphal said. "I doubt if Kevin would think that, either. I guess if I had to put any reason on his quote-unquote personality change, it was his energy level. He was criticized for being too open, too accessible, too involved in the community.

"I think that he said, 'Maybe that's right. Maybe that's taking away from my dedication to the thing that I'm getting paid for, so I'm gong to cut all of that stuff out, and I'm just going to concentrate on my job.' I think it was pretty much as simple as that."

KJ, early in the season said he hoped Barkley could make him into a better basketball player, and that he could make Barkley into a better person. But KJ was a better player than Barkley imagined, and Barkley was a better person than KJ envisioned.

"They both really care about winning a lot, and I think they really respect each other on and off the floor even though they have different personalities," Westphal said. "You need different personalities on a team. I really like that. It makes it fun to come to work every day, fun to watch the games."

Fitzsimmons, who knows both players well, said he was amused.

"Boy, I'd hate for everybody to be the same," Fitzsimmons said. "Charles loves people, loves to be out in it, was very sad that he couldn't go through the parade after the Finals because he loves people.

"Kevin would have preferred not to be in the parade. He would have preferred to be somewhere else. That's his personality. There's nothing wrong with that. It took me a while to try to understand that. I wanted him to be a little more outgoing like I am, and he's not that way."

But down deep, according to Fitzsimmons, KJ is like everybody else in some ways.

"He enjoys the accolades that were piled on him when we were making this drive to get where we are today," Fitzsimmons said. "He received a lot of recognition, and it hurts him like it would anybody else to lose it. But KJ wants to win an NBA title so he's smart enough that he put that out of the way. That's healthy. It was like, 'I'm gonna go this way, you're gonna go that way, but we are going to meet. And when we meet, we're going to meet for the same goal.' And that's what they did. It wasn't like a collision course, like, 'We're gonna meet and sparks are gonna fly, and we're not gonna be able to get this job done.' I think Kevin knew this was coming."

Playing slow and deliberately, waiting for Barkley to come down were foreign to him.

"That would be extremely hard for anybody, but I think Kevin looks at the pluses," Fitzsimmons said. "I think he was trying to play the way Paul wanted him to play, getting out of the way at times. And because of that, and I told Paul this, I think when you do give him the ball you take his initiative away. And a lot of times Kevin lost his scoring initiative."

Fitzsimmons always has regarded KJ as a scorer first, a passer second. John Stockton, the Utah Jazz point guard who annually leads the NBA in assists, is a passer first, a scorer second.

"There is a big difference there," Fitzsimmons said. "Kevin hurts his team, in my opinion, when he doesn't score."

Often, he was in no position to score. The Suns like to throw the ball in to Barkley with a bigger guard because it's easier and because the Suns' big guards also are their best three-point shooters. If a three-point shooter's man drops to double-team Barkley, he just kicks it back out for an open shot. So KJ often was on the opposite side, out of the action.

If Barkley were to throw it to KJ, he'd have to shoot the quick jumper, which isn't his best skill. He's a good driver, but not when the shot clock is about to expire.

"But a lot of times in trying to make his own adjustment, I felt Kevin Johnson took himself out of the game," Fitzsimmons said. "Then people would ask, 'What's wrong with Kevin?' Well, nothing's wrong with Kevin, but he wouldn't run down the court as fast with the ball and jump up and shoot it because he thought they wanted him to make sure they got the ball inside.

"So some of his initiative was taken away."

Everyone can speculate, but only KJ had the answer. And for the most part, he wasn't talking.

"I was on a mission starting in training camp," he said during a break at the postseason mini-camp in Prescott. "I know there were some stories written about me having a chip on my shoulder and not smiling much anymore. I was just trying to be purposeful. I'm a serious person by nature. I was trying to satisfy and please everyone. I had no time for myself, for the people I care about, for the other things in life I enjoy doing.

"Whether it was charity work, or the media, or autograph seekers, I just couldn't continue at that pace. So this year, I decided that I was going to do all that I was supposed to do, but not all the extras. Anything beyond what my duties entail, I don't need to explain. I've had a lot of time to focus and put things into perspective this year."

KJ said he would elaborate on the perceived "chip" after the playoffs, but when asked about it then, he declined.

"I'm going back to Sacramento for the summer, reflect on the season, and figure out what I can do to be more successful next year," he said. "I just want to look at what I need to do to improve my game.

"It was a great year, the most fun I've had playing basketball. A lot of people didn't think we'd jell as quickly as we did, but I thought it was reasonable to do it as quickly as we did because we had a bunch of guys who had a common goal, and a bunch of guys who were willing to sacrifice, who liked each other and who got along."

He acknowledged that it was his most trying season.

"But it's the farthest I've gotten in the NBA," he said. "My season was so fragmented, yet that stretch in March and again during the playoffs was probably my best basketball ever. It's just a matter of being healthy. But we still came up short, that's all that matters."

As Colangelo looks back, he can say it all worked.

"And it worked because people were willing to sacrifice egos," Colangelo said.

Give that assist to KJ, who in his own way was only doing what he'd been taught so many years ago to do.

*Chapter Seven*

# ADDING FUEL TO THE FIRE

There were five other new faces among the zanies in the Suns' clubhouse. And it was time for the change.

"If you have a team of 12 guys who are all alike, they become dull, no flair, boring, and that has been somewhat the M.O. of the Suns for years," Robertson said. "Going all the way back to the days when they won 50-something games a year with Alvan Adams, Paul Westphal, Don Buse, and that group of players, people said, 'Yeah, they're good, but they'll never get out of the Western Conference.' With one exception, that was an accurate assessment.

"So now you bring in all these people who all bring a different talent to the whole and it's sort of like living in the City of New York. It is a very vibrant, electric city, made up of many ethnic groups, talents, abilities, colors, and it all makes for a great city. And I think that's what has happened here with the Suns."

Prior to Barkley's arrival, the Suns had a clean-cut, choirboy image, consistent with what one might expect to find in a conservative resort/retirement community. Suddenly, joining Barkley were three fiery veteran players — Ainge, Frank Johnson, and Tim Kempton — and two talented but troubled rookies — Dumas and Miller. The chemistry obviously had changed, and not necessarily for the worse, according to Hollins.

"If you get guys to mesh on the court, that's all that's important. If they happen to like each other and hang with each other off the court, it's that much better. They were all competitors. They all had a fairly good understanding of how to play and they all had versatility: they could shoot, they could pass, they could dribble, and those are the things that it takes to win.

"There are guys who play basketball, and there are basketball players. We have a lot of basketball players."

The veteran Ainge, who would play in the Finals for his third different team, was a key addition. Not only were the Suns looking for an outside shooter to replace Hornacek, they were looking for another smart player, another player with a presence, someone who could perhaps be a bridge between Barkley and those who'd been with the Suns for some time.

"I remember our discussions internally regarding free agents, and all our basketball people were talking Herb Williams," Colangelo said. "I said, 'Huh-uh. It's Danny Ainge.' I said once we get past the fact that we need another guy who can shoot the ball, do you recognize who we're talking about here? What he represents? The kind of person he is? The kind of impact he can have on this team? He's a winner. He's a leader. He's been there on championship teams."

About the only negative about Ainge is that his phenomenal early-season shooting tailed at the end. Through 48 games, he was at 50 percent from the floor and an incredible 46.7 from three-point range. But in the final 34, those figures dropped to 40.3 and 30.3, respectively.

"He played more minutes than we'd planned, and he got a little tired at the end of the year," Van Arsdale said. "But he's one of the greatest competitors I've ever seen. He won't let you quit."

Ainge was in great shape, which allowed him to play 27 minutes a game, a pleasant surprise to the Suns. Among his points of contention with Portland the previous season, where he played 19 minutes a game, was that he was never used at crunch time. He felt his minutes could be better utilized.

Westphal gladly put him into the game in the fourth quarter. And Ainge proved that he was not too old to get the job done. He was an effective finisher who won several games with clutch shots.

"I think realistically in the future his minutes will go down here," Westphal said. "He's probably one of the guys who will lose some minutes to give Richard and Cedric some playing time. But the thing about Danny is that I always expect him to be a valuable contributor in the fourth quarter."

And as great as his value is at the end of the game, it is even greater in the clubhouse, according to Westphal.

"He comes to work every day, early, with a smile on his face, ready to go," Westphal said. "We have others like that, too — Majerle and Frank Johnson and Mark West can't wait to get there. The more you have like that, the harder it is for someone else to have a bad attitude.

"He appreciates this life and loves it. It's hard to find players who have enough perspective to appreciate how good they have it."

In Ainge and Barkley, the Suns suddenly had the two players you love to hate when they're playing against you, but who you love, period, when they're on your side. They're feisty, fiery competitors who not only know how to play the game, but how to get under your skin.

"That's why you want Danny on your team," Fitzsimmons said. "He loves to irritate you. He's a real pain. That's why I like him so well, and that's why I hated him when he played with Boston and Portland. I didn't hate him when he played with Sacramento because they couldn't beat us. I don't think you can be a winner without having a little devil in you. You don't think Michael Jordan has some devil in him? Guys have to have that in order to be a big winner, and Danny is a big winner, whether it be golf, baseball, basketball, anything you want to do, Ainge is going to try to beat you."

To the Suns, he was a perfect pickup, even at age 34.

"Adding Ainge to the mix was very important in the meshing of personalities," Colangelo said. "I just wish he was a few years younger."

The same can be said of Frank Johnson, whom the Suns brought in as an extra point guard to ensure they had enough players to go five-on-five in their informal workouts. He was in better shape than anybody else, and even at 6-foot-1, he had a presence about him. The players respected his veteran leadership.

The Suns couldn't get rid of him. They waived him the week before the season opener. He had no more than arrived home in Minneapolis and he was back on a plane to Phoenix because KJ was injured. He then stuck with the Suns for the season.

"One of the special moments for me was in Milwaukee," he said. "We were at a shoot-around. Paul pulled me aside and told me, 'You're here to stay for the year.' That was in December. It's been unbelievable. I couldn't have dreamed of a better situation, except for finishing with the championship."

As with Ainge, it was common to see Johnson on the floor in the fourth quarter, especially in those games in which KJ did not play. For a 34-year-old who'd been out of the league for three years, it was quite a comeback.

"Paul gave me the confidence to do the job by putting me in those situations," Johnson said. "You've got to take advantage of those to get other ones, and I think I did that. I gave him confidence that when he called my name, I was ready."

The Suns' brass credits chief scout Dick Percudani with finding Johnson in Italy, following his progress, and fighting to bring him in.

"Everybody lost track of him," Robertson said. "Percudani says, 'What about Frankie Johnson?' We said, 'Where in the world has he been?' From the first day he came in, he went head to head with Kevin Johnson. Kevin was going to take a few days to loosen up and warm up and get into the flow, and Frankie says, 'Uh-uh, you better get ready now.' He gave Kevin such a hard time it kinda woke us all up. The more we tried to figure him out of our plans, just from a numbers standpoint, the more he set his mind to proving he could make our team."

Knight had some nagging injuries, so Johnson loomed larger.

"Frank, for three years, labored in obscurity in Europe," Hollins said. "He saw an opportunity — not a guarantee, but an opportunity — and he grabbed it like a pit bull. He got his jowls on it and he would not let go. Even though he was released, he still hadn't let go. He had played and performed well enough to be on the team but there was not a spot for him."

The spot was Knight's.

"Then when Kevin got hurt and Negele didn't seize his opportunity, Frank ran with it for the rest of the season," Hollins said. "That's basically what happened to Negele. It was Frank Johnson."

The coaching staff knew exactly what to expect every time Johnson trotted onto the court. Whether he made shots or not, the coaches knew he was going to come out and get after his guy. They knew he was going to try to run what they wanted to run, and he was going to be tough-minded.

"I'm so happy for that guy, it's just a great story," Westphal said. "Frank probably doesn't get nearly enough credit. And everybody loves the guy — even Negele, and he's taken Negele's time. Referees love the guy. He's so happy to be around. And nobody — including Majerle, including Barkley — nobody works harder to stay ready. He doesn't know if he's going to play one second or 40 minutes. If he doesn't play, he goes in and works hard in the weight room to get ready for the next game, and he might not play in that game. Then he does it again. He never gets down."

Johnson survived. Veteran forwards Kurt Rambis and Ed Nealy, each of whom had a guaranteed contract, didn't.

"We ate over $2 million in contracts to keep a guy like Frank Johnson — or as I like to call him, 'Fourth-quarter Frank,'" Fitzsimmons said. "He made big buckets, made big defensive plays."

Even Johnson felt his chances of making it were slim. He already had arranged an interview with the personnel director of the Minnesota Timberwolves about getting into front-office work back home.

"I love stories like that," Colangelo said. "The things that happened for him and fell for him the past year are the things that books are written about. It was after some pushing by Dick Percudani, who said, 'Take a look at him. He finished strong in Europe. He's in great physical shape. If nothing else, he's going to push a few people.'

"And, of course, he came in and impressed everyone immediately. I remember after watching him for a couple of days, thinking, 'I don't think he's lost anything,' and that was thinking back to when he was a young player in the NBA when he was drafted in the first round.

"We could only pay him the minimum. We were over the cap. He was grossly underpaid for the contribution he made. I asked him two months before the season ended what was the most money he ever made in the NBA. He told me what that was. I told him, 'You're going to make more than that next year.''

On July 21, Johnson signed a one-year contract for the 1993-94 season for approximately $575,000.

"I believed then and I believe now that he earned another year on this roster," Colangelo said. "He's been a very positive influence on some of our people. There was definitely a bonding with Charles. They kind of hung around together. When you have a player like Charles who has so much that pulls and tugs at him, Frank also served as a buffer for him in many situations. I thought his role there was important. But Frank Johnson has just been a joy."

Never mind that with Ainge and Johnson, the Suns were 68 years older.

"When the fans and the media talk about the success of the Suns this year, all signs point toward Charles Barkley," Robertson said. "But, there also have to be some players on a team that the superstar respects. In Charles Barkley's case, this respect is directed toward Danny Ainge and Frank Johnson. "Why? These are two veteran players. Danny Ainge has won championships at Boston. Frankie Johnson is a mature player in his early 30s, is a bubbly, bright young man who has a wonderful personality. Charles respects both of these guys a great deal and he listens to them. They don't hesitate to say things to him to correct him if they think he's not acting in the best interest of the team. And he accepts it."

Robertson said if the coaches tried to say some of the same things to Barkley, he wouldn't take it the same way.

"These two guys are smart enough that they will make comments to Charles, sometimes in a laughing manner, but at the same time with a meaning behind it," Robertson said. "Charles will laugh with him, but they get their point over to him. I cannot emphasize enough how valuable these two players have been."

Younger players also look up to them.

"Basically, they do the right things on the court," Robertson said. "They're players who don't make waves. They're players who have balls to the extent that they're not afraid to take the big shot, make the big defensive play, do whatever it takes in a close game to help us win. And because of that, they're respected by everybody."

At the other end of the spectrum among the Suns' newcomers were two wild and crazy rookies, Dumas and Miller. They added 47 years to the roster. As for maturity, you can divide that figure by three. But they are the essence of the second generation of the Suns under Westphal's command. They are oddballs, but unbelievably talented players. Westphal had to fight hard to have them drafted. They tested his patience more than anyone.

"I feel it was a pretty good year," Dumas said. "I see what I need to work on: some defense, some strength, and I have some offense I still need to add.

"Being in the NBA, it's pretty good. I like it. I just hope to be here next year. We need another year, to learn from this, to mature."

How revealing. The Suns could only hope that Dumas was serious about learning from the past. In their cast of characters, his is a very unusual situation. He was asked to leave Oklahoma State following a series of personal problems that cut short his collegiate career.

He went to Israel, hoping to sharpen his skills in the pro league in Tel Aviv. It happened to be the winter of 1991. The Persian Gulf War was on. More than once, Dumas had to put on the gas mask and take shelter when air-raid sirens screamed the oncoming of Iraqi SCUD missiles. He didn't get in much basketball work that winter.

Everyone knew he had incredible talent. But everyone also knew that he had a substance abuse problem. Still, the Suns took a chance on him with the 46th pick in the second round in 1991, figuring that if he'd been straight, he'd have been a draft lottery pick.

On the eve of the 1991 season opener, Dumas was informed that results of his league-mandated random rookie drug test had come back positive. He was suspended without pay for a minimum of one year. It turned out to be a 13-month ban before Dumas was reinstated.

"He has come out now and adjusted, so far, to the fast life of the NBA," Robertson said. "He's married now. He has a wonderful wife and two children. Hopefully he has gotten his life straightened out."

Unfortunately, he hadn't. In September, Dumas admitted to a relapse, was suspended by the NBA, and is not expected to play in 1993-94.

Dumas quickly had to find his niche on a good team at mid-season. That's a difficult chore for any player, much less an immature rookie.

"He was trying to take his CBA game, his European game, which was strictly offensive oriented, into a team that already had outstanding offensive players," Robertson said. "Now, we look up and see we've got to work with him defensively or he's going to score 20 and give up 25."

The coaches sensed that they had to be very careful in their approach in correcting him, or when working with him to improve his game, because he was walking a tightrope emotionally.

"Sometimes you handled him a little more with kid gloves than maybe you would with a player who had no known problems like his," Robertson said. "He had a tendency when he was taken out of a game, or when he was corrected, to sulk and pout. I personally had a talk with him during the playoffs in Chicago about this. I told him that I would hope he would mature and become more professional in his approach.

"I said, 'You're embarrassing Paul, and Paul doesn't embarrass you when you make a mistake. Paul doesn't throw a towel, or throw a clipboard. He handles you in a professional manner, and I would hope that you would reciprocate and do the same.' We only had two games following that, but he handled himself, I thought, in an excellent manner. I hope that he'll remember that conversation."

The chat must have helped. In Game 5, Dumas torched Scottie Pippen, making 12 of 14 shots and scoring 25 points, as the Suns won and brought the series back to Phoenix.

The last person Dumas should want to embarrass is Westphal. He fought for the Suns to draft Dumas. He maintained personal contact with him throughout Dumas' 13-month rehabilitation. He basically handed Ceballos' job to Dumas when he was reinstated.

"First of all, Richard is just a pure talent," Westphal said. "He has so much potential. He's just a beautiful athlete. That's to his credit. That's my job, to get production out of guys who have some production in them. He still has a ways to go to come near reaching his potential.

"I don't think that we can relax and think that his troubles are over, because that's a hard battle he's fighting. When somebody has the abilities he has and is a nice person — and I think he is a really nice kid — you really root for them and hope they have every opportunity."

The Suns, who made walking the ledge a sport, know full well they are walking one with Dumas and Miller. In fact, after Dumas was suspended in 1991, Colangelo chastized his two young assistant coaches — Westphal and Hollins — for pushing for the drafting of Dumas. He said he hoped they'd learned a lesson from it.

There was a report in a Chicago newspaper during the 1992 Finals that Dumas was seen in a bar. In addition to drugs, Dumas has had problems with alcohol.

"Two things about that: First, Richard came up to me and said, 'That thing in the paper was false. I was in my room watching a movie with my wife, you can ask her,'" Westphal said. "I told him I don't need to ask her. I didn't believe it anyway.

"But second, if he was in a bar, Richard can go in a bar. Richard, everywhere he goes, at every hour of the day, there's a way for him to get into trouble if he wants to. And he can't just sit in his hotel room his whole life and not enjoy himself doing what other people do. He's just got to draw his line in order to keep himself from sliding.

"If he was in that place, it doesn't mean he was doing anything wrong. You can't be worrying about whether Richard is doing something wrong this minute or that minute, or getting a report he did this or that. He's got to take responsibility and make his own decisions."

Westphal frowns on putting superlatives on young players, but he gushed about Dumas, as if he was a five-year All-Star.

"I was trying to be reserved," Westphal said. "This guy's special.

He really is. It's rare when you can find a young player who is good enough to contribute to an excellent team the way he did, despite his lack of maturity. You can count probably less than 10 guys in the last 10 years who've come into the league as a rookie and contributed as much to a really good team. And he's just getting started."

Dumas played for the NBA minimum $140,000, about one-tenth what he was offered to play in Europe. He said he'd take the cut to stay with the Suns because they'd stayed with him.

"As I said a year ago, and it sounds terrible saying it this way, I didn't feel Richard was clean as we went through exhibition season," Fitzsimmons said. " I remember the last game in Toronto, that vision I see of him, one dribble, up over the top of Manute Bol, dunking, seeing that great potential, but never once thinking Richard was right.

"Sure enough, the NBA comes in, checks, he's dirty. It sounds crazy for me to say this but that was one of the happiest days of my life as far as my dealings with Richard Dumas. I knew because of that, he had a chance. Without that, he had no chance. He would end up for certain before that year was over in a terrible mess."

Fitzsimmons is convinced Dumas would have been on the all-rookie team, and would have averaged between 15 and 20 points.

A year later, clean, (Dumas was drug tested during the season, his relapse came during the summer of 1993) Dumas did just that.

"We said all along that he had a chance to be a star," Colangelo said. "The real question is whether he had the discipline to take care of his personal business. That means maturity, commitment and focus — all those things."

Colangelo says the measure of where his team is going to be lies in the development of Ceballos, Miller, and Dumas.

"All you can do is point a person in the right direction, try to monitor as best you can what is happening in their personal lives, encourage, support, and then hope for the best," Colangelo said. "You can't live their lives. People have to make personal choices. When I look at a talent like Richard, I hope and pray he can keep his act together because he's going to have a great 10 years in the NBA if he does."

Everyone in the organization knows it is day-to-day with a recovering addict.

"But what can I do? You're always concerned," Fitzsimmons said. He recalls having coached John Lucas before Lucas turned his life around. John Lucas and me are good buddies," Fitzsimmons said. "I tell two stories on Luke.

"One, I had him in San Antonio. We're in exhibition. The first shootaround, he misses. I get a call late in the afternoon, some crazy story. He borrowed somebody's car and he's outside of town, couldn't get to the shootaround. Meantime, between the time he missed the shootaround and the time he called me, I'd already traded him to

Houston. That happened to be who we were playing that night. So when he came in, I said, 'Luke, just go in the visitor's dressing room. That's where you are now.' We had a good relationship. The reason I could talk to him that way is because earlier in his career, after he was out all year because of drug abuse, I end up with an all-star team over in Japan and he's my point guard. The first game we played in Tokyo against another group of all-stars, I played Lucas 46 minutes. He'd been out most of the year. He about died. So when we came in for Game 2 two days later, everybody said, 'Luke, how you been?'"

Lucas told Fitzsimmons he was bushed and couldn't believe the old coach would pound him that hard his first time out.

"I said, 'You know why I did? Because I wasn't certain you'd show up for Game 2."

Even Lucas had to laugh. He now tells that story to recovering addicts he works with at his center in Houston.

"Because that's what it is, it's day to day," Fitzsimmons said. "And there's no need in speculating on this and that, you just take it a day at a time. If Luke can do it, because he was as low as you can get, anybody can do it."

Miller also reached a pretty low point, but his addiction wasn't drugs or alcohol, but food. It's been a long-running battle for him. He showed signs of taking control during the final two months of the season. He became a factor in the playoffs.

"I know what I did to get there, I'll know what to do again," Miller said. "I'll work even harder next year. I had a taste of success but there's a lot more there for me. Now, I want to be 270 coming into training camp, and by the end of training camp I want to be 265. If I keep doing the things I've been doing, I know I can take it off."

Even Miller doesn't know for sure what he weighed before Westphal read him the riot act in January. Miller had found a way to trick the scale. He said he might have weighed as much as 340. When he was activated in March, he weighed 280 — on the Suns' new, supposedly foolproof scale.

A very unusual guy, in the words of Robertson.

"Very immature. Spoiled. Great mother who loves her son and spoils him," Robertson said. "He's been allowed to do whatever he wanted to do. Because of that, he, in my opinion, had very little personal discipline. I think he always had the feeling that everything was going to turn out all right. He was always able to get out of any kind of jam.

"I'm not a professional in this analysis, but I've worked with a lot of people over the years. I think that was one of the reasons that he got so overweight. He has a lot of talent. He was able to get by playing with excessive weight, and he was allowed to do it. Therefore, there was no real incentive for him to discipline himself to get the weight off."

That perceived lack of discipline was evident in Miller's style of play, too. His floor game is brash. He's liable to snare a rebound and then take it the length of the floor, probably putting it behind his back along the way. He likes to finish the break with a dramatic assist pass instead of taking it in for the dunk.

As long as it results in a basket, the Suns don't care, although Westphal wants Miller to look to score more in his second season.

"He throws the ball from one end of the court to the other," Robertson said. "Sometimes, he makes a terrific pass that leads to a score. Sometimes it winds up in the 10th row of the arena. However, as a coach, you have to be very careful that you don't stifle this kind of talent. You try to work with him and show him that a long pass is a good idea at certain times of the game, and at other times, it might not be."

That isn't all bad, though, in Westphal's mind.

"Oliver made a lot of nice plays," Westphal said. "He has a lot of poise for a young guy. That's the thing that I value in a player attitude-wise more than anything — not being afraid to take a chance in a tough situation. It's never going to work if you're afraid."

Robertson noted that Miller not only is a relaxed person, but he came in and gave all the outward appearances of being a five-year veteran. He never felt that he was bound by the rules of a rookie.

"But he related very quickly to most of the players on the team and they accepted that from him," Robertson said. "That is very unusual. He's got a big smile. He wins you very quickly. But maturity is the answer for him as to whether he'll ever become a great player."

What are the odds, Fitzsimmons wondered, of a 300-plus-pound rookie being drafted, coming to Phoenix, looking at all the places in town, and then moving in next door?

"Oliver is my neighbor," Fitzsimmons said. "He moved next door to me. What would be the odds? Scotty Robertson had lived in that home for the last couple of years. So I traded that old assistant coach in for this rookie, wondering what kind of year I'm going to have. But the guy was great, was a great neighbor."

Fitzsimmons said he sensed during one of those basketball opera-tions "roundtables" that nobody but Westphal was enthusiastic about drafting Miller.

"They didn't want anybody that was that big, and just didn't show that he'd lose the weight," Fitzsimmons said. "But once we looked over the draft, there was really only one other guy we were interested in that we thought would be there when we picked, and that was Latrell Sprewell. But why do we need a small guy? We've got Ceballos, got Dumas, got Majerle, we were gonna get Ainge. How many times at 22 can you get a center? Here's a guy who can catch the ball. Here's a guy who can pass the ball, got a nice little touch. The way I like to describe him is he's a guy who could catch a ball in a darkroom. He's got those type of hands. So what's the gamble? There's no gamble."

Finally, according to Fitzsimmons, he told the gathering that he thought Westphal was right about Miller.

"I remember Paul, as we walked out of the meeting room, saying, 'I really want to thank you for going to bat for me.' I said, 'I didn't go to bat for you, I did what I thought was best for the franchise.'

"And I thought Paul did a nice job with him. He tried being Mr. Niceguy at first, did everything he could for Oliver."

Before the season, the Suns sent Miller to various "fat farms," but none of them worked. Strength coach Robin Pound gave it his best shot, and became frustrated.

"Finally, Paul took the hard route, said, 'That's it, this is the way it's going to be. You're either going to get yourself in shape or you're never going to play,'" Fitzsimmons said.

Hollins recalls that dreadful day in January when Westphal forcefully told Miller it was time to take action or take a hike. Miller accepted the reality. He voluntarily enrolled as an outpatient in a monitored diet plan that required him to spend his nights at a Phoenix hospital. He was allowed only 1,500 calories a day.

"It was a sad day, like when your kid wants to do something and you told him he couldn't, then he does something bad and you have to punish him. It's the same thing with Oliver," Hollins said. "It was a time of discipline, and the guy responded. If he was allowed to continue going in the direction he was going, we wouldn't have gotten into the Finals. So it was a sad moment, but it was also a monumental moment in the team's destiny."

Westphal had such high hopes for Miller.

"And I understood," Fitzsimmons said. "Paul bragged on him so much, and now the guy let him down. But that happens with coaches. That was just the first. There'll be a lot of others along the way."

It may have been one of the most important days in Miller's life, or at least his professional basketball life, according to Colangelo.

"That was literally putting the guy on notice that this was serious, this was a business, if he was going to make it in this league he had to show some commitment," Colangelo said. "I think it was a great move. It paid dividends. I think Oliver has come a long way, but still has a long way to go.  That was the turning point. The young man is blessed with exceptional talents at a position where it is very difficult to find people who can play, especially drafting late in the first round. He has demonstrated because of his passing, because of his great hands, because of his offensive ability and shot-blocking that he could be a factor in the NBA.

"Again, let's talk about the key words: focus, commitment, and how hungry he might be to be as good as he can be. Our goal with Oliver is to keep him focused. And again, he'll have to make his personal choices in terms of conditioning, and continuing to work on his game.

But we're excited about his future."

The common thread joining the two high-risk yet highly talented rookies to the best team in basketball was Westphal.

"It was unusual to have two guys like them, and we really walked the ledge with our rookies," Westphal said. "What are we going to do? That's the thing John Havlicek taught me. He was famous for taking the big shots and making them. He said the reason that he was able to do that was because he knew that if he missed, the sun was going to come up the next day and he was still going to be a great player. And the next time he had a chance, he'd still take the shot.

"I did push for us to get them. I have no idea what the decision would have been otherwise. We wouldn't have taken them if Jerry and Cotton and Van hadn't been convinced they were the right guys to take. I definitely pushed for both of them — hard. I didn't guarantee that they'd be what they are. All I said is they have a chance to be what they are, and better. They're just getting started. I acknowledged that both of them could fail and that we were taking a chance. I just said it's worth the risk. I didn't think I was selling something that wasn't there. I had no doubt that there was a great upside to those guys. But if you don't give them a chance, you don't ever find out. What I think is, absent a stress fracture and a substance abuse problem, we have two guys who would have been draft-lottery picks.

"Anybody can fail, but not everybody has a chance to succeed."

Westphal's spunk impressed his old veteran assistant coach.

"You've got a rookie head coach handling all these difficult situations, difficult personalities, and handling them for the most part extremely well," Robertson said.

When added to the existing cast of characters on the Suns roster, the new kids on the block gave them quite a lively mix.

"For some reason," Frank Johnson said, "we're all out in different places, a totally different group. But the minute we stepped on the court, somehow everyone found a way to come together. Look at some of our games. We'd be way out of them. It was like, 'What is going to happen?' And somehow, the last quarter, the last six minutes, we always found a way to pull it out. There were so many times when we were not sure, like, 'What are we going to do now?' That really is what this team is all about. I am shocked that it all came together for us so quickly because of the number of new guys we had coming in here and the number of young guys who played important roles. It doesn't happen that quick. It takes a year, maybe two years. But our confidence came in December, when we swept that first long trip."

Robertson, also with a lot of years to draw upon, is baffled and amused by what he saw unfolding before his eyes.

"I've been both fortunate and unfortunate in my associations with other NBA players on other teams," he said. "I've had Pete Maravich, who was one of the most colorful basketball players in the history of the game.

"I've also had Marvin Barnes, who was a completely different kind of guy. If the team was to report at 6:00 for a 7:30 game, he would walk into the dressing room at about 7:15 when we were in the final words of our pregame meeting. He'd have a big smile on his face when he sat down and he'd tell the ball boy to go get him two hot dogs while he dressed.

"I've had Bill Laimbeer, Isiah Thomas, Kelly Tripucka, Moses Malone, Rick Barry — now there was a very interesting player. Rick Barry was a player who at timeouts would very quickly tell us all what needed to be done and quite frequently then would go out and make the mistake that he'd just told everybody else not to make. But I respect Rick Barry a lot, and I consider him one of the finest players I've ever been associated with.

"But moving from those players to the players on this year's Phoenix Suns team, you go from a situation where you might have one unusual player to a team that's just loaded with diverse personalities."

And that wasn't restricted to the newcomers.

## Chapter Eight

# COMING BACK FOR MORE

Anyone who embraces the "If it ain't broke, don't fix it" philosophy had to look at any changes Colangelo and Co. might make with skepticism. The Suns had a nucleus of players in place who were accustomed to winning.

Majerle was an interesting case. Suns fans booed when his name was called at draft headquarters at the Phoenix Civic Plaza as the 14th selection in the first round back in 1988. Fitzsimmons assured them they would rue the moment they treated this unknown young man with disrespect.

At the time, everyone figured it was just more of Fitzsimmons' bravado. But time — and Majerle — proved him correct. Today, Majerle is probably the second most popular Suns player.

Colangelo denies that he has Majerle on the roster just to keep women interested in basketball. Females comprise the bulk of the fans of the muscular, chisel-jawed — and single — Majerle.

"What a story, when you consider where he was at the start," Colangelo said. "I'll always remember the day he walked into Phoenix, Arizona, for the first time — it was about 115 degrees — with his double-twisted wool sport coat from Northern Michigan, and perspiring buckets when he showed up after we drafted him."

It took him less than a year to capture the hearts of the fans. He won them over with hard work.

"He's terrific. He is our blue-collar guy," Colangelo said. "His legion of fans just keeps growing and growing. And Dan being a single guy, females probably outnumber the males, three to one. He's made himself into an outstanding NBA player."

Majerle missed a large portion of his rookie season with mononucleosis after arriving at training camp worn out from the 1988 Seoul

Olympics. His work off the bench, especially guarding the opponent's hot shots, enhanced his reputation as both a sixth man and as a defender. He began picking up votes in both categories in the NBA's post-season honors after his second season.

By 1991 it was becoming obvious that Majerle was a bargain-basement special. Colangelo was reworking the contracts of several other players, but hadn't yet gotten around to Majerle.

As the regular season was winding down, Majerle began experiencing weakness and numbness in his leg about the time he and Colangelo finally went to the bargaining table. A new deal was worked out in which Majerle would receive a windfall, but because of the Suns' salary-cap situation, the contract extension would not kick in for two more seasons. In the meantime, doctors discovered that a small cyst was pressing against a nerve in his back. Surgery was necessary.

Colangelo signed Majerle to the extension before the surgery, knowing the procedure was potentially career-ending. The new package was fully guaranteed, regardless of the outcome of the surgery. Colangelo said it was his way of thanking Majerle for playing for well below his market value for all of those seasons.

"That little story is very special," Colangelo said. "It was very serious. It would have been a very simple thing to say, 'We're not going to continue with this until we know what's going to take place ultimately.' But I called him in and said, 'Dan, I just want you to know what I'm going to do. I'm committing to this contract in advance of your surgery. I just want you to know what I feel about you, and I have all the confidence and faith that everything is going to work out.'"

Majerle's contract extension kicks in in 1993-94, and his salary will jump to $3 million. It seemed astronomical when he signed it, but he has fully recovered from back surgery, has gone from being the backup small forward to the starting shooting guard, and has earned successive trips to the All-Star game. The payment now seems no more than commensurate with Majerle's contribution.

Van Arsdale, who was a similar kind of player to Majerle — hard-nosed defender who swung from guard to forward — says what Majerle did in the silver anniversary season in moving from small forward to shooting guard was largely unappreciated.

"It's more difficult to defend the 'two-guard' than the 'three' because your back is to the action," Van Arsdale said. "You don't have the baseline and sideline to work with. I think it's much more difficult, much more exhausting defensively. And, granted, when you play the 'three' it's a bigger player and there's much more contact, but it's much harder on your legs to play the 'two' spot when you're a small forward like I was. The 'two' is quicker. Playing a 'three,' the guy's not as quick, you have more help, there's not as much room to cover."

In Fitzsimmons' estimation, it doesn't matter whether you call Majerle a guard or a forward.

"Dan just plays," Fitzsimmons said. "The one guy both Paul and Dan's former coach never worry about is Majerle. We just pencil him in. Dan's the easiest guy in the world in that regard to coach. Just put him in and forget to take him out. He's the guy who brought things to this team that this team needed, a sense of toughness, determination. You saw how quick Charles bonded with Dan because Dan's a guy you go to war with."

Westphal, who unlike Van Arsdale isn't remembered for his defense, nevertheless tends to agree with those assessments.

"I don't think you can give that guy enough credit," Westphal said. "Dan's an amazing athlete. He's starting to get appreciated for what he does, guarding those guys every night. It's Sean Elliott one night, Clyde Drexler the next, Ron Harper, Chris Mullin, Jeff Malone. Every night there's somebody. It's a tough thing to do and then still be effective offensively on top of it. Dan's fun. You can yell at him. I never yell at Dan, but I know I could if I wanted to."

There were those who wanted to, though, including Fitzsimmons and Robertson, the old traditionalists, and Van Arsdale, the purist. Instead, they took the calm, reasoned approach when Majerle began jacking up three-pointers unjudiciously. While Majerle set club records by launching 438 and making 167 from long range, and then tied an NBA playoff record by making eight in Game 5 of the conference finals against Seattle, and won several other games with his three-point shooting, the feeling grew that he lived on them a bit too much.

"He got so hooked on three-pointers," Fitzsimmons said. "Dan Majerle, to be a total player, needs to slash and cut to the basket, get those cheap buckets, get some offensive rebounds and put them back. At times, because the Suns lived off the threes so much, he could have put a tent out there around the three-point line. At times he needed to be more active."

Ditto from Robertson, who made his point to Majerle in a private chat on the eve of Game 5 of the Finals in Chicago, a game the Suns had to win if they wanted to play a sixth game at home.

"Dan Majerle is a player that I feel very close to," Robertson said. "He's a young man that I respect so much. He's used to hard work. But I said to him, 'You know Dan, before this season started, if a person mentioned Dan Majerle's name, what would people think?' And he said immediately, 'Defense.' And I said, 'That's right.' Then I said, 'You know, you've forgotten who you are.'

"Now you have to remember this was following Game 4 when we played probably the worst defense that's ever been played in the history of basketball. And I said, 'All you want to do now is run down the court and spot up in the three-point area. We need that. I don't want you to quit looking for that shot, but we need you primarily to do a job for us defensively, and you're just not doing it now. It's amazing in this playoff series how few personal fouls you have. You don't foul anybody anymore. I'm not saying that fouling is a prerequisite to playing good defense, but it shows me at least a person is being aggressive. You have just forgotten who you are and I would like to see you, starting in tonight's game, get back to being the defensive player that we all know you can be.'

"Well, he was terrific that night defensively."

Van Arsdale says he likes Majerle so much as a player that he'd like to overlook any weaknesses he has. But he couldn't.

"He'll take that three-point shot when he could go to the basket," Van Arsdale said. "Of course, the coaches gave Ainge and Majerle the green light to shoot the three, and it turned out to be a good move overall. I think when Dan gets into a situation where he realizes he's in a slump, he goes to the basket more. When you have to play both ends of the court, its tiring."

No longer some hick from Traverse City, Michigan, Majerle is one of the Suns' most marketable players. He's on local TV pitching everything from automobiles to hamburgers. He has his own line of underwear. Majerle's Grill, two blocks north of the Purple Palace, is the hottest spot in downtown Phoenix on game nights. It was open for only five months before the building next door was purchased, the walls knocked out, and the facility expanded to meet the public's demand.

When people think of Majerle now, they think less of him as some blue-collar role player and more as an enterprising playboy with a good tan, a square jaw, mischievous eyes, and a big grin. There's no need to begrudge his business success, though. He does know how to handle it. At least so far.

"Whatever you have outside basketball is earned because of basketball — the house you live in, the cars you drive," Hollins said. "Sometimes players realize it, but sometimes it's too easy. I've always said that the guys who love the game are the guys who could be getting nothing. They're still going to give you a day's work. I still think Dan falls into that category."

Robertson hopes so.

"He's a guy that his popularity has come on so strong every business in Phoenix would like to use him from a publicity standpoint, and most of them have," Robertson said. "He's a good person, one who has not let this go to his head. Sometimes I'm a little bit concerned that people take advantage of him at times because of his goodness. I hope that he doesn't get caught up in the fast lane. I hope that he always remembers — and I think he will — who he is, where he came from. I think that's his only way to continue to be a great player in this league.

He will never be a guy with great flair and fancy moves, but he knows this. I certainly hope that he maintains that throughout his career."

On the other hand, the Suns were concerned as recently as the beginning of the silver anniversary run that Ceballos had a big head.

But having his job handed to Dumas, maintaining humility, continuing to be ready when called, continuing to work on his game, handling a heartbreaking stress fracture that required surgery and knocked him out of the Finals all were part of a maturing process that won Ceballos a great deal of respect around the Purple Palace.

"I thought he handled his situation with professionalism and class, being a starter, being a nonstarter; playing, not playing at all," Colangelo said. "If Paul was anything with his personnel at certain positions, it was inconsistent in terms of people knowing for sure how many minutes they were going to play. It applied to Cedric."

Westphal, faced with juggling two talented, explosive small forwards, actually had help because of their injuries. It seemed either Ceballos or Dumas was always out. Consequently, each had opportunities, and each had runs of outstanding basketball. The Suns would like to have had both available in the Finals. The Suns want to believe the injury to Ceballos was the difference between winning the championship and not winning it.

"That was an important loss for us," Colangelo said. "I think Cedric Ceballos is on the verge of making a major step forward."

Ceballos has shown incredible improvement for two years.

"You talk about a guy who really grew up and took responsibilities for his weaknesses and worked on them, that's Cedric," Westphal said. "He didn't blame anybody else, didn't hang his head, just kept working harder. He's turned into an excellent pro. He's a real example for other young people. The problem with most players is they don't have a sense of history and don't learn from the mistakes of people who went before them, or from the good things from the people who went before them. In Cedric's case, he did learn. He'll have a great career because of it."

Hollins likens picking up Ceballos in the second round to finding him on a doorstep. He was talented, but immature, self-centered.

"He had the tools and ability to play winning basketball but the only way he was going to be able to do that as a pro was to mature and understand that he wasn't the most important thing in the universe," Hollins said. "He went through a lot of difficult moments. He overcame them and he gained a lot of respect from everybody within the organization — including the players. In fact, I think the players may have respected him more than they respected Richard in that regard."

The Suns look at Dumas and see Ceballos three years ago.

"That's the difference in their games right now," Hollins said. "Cedric has improved his ball handling, improved his shooting, improved his free-throw shooting, the whole gamut, and Richard is just back there coming. A lot of admiration goes out for what Cedric has accomplished thus far. He still can go further, and he will go further, and he will be a solid player in this league."

Ceballos now has the ability to hit an outside shot, but you very rarely see him take one. He scores 20 to 25 points because he is active around the basket.

"He came into this league a borderline player, a guy that you really didn't know how solid a person he was," Robertson said. "But through hard work and through some special attention given to him by Paul Westphal and Lionel Hollins when they were assistants to Cotton, he improved his offense, improved his shooting skills, and through maturity he has developed into a much stronger person. He's made himself into an NBA player.

"This year was not easy on him. All of a sudden, in comes a rookie, Richard Dumas, who probably did not win a starting position but it was decided by Paul, Lionel, and myself that it was time to move him into the starting spot. I don't think Cedric was a negative influence on our team, and he had reason to be. If you weren't pretty strong character-wise, and if it had been Ced's rookie year, it might have been a problem.

"I think the position that Ced found himself in this year required that he mature or get lost in the shuffle. He's proven that he belongs in this league, and I think next year you'll find him at his best."

Fitzsimmons can remember when he doubted such a day ever would come for Ceballos and the "too cool for school" persona he brought with him from his college days at California State-Fullerton.

"He was like a lot of rookies I've brought in: Everytime he got hit, he liked to fall on the floor and liked to stay on the floor while the other team was playing five against our four," Fitzsimmons said. "I probably broke his chops as hard and as tough as anybody I've ever had — I'd say him, Tim Perry, and another kid years ago, LaSalle Thompson."

Ceballos fought it. Fitzsimmons not only put him on the end of the bench, he didn't even put him on the floor for practice drills.

"Didn't even let him practice if he's not going to get up and down the floor," Fitzsimmons said. "But of all the guys that I started with here, Cedric has come the furthest. He was a soft player. He wouldn't even try to cover people. He would take terrible shots, wouldn't work on his shot, wouldn't work on his free throws.

"Paul got with him. And Lionel. And eventually, Cedric started coming around. Whatever he does, whatever he gets, he deserves because he has worked for it. In my mind, Cedric's a man. He grew up."

Ceballos had a good example to follow just a few lockers down in West. The ironman. The professional. West is a worker who doesn't complain, doesn't get respect from referees, doesn't get much credit. But the Suns have been big winners with Mark West in the middle.

He's the quiet giant. He's consistent.

"Really, when you think about the journey he's had in the NBA, being waived twice and ending up as the starting center on the team that's had the success that the Phoenix Suns have had, that's a remarkable story in itself," Colangelo said. "Class guy. Articulate. Intelligent. The kind of individual you want representing your franchise.

"When I think back to the trade with Cleveland that brought him here, he was a very important acquisition. We didn't have a center at the time. We added a center who has given us more than our money's worth."

West does have the respect of the team.

"He's a tough guy who does his job, and certainly doesn't get any respect from the officials," Westphal said. "It's just the NBA. They've gotta call fouls on somebody. Every game isn't going to be both teams shooting the exact same number of free throws, and having the exact same number of fouls. They don't have to be equal, but there is such a push for things to be numerically evened up that I think it even affects the officials sometimes, subconsciously, if not consciously.

"They think, 'We haven't called a foul on this team for a long time.' Then there's Mark West standing there, looking a little clumsier than everybody else. They definitely call fouls on him they wouldn't call on David Robinson, Hakeem Olajuwon, or Patrick Ewing. But you have to deal with it. Kurt Rambis his whole career had to deal with a foul being committed by the Lakers and the referees not quite sure who it was on. It was like the referee would say, 'Well, it's on you. No, that's Magic. Then it's on you. No, that's Kareem. Well, the foul's on you. No, that's Worthy. Hmm. Rambis! You fouled him.' That's what Mark is on our team."

Even at 33, West shows signs of being able to play for several more seasons, especially if Miller steps up and takes a few more minutes, or if free agent Joe Kleine, signed in August, can give some relief. Big guys have a tendency to last for a while. They don't have to run much, just be tough around the basket and take up space.

"It's not like he's such a huge scorer that his skills will be eroded," Westphal said with a smile. "If his back feels good and he doesn't get injured, he should be able to play for several more years."

It's as if West has a license to be insignificant when the Suns have the ball. He's one of the game's highest percentage shooters — he's never failed to reach 60 percent in his five seasons with the Suns! — but rarely does he have enough attempts to qualify for the NBA field goal percentage title. He doesn't have much of a repertoire around the basket, although he has an effective up-and-under move. His shooting range is limited, as evidenced by his field-goal percentages being higher than his free-throw percentages.

Probably the biggest detriment is his inability to catch.

"You can't get mad at the guy," Westphal said. "He's tried to do some things — drills with tennis balls, catching them after bouncing them off walls, had his eyes checked, all kinds of hand-eye coordination things. He caught more this year. Sometimes he makes some amazing catches. A guy will throw one really fast and he'll just catch it and put it in. Maybe it's the slow balls he has trouble with."

It's on the opposite end of the court where West's shot-blocking, rebounding, and guarding the basket keep him in the league.

"I get tired of people complaining about Mark," Fitzsimmons said. "All I know is this: we acquired Mark, we win 55, 54, 55 , 53, and 62. That's what I tell the fans that criticize him. All I know is he's a big part of it because he'd come up big in big games. He has a difficult time on the court because his name is synonymous with fouls, whether he does it or doesn't do it. I've got a TV monitor in front of me now as a broadcaster, so when Mark takes a charge and they call a block, I let the refs know it. We took Mark because we needed to start over, we needed guys to show some character and leadership. He's done it."

West goes into the 1993-94 season with a string of 419 consecutive appearances — an ironman streak that covers more than five seasons.

"It's been very interesting to me to see Mark West's reaction to some of the people on this team," Robertson said. "He reacted in a different way than I thought he would. For instance, we were hopeful that his steadiness, his calmness would be an influence on some of our rookies and some of our younger players. And it has.

"However, my personal feeling is that he gravitated toward some of these guys and began to be a pretty integral part of the Oliver Miller-Cedric Ceballos-Negele Knight-Richard Dumas group, laughing, joking. In my opinion, they influenced him more than he influenced them. I've never discussed this with anybody else but from my observation, I thought that was somewhat unusual, somewhat surprising."

Even West admits he was surprised at the quick bonds that were formed in the clubhouse, but less surprised with the successes on the court.

"We jelled early, and sometimes it takes time to do that," he said. "But for us it came fairly fast, and we ran with it. Looking back, it was a great thing. But I can't really say that I am surprised because of the personalities on the team and a good part of the nucleus already was here. Then when you bring in charismatic players like Danny and Charles, you're putting together a formula for good chemistry that accelerates the process of coming together. It was an unusual cast of characters, no question, but you need that diversity in personalities as well as styles of play."

While West was stepping back into the starting lineup to reclaim the job he'd lost the season before to Andrew Lang, Chambers was going in the opposite direction. He generally was very testy with the media.

Chambers broke the Suns' single-season scoring record in each of his first two years after signing on as a free agent in 1988. Those outputs became his measuring sticks, and he only went downhill during his final three seasons. So the perception of many in his final years in a Suns uniform was that Chambers was washed up.

His skills diminished and his role was reduced, further complicating his effort to be productive, but Chambers still had some basketball life left. He couldn't score 25 points every night, but he still was a threat to do it once in a while. Defenders still had to take him seriously. Would you want to lay off him and have it be the night he goes for 25?

At nearly 7 feet, Chambers still has the versatility to play all three front-line positions, although he was becoming a step slow when going against a "three."

Westphal said that Chambers no longer would be in the lineup just because he is Tom Chambers. His playing time now would have to be earned. After Mustaf quickly washed out, Westphal did not turn to Chambers, but to Ceballos and Dumas.

For the first time in his pro career, Chambers did not start a regular-season game. He didn't like it. Had it been on any other team, he probably would not have accepted it. But Chambers was in the final guaranteed year of his contract, and he knew this might be his last chance to win a championship. He was effective.

With the Suns in the dramatic seventh game of the conference finals against Seattle — the team Chambers had bolted to sign on with the Suns — Westphal started Chambers. After 91 games coming off the bench, Chambers had his chance. His 17 points, six rebounds, and two blocked shots helped the Suns move to the Finals.

Westphal said he did it because of matchups. Seattle's tall forwards were tough for Dumas to defend, and Ceballos was out with his foot injury. Westphal admitted that in the back of his mind, he suspected Chambers might be fired up, knowing this probably would be Chambers' final game as a Sun if they lost. Westphal thought about all those successes Chambers had early in his career that helped turn the franchise around and create the fan support that led to the building of the new arena.

"That helped make me feel comfortable that it was the right decision," Westphal said. "Tom just has a way of rising to the occasion. In my opinion, he doesn't have the ability he used to have to bring it every night. There were times he'd play 40 minutes and have 35 points. It was like setting your watch. He can't do it every night anymore, but he can do it some nights. I just felt that in the biggest game of the year, I wanted to give him the chance to do it, and have that be his night."

And it was. Even the stoic old Chambers was moved by the thunderous response when Westphal took him out of the game in the closing minutes.

"One huge highlight, I'd have to say maybe even bigger than beating Chicago back there in the regular season, was Chambers coming off the floor," Westphal said. "I was so happy for him, for what that meant, for what he had done, and what he had gone through the whole year. It was different than anything he'd been through in the past. And here he is in the biggest game, getting taken out to the applause. That summed up the year for me really well."

Even in his advancing years and with declining skills, Chambers had an impact playing 24 minutes a game off the bench.

"I'm real happy for him to be able to swallow his past, not liking it and not agreeing with it, but still having a great attitude," Westphal said. "Once you've been around enough to know what it's all about, that the only thing you really want people to say about you is that you are professional. That's what you have to say about Tom."

Although Chambers and Fitzsimmons began to butt heads before Fitzsimmons retired as coach, it was Fitzsimmons who actually resurrected Chambers' career. When he came to Phoenix, Chambers was allowed to play the way he wanted to play — at small forward out running. Fitzsimmons never tried to make Chambers into something he wasn't, as most of Chambers' previous coaches had. When Fitzsimmons saw his offensive skills beginning to erode, he harped at him to work harder on his defense and rebounding, the ticket to staying in the league. Chambers didn't take it well.

"I give Cotton credit for handling him when he came here as a free agent," Robertson said. "Tom Chambers became the player that he could be with this team. He played relaxed for Cotton until the last year of Cotton's contract, and then the relationship there soured. Because of that Tom came into this year not knowing how he would fit into this basketball team, not knowing whether he would be a starter or come off the bench. Tom has been a great player in this league. Tough mentally. Will take the big shot. But it was a little bit sad to see him decline in ability as this team improved so much."

After the Suns were eliminated in the Finals, Chambers did not stick around for the parade in downtown Phoenix that attracted more than 300,000 spectators — more than had come out to see the Pope six years earlier. Everyone knew the end had come. Colangelo was delaying official announcement that he wasn't picking up Chambers' option for 1993-94 until the following week, but Chambers knew.

It would have been a nice way for Chambers to go out, to say good-bye to the sellout crowds that cheered him on during those early years. It would have been a nice way for them to say thank you for his five years, the most successful five-year stretch in Phoenix Suns history. But while the crowds swelled in downtown Phoenix, Chambers and his family were on the beach in Hawaii.

Sometimes it is difficult to accept a diminished role at a place where you've been something more. People only want to compare you with the past. Sometimes it is better to move on. The Suns wanted Chambers' salary slot to sign a younger free agent who could give them more than he could. In September, they used it to sign A.C. Green. Chambers needed to move on to a new setting, where everyone knew coming in that he isn't what he used to be, that he was coming in to be a bench player.

In August, Chambers signed with Utah for $650,000. He also will receive a sum nearly the equal of that from the Suns that he restructured to allow them to sign Ainge.

It was over for him in Phoenix, but he left without saying good-bye. That's Tom Chambers.

─────── *Chapter Nine* ───────

# HAVE GRIPE, WILL TRAVEL

Imagine being a talented young player and having the chance to break in with a team like the Suns, to learn your craft every day around the likes of Barkley, KJ, Majerle, Ainge, West. It is the opportunity of a lifetime for Knight and Mustaf, who've been in the NBA for three seasons.

Their response? They're unhappy and want to be traded! Their whole careers are ahead of them. They have a chance to be a part of a championship team and they want out.

"When we're paying the kind of salaries that we're paying, I'm not necessarily interested in what a player wants or doesn't want," Colangelo said. "Contracts have to work both ways. If I can ever be in a position where if I don't want a player anymore that I can just tear up the contract, then I'd be more open to appeasing players the other way."

Two summers earlier, the Suns were turning down first-round picks for Knight following his impressive rookie season. He had plenty of chances in the Suns' run to the Finals, what with KJ's numerous injuries, but he struggled. It is Knight's contention that he hasn't received a fair shake, that's he's much better than he's been allowed to show.

"When Negele Knight came in as a rookie and got his opportunity to play, he did a great job, he really did," Colangelo said. "I think what's happened with him in his career here is that he's lost confidence, or felt that people lost confidence in him. So it's been kind of a rollercoaster ride for him."

Knight has indicated that he believes he could start on a lot of teams in the NBA.

"I don't think that's off necessarily because I've always kind of felt that way," Colangelo said. "Whenever Kevin's been down, we've played well with Negele Knight. The record speaks for itself. The statistics when he played that one season — the 20 points, 10 assists for a stretch — were outstanding. But circumstances have dictated that he's been a nonplayer after he's been a starter. That's tough on a guy to accept. I'm sure there's a great deal of frustration. Today, I would say that he is a point guard who could start for a lot of teams in this league and do an adequate job. But unless we change our mind, he's still here."

Knight simply was beaten out of the backup job by Frank Johnson. He had a tough season shooting the ball, making less than 40 percent.

"Negele is a good player, he's proven that," Westphal said. "Maybe something happened to his confidence. Maybe he started pressing. At some point, the coach has to say, 'I feel bad for the guy, but I've got to play somebody who can do the job.' For whatever reason, I think he took a little step backward this year. Maybe it was just a bad year, just bad shooting luck. We were never able to give him the playing time to work his way out of his slump. That's unfortunate, but we've got to move on. We can't wait for a guy who you don't have to wait for."

Even when KJ was hurt and Knight got the call, the nightly scenario was similar game after game: Knight started and played the first quarter, came out, came back to open the third quarter, played a few more minutes, then took a seat for the evening. Of course, when KJ was healthy and starting, Knight rarely played at all.

"Even though Negele wasn't necessarily a big impact guy all the time, the team won, and that's all I can base things on," Fitzsimmons said. "I think we were 26-5 with Negele starting, so I'm saying to you that he can play. He just can't play here.

"In Frank Johnson, Paul made up his mind he's going with a veteran player. A lot of people say Negele has a bad attitude. He doesn't have a bad attitude. How can you have a good attitude if you never play, and you know you're never going to play unless Kevin Johnson gets hurt, or Frank Johnson gets hurt? I have to agree  that Negele would be better off someplace else. And if that opportunity presents itself, that's exactly what we'd do."

All the things the Suns liked about Knight when they drafted him no longer were there; he was tentative.

"Negele is a wonderful guy, a great teammate, a really nice genuine person, and all the guys do like him," Hollins said. "Then to come out the first game and go 5-for-18 and have the crowd starting to boo just shot his confidence. He was not the same player he'd been when Kevin went out at the end of Negele's rookie year and he had the 20/10s. And Frank was hungry. It's as simple as that."

Knight knows that KJ is young. He sees the possibility of being a career backup if he stays with the Suns.

"The second season, and subsequently each season following, Negele turned out to be injury prone." Robertson said. "He at times showed the brilliance he did as a rookie, but he has not been consistent in that regard since then. Therefore, his future here with this team is clouded.

"In our opinion, and in his opinion, too, he needs to be put into a situation where he can be the starting point guard, and in so doing, allow his talents to blossom again and allow him to get back to being the type of player everyone thinks he can be. I doubt that will ever occur here in Phoenix."

Tough as his situation is, Knight's future in Phoenix has to be brighter than that of Mustaf's. He, too, thought he was burned in a promise for more time. But Mustaf apparently mistook an opportunity for a guarantee. The Suns gave him the chance, but he did little with it.

Still, he got huffy when his minutes disappeared — that after the Suns extended his contract in the summer of 1992 to pay him more than $5 million over the next three seasons, fully guaranteed. Mustaf's daily effort seemed to say, "I've got my money, so to heck with it."

Westphal was excited about Mustaf's potential, pushed for the contract extension, and planned to give him a real shot in training camp. Then Mustaf opened the season on the injured list.

"He never got into a groove," Colangelo said. "As it turned out, the whole year was kind of a wash where, as Paul said to me, the one thing we didn't do is find out whether he can play or not. There's been a lot of speculation about what's going to happen to Mustaf. One of the things that may happen is he's going to come in here and we're going to find out. It may be a year later, but Paul feels there is talent there.

"Jerrod has to show us that he really wants it, too. The bottom line is the jury's out on Mustaf. He's a young athlete with a lot of skill, seems to have a lot of things on his plate in terms of other interests. Not that a player can't do that, but you can't lose focus on what it's all about. Your livelihood is basketball."

Although Mustaf horrified the coaches with his summer league showing in 1992, they still were hoping he would come into training camp, establish himself, and take off. His failure to emerge hurt them badly in the playoffs. He was the player ticketed for duty against the Derrick McKeys, the Elden Campbells — young athletic forwards with size and range. With Mustaf at the end of the bench, the Suns really had no other players who matched up well. Those kinds of players hurt them all season long, but especially in the playoffs.

"It's just unfortunate, but I will not criticize him, and I don't think it's fair to criticize him for circumstances," Westphal said. "We had high hopes for Mustaf. But he got hurt at the wrong time. He got hurt when the team was being formed, and it formed without him. That's all you can say. He was in the plans, then all of a sudden he was not there, and the plans changed. That's too bad for him.

"I won't say it's his fault, but I won't say it's anybody else's, either. It's time for him to find out what kind of player he is."

That's difficult to do when you're injured, and nobody but Mustaf knows what kind of pain he had. Others might have played through it. Mustaf is the only one who can answer that.

"Maybe somebody else would have said, 'This is my chance, you're going to have to put me in the hospital to keep me out,' " Westphal said. "But if you're hurt, you're hurt, too."

The Suns don't view Mustaf as somebody who, given an opportunity, will not be denied.

"Majerle is probably the best example of that attitude I've ever seen," Westphal said. "When he separated his shoulder, he was out. That's what it took to put him out. You can't play with some of the injuries he's had."

Mustaf can't make that claim. It's called seizing the moment. When the door of opportunity opens, you have to be prepared.

When the Suns scouted Mustaf in a predraft camp in Chicago in 1990, they liked what they saw: a guy 6-foot-10, about 220 pounds who had come out of college two years early, so they believed he was going to get bigger and stronger. He could run, he could jump, he could shoot around the basket with either hand.

But New York drafted Mustaf a few picks ahead of the Suns. A year later, following a promising rookie season with the Knicks, they traded him to the Suns for Xavier McDaniel. McDaniel had a provision in his contract that allowed him to buy himself out and become a free agent. The Suns were certain he would do it, so they had to move him while they still could get something in return.

"I think Jerrod still has the ability to be a solid player," Hollins said. "A star, we don't know. To reach that level, there are a lot more factors that would have to enter into it.

"One thing I've learned in this league is that I don't know if a lot of these younger players realize that financially the worries and the struggle are over, but athletically it's only beginning. Like watching the draft, each one of these guys in the top 11 is going to be a millionaire, but whatever he accomplished on the college level is over. What now happens is you start from zero, and you build and establish yourself all over again. In the pros, you have to do it every day, every year you're in the league because there are new guys coming in, there are guys sitting on the bench getting new opportunities. And they keep coming."

Mustaf has not meshed a hungry attitude with his physical ability. He seems more interested in his bookstore and production studio in Phoenix, and his foundation in Maryland that helps troubled teens.

"For whatever reason, he hasn't," Hollins said. "He has a lot of outside interests. He has a lot of different agendas there that cloud his ability to come and be the first one to practice. He doesn't drag me or any of the coaches out of the locker room to come with him to work on his game. He isn't the last one still out there working, or the first guy in the line drills, or the guy that gets every rebound in practice, whether he plays or not.

"Many young players come in, look at guys who are playing and say, "If I got the opportunities, I could do what he's doing." But opportunities are earned. Frank Johnson, for example, earned his. Every day in practice, Frank said, 'Don't cut me,' without saying a word. Every day his play said, 'Don't cut me.' A guy like Jerrod has to have his play say every day, 'Give me playing time,' to where you say, 'Hey, we've got to find some place for this guy in the game.'

"But if you come to practice just on time or only five minutes early, or as soon as the whistle blows and it's time to shoot free throws you walk out the door and you're gone, or if you've got other interests outside of basketball that are diluting that intensity that you need on the court, you're never going to achieve. Financially, he has it made. But athletically, he's at minus-zero."

Others have juggled their outside interests more effectively. Ainge has a hat store; Majerle, the restaurant; KJ, the St. Hope Academy. They all handle it.

"I don't even know what Jerrod's interests are, but something is taking away from him spending more time at his craft to get better," Hollins said. "He has something because he doesn't stay there and take care of business in the basketball arena."

The new coaching staff felt Fitzsimmons made a mistake in not giving Mustaf more playing time after the Suns acquired him. They all put their eggs in his basket verbally when Westphal took over.

"But it was up to him," Robertson said. "I pointedly told him in that meeting, 'Moose, you have never done anything yet in this league. You were a first-round pick, heralded as a future star, but you've never done it yet. We believe you can. But until you do, the verdict is out.'

"So we took him to the summer league and our plan was to work with him and prepare him to be a starting forward. He and Barkley, in our minds, were to be our starting forwards. Well, Moose's summer league was terrible. He didn't rebound, he didn't score, he didn't run, he didn't guard. He did nothing.

"So now, all of a sudden, we say, 'Oh, my goodness, we've got to change our thinking.' We started the season working very hard with Moose, gave him some starting assignments, and things just didn't work out. So Paul decided he would move Barkley to the power forward position, and Moose would have to earn his way from there, which he never did. Paul never had confidence in him anymore.

"Now, we're going to approach it the same way for this coming year. We're going to work with him. As coaches, we're paid to bring out talent in players. That's gonna be a big challenge for us."

It became more of a challenge when Mustaf ditched summer camp and summer league play after the Finals, saying that he was too good for it, that he couldn't improve his game against those stumblebums, and why should he participate after the Suns put him on the bench?

Colangelo said publicly that if there was any demand for Mustaf, he would have been traded long ago. Colangelo added that he has no plans to eat the remaining three years of Mustaf's contract, but that if Mustaf doesn't want to be a Sun, he'd be willing to tear up the contract and forget the more than $5 million in guaranteed payment.

Mustaf declined that offer.

All of this occurred prior to a bizarre series of events in July 1993, in which Mustaf was questioned and a search warrant issued on his home in connection with the fatal shooting of a woman in Glendale, Arizona. The parents of the slain woman, Althea Hayes, said that Mustaf is the father of the three-month old baby she was carrying. Mustaf acknowledged that he knew the woman, but denied that he was the father or that he had any involvement in her murder. By late summer, the investigation was continuing.

Few among the Suns took to Mustaf. Barkley, whose locker is next to Mustaf's, early in the season called him "the second coming of Armon Gilliam." Mustaf occasionally burned incense at his locker.

"He is a mystery man," Fitzsimmons said. "Jerrod has all this potential to be a good player. We were going to trade Xavier because we knew what his contract was. We knew he'd buy himself out and we'd already given up two firsts and given up Eddie Johnson for Xavier. So we wanted to get something. We took Mustaf. He had this potential, but he certainly hadn't reached it yet after he came out of Maryland early. And we're still waiting for him to reach it — if he does.

"His whole thing will be the focus. Some people, you can give them the money, and it won't affect them at all. You can give Majerle all the money you want to give him, and he's going to go play the game. But some guys you give the money to, and it affects them, and they don't see the big picture. As long as the money keeps coming in, maybe you don't get the effort that you think you should get. That's the way I see Mustaf."

There are wildly diverse personalities on many teams, but they tend to receive more focus on a winning team like the Suns.

"You need a couple of guys on your roster who are going to keep you loose," Colangelo said. "You need a couple who are going to push and shove. You need a jokester here, and you need this there. It's just kind of neat the way it comes together, and also, who kind of jumps out at you at various times."

The biggest concern the Suns had going into the silver anniversary season was how some players would adjust to bringing on a player bigger than life.

"In retrospect, I think our guys, in particular Kevin and Tom, sacrificed," Colangelo said. "I think Charles attempted in the best way he could to bring attention to his teammates and share in that, but mostly the media wanted him. I'd say we had a tremendously successful year in terms of blending these personalities. You never know how personalities are going to come together, even in the best-laid plans. Like some marriages, it doesn't always work. The true test is when things get a little testy."

They were, indeed, as Bulls Coach Phil Jackson described them, "a team of oddities."

*Chapter Ten*

# GETTING ACCLIMATED

Never had there been so much excitement in the Grand Canyon State as on the opening day of Suns training camp.

Love him or hate him, everybody recognized the impact of Barkley. He was one of the top five players in the game before the Olympics. He had transcended that on the basis of his play on the Dream Team.

Already, Barkley was building quite a following with his outrageous quips. A lot of great athletes have passed through Arizona in various sports, but here was the first big-time sports personality the state had ever been able to claim as its own.

Informed that the Suns conduct preseason camp in Flagstaff, about a 3 1/2-hour drive north of Phoenix, Barkley wanted to know, "Ain't that where Mel's Diner is? Is Mel's Diner for real?"

Also informed that Flagstaff is at an elevation of 6,905 feet in rarefied air that has claimed a goodly number of unsuspecting first-timers, he deadpanned, "Oooo. We'll be a little tired up there, then, huh?"

This was after he'd just returned from Japan pumping his new Godzilla TV commercial for Nike. "Even though it is shown on TV here, the spot was made for Japan," Barkley said. "Godzilla is big there."

And Barkley is big here.

Record numbers of reporters from around the world paraded in and out of the Suns' camp. Barkley was scheduled for in-depth interviews with somebody almost every day.

"I'll be glad when we start playing games so I can get this stuff over with," he said.

He didn't have to accommodate anybody, but he didn't turn anybody away. He was already winning friends and influencing people. At least in the media.

He seemed eager to establish a different kind of relationship than the rocky one he had with reporters in Philadelphia.

"The biggest difference out here is that they don't go over every single thing you say with a fine-tooth comb trying to find something they can use against you," he said. "In Philadelphia, they were just looking for it. Here, if I say, 'We didn't play well,' they write, 'Charles said they didn't play well.' In Philadelphia, they would have written, 'Barkley rips teammates.' That's the difference."

He quickly became just as popular with his teammates, though not without a few tests.

"I can remember whenever we played Philadelphia that I hated to play against Charles because he'd always foul me hard," KJ said. "I remember one year he put me into the basket support the first time I drove. Nobody stood up to him. It set the tone for the whole game. I really didn't like his game.

"But being on the other side of it now, I've got to love it. Charles dishes it out and he can back it up, and it's a good feeling to know he's on your side making life miserable for other point guards now."

KJ, incidentally, reported for his first workout with extremely close-cropped hair, emulating Barkley's shaved head.

"Charles cut me on the bus ride up," KJ said. Barkley denied it. "If I'd done it, it would look a whole lot better than that."

Westphal, while amused, said chances were slim he'd join in the fun. "I'll shave my head when Majerle does," Westphal said. "But here's the thing: We've now got two starters with shaved heads, so the next three guys to shave their heads start."

It didn't start a trend, and KJ quickly let his hair grow back. He said he'd actually lost a bet to Barkley on the bus. He wouldn't say what the bet was. A light tone was set. This was going to be a fun, loose group, as long as the levity didn't impede the development of the team.

Westphal initiated a policy in camp that he continued throughout the season of taking it easy on the veterans. Barkley, coming off his long summer with the Dream Team, was allowed to opt out of some sessions. West, Chambers, and KJ had the same privilege for morning sessions. The evening workouts included scrimmages, so everyone worked. Westphal wanted to see the pieces he had put in during that morning's session executed in live settings.

Barkley was among the few vets, though, who ran on his own during the morning.

"These two-a-days ain't no joke," he said. "You don't just show up to be a good team. You take every practice seriously."

The Suns took the evening practices seriously. They were lively, often heated battles, and on the third day Barkley laid down his first serious challenge to his new teammates.

"I had heard about how the Suns were soft," Barkley said. "Everybody told me that Kevin, especially, was soft. I wanted to see."

Barkley leveled Ceballos from behind as he drove for a layup. First on the scene to castigate Barkley were KJ and Ainge. "That's bogus, Charles," KJ said. Ainge used a slightly stronger word beginning with "B".

"Charles is good at giving criticism, but he's good at taking criticism, too," Ainge said. "You can't be afraid to tell him when he screws up. We owe that to each other."

It came during a workout in which tempers flared throughout. Rambis and Mustaf wrestled with each other. It hadn't taken the Suns long to determine that they had something special, and that not all of them were going be part of it. There weren't enough roster spots.

"It was like playoff basketball," Westphal said. "That was amazing. Guys are trying to stake out some territory, and I think everybody picked up on how hard KJ and Charles were playing."

Westphal always placed Johnson and Barkley opposite each other during scrimmages, perhaps laying down a little test of his own to see how they would respond to leadership roles, and how their teammates would respond to them.

"It was unbelievable how much intensity there was," Hollins said. "A lot of that can be attributed to the competitive nature of the players. But it's also the way Paul has it set up."

Bandages began appearing everywhere. The team of oddities looked like a team of Les Nessmans.

"Yeah, it's more physical out there this year," said Mustaf, a patch covering his right eye. "Anytime you've got a guy like Charles it's going to be physical. When you get down to it, we weren't a very physical team before. That was one of our shortcomings. We didn't have that mentality. This year, we're trying to develop that in training camp.

"There are all sorts of ways you can lose a basketball game, but I see us building the discipline it takes to do all the little things that add up to a championship team."

Interesting that those words came from him, but it was hard to argue.

"I challenged them every day," Barkley said. "They stood up to me. I like that. That's the way it's supposed to be. I tried little mental games. I wanted them to fight me back. If they'll fight me, that means they'll fight Karl Malone, Tim Hardaway, Shawn Kemp, the guys we have to fight."

All in all, camp was an interesting week of feeling out egos, personalities, and playing styles.

"Charles came in here testing people, and he likes the fact that they stood up to him," Westphal said. "There was a mutual respect built. If nothing else, that will be valuable."

Most eyes were on the interaction between KJ and Barkley. "I can't wait to go to the basket and see the faces of those big guys who usually threaten me," KJ said. "My confidence is way up. I may even turn my trash-talking up with Charles back there. He's going to make all of us a little more physical, a little more feisty."

A revealing statement, as it turned out.

Johnson was the one who had to check his ego at the practice-gym door.

"I think there's going to be a synthesis," Johnson said. "Everybody can have their personality and still work within the context of the team. I'm the point guard, so whether I want to be or not, I'm a leader. I've always played with enthusiasm and encouraged people. That's not going to change at all.

"But Charles is unpredictable. He's going to go off at any time, so you don't know what to expect. You do know to expect it at some time. I think there are some unspoken things communicated out there on the court. People understand their roles and fall into them. Charles isn't going to sit back and let others run the show and him just respond when things aren't working. I know that, and I accept that."

The on-court execution was acceptable, also.

"I think if I were coaching against us, I would feel like I wanted to play with six guys," Westphal said. "You really have to double-team KJ. And now you have to double Charles. After a while, you say, 'Hey, I'm running out of people.' Hopefully, our offense will be set up to make people pay when they double either of those guys."

The acquisition of Ainge, the drafting of Miller, and the improved range of Majerle were obvious factors early.

"It takes a great deal of pressure off my role as point guard," KJ said. "I think I can work on things I should be better at, and still contribute in ways I have in the past.

"Charles and Danny are guys who are going to take good shots, and know what it takes to play consistent basketball day in and day out. They know what it takes to win. Hopefully, you'll see a lot more guys contributing instead of a few guys having to carry us. I've been an All-Star. I've been a second-team all-pro. I want to win, and whatever happens within the context of us winning is fine with me. One thing Danny has taught me already is to not get caught up in the numbers game. I used to challenge myself to average 20 points and 10 assists just to have a goal out there. You can get too caught up in that, reach those goals, and say, 'Hey, I did my part.' Numbers can become a defense mechanism. I don't want that. If my numbers are down, and we win the NBA championship, that's where I want to be."

By the end of camp, the synthesis was well under way.

"I like what I see developing," Westphal said. "We have established a mentality for this team: toughness, mutual respect for our talents, mutual respect for the depth of this team. I want everybody to adopt the attitude of the Dream Team, that being, 'We're after the win.' There's probably not a guy on the team who will get as much time as he'd like to get because we do have a lot of guys who deserve to play."

Barkley was mobbed everywhere he went in Flagstaff, a tiny community most noted for its many truck stops (no, Mel's Diner is NOT there). He registered at the team hotel under an assumed name to ward off visitors and callers.

When the Suns wrapped up camp with an intra-squad scrimmage at the Northern Arizona University domed football stadium, players were positioned at tables around the football field for one hour before the game to sign autographs. Barkley's line stretched around most of the 220 yards of the indoor track.

Before he would let the team break camp at week's end, Westphal assigned strength and conditioning coach Robin Pound to put them through a final one-hour torture test. Everyone was doubled over, gasping for air.

"I struggled with the elevation," Barkley conceded. "I'm looking forward to getting back to some level ground and back down where I can breathe."

The Suns were to make their pre-season debut on Sunday, October 18, against the Boston Celtics — the first basketball game ever played in the 19,026-seat America West Arena.

"I told Charles the place would be full the first time he played here — and that it would have happened with him or without him," Fitzsimmons said. "I said to him, 'See these blocks and mortar? You didn't put any of them there.' Then I said, 'Look up there in the rafters. Do you see any banners up there? Well, that's your job: Hang a flag.'"

Westphal, out of respect, started the veterans who had produced four successive 50-game winners under Fitzsimmons: KJ, Majerle, Chambers, Rambis, and West.

"This building never would have been built without the contributions of those guys," Westphal said. "I think it's a nice honor for them, and I think the fans will enjoy seeing the guys who played a big part in making this building a reality out on the floor at tip-off."

Indeed they did. The sellout crowd rose and cheered as the Suns came onto the court for the tip.

Then KJ made good on his promise to score the first points in the new arena. The Suns won the opening tip, the ball coming to KJ, who quickly jacked up a rare three-point try that missed. He was fouled on the offensive rebound and made his free throws. Mission accomplished. Rambis scored the first field goal a few seconds later.

"That doesn't count," Johnson said. "The first ball to go through a goal in the new arena was by KJ, No. 7. I predicted it. I had to get the first points. Now I have to do it in the regular-season, too, because they may try to throw the exhibition-season records out."

The vets really appreciated Westphal's starting them.

"Paul's a players' coach," KJ said. "Normal coaches wouldn't think of that. He understands that those little things make a difference, and that they're things players will never forget."

The crowd also will never forget its first look at Barkley, who like Ainge and Miller, was understanding of Westphal's honoring the veterans. They took a seat and waited their turn.

Once in action, though, Barkley was Barkley: Fittingly, he was thrown out of his first game with his new team in its first game in its new arena.

"I think it's poetic justice, that's the way it ought to be," Westphal said, amused after the Suns gave an accurate portrayal of things to come with a 124-112 reaming of the Boston Celtics.

With 6:45 to go in the first quarter, Barkley stood, ripped off his warm-up suit, and reported to the scorers' table.

"That was difficult," Barkley said, "because that made it official. When you've been doing the same thing for eight years and you change, that's difficult. But it was also nice. It's a new team, new players, and the fans were excited. I didn't want to let the fans down."

And with 27 points in 27 minutes before referee Hue Hollins dismissed him, Barkley was anything but disappointing.

"During training camp, we were always going against each other on opposite teams, so it was like he wasn't my ally, but my nemesis," KJ said. "I have to admit when I finally saw him run onto the floor in that purple and orange uniform, that was the first time it really sunk in that he's on our side now. It's going to be nice to have him with us instead of against us."

Robert Parish of the Celtics, who'd just witnessed Barkley's coming out in the desert, agreed with KJ's assessment.

"They've got a go-to guy now," said Parish, familiar with the Suns' new warrior from their Atlantic Division clashes. "They've got somebody with the ability to get a good shot every time down — not to mention that in anything that's close, they're going to get the call."

But Chris Ford, the Celtics coach, was more taken by the Suns' complementary pieces around their new superstar. Double-team him, and Barkley will find the open man.

"And you're talking about a lot of guys who can do something with the ball," Ford said. "You're talking about an awful lot of fire-power."

Barkley's second "T" and his pink slip came for hanging on the rim with 2:20 remaining in the game — a far cry from most of his transgressions.

Barkley later kidded that he wanted the early release because he had a six-pack waiting in the Suns' new Jacuzzi.

"I just wanted to get back here to the TV to see who was winning the World Series," Barkley said.

Later, Miller, whose locker is next to Barkley's, was kidding him about being a poor example to the Suns' young players by getting the heave.

"Hey, Fat Boy," Barkley shot back, "you can't even jump high enough to hang on the rim — unless they put a Big Mac on it."

Miller's debut had been impressive as well. Though overweight, Miller showed that he can handle the ball like a tennis ball in his large mitts. He could also pass, move, and shoot. Westphal enjoyed watching him.

"I see Oliver Miller playing a lot of center," Westphal said. "If I had to pick one guy so far, I'd say I'm especially pleased with him. He's playing like a veteran. He's working hard. He's going to be a good addition to our team."

Miller and the Suns played a game of cat-and-mouse all summer on contract negotiations. The Suns didn't want to make a long-term, heavyweight commitment (no pun) until Miller demonstrated that he could reduce and control his weight. Try as he did, it was difficult to get the pounds off.

The Suns used all but $77,000 of what they had available under their salary cap to sign Kempton, their insurance policy. "I know they just did that to light a fire under me," Miller said.

It didn't seem to do the trick, though.

Finally, the day before the Suns boarded the bus for Flagstaff, Miller, hovering around 300 pounds, and the Suns came to terms. It took an assist from — who else? — KJ to get it done.

KJ agreed to restructure $310,000 of the $2.2 million he was to receive. When combined with the league-minimum of $190,000 the league allows a team to pay a first-round pick regardless of its position relative to the cap, Miller got $500,000, jumping to $650,000 in the second year. Miller promised to prove to KJ that he's worth it.

One of the most dazzling plays of the intrasquad scrimmage in Flagstaff was Miller's no-look, over-the-shoulder dish to Ceballos, who was slashing for a dunk.

"My friends in grade school used to call me Baby Magic," Miller said. "When you're young, you always watch the legends like Magic Johnson, and you try to do what they do. I would watch him on TV, then go outside with a tennis ball and try to make those passes. It always made me feel good to hear the fans ooh and aah."

The big fella also loves the length-of-the-floor inbound toss, which can be a blessing and a curse. He has burned a few unsuspecting laggards who are slow to retreat on defense, but more often than not,

Miller tends to over-throw it. His affection for the bomb came from playing quarterback in street football games.

"The thing that amazes me about him is the number of high-risk passes he throws that connect," Westphal said. "He does it without making a whole lot of turnovers, that's rare in a young player."

Twenty-one other teams passed on Miller in the first round, and Westphal was hooted when the Suns took him. But Westphal loves versatile players. Miller can hit the outside shot, he can post up, pass, dribble, rebound, and block shots. Late in the season, after finally shedding weight, Miller played power forward.

Arkansas had two others who were first-round picks, Todd Day and Lee Mayberry, and another, Isaiah Morris, who was a second-rounder.

"I wonder how many of those guys would have been picked where they were if they hadn't played with Oliver," Westphal said. "I love Oliver. A lot of people took cheap shots at him, but I said all along he can play, and he showed it every time he went out there."

Barkley and Ainge could see it, too. They also could see that Miller wasn't going to last long at 323, or 312, or even 290. They continually gave the rookie pep talks on continuing his battle.

Barkley could identify with the problem because he conquered it himself. Remember "The Round Mound of Rebound," as he was called when he came into the NBA?

"The worst thing in the world for you is eating late at night, and it's the hardest thing to avoid in the NBA," Barkley said. "You get back to the hotel after a game and you want to eat. You just have to be real careful. For me, beer and pizza were the worst. It's not an easy thing that Oliver is dealing with. It's a serious problem."

As the season unfolded, Miller would reveal to the world exactly how serious it had become to him.

That preseason opener was very telling. The Suns weren't exactly the Detroit Pistons defensively, but they slowed the Celtics enough to win.

"We didn't get Charles for his defense, and we didn't get KJ for his defense, either," Westphal said. "They'll make some steals and they're a net plus, but they're primarily offensive players."

True. The Suns had little trouble scoring with their diverse and deep arsenal.

"When we play together like that," the normally reserved Westphal said, " I like our chances to win the game."

Apparently, so did Miller.

"He's a dumb rookie," Barkley said. "He was saying in the fourth quarter, 'I see a parade in my future.' I said, 'Sure, son. It's the first exhibition game, and you're talking about a parade already.' That tells you right there he's not playing with a full deck."

Maybe Miller was a little more perceptive than Barkley realized.

The Suns' second preseason game, their first on the road, was essentially a testimonial to KJ, played in his old college gym, Harmon Arena, at the University of California against the Golden State Warriors. Cal was retiring KJ's jersey No. 11. Westphal allowed him to go to Berkeley a day early for the festivities.

"I yearn for this environment," KJ said. "Whenever I get the chance, I try to soak up as big a dose of it as I can get. I love this place."

So after KJ had his fix of visiting the library, his old dormitory, and his old favorite coffee house, he saw his jersey become the first ever retired at Cal. The feeling was that his school-record 1,655 points didn't have as much to do with the honor as with the way he has represented himself, as a pro athlete and a humanitarian, since leaving. That, in some ways, contributed to his reputation for being soft. He just seems like too nice a guy, which shouldn't be a crime. At times, it seemed that basketball was secondary among his interests. And it might well have been.

"But I can't ever lose sight of the fact that everything I want to accomplish in life, the opportunity to do the things I want to do, are all made possible because of basketball," he said.

After the ceremony, KJ made the first basket nine seconds into the game.

The Suns had 29 turnovers against a banged-up Warriors team that was playing without Tim Hardaway and Chris Mullin most of the way, leading Westphal to quip, "We were lucky we didn't have people in the stands hurt by some of the passes we threw."

The Suns also went to the free-throw line 51 times, which would be an early-season trend.

"If we go to the line 50 times every game, you can write us down for the championship," Westphal said.

The Suns got by, 135-129, still unblemished in the Barkley era. Barkley, though, had some fun with the KJ hoopla.

KJ commemorative T-shirts were being hawked in the stands by a young woman. During pregame warmups, Barkley ran up to a vendor, grabbed a handful of shirts from her, and began tossing them to the sellout crowd in the stands. Barkley hugged the young woman, and then pointed to Westphal.

The Suns coach reached into his pocket and withdrew $100. "I thought she'd go away happy, but she made me reach back for another $20," Westphal said. "and I didn't even get a shirt." For several weeks, Westphal was kidded about whether Barkley had repaid him.

"I haven't heard a word from Charles yet, but he's an honorable man and I know he'll do the right thing," Westphal said. "I'm not going to say anything to him. I might ask him to repay me in other ways."

By the end of the season, Westphal would consider the debt squared. But that was a long way off.

Barkley had proven adept at drawing, and breaking, double-teams. KJ always had the ability to explode to the basket. Majerle and Ainge were outside threats.

If the Suns had a center who could catch, he'd get a lot of dunks.

"Because if they don't double-team me," Barkley said, "I'll score a hundred points."

All West had to do was guard the basket, be a help if somebody got beat out front, clean the boards, and trigger the break. Then, simply be enough of a threat inside to give a defense pause. West was ready for the challenge.

When teamed with Barkley, the Suns finally had the strength and nastiness they thought they were getting when they traded for Xavier McDaniel two years earlier.

Who better to test them than the Pistons? True, they had degenerated into a shadow of their championship teams. But Laimbeer still was on the roster, and the sight of Laimbeer to Barkley is like waving a red cape in front of a bull.

Olden Polynice, a well-traveled, sharp-elbowed, nasty-tempered center, also was on the squad when Detroit visited America West Arena for the third preseason game. It didn't take long for pushing, shoving, and trash-talking to become the order of the day.

Shortly before halftime, Polynice grabbed Chambers around the neck and bulldogged him to the floor. Chambers got up and punched Polynice. Both benches emptied, but there were no other altercations. Laimbeer was headed for the melee until he saw Barkley running to the scene. Laimbeer backed away. Barkley once received a $20,000 fine for flooring Laimbeer with a punch in the face.

"I respect the hell out of Bill Laimbeer, he's a great player," Barkley said. "I also enjoyed hitting him in the face."

This time, Chambers was ejected. Polynice later was ejected after mouthing off to official Ed T. Rush — who would see an even bigger battle at America West Arena before the season was over.

"I don't see any indication of anybody on this team backing down since I've been here," Ainge said. "I think the 'soft' label is false. I don't think it will be a label here now."

KJ, supposedly the softest of the soft, knew physical play would be necessary for the Suns to go beyond where he'd taken them.

"I said at training camp that the addition of Charles would make a lot of other guys play more physical," KJ said. "Now it's coming out on the court."

Still, Westphal was incensed by the rough play.

"There's no place for that in basketball," Westphal said. "They're just trying to hurt someone. We did what you're supposed to do when somebody tries to pull that crap: We kicked their butts by 40 points." Final score: Suns 147, Pistons 105.

Each season, the Suns try to schedule a killer trip worse than anything they face during the regular season. They simulated an extended Eastern trip in this preseason with visits to Milwaukee, Miami, Detroit, and Boston. On this one, they were taking a hard look at the forwards.

If Rambis was to play at all, he had to be in the starting lineup. Westphal made it clear to him: Win the job, or you probably won't play. Like West, Rambis was motivated to reverse a frustrating season in which Fitzsimmons relegated him to the end of the bench.

Rambis was one of the fans' favorites from the day he arrived in December 1989. People appreciate his willingness to do the dirty work: box out, set screens, rebound, defend. When he stepped into the spot vacated by Armon Gilliam, Rambis drew on his championship years with the Lakers to lead the Suns. He called team meetings. He counseled younger players. The Suns respected Rambis. They knew that he knew what he was talking about.

Late in 1992, Fitzsimmons finally began using Rambis in spot duty, claiming that it always had been his "master plan" to do so. Fitzsimmons said he feared that playing Rambis regularly during the season would cause him to break down. It was true that Rambis, 34, was aging and he does have a long history of leg injuries. Nobody was buying Fitzsimmons' "master plan" story, though. Least of all Rambis.

"At least, Paul was honest with me and told me that if I could win the job, it would be mine, and if I didn't, well . . . . ," Rambis said.

An example of the Rambis touch came during the fourth preseason game against the Milwaukee Bucks in Madison, Wisconsin. This was an example of why preseason trips are killers. It's not easy to get here. At least NBA cities are fairly accessible by air.

Nevertheless, the Suns came, saw, and conquered the Bucks as Rambis yanked nine rebounds in 13 minutes.

"He made only one basket, but each quarter that he started, the lead grew, and that's the measure of Kurt," Westphal said.

Rambis had played only 380 minutes in 28 appearances in that frustrating 1991-92 season.

"It's just been fun playing again," Rambis said after that 116-102 win. "I don't have any problems — not physically, anyway. I'm not a broken-down old horse."

Like West and Chambers, Rambis had worked hard during the summer.

"It wasn't a whole lot of fun last year," he said. "It's tough to just sit there. Imagine going to work and sitting there doing nothing. Then see how long your day is."

With the season opener two weeks away, it appeared Rambis was successfully reclaiming a starting position. Barkley wasn't having much problem at small forward. He'd scored 99 points in 99 minutes in his first four outings.

Ceballos, at that point, was Barkley's backup. "I have to fill a small uniform when I come in the game," Ceballos joked. Westphal was beginning to wonder if it was a good fit, though.

Ceballos was so active. With his lively body, he is quick, explosive. He couldn't guard anybody, though. Not that Barkley did, either.

When Ceballos came into the league, he was known as the "Point-a-Minute Man." It was never clear if that was in reference to his offense or his defense.

Either way, he once scored 32 points in 20 minutes against Denver the night the Suns ripped the Nuggets for an NBA-record 107 points in the first half and tied the league record for a nonovertime game with 173. Ceballos had established that he was the kind of player who could come off the bench and change the tempo of a game. He has an uncanny knack of getting the ball to fall,  no matter how wildly he contorts or gyrates going to the basket. And he is an excellent garbage man. He does a lot of scoring with lightning-quick put-backs.

He also established that he had some growing up to do. Ceballos was so cool, he had taken the nickname "Ice." Fitzsimmons brought him along slowly through his first two seasons. If you're going to play small forward in this league, you have to be more than a dunk master. You have to have an outside shot, and Ceballos really didn't have one.

"It got to the point where the coaches reconstructed my shot," Ceballos said. "But I didn't have the confidence to shoot it all the time."

His work through the first four preseason games indicated to Westphal that Ceballos now was ready for an expanded role. After all, how do you ignore averages of 19 points and 5.5 rebounds when coming off the bench behind Barkley? And Ceballos had elevated his shooting percentage nearly 20 points, to 65 percent. Ceballos was really making a case for himself.

"I'm not worried about my shots anymore. I take them, they feel good, and they're going in," he said.

That opens up the best part of Ceballos' game. When he gets a defender to take his outside shot seriously enough to come out on him, Ceballos then can use that explosive slashing ability of his and blow past him for a dunk. As for his defense, Ceballos was so physically weak, that when he was in good position to defend, he was often outmuscled.

"Now I can stop some of them. I can at least put a forearm on them and get results."

Just as Westphal's head began spinning about whether Ceballos belonged in the lineup beside Barkley instead of behind him, Westphal's mother-in-law passed away. Westphal left Hollins and Robertson to handle the final three games on the long trip.

Kevin Loughery, coach of the Heat, made a lineup change that in a backhanded way hurt Rambis' future with the Suns. Loughery moved Willie Burton into the small forward spot against Barkley, and Burton responded with 23 points and nine rebounds compared with Barkley's 18 points and nine rebounds.

"He's good," Barkley said of Burton, "but not as good as I made him look. I've been saying that we needed to defend and rebound, but I didn't expect it to be me."

The Heat hammered the Suns on the boards and won, 124-120.

It was the first loss of the Barkley era, and it was revealing— maybe Barkley would be more effective at power forward. The coaches later said they suspected as much, but were simply giving Rambis his shot.

For the time being, Hollins and Robertson didn't have to worry about the decision. They had their hands full with the next assignment: a rematch with the pugnacious Pistons at the Palace of Auburn Hills without KJ, who was resting a sore back.

As it turned out, everyone was on good behavior, and Barkley produced the game-winning free throws in the closing seven seconds after Polynice fouled him on a post-up.

The 96-95 decision was the kind in which the Suns rarely had prevailed. This was the kind of game Colangelo envisioned Barkley influencing.

During the previous four seasons, if the Suns didn't reach the 100-point mark, they didn't win. And if a game was on the line and required execution of a half-court play, the Suns were at a loss because they didn't really have plays. How many playoff games did they lose to Portland because they couldn't make a basket in the final 30 seconds? Well, there were three in 1990, and three more in 1992.

It was only an exhibition, but it was encouraging.

"It's easy to execute when you have Charles," said Knight, who got the call while KJ rested. "We got so tired of seeing other teams do it to us."

Barkley had to bail the Suns out of a 10-point fourth-quarter deficit caused by some normally reliable shooters who couldn't hit the ocean. Chambers went zero for nine, Ceballos, one for eight.

Two nights later, when the Suns had a rematch with the Celtics in the Hartford Civic Center, Barkley missed a late shot to tie it, and the Suns lost, 103-101.

Barkley pump-faked Kevin McHale, whom he rates as the best player he's ever faced, and got the shot away, but it bounced off the rim.

"If it goes in, great," Barkley said. "If it doesn't ... preseason is just a way to steal money from the fans."

Hollins treated it as a learning experience for Miller, though. He started the chubby rookie against Parish.

"When they played us in Phoenix, Oliver was taunting Parish a little when we had the game won," Hollins said. "I knew Parish would remember that."

Miller played 25 minutes, with four points and nine rebounds to show for it. Parish countered with 17 points — including 13 tries from the foul line — and 10 rebounds. "I learned not a few, but a lot of lessons from the 'Chief,' " Miller said.

With one preseason game remaining, at Utah, the coaches now had seen all the combinations. It was just a matter of making decisions.

If Loughery's move in Miami had started the wheels in motion, the Utah Jazz shifted them into a higher gear. The Suns were absolutely mauled in Salt Lake City, finishing with three losses in their final four exhibitions following that 4-0 start.

The Jazz were the biggest and strongest of the Suns' preseason foes, and they exposed their weaknesses as no other team had. The Suns were down by 26 points in the fourth quarter before losing, 126-112.

"We've got to get back our training-camp intensity," said Westphal, who rejoined the team. "We were tough and focused coming out of Flagstaff."

There was more to their struggle than coming off that grueling four-game Eastern trip, and more to it than stumbling while Westphal was away.

It was obvious that Barkley's best position would be power forward — good news to Ceballos, who would move into the lineup, but terrible news to Rambis, whose days now were numbered.

"I'm sure Paul didn't say he's leaning toward me and then go etch it in stone," Rambis said. "I've done all I can as a player. I've stayed in shape, played well, stuff like that. I've left it up to him."

The Suns and their coaches took the Utah beating seriously because by most accounts, anyone wanting to win the West had to come through Portland and Salt Lake City to do it.

The Suns still were an unproven entity. And this game illustrated that they had plenty of room for improvement. They had been crowing about their bench, but the reserves allowed the Jazz to score 40 in the second quarter. But then, the Suns' starters gave up 34 more in the third.

"I would prefer not to go into the season with this type of beating," Barkley said.

Ultimately, these are the numbers that caused Westphal to make some hard decisions: the Suns shot a preseason-low 44 percent, they were outrebounded, 49-41.

"Cedric was just eating Charles up in training camp," Westphal said. "It's not that Charles is not quick enough to play the small forward, it's that he has to use so much energy chasing them around and it takes him away from the basket. He would either relax and not chase the guy and get killed, or he would use so much energy and not be the inside force we want him to be. He'd be out on the perimeter.

"I think that there's no better inside player in the game than Charles, so why do we want him outside, using up a lot of energy that he doesn't want to use up? Really, in training camp we decided he had to play power forward. I still wanted to take a look at him at small forward in exhibition. But we concluded that we got this guy to be a power player, let's put him in a power position."

The players were mulling their recent downturn before any personnel decisions were announced. KJ said the Suns had it "too easy, too fast."

"I think we took a look around the locker room and said, 'Wow, this is a great team.' We took it for granted."

As Barkley put it, "This is what separates the men from the boys. We've got all the talent in the world, but it doesn't mean nothing. We've got to get it together, or it's going to be a long year. If we don't start now, you can't expect us to suddenly start playing good defense in the playoffs."

Westphal got them started by putting them through a 2 ½ hour practice the following day. That was on Tuesday. Their 12-man active roster for Saturday's opener had to be declared by Thursday.

The cut-down moves seemed obvious: replace Mustaf, who had missed the end of preseason with a shin bruise; waive Frank Johnson and Alex Stivrins. Some last-minute surprises prevented the Suns from doing the obvious, though.

KJ had complained of pain in the area of his groin since having playfully lifted the hefty Miller during warm-ups in an exhibition game. It was feared that he had suffered a hernia. Surgery to repair it could cost him two months.

To get to the 12-man limit, the Suns placed KJ and Mustaf on the injured list, recalled Frank Johnson, who had been waived, and then waived Ed Nealy.

Stivrins, a small forward, so impressed the coaching staff that he was given a roster spot on opening night. He had played in France, Spain, and Italy for six years. He assumed he'd be returning to Italy. He lived in Phoenix during the summer in the condo a friend had persuaded him to buy as an investment. He rents it to winter visitors while he's off touring the world. Stivrins was looking for summertime pickup games to stay in shape. A friend put him in touch with the Suns, who said, "Come on down." Stivrins was at informal workouts from the first day. "And every day, he showed he belonged," Westphal said. He so impressed Westphal and associates that they invited him to Flagstaff. Stivrins knew his chances of making the roster were slim. He was actually awaiting word on his situation in Europe from his agent, who was negotiating with a team. "The funny thing is if the negotiations hadn't dragged on, I would have been over there in August," Stivrins said.

Stivrins knew he was there only as long as it took Mustaf or KJ to heal, or for the NBA to reinstate Dumas.

The Suns received results of KJ's medical examination about an hour before the roster deadline: strained groin, not a hernia. "Two weeks is a lot better than two months," Westphal said. "But it's still a tough way for us to start the season."

With expectations so high for Barkley's debut, the Suns now would be directed by Knight and Frank Johnson. Knight rallied the Suns from 10 points down in that preseason win at Detroit, but he is no KJ.

Suns fans wondered if KJ's injury was more serious than the Suns were letting on, something that really could cause a long-term absence? Where would this team, with all its expectations, be when KJ was healthy enough to return? Out of contention, or still within striking distance? There were scary questions for the Suns. Suns medical personnel reassured Westphal that if KJ went on the injured list for two weeks, the rest would heal the strain and reduce the possibility of its becoming a hernia.

The other blow to Suns fans was Nealy. A popular player who'd had two stints with the Suns, Nealy never was properly used in the eyes of many. He came to the Suns during Fitzsimmons' first season, 1988-89, and played in 30 games off the bench. He was traded to Chicago — where he'd been the season before — for "future considerations." In other words, the Suns gave him away. They never received any of those "future considerations."

The Bulls knew how to use him — at crunch time to set screens that freed Michael Jordan, and as a rebounder. He proved his worth in the 1990 Eastern Conference finals. Jordan said there were few players he'd rather have on the floor with him at crunch time, because Nealy is a smart player who knows his role. Nealy, ironically, was especially effective against Barkley and the Philadelphia 76ers in the Eastern Conference semifinals. The Bulls had made noises about making him an assistant coach when his playing days were over. There was a minor disagreement about when that might be, though.

After the 1990 playoffs, the Bulls were torn between re-signing Nealy, an unrestricted free agent, or picking up Cliff Levingston. The Suns beat them to the punch, quickly offering Nealy a multiyear contract for more than the Bulls were prepared to pay.

So in July 1990, Nealy was back. Fitzsimmons was crowing about how, this time, Nealy would be used in a meaningful way. The Suns needed his size, toughness, savvy. All true. The overlooked part of Nealy's game was his shooting. He is a terror from three-point range, something you don't often see in a man who is 6-foot-7, 240 pounds.

Colangelo was a bit more tempered in his enthusiasm. He said Nealy was being signed primarily as an "insurance policy," although he did mention he enjoyed the fact that while Chicago essentially got Nealy from him for nothing a year earlier, the Suns were getting him back from them for nothing, since he was a free agent.

After averaging a little over 10 minutes in 55 appearances in 1990-91, and only 9.7 minutes in 52 games the following season, it was obvious that Nealy had no more of a role this time than during his first stint.

"He belongs in the NBA," Westphal said. "You could put Ed in a playoff game and he'd know what to do, and he'd respond. A lot of guys, you can't say that about. We just had too many guys."

It was Thursday, November 5. Two days before the opener. Westphal still wasn't saying publicly who he would have in his opening-night lineup for the debut in the "Purple Palace," the moniker given the new building by a staffer of *The Arizona Republic*.

Further complicating last-minute preparation was an open-house practice, the last hard workout the Suns would have before tapering off Friday. It was the first in a series of public viewings. The Suns charged one can of food, to be donated to a food bank, or $1 admission. Colangelo liked the idea of helping worthy ventures, and of giving people who couldn't afford, or couldn't obtain, tickets to games a chance to see the Suns up close. Most of the lower level of purple seats was filled — 9,140 by the Suns' count.

Westphal, not crazy about the timing of the viewing, got a little testy when chants of "We Want Barkley, We Want Barkley" rang up. The new hero had a bruised thigh, and Westphal was resting him, hoping he'd be ready for the opener against the Los Angeles Clippers. Westphal, irked, had the public-address announcer remind the crowd that this was a real practice, and to cut out the chants.

"I guess if we play games with people in the arena, we ought to be able to practice with them in there, too," he said. But later, he took the Suns down to their practice gym away from the crowd to go over the scouting report.

# Chapter Eleven

# FALSE START

The Valley of the Sun had been building for this all summer.

Colangelo had a gala planned for the opening of the Purple Palace. Banners commemorating the four Suns whose jerseys have been retired — Connie Hawkins, Dick Van Arsdale, Alvan Adams, and Westphal, were hoisted in a ceremony before tip-off.

The fans knew Barkley had a history of coming up big on opening night, and it was a good thing. The Suns were beaten up from the intense preseason. West had a hamstring strain. Rambis suffered a hyper-extended knee in a light workout the day before the opener. Barkley was sore. And, of course, KJ was out.

"This will be a good little test for us," Barkley said, adding that it was difficult for him to start and stop.

By now, it was apparent that Barkley would be the power forward and Ceballos would start at small forward. "I have to play the '4' because we can't rebound," Barkley said. Barkley was no stranger to the power forward spot. That's primarily where he played on the Dream Team.

The Suns wouldn't necessarily have to alter their style with Knight at the point. Their primary objective still would be to get the ball to Barkley in the low post. But Knight isn't the penetrator that KJ is. One advantage to starting, Knight said, is the coaches are more inclined to stay with him through mistakes.

"You know they'll work with you until it becomes right," he said. "They're not going to just yank you."

How prophetic those words were.

From the moment the ball went up, Barkley was relentless. He simply wasn't going to let the Suns lose on such a special night. Of course, it turned out he wouldn't let the Suns lose on a lot of nights.

This one wasn't going well, however. The Clippers were shooting over 50 percent. The Suns, with all their great offensive weapons, couldn't find those new baskets and finished at 38 percent. Eighty-one games later, they still hadn't shot worse.

The only thing that saved them was Barkley's rebounding — 21 in all. He also scored 37 points and came within two assists of having a triple-double in his debut.

But poor Knight. He found defenders slacking off him to double-team Barkley. Knight's two-for-17 opening-night shooting gave them no reason to do anything else.

"Negele could have looked for a rock to crawl under but he kept defending and making big plays, and getting the ball to the right people at the end," Westphal said.

Ironically, Knight said during preseason that he'd rather play and shoot 0-for-75 than sit as he did during most of the previous season. "I was close," Knight said. "I had shots that high school guys knock down." Knight was booed by the sellout crowd as his bricks continued to bounce off the rim, which did nothing to enhance his confidence. "I did hear one fan yell at me, 'Let somebody else shoot,'" Knight said. He did have seven assists, including dish-offs to Ainge and Majerle for a pair of three-pointers in the closing moments. His only two turnovers were early.

But the real key was defense, something for which the Suns weren't noted. On six of seven Clippers possessions in the fourth quarter, the Suns got stops. They made the most of it, going from five points down to eight up in a 111-105 win.

"It would have been a bummer to lose the first one," a relieved Colangelo said.

There was relief all around. The Clippers had been a menace to the Suns all through the Fitzsimmons years. In fact, they had won the series, 3-2, in Fitzsimmons' final season. With tall, athletic young players, the Clippers are among the teams that pose matchup nightmares for the Suns.

The difference was that the Suns now had a low-post threat, and he made all the difference.

Late in the game, Barkley demanded so much attention that Ainge and Majerle were free on the perimeter. They had been cool-shooting most of the way, but they heated up at the appropriate moment for the Suns. Ainge scored 15 of his 20 points in the fourth quarter, Majerle scored eight of his 18 in the final 2:25.

"We have a lot of great shooters who had bad nights," Majerle said, "but Charles put us on his back and carried us. Our best play was to keep putting up bricks and let Charles go get them."

The first two points ever scored in a regulation game at the Purple Palace were by Barkley — sorry KJ — off an offensive rebound.

They came 39 seconds into the game, and began a 51-33 domination of the Clippers on the boards.

"I've been waiting for this since Barcelona and the Dream Team," Barkley said. "I was a little nervous. This was a very emotional game." It was the first real indication of the Suns' new toughness. How many teams could lose a Kevin Johnson and keep on rolling?

"If we compete like we did the last five minutes," Barkley said, "we'll be something special. There is something special brewing here, but we're not there yet." No, but only 81 to go.

And next up would be a monumental early-season challenge: visits to Portland on November 10 and Utah two days later.

The Trail Blazers had been in two of the previous three NBA Finals, losing both. They had eliminated the Suns each time — in the 1990 Western Conference Finals and in the 1992 semifinals that led to Hollins' infamous quote. Utah had been a thorn to the Suns as well. The Jazz sent them home in the first round in 1991 when KJ and Majerle were injured and missed most of the series.

"When you get down to it," Barkley said, "you have to go through Portland and Salt Lake City to win the West. They're probably the two best teams out there."

But the comeback against the Clippers proved that with Barkley, the Suns could be a threat, too, even without KJ — and that's something they soon would get used to.

"It's great to have defense and offensive rebounding," Westphal said.

The only problem with having a dominating player of Barkley's ability is that you tend to lean on him too hard. Would the Suns begin to simply throw the ball to him and then stand and watch? Did they know how to play off him effectively? The visit to Portland indicated they weren't quite sure.

It was Ainge's first game against his old team. His leaving got nasty. The Blazers alleged tampering, but they never lodged a formal complaint against the Suns. "That's because there was no tampering," Colangelo said. Nevertheless, it had been embarrassing for Portland and its front-office staff to see a player of Ainge's stature walk. But Ainge had tired of hearing promises that never were kept. When he was traded from Boston to Sacramento in 1989, the Kings said they'd rework his contract. They never did. When Portland acquired him, a similar promise was made. Beginning in training camp, 1991, as Ainge went into the final season on his contract, he assumed the Blazers would be talking to him. They never did.

The Blazers thought they could string him out. They thought they had a sure thing. They badly underestimated Ainge. They also underestimated his remaining value; Ainge hadn't played all that much during their run to the 1992 Finals. With the Suns, he was undeniably their sixth man, a central figure in their offense, and a welcome addition. Not only could he fill the outside shooting void left by

Hornacek, he could impart the experience of playing in the Finals with two teams to his new teammates, who expected to get there themselves. And he would play in late-game situations with the Suns.

Ainge grew up in Eugene, about 120 miles down Interstate 5 from Portland. He has a lot of family and friends in the Pacific Northwest, a lot of history.

"Going back to Boston for the first time after being there eight years was emotional," Ainge said. "I don't think anything can match that. This isn't anywhere near that. "I knew for a year that I might be leaving. I know there were a lot of letters to the editor in Portland from people who said they were supportive Danny Ainge fans, and some letters to the editor saying they were disappointed in Danny Ainge."

So he wasn't sure what to expect from the sellout crowd at Portland Memorial Coliseum. They gave him a standing ovation. That was before he made only one of 10 shots. "No question, I forced some," Ainge said.

Knight shot better than he did in the opener, but his 20 points weren't enough to carry the game, which the Suns lost, 100-89.

"Portland is a great transition and rebounding team," Ainge said. "A big advantage they used to have on the Suns was on the glass, but now Charles alleviates that. One guy who has given them lots of trouble is KJ. I'm sure they were happy he was out. They've had the same five guys starting for five seasons now. They know what they want to do and how to get it done."

That is something the Suns still hadn't figured out. When the ball went inside to Barkley, the offense broke down.

"We're getting into the offense late, then the shot-clock runs down and we have to take one-on-one shots that we don't want," Ainge said. "Sometimes, we're trying to make too many things happen. Our execution is not good. What's happening is when we get the ball down low to Charles, when he's double-teamed and finally throws it back out, we only have a few seconds left to create a shot."

Barkley didn't get an offensive rebound in Portland, although he had 14 defensive rebounds to go with 21 points and seven assists.

"Kevin wasn't here missing shots and throwing bad passes," Barkley said. "If we start using Kevin as our alibi, we might as well forfeit." All true, but there is no question that KJ knows how to create a shot on short notice.

Of more interest to the Suns than what they didn't have was what the Blazers *did* have. They, too, had done some off-season fine-tuning, signing Rod Strickland after Ainge left for Phoenix, and Mario Elie, a gritty bench player. Elie scored 13 of his 17 points in the final quarter to make sure the Suns didn't pull out another one late. The Blazers outscored the Suns, 33-20, in the fourth quarter.

Coming up were two of Barkley's Dream Team buddies, Karl Malone and John Stockton, in the Delta Center. Still fresh was the pounding the Suns received there in their final preseason game.

And fresher still was the way their offense went belly-up in Portland when they were in position to win the game. There was a team meeting before their practice in Salt Lake City in which they talked about how to play off Barkley so he could get the ball to them quicker out of double-teams.

"That's a problem," Westphal said. "We need everybody looking to score instead of just Charles. And Charles has to recognize the double-team and get rid of the ball earlier."

The Suns hadn't run much in their first two games, and running was the trademark of their four high-scoring years under Fitzsimmons. Part of their problem was attributed to Knight.

"We've been walking the ball up the floor, and that's not because that's what I wanted," Westphal said. "Seldom will I try to control the tempo. It's against my will. I love easy baskets. When you don't get easy baskets, you shoot a low percentage." And at Portland, the Suns made only 43 percent, barely lifting them to 40 percent through their first two games.

Westphal admitted he was "floundering" to find a substitution rotation that was effective, too. He had expected his bench to be one of the Suns' strengths. "You can't tell if we've deviated, because we haven't had a plan yet," he said.

All in all, it had been anything but a rousing dash out of the gate, and the Jazz weren't likely to change that. But they did.

This was the beginning of a terrible skid for Utah. The Dream Teamers were worn out. The Jazz really never were in the hunt for the Midwest Division title after January. First, San Antonio, under new coach John Lucas, took off. Then Houston, with Hakeem Olajuwon's play rejuvenated under new coach Rudy Tomjanovich, became the hottest team in the NBA after the All-Star break. Jazz coach Jerry Sloan could see it coming, and began telling friends privately that he expected to be fired.

They had been nearly impenetrable at the Delta Center when it opened in 1991, losing only four home games, fewest in the NBA.

But this early game started a new trend — for both teams.

Ceballos slashed, cut, and dunked his way to 24 points, and grabbed 12 rebounds. Barkley added 25 points and 14 rebounds. More important, he found open shooters spotted up before the shot clock wound inside four seconds. And Westphal, in a brilliant move, assigned Mark West to cover Malone. West always has been able to throw Malone off his game.

"Needless to say, it was a big win," Westphal said after the Suns pounded the Jazz, 102-91. "You can't say that it was expected."

The Suns, who hadn't won a regular-season game in Salt Lake City in 2 1/2 years, made a conscious effort to get into their running game.

"If we go to Charles and everybody just stands and watches, we'll look just like Philly when he was there," Westphal said. "But when we get everybody involved, it's a lot easier for Charles to do his thing."

The Jazz aren't used to playing to many empty green seats, but the sellout crowd left early.

Although Malone scored 32 points and grabbed nine rebounds, he shot only 11 free throws — a low figure for him. He is the annual league leader in attempts. Most of his points this night came late in the game, after the issue was decided.

"You just try to make him earn everything," said West, who passed his first major test with his redeveloped body. "The biggest thing is don't let him get to the free-throw line, especially after one of his power dunks."

Ainge said the meeting the previous day had been beneficial. "Before, I think we were standing because we didn't want to take our defensive man into Charles' territory," Ainge said. "We wanted to help him, but not get too close so that our man could double him. Tonight, I think we figured out how to keep moving and create confusion for the defense so that they didn't know where to double him from."

As for Ceballos, "Ice" wasn't talking to the press. He said he was miffed because none of the reporters who cover the team had bothered to feature him in a preseason story. When it was brought to his attention that he'd been given a big spread in *The Arizona Republic*, Ceballos then said he didn't think he should give interviews because he hadn't earned the attention yet. Yet he did go on the radio with Suns play-by-play man, Al McCoy, where Ceballos wasn't a bit bashful about accepting a free gift.

Ceballos obviously was a splendid raw talent whose maturity hadn't yet caught up with his physical skills. But he hadn't earned the "Point-a-Minute Man" nickname for nothing. He scored seven of the Suns' first nine points and had 14 in the opening quarter when they stunned the Jazz.

"We told Ced before the game that he hadn't shot a free throw and he had one defensive rebound in our first two games," Westphal said.

"If he's not scoring," Barkley said, "he can't play bad in the rest of his game. Some nights he's not going to score those quick points. Those are the nights he's got to do other things. He's got to play consistent."

That would be the early-season lament of the Suns: a lack of consistent play from their rotation of small forwards. With Dumas still not on the scene, the responsibility belonged to Ceballos.

Back above .500, the Suns moved on to Minnesota to complete the early-season three-game trip on November 14. The Timberwolves never had beaten the Suns, and there probably wasn't a person in the locker room who expected that to change. They had drafted Christian Laettner, who led Duke to two national championships and was the token college kid on the Dream Team. But nobody really expected them to be a threat to the Suns — or to anyone else. Trading for Chuck Person and Micheal Williams had given them some help. Person, despite his reputation as a trash-talking jerk, is a big-time scorer, something the Wolves hadn't had in their first three seasons. Williams is a competent point guard who began his career with the Suns. They kept Knight instead.

The Suns rode into the Twin Cities on their unexpected early defensive success. Here was a team full of potential big-time scorers shutting down the likes of the Clippers, Trail Blazers, and Jazz, all playoff teams. Through three games, the Suns were allowing just under 99 points and 44 percent shooting a game. Strange as it sounded, Westphal said having Ceballos in the lineup made them better defensively. Ceballos, while not regarded as the Rock of Gibraltar, is quick. By playing Ceballos at the "three" spot, Barkley then takes on the opponents' power forward. When it's working, it usually spells extended bench time for Chambers, unless Westphal can find a few minutes for him at center. Or unless there is a good matchup for Chambers at forward, as there was against Laettner.

After playing only six minutes against the Jazz, Chambers played 35 minutes against the Timberwolves and made the most of them with 28 points, nine rebounds, and five assists. That came in awfully handy as the Suns overcame a 17-point deficit in the first half and moved to 3-1 on the season with the 108-101 win.

"Charles certainly didn't carry us this time," Westphal said afterward. Barkley didn't disagree, saying he had one good play in 44 minutes, that being a block on Laettner, who was going for what appeared to be an open layup in the final minute before Barkley sprang after him, and ended the Wolves' upset hopes.

Barkley, assigned to Person, limited his former Auburn buddy to three-for-16 shooting. But Barkley made only eight of 24 himself, scoring 20 points.

"I'm just sorry I was terrible," Barkley said. His apology was accepted, but only because Chambers rose to the occasion.

Chambers said he had his shooting confidence, because he and Rambis had scrimmaged against each other the day before, and the shots were dropping against Rambis, a player Chambers respects as a good defender.

The Suns fought through Barkley's first off-night to take an important step in their development.

"Defense has turned out to be a real strength for us, especially in the fourth quarter," Westphal said. "I hope that will be our identity, but I think we're still searching to find our true identity right now."

Time would show that this was the embryo of their true identity, and it was formed without KJ and Dumas. It also was formed with Majerle struggling with his shot. There was no question that he was favoring the left knee on which he had arthroscopic surgery in August. Majerle never has been among the league's field-goal percentage leaders, but the 29 percent he'd thrown up through four games indicated his struggle.

"It's like Ainge says: If you keep throwing enough mud up there, something has to stick," Majerle said.

With undefeated Seattle coming to the Purple Palace on Nov. 16, it would take quite a bit of mud-throwing to emerge victorious.

Majerle finally got some to stick. He made seven of 13 shots and scored 13 of his 22 points in the Suns' crushing 40-point first quarter. He made four of his first five shots, two of those being three-pointers. The biggest difference for Majerle was that he began taking the ball to the basket. He viewed his role as replacing Hornacek as the Suns' primary outside shooter. He wasn't entirely incorrect. He has improved his long shooting considerably through the years, particularly his three-point accuracy. But many observers believe he did it at the expense of his trademark thunderous drives.

This was an important test for the Suns, not only because the SuperSonics figured to be one of their primary challengers in the Western Conference, but because it marked success against a taller team. And nearly every team the Suns would face would be taller. Derrick McKey and Shawn Kemp are the kind of mobile, young skyscrapers who can hurt the Suns.

"This was probably the best team we've played so far," Barkley said. "Seattle, Utah, and Portland are all just a little bit better than us right now. They're bigger and stronger than we are, and they've been together longer. "So it's going to take a good effort to beat them."

That's what the Suns gave. Kemp and McKey each got into early foul difficulty, thanks to Majerle's assault on the basket in the 117-108 win.

Also on that November 16 evening, team physician Richard Emerson cleared KJ to return to practice. With the two-time defending champion Chicago Bulls coming in on Sunday, it meant that KJ had enough time to perhaps be activated for that early-season showdown.

Mustaf also was cleared to resume practicing. Westphal was anxious to get Mustaf back because he wanted to determine whether the lanky youngster had any future at small forward. Mustaf has good mobility, a decent shot, good basketball skills and instincts. He thought there was a chance Mustaf could slide into the spot next to Barkley, and at 6-foot-10, Mustaf had height the 6-6 Ceballos lacked.

In the meantime, the Suns had to find a way to get excited about a visit by the Sacramento Kings. Nobody gets fired up to play the Kings.

Everybody expects a guaranteed win. The Kings, despite having all those high picks and negotiating a trade for All-Star guard Mitch Richmond, still haven't put it together. New ownership and a dynamic new coach, Garry St. Jean, a former assistant to Don Nelson at Golden State, gave the Kings hope.

But if the Suns weren't worked up to play the Kings, they were worked up knowing that some difficult roster decisions were upcoming. Kurt Rambis and Tim Kempton sensed it. They suspected that they were battling for the right to stay with the Suns when Mustaf was ready to come off the injured list. In practice, Rambis and Kempton, who'd been best buddies in training camp, got into a fight.

Miller was showing his first signs of complacency. He was assigned additional conditioning work after practice. "We want him to know we love him," Westphal said. "But he's got to keep working. I don't want him to be satisfied." So putting the hefty rookie on the injured list also was an option.

The Kings rolled into town, and the game was just what everyone expected. The Suns' frontline players, some of whom were fighting for their jobs, outscored the Kings, 60-14, inside. Ceballos went for 30 points. Miller scored 19, Stivrins 12 in the 127-111 blowout. Miller also showed why Westphal loves him: five assists. "That's the strongest part of my game, passing," Miller said. The subs picked a good night to be hot. Barkley made only three of 13 shots.

"The good thing," KJ said, "is we're 5-1 and we're not even playing well." KJ wanted to be activated for a game against the Clippers three nights later in Los Angeles — the night before the Bulls were to visit the Purple Palace.

"I can't break out against the Bulls," he said.

On Friday, November 20, KJ was activated, but it was the low point of the year, Westphal said. That's because to make room for him, the Suns waived Rambis, a shocking move. The Suns had decided, at least for the time being, to ride with Stivrins and backup point guard Frank Johnson. They were going small. They would eat the final season on the $1.1 million contract of Rambis, 34, even though he made considerably more than Kempton ($550,000) or Stivrins ($140,000, league minimum).

"That's a guy I have all the respect for," Westphal said of Rambis after the season. "I wish that he could have been a part of this."

Then, Westphal revealed that the Suns had tried to get Rambis back late in the season. He signed a one-year contract with the Kings, but he wasn't playing much.

"We tried to get Sacramento to waive him and pick him up to have him on the team for the playoff run, but they wouldn't do it," Westphal said. "In my mind, Kurt is a big part of what's gone on here, too, and I wish he could have been a part of it in the playoffs. Having to cut him was definitely the worst moment of the year."

At the time, Westphal said that Rambis' fate hinged on where Barkley played. "If I played Charles at 'three,' we needed Kurt. If I played Charles at 'four,' Kurt became a victim of the numbers game," Westphal said. "It's a sad day. I told the team that Kurt is a warrior. I respect him as a person and as a player. The guy got every bit out of his ability."

Colangelo demonstrated that he has a healthy appetite for a championship. The previous season, he ate nearly $2 million in guaranteed contracts after waiving Joe Barry Carroll and Trent Tucker. The difference was that both of them seemed to be in it for the money. This season, Colangelo was eating nearly $2 million more in guaranteed salaries of Rambis and Nealy, both dedicated hard-working role players. It didn't take Rambis and Nealy long to find employment elsewhere in the league: Nealy went to Golden State and later back to Chicago. It was an emotional decision. Rambis had meant a lot to the rebirth of the franchise.

"He brought so much to the team, whether it was his understanding of the game, or being effective because he's so fundamentally sound, or being a good complementary player to guys who might have a little more talent but didn't know quite as much about the game," KJ said. "If he didn't play for five games, you could bring him in and know he'd get the job done."

Rambis, who never lost his humility or his bearings, managed a soft chuckle about his fate. "I guess I went down faster than the Roman Empire," Rambis said of his decline from starting power forward five days before the opener to the waiver wire only six games into the season. "It was a quick downfall from starter to garbage time."

But, Hollins said, the coaches felt all along that Barkley had to play power forward, no matter how hard Rambis worked or how well he played.

"But we were trying to give Kurt the first shot at starting, then give Tom," Hollins said. "It wasn't my suggestion, but Paul wanted to give the older players the opportunity. It was their job to lose. Paul came from a program in Boston where tradition meant something and younger players had to earn everything.

"Initially, that was his thinking. We're going to play our veterans until somebody else takes them out. Eventually, the cream rose to the top. That was basically why Charles was initially a 'three.' It wasn't because we thought he was this superhuman guy. Maybe when he was 26 or 27 he could have played that spot. On occasion, he can play it now. The way Charles makes demands on his body, with his rebounding and scoring, at this point in his career, it would have just ruined him to try to play him at the 'three.'"

The good news out of all of it was that KJ was ready. He served notice with a sharp performance in practice. KJ made his debut in Los Angeles with 10 points and seven assists in 41 minutes — a big workload for his first time out. It was hard to get an assist the way the Suns were shooting. They tried a club-record 28 three-pointers, forced outside by the long arms of the Clippers. They made only seven.

Westphal was livid after the 111-107 loss that ended a four-game streak. Ainge made one of eight from three-point range, Barkley two of eight after missing his first 12 tries of the season, and Majerle four of 11.

"Ainge is hitting a good percentage and he's been around, so I'm not going to question his judgment," Westphal said. "One reason he's out there is so the other team has to guard him. Same with Dan. He's a good shooter. "But you've got to have enough good games to balance out the bad ones, and our overall shooting percentage this season is terrible. After a while, you've got to ask yourself if they really are good shots. You've got to take shots you can make."

For Westphal, that was quite a tirade. It wasn't lost on Majerle.

"It's tough to turn them down when you're that wide open, especially when you usually hit them," Majerle said. "I don't know if we need to take that many. We need to get more points inside."

Barkley did what he could to keep the Suns in the game with his 44 points and 17 rebounds. Even he questioned the judgment of his teammates. "I think we're playing hard, but it doesn't mean anything if you don't play smart and don't get the win."

The Suns seemed to welcome the chance the next day to put this one out of their minds, even if it meant going home to play the two-time champs.

But as Barkley would put it after Chicago's 128-111 coast, "If you're going to play like a puppy, you shouldn't be on the floor with the big dogs." The Suns gave up 43 points in the first quarter in their first loss in their new home, and 74 in the first half. "Everybody on this team needs to go home and take a long look at themselves in the mirror," Barkley said. This was their first bona fide skid. Westphal took it hard, blaming himself for not having his team ready to play. Maybe he'd tried too hard to be their buddy instead of their coach, he wondered.

Jackson, the Bulls coach, was surprised to see the Suns try to make it a running game, considering they had played a tough one on the road the night before. "I thought they were opening the gates by making it a running contest," Jackson said.

The Bulls simply didn't respect the Suns short frontline or their interior defense. They went right after them.

Figuring Michael Jordan was unstoppable, Westphal assigned Ceballos to cover him and put Majerle, the defensive stopper, on Scottie Pippen. Pippen made eight of nine shots and scored 18, complementing Jordan's 40.

"I didn't think we played hard, and it's really disappointing," Majerle said.

"We're just not in their league," Westphal said.

KJ observed that the Suns had "played soft, just like in the past. With Charles on this team now, we have to intimidate."

Barkley didn't disagree. "We've got all this talent, and we don't play hard because we don't have a fear of losing," he said. "Hey, we should have been mad about last night. We should have been so mad that we should have come out right away and established how this one was going to be played. "Look at the Bulls. They lost to the Lakers the other night. They came out determined to change that. We live in the desert. It's 90 degrees outside. We can play golf every day. We don't fear losing. We've got to get that. It's not about physical toughness. It's all mental toughness. It has to be life or death every night."

It never had been that way with the Suns, and Barkley was playing with the nucleus that wasn't overly distraught about its position in the pro basketball world. Maybe this place does it to you. Xavier McDaniel came to town with a nasty reputation, but he turned out to be a nice guy who was traded less than a year later.

Then there was Westphal, who made a rookie mistake by playing KJ 41 minutes against the Clippers.

"I was stupid to do that," Westphal said. "I was not very pleased with the way I coached. We looked tired for a lot of reasons, and we played like it. We're not ready to challenge them yet. Maybe by the end of the year we will be."

How prophetic that statement would become, but then Westphal would go on to make a number of whopping statements that became prophetic as the season rolled along, into the playoffs.

"We're going to go after each other in practice tomorrow," KJ said. "If it's too hard or too physical, then you shouldn't step onto the court."

At 5-3, the Suns already were soul-searching. And guess who was coming in next? The Portland Trail Blazers.

# Chapter Twelve

# AND THEY'RE OFF!

Portland was the league's only remaining undefeated team. The one that had put the Suns out of the playoffs two of the three previous years. The one that prompted the Suns to make the move for Barkley.

Statement games are overrated, but this one certainly seemed to have more significance than most, and it was coming at a time when the Suns were sputtering.

Westphal already was contemplating changing his lineup. Mustaf still hadn't been activated, but Westphal was itchy to slide him into Ceballos' small forward spot for a test drive.

"I want to see if this game got everybody's attention first before I make any changes," Westphal said. "We don't have a rotation yet. We're still trying to find guys who deserve to be in the lineup by the consistency of their play."

But, untrue to KJ's word, the next day's practice was tame. Docile. Uninspired. Considering their back-to-back losses, Westphal was steamed, so he took matters into his own hands — well, actually, into his own foot. He didn't literally kick butt, but he interrupted practice and screamed at his lethargic players, capping it off by kicking a basketball high off the wall of the Suns practice gym.

He had popped his cork. What a rare display. He knew it. The players, who could only imagine what Westphal was kicking figuratively, knew it.

He was morose when talking with reporters afterward. "Nobody knows this team yet," Westphal said. "I don't claim to. We're still growing. I just hope they're not too happy. I guess I'm surprised by their soft attitude. "I said when we were 5-1 I didn't think we were playing that great. KJ hasn't stepped on the floor and been KJ yet. It's going to take him a little time. He's also running a new team. It's not like he's stepping in and familiar with everybody. It's not an easy thing we're asking him to do. It's going to take him some time to be KJ. How long, I don't know, but I'll know it when I see it.

"It's not time to panic. If you make an honest assessment of this team, you have to understand everything. We're far from where we want to be, but there are reasons. I just want to see us make progress."

The Suns took the challenge in that November 25 meeting at America West Arena, coming out rough and tough and coming away with a 121-117 decision.

"Well," Blazers coach Rick Adelman said, "I didn't expect to go 82-0."

The end of Portland's 8-0 early-season run was the beginning of a number of setbacks that would culminate in a first-round playoff elimination by San Antonio.

Mustaf was activated, but he played only five minutes off the bench, grabbed one rebound, and missed all four of his shots. Stivrins' storybook run ended. He was waived to make room for Mustaf. "He was just a little overexcited," Westphal said of Mustaf's debut. "I plan to give him more time."

But Miller suffered bruised ribs and had to be taken to a hospital for X-rays during a rough sequence that illustrated the rededication by the Suns.

"We don't have soft players on this team," Ainge said. "When you're not 100 percent sure of how you're supposed to play, you are tentative in your execution. I think tonight is more characteristic of this team."

The Suns were heartened by their ability to take a tie game with 5:33 to go and turn it into something good with a crushing finish. They limited the Blazers to one field goal for nearly 5 1/2 minutes while pulling away.

But it never would have been that close had the Suns not missed 16 free throws and coughed up 24 points on turnovers — of course, the Blazers' defense has to be given some credit for the latter.

"But we controlled the game because we played hard," KJ said. "If we do that, we're going to be in every game at the end. This is not the same Phoenix Suns as in the past. We can be ahead of a team by four points late and win by four points. Before, we had to be up 16 points going into the stretch because we couldn't stop anybody. We don't rely on finesse anymore."

An example: The Suns outrebounded a team that has been among the best in the league at it for three years.

"The good thing about Paul is that he is carefree and mild-mannered," KJ said. "But he can put his foot down. The last two games were embarrassing the way we were outplayed, the lack of intensity. Like Paul told us, we played like chumps. It's not his normal tendency to explode like he did. I think he made his point."

Barkley thought so, too. "Yeah, Paul was pissed off," Barkley said. "And he should have been. He was yelling and raising hell. He wasn't our friend. But if you want a friend, you should get a dog. He's our coach, not our friend."

This was a turning point for the Suns, a launching pad to a big run. At 6-3, the Suns were to close out November with back-to-back games against the Warriors, who were badly injured.

The Suns were having better luck getting through their injuries, although KJ said he still found nothing to be very comfortable. "Before, when I'd come back from an injury, at least I'd know what we were running," KJ said. KJ was throwing balls out of bounds because he wasn't yet accustomed to where Ceballos, Ainge, and Majerle wanted the ball, and he would have his hands full with Tim Hardaway, who displaced him on the All-Star team in 1992.

The Suns and Warriors have had many entertaining, high-scoring games over the past five years. Coach Don Nelson has gotten the most out of unorthodox combinations of players. His small lineups have disrupted many teams, but the Suns had success because they could play just as fast but with taller players. Golden State was one of the few teams against whom the Suns could claim a height advantage. The Warriors were getting killed inside by everybody because, Nellie said, of the league-mandated stricter enforcement of inside defense. "The new interpretation has just about put us out of business with a small team," said Nelson.

That's bad because small is the only kind he has.

"Whatever good things we've done in the past to be able to win games, it's almost impossible to do now when you play a bigger team. They're almost forcing us to go big against big, and it's really a shame because there's room for small teams in the NBA."

Having said that, Nelson neglected to point out that in five years on the job he still hadn't brought a legitimate big man to the Warriors. While he is regarded as a coaching deity, Nelson was beginning to cultivate doubters about his skills in acquiring personnel.

All of this did not escape the attention of Westphal, who finally made good on his desire to start the taller Mustaf in place of Ceballos at small forward. Mustaf responded with 12 points, as the Suns made a concerted attempt to pound the ball inside. Barkley scored 29 in the 121-107 romp.

"Considering I was coming off five minutes in the last game and I hardly played in preseason, I was really surprised," Mustaf said of the start. "I feel like I'm part of the team again."

But just as KJ was beginning to feel like part of it again, he suffered a strained hamstring in the third quarter.

It was a pretty easy win, but even so, there were danger signs for the Suns, the most obvious being the Warriors' 45-31 rebounding advantage. The Suns' tall  front line had trouble boxing out the little fellas.

"The difference was we outshot them, and that's going to be hard to do up there," said Ainge, who scored 16 of his 22 points in the fourth quarter.

It would prove really hard to do with KJ staying behind. That put Knight back in the lineup for the rematch the following night in Oakland.

"He's better as a starter than off the bench," Westphal said of Knight, in what  would prove to be a significant statement.  Knight suffered from comparisons to KJ, and their games are not really comparable. "They're used to the style that Kevin plays and they try to get me to play that way," Knight said. "I get yelled at for not being Kevin."

KJ was going out of business for a long time with his hamstring strain; like it or not, Knight would be at the point. The Suns were about to become a pedestrian bump-and-grind team. They weren't going to run away from many opponents.

Even without KJ, they expected to get past the Warriors again. The Suns figured to work it in to Barkley and overpower them in the low post again.

Surprise! Nelson scraped together what big players he has and stuck them in the starting lineup. He had nothing to lose going with Tyrone Hill, Victor Alexander, and Billy Owens.  They ganged up on Barkley and limited him to nine for 24 shooting, although he scored 28 points and took 18 rebounds. Meanwhile, the Warriors shot 62 percent, and Chris Mullin scored 36 points as the Suns fell, 134-131.

At the end of the first month: seven and four, and unfulfilled.

When the Suns got home from Oakland, there was bad news waiting for them. KJ would miss at least two weeks. "We would rather attack it now than be faced with it in the spring," Emerson, the team physician, said. KJ has a long history of hamstring problems, so caution has become the key word at any sign of trouble.

That meant Knight was secure in the starting lineup for the immediate future. The rapidly improving Frank Johnson and Ainge would rotate in as reserves.

Still, Westphal was more than a little steamed, claiming KJ misled him about how his leg felt. "Kevin is Mr. Boy Scout," Westphal said. "He never tells a lie. I'm never going to believe him again."

Although this injury was not the same as the groin injury that had him out of action for the first six games, Westphal is convinced KJ came back too soon and suffered this one while compensating for the previous one.

"He said he felt great. Now, he says he really didn't feel that great and just wanted to play," Westphal said.

CHARLES BARKLEY brought to Phoenix the intimidating physical force the Suns had lacked in previous years.

KEVIN JOHNSON was the best penetrator on the team and a consistent floor leader at the point.

DAN MAJERLE'S hard-nosed play made him a favorite in Phoenix and an All-Star in the NBA.

MARK WEST (right) was the Suns' starting center throughout the year, but many of his minutes eventually went to OLIVER MILLER (below) as the season progressed.

DANNY AINGE, signed as a free agent in the off-season, added fire power and championship experience off the bench.

KJ's ability to drive and either pass or score made it nearly impossible for teams to double team Charles Barkley.

TOM CHAMBERS, long the star in Phoenix, grudgingly accepted a reduced role when Barkley was acquired. Chambers' contract with the Suns expired at the end of the season, and he left via free agency to play for Utah.

RICHARD DUMAS is another player the Suns will have to do without in 1994. Dumas' violations of the NBA's drug policy led to his most recent suspension in the summer of '93.

CEDRIC CEBALLOS (left) and
FRANK JOHNSON (below)
were called on to add a spark
from the bench.  With several
team  injuries during the
season, their roles became
increasingly important.

JERRY COLANGELO, the president and one of the owners of the Suns, is credited with keeping the team in Phoenix and building the Suns into the power they are today. Around the NBA, Colangelo is considered to be one of the sharpest executives in the league.

In the '70s PAUL WESTPHAL led the Suns as a player, and in the '90s he has proven himself to be the perfect coach for this "team of oddities."

THE FANS in Phoenix immediately took to Sir Charles. Over 300,000 people came to the rally after the finals to show their support for the Suns' 1994 drive to the NBA Championship.

In just one year, CHARLES BARKLEY has become the heart and soul of the Phoenix Suns and has already promised a return trip to the finals.

Knight also had some getting well to do of a different kind. His nose was bent out of shape because Frank Johnson was playing more minutes.

"I'm not going to guarantee him minutes," Westphal said. "I think Negele is a good player. When he gets his chances, if he plays well, he'll play more."

The Suns were pleased to see seven home games on the schedule in December, many against teams they expected to beat. Beyond that was an ominous January that had them playing 11 of 14 on the road. Certainly, they would need KJ for that span.

The Suns opened December with a home battle against Charlotte, off to its best start ever thanks to 1991-92 rookie of the year Larry Johnson and Alonzo Mourning, who would become 1992-93 rookie of the year runner-up. The Hornets couldn't quite match the firepower of the Suns but they'd certainly made strides through the draft lottery.

Still, the Suns smothered them, 109-90, limiting them to 42 percent shooting and out-rebounding them , 53-37.

The Suns might have found a spark that ignites Mustaf — albeit one they can't count on every night: two days earlier, a daughter was born to Mustaf and his fiance. He went for 16 points and five rebounds.

The Suns also got a boost from their bench, something they knew they were going to need on a long Eastern Conference trip just ahead. Ceballos gave them 20 points in 22 minutes; Chambers, 18 points.

"It's amazing what can happen when you're working, isn't it?" Westphal said. "Those guys were really digging."

The Hornets' bench had been outscoring foes by an average of 47-34, but the Suns' reserves beat them, 54-22.

"I think you've seen my substitution pattern by now: whatever I feel like — and they better be ready," Westphal said. "Ced is a guy who knows where the basket is, but he stayed in the game because he was active on defense. He was one of the guys I singled out before the game about defense. As quick as he is, to get one steal every other game is ridiculous. The ball ought to slip out of the other guy's hand at least once a game. Tom did a nice job, too. These guys know they'll get to play more as long as they cover."

Barkley, who had the flu and made his plight worse by jamming a finger in warm-ups, still came within reach of a triple-double with 13 points, 14 rebounds, and seven assists. Afterward, he claimed he threw enough passes to get the additional three assists.

"But these guys keep missing these damn layups," Barkley said. "I'm going to stop passing the ball. Next game, I'm going to give each guy one chance. First missed shot, he ain't seein' it no more." While said tongue-in-cheek, there was an element of truth to it.

Ironically, the excitement about Dumas' impending return came the week that Majerle opened — of all things — a bar. Majerle went one-for-12 against the Hornets the day before the opening and said it was because he was distracted.

Getting into Majerle's Sports Grill on opening night proved to be a task just as difficult as getting a ticket to a Suns game. The line began forming at about 3 p.m. By 7, it stretched around the block and down the street, and extra Phoenix police officers were dispatched. Many customers waited in line for more than two hours before gaining admission.

Once inside, it was wall-to-wall people. Ainge, who had suffered a freak ankle injury a week earlier while boarding the Suns' charter jet, aggravated it during the gala grand opening when he stepped on somebody's foot in the crowd. It would become a popular watering hole, where the elite meet to eat.

Soon, though, the focus was back on hoops. Once one of the most hated teams when it visited the Valley of the Sun, these clearly weren't the same Los Angeles Lakers who paid a call on Friday, December 4. Only Byron Scott, A. C. Green, and James Worthy remained from the Showtime era, and they were getting along in years. The Lakers had become big, slow, and old. Their game now was powering the ball into the low post and keeping the tempo slow. In other words, they had become the Celtics of the West.

"I guess I'm going to have to go down to K-Mart and get me a jumper," Worthy said after he and the Lakers were bombed by the Suns, 103-93. Worthy missed nine of his 12 shots. A career 54-percent shooter, he was shooting 39 percent through the first month of the season.

It was the Suns' oldest player, Frank Johnson, who bailed them out of this one. Frankie might be 34, but he's taken great care of his body. He figured he'd be around only as long as it took KJ to prove to the world that he finally was healthy.

"I liked my chances because they said they wanted me," Johnson said. "I went to Denver's camp the year before but their attitude was like, 'We'll bring you in and take a look.' Phoenix's attitude was more like, 'We want you in camp, please come in.'

"As Paul said, there was a math problem. He had 13 players with guaranteed contracts, and I was not one of them. That made it tough, so it was up to me to make them want to keep an extra guard."

Westphal said Frankie earned the opportunity. "He belongs in the NBA," Westphal said. "He's a lot better than most backup point guards."

Frank responded, "When a coach shows confidence in you, you want to do your damnedest to help win games."

He would do that the entire season. In this one, the Suns let a comfortable lead slip away and found themselves only a point in front of the Lakers with 3:18 to play. Westphal subbed Johnson for Knight, as he often did in late-game situations. Johnson keyed three straight defensive stops, first by stripping the ball from Lakers point guard Sedale Threatt, and later by stepping in front of an entry pass intended for Sam Perkins.

"To tell you the truth," Westphal said, "I don't know who are our bench guys and who are our starters anymore."

Upcoming was a five-game Eastern trip that would reveal their identity.

# Chapter Thirteen

# REVEALING THEIR TRUE IDENTITY

It was a nasty day in Milwaukee — cold, windy, the snow began falling by mid-afternoon on Saturday. The game was the following evening.

It was here that Barkley learned the Sixers finally had pulled the trigger on his trade to the Suns moments after he was acquitted on charges of roughing up a drunk who had accosted him in a late-night incident the previous season.

Barkley spent most of this evening in the hotel bar with reporters who cover the Suns watching the Michigan-Duke game on television. He knew everything about every player. It was obvious that he is a huge fan of the game, of sports. He said the Fab Five would remember the whipping they took at Cameron Indoor Stadium and put it to good use as the season progressed. He proved to be right. The Wolverines reached the NCAA championship game.

He signed autographs for a steady stream of people. It was orderly. Nobody even mentioned his incident. Barkley solicited opinions from the writers about the Suns' progress thus far, and then volunteered some of his own. He thought they needed another big player to share some of the rebounding burden with him. He thought they needed to arrive at a decision at small forward and discontinue the policy of playing it by committee. He suggested that Westphal would be well advised to start Stivrins. Barkley thought the Suns had enough stars on the floor. Stivrins is a solid, smart player, a complementary player.

"This is a scary trip for us," Barkley said. "We could win them all, or we could lose them all."

As the evening wore on, Frank Johnson stopped by to join the group.

There was a convention of farm-equipment salesmen staying at the hotel and one of them, who'd had more than his share of hops harvested with farm equipment, hollered to Barkley, "Hey, Ace! Why don't you buy me a beer?" Barkley and Johnson laughed at the guy, but Barkley put another beer on his tab and said to those around him, "He LOOKS like he ought to be on a tractor." Barkley got through the off-night without incident.

By Sunday morning, it was snowing hard. The Packers were playing one of their annual home games in Milwaukee, but some of the Suns who had planned to go changed their minds.

It wasn't a bad idea to begin getting focused on the Bucks. They were doing surprisingly well under new coach Mike Dunleavy. Their 9-3 run through November earned him the Coach of the Month award from the league.

It is an unusual arrangement between Dunleavy and Herb Kohl, a U.S. senator from Wisconsin who owns the Bucks. Dunleavy had two years remaining on his contract with the Los Angeles Lakers and was ready to discuss adding two more. He had taken the Lakers to the Finals in 1990, upsetting Portland for the Western Conference title. In 1991, he got the Lakers into the playoffs despite the first retirement of Magic Johnson and numerous injuries to key players. He'd done a fantastic job in Los Angeles. That is precisely why Kohl wanted Dunleavy to rebuild the Bucks.

Kohl negotiated a settlement with the Lakers in which he paid them two second-round draft picks in exchange for them allowing Dunleavy to break his contract. Then Kohl signed Dunleavy for $9 million over eight years and gave him the additional title of vice president of basketball operations. Dunleavy has nearly total control in Milwaukee. If that doesn't get a player's attention, nothing will. The Bucks made some deals that dropped their average age from 30 to 27 years. He believes he has assembled a unit that can be competitive early into the next century — when his contract expires.

They showed their scrappiness against the Suns by building a quick five-point lead before Westphal turned to his bench, which responded well in a 122-112 win. Barkley got off to a terrible start, missing his first nine shots. He had one point at halftime.

When Frank Johnson, Chambers, and Miller came into the game, the Suns went on a 16-2 spurt. With Knight, Majerle, Mustaf, Barkley, and West in the game, the Suns opened the third quarter with a 13-0 run that gave them a 21-point lead.

When it was over, Knight had a season-high 22 points, Ceballos 21, Miller 15 — with 12 rebounds, six assists, and three blocked shots — and Ainge 14.

"I can't tell you what a good feeling it is to finally be on a team where I don't have to be Charles Barkley every night in order for us to win," Barkley said after his 12-point output with four-for-14 shooting.

The Bucks took Barkley out of the game early with their double-teams, then Barkley moved the ball and made them pay. "That's pretty nice when you can score 122 with Charles at less than his best," Westphal said. "I've said all along I like teams with depth and versatility, and you're going to see a lot of that from this team. "

The Suns' next stop, New Jersey on Tuesday, December 8, also would be the first real media circus for Barkley. New Jersey is conveniently located between New York City and Philadelphia, and every reporter from within 150 miles who owns a mini-tape recorder hit the press room at Brendan Byrne Arena for Barkley's first trip back East following his Dream Team summer and the trade. He didn't disappoint them.

Barkley had made no secret about his feeling toward the Eastern media: they were dishonest, unfair, malicious. He believed the Philadelphia fans had a much different view of him than those who reported his daily activities.

The Suns finally moved the media horde out of the locker room and got a smaller, vacant dressing room so Barkley could hold court.

"I'll always be a 76er," he said.

In fact, he said he planned to continue to live in Philadelphia during the off-season and would consider going back to work for the Sixers in some capacity after retirement—for a price. "I can be bought," he said. "If they paid me enough, I'd even go to work for the Klan."

He launched into a tirade about the way the Sixers treated their players, how his old buddy Katz made lousy personnel moves — and how the Sixers notified the players about them.

"The fans were great to me," Barkley said. "But do I have resentment for the organization? Yes. I don't like the things they did, the way they treated people in general."

When they made a trade, they never got a player better than the one they let go, he said. "I felt like Custer out there last year. It ain't no fun getting beat on every night. Like when they traded me. I thought they'd be better than they are with the three guys they brought in. I'm gone now, and they're still bad."

He said he watches Sixer games all the time in Phoenix on the satellite. "After I get off my knees from giving thanks that I'm not there anymore, I'm sorry to see what's happening. I don't wish anybody bad — except Bill Laimbeer."

Not even Armon Gilliam, the Sixers forward who said Barkley was disruptive and that the Sixers should rid themselves of him. "Armon said the only reason I'm better than he is is because I get the ball more. Well, he gets it all he wants now. We'll have to compare notes at the end of the season and see how much I was holding him back."

Barkley also was asked about the Suns fans. "Suns fans cheer even when we lose. Chicago came in and spanked us real good and told us we're not ready for the big time. The fans were still cheering. I thought, 'This is definitely not Philadelphia.' "

In Philly, the Sixers barely had enough able players to fill a starting lineup. The Suns suddenly had so many, they were playing several positions by committee.

With KJ out, Knight and Frank Johnson were dividing time at the point. Miller and West were dividing minutes at center, even though Miller still was well beyond the weight the Suns had hoped he would reach.

Small forward was the most unsettled position, where Westphal was rotating five players — none of whom was the still-absent Dumas.

Amazingly, the Suns had won three in a row and five out of six as they took on the Nets, who were on an impressive run of their own — six straight — under new coach Chuck Daly, who'd coached Barkley on the U.S. Olympic team in Barcelona.

"It's definitely small forward by committee," Westphal said. "That might not be the way we envisioned it, and that might not be the way it is at the end, either. If we stop winning, then I'll address it as a problem. If we keep winning, I'll just accept it as the way it is."

The way it was in New Jersey, Mustaf started again. When Westphal doesn't like the matchup, he has Ceballos to turn to. Chambers saw time at small forward. So did Barkley. Majerle often wound up there in the fourth quarter.

"I need to see more of Mustaf at the 'three' spot," Westphal said. "It's hard to say that I'm going to give him 20 minutes every night. If he plays just a few and doesn't come back, that doesn't mean he's done something wrong. Same with Ced. He's had some games where I've played him only a few minutes. It just depends on the situation and who has the hot hand. There are just too many players to give any one of them consistent minutes there."

Rumors were swirling that the Suns were trying to trade for San Antonio Spurs small forward Sean Elliott. But Westphal couldn't help but look ahead to Dumas and salivate.

"He is our most pure 'three-man,'" Westphal said. "That really is his position. I really hope we'll be able to get that out of him. He has the ability to be an NBA all-purpose 'three-man.'"

Indications were growing that Dumas would be in Phoenix waiting for the Suns when they came home from this trip. KJ's return also wasn't far away. "I would never gripe about adding Kevin Johnson and Richard Dumas to our team," Westphal said. "I'm sure we'll find a way to work them in."

In the meantime, the Suns weren't doing badly with what they had. Majerle, assigned to guard Drazen Petrovic, the Nets' sharpshooter, took him out of the game.

"You know," Barkley said, relaxing in front of his locker after the 105-100 win, "I'm really getting sick of Majerle taking over my role as defensive stopper." Even Barkley couldn't get it out with a straight face.

Not that Barkley didn't put on a show of his own for the big media crowd: 34 points, 12 rebounds, six assists, three steals, two blocked shots.

Majerle limited 'Petro' to 16 points, seven below his average. "Sometimes," a peeved Petrovic said, "he gets away with pushes."

Daly called Barkley one of the three best players in the world and said, "Phoenix isn't a bad team right now, but they're going to be very tough come playoff time."

The embattled Knight actually made the play of the game. With Petrovic looking down to check his foot placement for a three-point try that could have tied the game, Knight stripped the ball from him and fired it ahead to Barkley, who finished off the game and the Nets with one of his ferocious, hang-on-the-rim  dunks.

"If we get another big man and get KJ back, watch out," Barkley said. "But I'll tell you what. If we play defense and rebound, we can compete with anybody right now. Dan sacrificed his game to play defense. That's why we're a good team. You have to sacrifice a little of yourself. "The other night in Milwaukee, I scored one point in the first half, and we were ahead by eight. I was happy. Tonight, I scored a lot but Dan got the big stops on Petro."

And then, with a final shot for his New York and Philadelphia media buddies, Barkley said, "We've got a lot of guys who can play — unlike the team I was with last year."

Then came Barkley's first brush with trouble. After he completed a radio interview on the court, arena security personnel failed to head off a drunk who abused Barkley verbally and refused to get out of his path to the locker room. Barkley delivered an open-handed stiff-arm to the drunk's face that cleared the path effectively. The unidentified man wanted to press charges against Barkley, but police refused to do so after interviewing several witnesses and arena security officers. Byrne Arena, coincidentally, was the site of one of Barkley's most forgettable moments: when he tried to spit on a heckler but missed and hit a little girl.

"That's one of the few things I've ever done that I was ashamed of," Barkley said. "I apologized to her."

There was little time to get smug. The game with the Hornets was the next night. Back-to-back games never are easy, but they're especially demanding in the middle of a long trip.

The victories over the Lakers, Bucks, and Nets indicated the Suns were finding ways to pull out close ones. It was a good trait to have absent the explosiveness of KJ, who could have turned some of those white-knucklers  into comfortable wins.

The Hornets were the  next to get a dose of it. And it was a momentous occasion: Wednesday, December 9, 1992, the Suns' 110-101 win coupled with Portland's loss to the Los Angeles Lakers put the Suns atop the NBA with a 12-4 record.

"Something like that doesn't happen very often," Barkley said, "so you'd better enjoy it. And you'd better take advantage of it." They did. It was a position the Suns would not relinquish until June 20.

With 23 points, 12 rebounds, and 10 assists, Barkley had just completed his first triple-double in a Suns uniform.

"Hey," he shouted in the locker room, "it's about time you all made some layups."

Barkley had missed triple-doubles by three or fewer assists four times, causing him to joke that his teammates were killing him because they couldn't catch.

Ainge, checking a statistics sheet, grinned and shot back, "Hey, Chuck, look: You came within five turnovers of a quadruple-double."

There were a number of come-through performances in the final three minutes when the Suns took control of another tight game. Knight, Ainge, Chambers, and Frank Johnson each made a key steal.

Majerle's three-point basket, part of a 21-point, 11-rebound performance, gave them some breathing room. But Barkley snared two humongous defensive rebounds that sealed it.

On one in the final minute, Barkley was sandwiched between Larry Johnson and Alonzo Mourning. Barkley outleaped them both for the ball. "He just kept going up," said Mourning, who is a half foot taller than Barkley.

"Isn't that why they brought me to Phoenix?" Barkley said. "We were tired. Me, I was sick and tired (he had the flu). It's difficult to fly, play, fly, and play again, but you've got to do it if you're going to be good. You've got to win on the road and this was a great win because the guys we have here have guts."

Next. the Suns had to deal with rookie sensation Shaquille O'Neal on the road.

"He's big, he's strong, and he's probably going to be everything they say, but he's a rookie," Barkley said. "I don't put any rookie up there with players like Michael Jordan. Shaq can be dominating, but any rookie has to do it for three or four years in the league before he gets my respect. . . well, maybe Shaq is an exception to that."

West is foul prone, but then, everybody who covers Shaq is foul prone, because he is well taken care of by league referees. O'Neal already was in the league's top five in scoring (22.2), rebounding (14.7), and shot-blocking (3.69). Matt Guokas, the  Orlando Magic coach, was comparing the 7-foot-1, 301-pound rookie to Wilt Chamberlain, whom Guokas played with. But O'Neal, while powerful, doesn't yet have the offensive repertoire of Chamberlain and hasn't proven to be a consistent 40-point scorer.

"But he's facing more sophisticated defenses than Wilt did, too," Westphal said, adding he was inclined to play O'Neal straight up. "I'd like to see him shoot some threes, too, but he seems to want to stay under the basket," Westphal lamented.

The Suns coach also had seen enough of Mustaf at small forward. Even though the Suns had won five in a row and were on top of the world with Mustaf in the lineup, Ceballos was reinserted.

"We're winning, so you don't want to change that," Westphal said. "I'm pleased we are where we are. We can play better, is what I am saying."

It was something of a landmark. It established Ceballos as one of two primary small forwards for the remainder of the season. The other one hadn't yet arrived. The revolving door, which spat out Barkley, Chambers, Majerle, and now Mustaf, was beginning to slow.

And it didn't seem to hurt them because they slipped past Shaq and the Magic, 108-107.

What other team but the Suns actually would encourage the Magic to throw the ball to Shaq in the closing seconds of a tight game? That's just asking for a Shaq Attack, right? Not necessarily. The object was to foul him quick and hard before he could get off a shot with those powerful arms.

Although Shaq scored 26 points, he missed two of four free throws in the closing 6.5 seconds. The Magic were hoping to go to Dennis Scott the first time (covered by Majerle) and to Nick Anderson the second (covered by Ainge). Instead, they had to throw the ball to Shaq.

"I'd rather see him shoot four times from 15 feet than twice from one inch," Westphal said of the 53 percent free-throw shooter.

Now the Suns were in position to sweep the trip, improve their six-game streak and their league-leading 13-4 record with a visit to Miami the next night, Saturday, December 12.

The bench, particularly Miller, Chambers, and Ainge, was getting them through. Chambers scored 27 against Orlando and Ainge 10 of his 16 in the fourth quarter as the Suns' bench beat the Magic's bench, 48-29. That made it 308-168 for the Suns' bench over four games.

"The old guys are having a great trip," Westphal said. "But we really don't have a bench. Tom and Danny come off the bench, but they're legitimate starters. We just choose to bring them in and spot them so we don't wear them down over the course of the season."

The Suns made eight of 19 three-pointers, which was becoming an ever-increasing weapon for them. "They're a double-edged sword, you have to accept some misses," Westphal said. "I don't want us to be three-point happy, but with Dan, Danny, and Charles, we have three guys who can make better than one out of three. That's a good return."

The great secret about the Suns, though, continued to be their late-game defense. The Magic might have shot 52 percent, but they were outscored, 14-6, over the final 4:23 when the game was on the line. That came after the Suns shut down Charlotte, 8-2, during the final 2:41 two nights earlier.

"In the final three or four minutes we pull together reasonably well," West said. "I think we're more aware of helping each other out. Over the course of the game, it's more individual man concern. "But at the end, it's more a team thing. We're making sure we get the rebound instead of running out. We're stepping up on the drive rather than letting a man get to the basket because it's for all the marbles."

Sounded good, but the Suns nearly blew the Miami game in the closing seconds with turnovers and fouls. They eventually prevailed, 122-118, when Willie Burton of the Heat pulled a Shaq and missed two free throws that would have tied it with 14 seconds left. Then Ainge, who scored 11 fourth-quarter points, iced it with two free throws with 11 seconds to go.

"There," Westphal said. "We won two games with our free-throw defense. We work on that a lot. I have to credit good coaching."

It seemed like good coaching when Westphal put his veterans on the floor in the closing seconds to try to bring home the sweep, but it was Barkley and Chambers who were responsible for the mistakes that allowed the Heat to get close after the Suns were up by eight with 41 seconds left.

Still, it was a sweep. The streak had reached seven games, and the Suns were coming home with a league-leading 14-4 mark.

This trip had been instrumental in the Suns' development:

They established that they had depth, with the bench outscoring opponents by an average of 49-29.

They established that they had grit, pulling out each game in the closing seconds.

They allowed five home-standing teams to average only 103 points a game, proving that their defense was better than reputed.

They made it clear that the three-pointer was going to be a valuable weapon.

They averaged seven more rebounds a game than their opponents.

"It's not like they panic," said Heat center Rony Seikaly. "They get the ball to the right people. They're very smart." And they did it all without KJ and Dumas, two of their best players. The Suns had established that they were a real team led by a ferocious team player in Barkley.

"That trip established the identity of our team," Hollins said. "Although we won 62 games, it was the same identity we took into the playoffs. We were called inconsistent, but that was our team the whole season. We'd stay close enough and then do everything right at the end to find a way to win. That was our team, regardless of the opponent and the caliber of the team.

"When we beat everybody and we were gutting out wins and showing a lot of mental toughness, things that in the past we hadn't accomplished, it was gratifying because it used to be that we would go out on the road, get down, try to come back, and fall short. This team got over the hump all the time."

His work on the road sweep brought Barkley the NBA player of the week award.

# Chapter Fourteen

# A CLEAN SWEEP

The road had taken its toll. Westphal stopped practice after less than an hour on Monday, December 14, the day before the Suns took on the Washington Bullets. Barkley had fluid on his knee; Miller had X-rays taken after experiencing twinges of pain in his right foot, which was fractured in college; Knight had a sore calf; Kemtpon had pain in his right heel (he had surgery on the Achilles' tendon at season's end); and West had sore hamstrings.

Miller's condition was termed a "stress reaction," and he was placed on the injured list. The report on KJ was not encouraging, either. He would likely miss at least another week.

Still, Westphal was excited. Dumas finally was due to arrive that night. Van Arsdale said the Suns would proceed slowly with Dumas, first carefully examining a knee he injured in a pickup game, and then making sure that he was mentally ready to resume his career.

But Westphal wanted the pace accelerated. "The league will let us have some time if we want it, but I don't want it. If he's in shape, I want him on the roster. He'll have a uniform Friday (for a game with the Lakers)."

As Westphal raved on, most reporters looked at each other with a wink. Maybe the guy was just trying to cover his butt because it was his idea to draft Dumas.

"Richard is an NBA small forward," Westphal said. "The ideal 'three-man' has to be one of the best athletes on the team because he has to handle the ball, go inside and rebound, shoot it, put it on the floor, go to the basket, and defend the greatest athletes in the world. Richard has the ability to do that. Nothing will stop Richard from being outstanding as long as his body stays healthy and his substance problem does not reoccur."

In his first meeting with reporters, Dumas said he had learned that the most important thing in his life wasn't dunking a basketball, but taking care of himself. "I feel good. I'm confident of the situation. I'm ready to go."

The time in John Lucas' after-care program in Houston "helped me become a better person, which I had lacked. I put myself first and basketball second. It's part of life," Dumas said of his recovery. "Things happen quickly, things happen slowly. This happened to take some time. It was a frustrating 13 months. But I never doubted that I'd get a second chance to be here. I put my faith in God and go from there."

Dumas sat with Colangelo and Van Arsdale while watching the Suns wallop the Washington Bullets, 125-110.

Even on his sore knee, Barkley made 13 of 17 shots, scored 36 points, and took 10 rebounds. But in the second half, Barkley shifted into cruise control and Bullets rookie Tom Gugliotta, who'd watched Barkley in admiration in the first half, scored 19 of his 27 points. That's after Westphal made a defensive switch because Harvey Grant scored 19 of his 22 in the first half against Barkley.

"I'm not going to say Gugliotta is another Larry Bird like Pat Riley did," Westphal said. "Charles just made him look like Larry Bird."

Barkley, in his defense — the only defense from him on this evening — responded, "I only score and rebound. If they want me to play defense, they're going to have to pay me another $2 million."

He could use it to pay his league-imposed fines. Barkley was nicked $5,000 by the NBA for his comments about referee Mike Mathis following the New Jersey game. Barkley and Mathis have a long-running feud. This time, Barkley said of the curly haired arbiter, "Mathis is just a bad official. He's hurting our team. Rod Thorn (NBA operations chief) has to have some balls and go after him."

Dumas could have rejected the opportunity to return to the Suns and gone to Europe for 10 times more salary. The Suns signed him for one year for the league-minimum $140,000. But Dumas said he wanted to stick with the Suns, because they had stuck with him, especially Westphal, with whom Dumas had developed a strong personal relationship.

Westphal phoned him often and visited him while Dumas was playing for the Oklahoma City Cavalry of the Continental Basketball Association.

"Everything is a gamble, but I don't think this is a very big one," Westphal said. "I think he has had a lot of adversity in his life that contributed to his problems. During this last year, he went through something he didn't have to. If he didn't want to play in the NBA, he had a lot of overseas offers. If he wanted to get high, he could have gone over there and gotten as high as he wanted as many times as he wanted.

"I hope everybody understands that he isn't just a raw talent. He's a very intelligent, versatile player. He knows how to play basketball. He's going to be on some highlight films. I think he has grown up a lot.

I think he's finding out that he's a much better player straight than when he was high. I think Richard was a little bit afraid to play straight. The best thing in the world for him was getting busted."

So Dumas had seen it all — Israel before the bombing of Tel Aviv during the Persian Gulf War shut down the pro league there, the CBA, the USBL, LA summer pro league, pick-up games among his friends in after-care.

But this was the big show, and Dumas was eager to show what he could do. "I have played at every level except the NBA. I want to play here," Dumas said.

Dumas hit the big leagues just in time to witness Ainge on a major-league tear. Over an eight-game run, Ainge was shooting 54.5 percent overall and 56.8 percent from three-point range — an amazing statistic. He also was scoring 15.4 points a game.

"We've had a lot of tight finishes," Ainge said. "I've been in those situations a lot more than most players, so I feel confident out there. I've also played a lot more minutes this season than I did last year in Portland, so I get a better feel for the flow of the game."

Opponents know Ainge is one of the most successful three-point shooters in the history of the game. That's a valuable ally for Barkley. The Suns also know that for every "up" streak, there is going to be a "down," and Ainge would have that, too, before the year was over.

As the first quarter of the season drew to a close, the Suns were showing signs of being for real. Amazingly, they were doing it without their "real" team.

Dumas proved to be another valuable piece, and it didn't take long for those who were skeptical of Westphal's lofty praise to see why the coach was excited. The first time he stepped onto the court, in the second quarter at the Forum in his first official NBA game on Friday, December 18, Dumas took a pass near the free-throw line, put a move on A. C. Green — actually appeared to travel, but there was no call — rolled past the startled Lakers veteran who is one of their better defenders and delivered a soft finger-roll shot through the hoop.

Oh, my.

Of course, the Lakers were coming off a loss to Dallas, a team that challenged the all-time-worst record right up to the final month of the season, so it was understandable if they all were a little startled. The Forum fans booed them loudly as the Suns outscored them, 35-14 in the opening quarter and coasted to a 116-100 win.

This was the night the Suns' troublesome small forward position became a strength. Ceballos, still in the starting lineup, scored 18 of his 24 points in the first quarter, perhaps feeling some heat from Dumas' arrival. Dumas played only 17 minutes, but scored 16 points and made two steals.

"We are the weak link because everybody else on our team is proven," Ceballos said. "But that doesn't mean we're weak players. I talked to Richard before the game and we said whoever starts and whoever plays, we're going to back each other. If you add up our stats, we had a hell of a game."

Barkley, after a routine 25 points and 23 rebounds — which gave the Suns a 60-36 edge on the boards — said, "We needed a win like this. We went back East and beat some teams that people think are lackluster." Of course, most people were beginning to draw the same conclusion about the Lakers. It was a night in which Majerle equaled his career high with six steals. And the hits just kept on coming.

On December 22, a Tuesday, the Suns tied the franchise single-season record with their 10th straight win, 106-104, over Golden State.

Guess who was the spark plug? Barkley scored the Suns' first 15 points, setting a club record. Then he scored the most important ones — the last two with 19 seconds left, giving him 35 in all. And when the Warriors missed their chance to tie it, Barkley was there to smother the final rebound, his 16th of the evening.

A sign in the Purple Palace seemed to sum up a growing feeling in Phoenix: "Santa Claus is bald and he's bringing an NBA championship to Phoenix."

Nellie, whose team successfully outruns most of the league, uncharacteristically slowed it down, and it almost worked. But the Suns found a way to pull out another close one.

Afterward, they received some long-awaited news that might help them avoid these nail-biting finishes: KJ would be reactivated for a December 26 home game with Seattle. Before that, the Suns would have to go to Denver to play one last time without him.

They also would have to play most of the evening without Barkley on December 23, when they had a chance to break their single-season winning streak record. Barkley got the heave in the second quarter from referee Ron Olesiak.

That left Majerle to rally the troops, and he did, 111-96. It sounds easy, but the Suns led by only three points going into the final quarter.

"Charles has been getting a lot of credit, and deservedly so," Westphal said. "But we're not a one-man team. Majerle played better than he usually does, and he's usually fantastic. "

His line: 10 of 13 shots, four of five treys, 25 points, five rebounds, five assists, three steals. As Barkley put it, "The Ritz Twins — Dan and Danny — really came through. They're no ordinary crackers."

At the quarter mark, the streaking Suns were 18-4 and beginning to make believers of most of their skeptics.

"This team has shown that it has something special," Westphal said. "It has shown an ability to find ways to win. That's the greatest trademark you could hope for a team to have."

Colangelo was grateful, if not mildly surprised. "I thought there would be a period of adjustment, and that hasn't been the case," he said. "The good news is we're building a nice cushion of victories. It's been my experience that when you're on a roll like this, you milk it for all you can for as long as you can. Right now, they're all chasing us, and that's a good feeling."

The Suns' commitment to retool with smarter, more versatile players was paying off. "We've kept all-around players who you can put at different positions on the floor, who can pass," Westphal said. "That's a real luxury, especially at center. That's been the major change. And this team is confident. You don't execute in the fourth quarter the way we have without that."

Beating Denver on the road without Barkley only boosted the Suns' confidence.

"It was important to demonstrate we can do it without Charles, important to ourselves, to Charles, to observers," Westphal said. "And we demonstrated that decisively."

The rookie coach expressed gratitude to his players "for how willing they have been to sublimate their egos." As Westphal pointed out, "Any NBA coach's worst nightmare is player refusal to accept, because there's not much you can do to them. You can't take their scholarship away. It's good this stuff has worked so far. It sort of proves to them that I'm not crazy. The big test will be if we go on a long losing streak to see how things hold up."

And with a killer road schedule coming up in January, a skid appeared to be a possibility.

"Paul has done an exceptional job of blending personalities and talent," Colangelo said. "And he is a good bench coach because he is creative, perceptive and willing to take risks. He's a bit unconventional, but he has used his strengths to his advantage."

The Suns closed out December with home games against Seattle, Denver, and Houston. There's never a bad time to get a Kevin Johnson back from an injury, but this was looking like a particularly good time from the Suns' standpoint. But how much better could KJ make a team that was leading the league, had won 11 straight and 16 of the past 18 games?

"I know some people have said some negative things about what my return will do," KJ said. "But I know I can help this team. We are playing good basketball, but we are not playing great basketball. We're playing great in the fourth quarter to pull games out, but there have been a few teams in there we should have buried."

Westphal was incredulous that the question of KJ's value even would arise. "I don't believe in psychiatrists, but those people need some help. I don't think it will be that hard to blend what we've been doing with his skills. We'll just be that much tougher to guard."

When healthy, KJ still has a killer first step. There are few who can stay with him.

He saw the shift in the Suns' game coming. In many situations, he would effectively be a shooting guard when others bring the ball up the floor, and when Barkley takes command in the low post. KJ's greatest asset — that killer speed — still is always there. It now would be a matter of picking his spots instead of having to use it every time down the floor.

"A lot of times some quick baskets would have helped us," Westphal said. "We've had to grind out a lot of games we maybe could have opened up with a spurt had KJ been there."

KJ said he'd actually been ready to return for a week, but don't forget, that was KJ talking. Remember when he said he was ready to come back earlier? When he came back too soon, disguised his true condition, and suffered a compensating injury? So the Suns were ultraconservative this time. The decision was left to the medical staff and Westphal. KJ was out of the loop.

Knight started against the SuperSonics, but KJ played 15 minutes off the bench, producing only two points with one-for-four shooting, only one assist, and suffering five turnovers. Needless to say, that didn't spark the Suns to a blowout. They had to grind once more, and they did it successfully once more, 113-110. Had the Sonics not missed four free throws in the final 40 seconds, it might have been a different story.

But it was 12 wins in a row, a Suns all-time record, and it took 33 points from Barkley and more bench work from Frank Johnson, Ainge, and Chambers to get past the team that now had the second-best record in the league. Chambers made a couple of clutch free throws to pull it out after he was hacked on a drive. Barkley had to give it up to him after being quadruple-teamed.

"I really believe our experience has been a factor in the streak," Ainge said. "Tom is not afraid to fail, and an inexperienced player might not have reacted like that."

Westphal's practice of no practice now was in effect. He'd given the Suns the previous two days off.

"I almost blew the game for us," Westphal said. "We were rusty."

Barkley didn't think that was really the problem. He proved prophetic — who on this team isn't prophetic? — when he said of the Sonics, "I've got a real bad feeling we're going to run into them again. That's a damned good basketball team."

Twelve straight wins was something few on the Suns' roster ever had experienced. Ainge was an exception. So was Westphal during his playing days with the Celtics.

"My first year, we won 68 games and never lost more than two in a row," Westphal said. "In this league, when you're winning, it seems you keep winning, even if you don't play great. We're on a nice roll now."

"And when you're losing, you can play great and have your heart broken. We know we're going to lose at some point. We might even go on a bad streak. We really don't talk about it. We just have guys who enjoy winning and really don't enjoy losing."

Ainge, who'd been to the Finals with the Celtics and Trail Blazers, added, "I don't think we're good enough to win a championship at the moment. Portland and Chicago have done it. They know they're capable of getting to the Finals. We don't know what we can do yet, except win 12 regular-season games. Eight or nine of those were against teams we should beat."

A rematch with Denver was up the following night, Sunday, December 27, at home. The Suns had no trouble making it No. 13 with a 129-88 rout, thanks to Dumas' major-league coming-out party: 27 points and four steals in 27 minutes off the bench. With five steals the night before, Dumas was proving to have great anticipation and quickness. Slam after slam he threw at the Nuggets, who with an 11-game skid were headed in the opposite direction of the Suns.

Westphal said he liked the idea of running a play called "Three-Up," in which KJ has the ball and Dumas comes to the top of the key to screen for him.

"I like them both, period, but I like them together on that play because they are extremely quick and have the ability to pass as well as score," Westphal said. "If their men switch, KJ has a small forward on him and Dumas has a point guard. They can take advantage of that, especially if we have other shooters on the floor. They're too quick to guard. They're creative. I like to put them in those situations so they can take advantage of their skills."

KJ called the play "almost impossible to stop."

"The two-man in the past has been our bread-and-butter, but this play is even more effective," he said. "If you get this guy the ball against a point guard, it's over. "

It was almost over for KJ in the third quarter, when he was given a technical foul for arguing no calls on his drives — he made only five of 13 shots — and was on the verge of getting a second "T" and the boot.

"I play 27 minutes, I go to the basket hard on almost every play, and I shoot two free throws," KJ said. "Darell Garretson (chief of NBA officials) must have told the referees at their orientation this year to only let me shoot four-to-six free throws a game. "

Then KJ offered his explanation for uncharacteristically popping his cork. "My mom is here for the holidays and she was sitting down there by the basket. The only reason I got the technical was if I didn't, she was going to. So I stepped up for her."

This was a 27-minute off-the-bench outing for KJ, good for 12 points and 12 assists.

"I told our guys I'm tired of fourth-quarter heroics and let's blow one open," Westphal said. "I blame myself now for all those nail-biters. If I had known it was that easy, I'd have told them to do it sooner."

Dumas certainly took it to heart. "This team is loaded with talent, there are a lot of great players around here. It's really hard not to look awful good."

It also seemed to be getting easier for him to put his life back together. "My wife (Angela) and my two sons make a huge difference for me. A year ago, my mother told me to grow up, get my priorities straight. My wife tells me that, too. I've listened to them."

Barkley had some fun with reporters who had gathered around Dumas: "Hey, let's get this straight: Even when I play shitty, you come to me first."

At 20-4, the Suns were off to their best start since 1981, when that club set the franchise record with 57 victories.

And at 13-0 for December, all that was standing between them and an unprecedented unblemished month were the Houston Rockets.

"They scare me to death because they have good inside people and good outside people," Westphal said. "You don't want to run into them on a night when they're on."

It was a timely game for Miller to be activated. He'd been trying to lose weight in hopes of reducing pressure on the stress reaction in his right foot. The Suns were the second-shortest team in the NBA, and Houston's front line included not only Hakeem Olajuwon but also Otis Thorpe and surprising rookie Robert Horry.

"Size doesn't mean anything," Westphal said. "I don't consider us to be small because we rebound well. "Somebody asked me if I thought it was unfair to have Charles, a 6-4 guy, at power forward. I wanted to know who it was unfair to, Charles or the guy he's playing against."

The Suns capped their historic undefeated run through December with a 133-110 rout of the Rockets, making them 14-0 for the month and 21-4 overall. Their month tied the 1971 Los Angeles Lakers for the third-best in NBA history.

KJ moved back into the starting lineup just in time to tune up for January, and quickly and emphatically answered the question of whether he could coexist with Barkley. KJ scored 25 points, his season high, by making 10 of 13 shots. He also had 10 assists. That was on a night when Barkley had his second triple-double: 25 points, 17 rebounds, 10 assists. KJ termed speculation that he couldn't make the Suns more effective "a foolish assessment." He and Barkley worked smoothly together.

"When I get doubled and can pass to a guy who is making his shot like Kevin did, that makes the double hesitate a bit," Barkley said. "And that makes my life a whole lot easier."

Seven baskets and three assists by KJ took the Suns from a point down to 19 up during a third-quarter blitz.

"I told Paul at halftime I thought we were close to burying these guys," KJ said. "We were ready to open it up, and that's where I feel I can help this team. When things get close, I can get aggressive and help put teams away."

KJ said he still was not ready to go 40 minutes. "I played 27, and it felt like 40. It still takes so much to do the little things that normally just flow. "But all our roles have changed, and I can be just as effective in 30 minutes as I used to be in 40. We're playing with a confidence that I haven't seen before. It's different this year because we have Charles who can clean up every mistake we make."

Westphal was impressed with the continued improvement of Ceballos, who seemed motivated by Dumas to keep his position.

"Ced has gone from somebody we just put out there to earning his spot," Westphal said. "Ced would have one good game then, I don't want to say he'd coast, but he wouldn't put good games together back-to-back. He's been putting them back-to-back since Richard's been here."

When you are the top dog, according to Barkley, you have to change mentally. "We're not a regular team anymore. We are an elite team now, and because of that, we're going to be a marked team on the road."

The record run through December earned Westphal the NBA Coach of the Month award in only his second month. "You saw what it did for Mike Dunleavy," Westphal quipped about the Bucks coach who, after winning it in November, saw his team go skidding off the face of the earth in December. And Barkley received the NBA Player of the Month honor.

It had been a sweep through December for the Suns, with an unblemished record and the two major awards. And, with Dumas so far making a successful comeback from substance abuse problems, it could be termed a clean sweep. Now, they all faced monumental tasks.

"It's the oldest cliché in basketball: Just look at the next game, at each team, and not focus on the drudgery of January," Westphal said.

KJ said where the streak will make a difference "is each team we face on the road in January will be out to play its best against us. Sometimes we forget that the reason teams like Chicago and Detroit got to be so good is because the teams they play are always at their best."

Ainge said the roll makes it more fun to come to practice every day — assuming one is scheduled.

"Pressure? This isn't pressure, it's fun," Ainge said. "Some guys say they don't think about the streak, but I do. It's fun."

# Chapter Fifteen

# THE ROAD WARRIORS

All right, December wasn't a bad little month. While January didn't look as promising from a scheduling standpoint — three home, 11 road — at least the Suns were tackling it with a full army for the first time.

If they could do what they'd done playing musical chairs, maybe, just maybe, they could get through this thing without taking too many hits with KJ, Dumas, and Miller back in action.

"Now we're going to find out how good we really are," Barkley said. "We're always going to be there at the end, and we're going to be there to kick some ass. I'm really looking forward to '93."

With Miller activated, this was the first time the Suns had what they considered to be their top 12 players on the active roster at the same time as they headed for the Texas Triangle to meet San Antonio, Houston, and Dallas in succession on January 3, 5, and 7.

The Suns were on the league's biggest streak, but the Spurs were on a roll themselves, having won four of five games since John Lucas replaced Jerry Tarkanian as coach.

The Suns were in control all the way. They led by 12 late in the third quarter, by nine midway through the fourth, by five with 20 seconds to go, and still by two with 4.3 seconds remaining, when all they had to do was execute an inbounds play and perhaps make two free throws.

For the record, the Spurs swiped the pass and scored, sending it into overtime, where they pulled out a 114-113 win that ended the Suns' franchise-record streak. It would become one of the most controversial games of the season, one in which the Suns filed an official protest with the NBA.

'We had this one counted," Westphal said. "It just goes to show that you can't go into your home run trot until the ball clears the fence."

Barkley called it a "giveaway."

Lucas said afterward, "I'm one who believes in miracles, and I think that we saw one tonight."

Westphal said what Lucas actually had seen was "offensive discombobulation."

The Suns deferred to each other in the fourth quarter. Where was that brazen step-up-and-take-the-big-shot attitude that carried them through all those white-knuckle fourth quarters in December?

"We were hesitant, and that's probably my fault," Westphal said. "I still think this is an adjustment period with Kevin. We're still getting used to him, and him to everybody else, because he runs things a little differently."

Majerle, who threw away the inbounds pass, admitted that he should have called timeout: "I forced it in, and there were just too many people in a congested area."

Westphal agreed that the Suns made more than their share of execution mistakes. "If we're going to be a good team on the road, we can't let these kind of games get away. We would have beaten a good team on the road if we had inbounded the ball."

It turned out the officiating crew of Joe Forte, Lee Jones, and Tommie Wood made more than their share of execution mistakes, too.

As San Antonio attempted to inbound the ball with four-10ths of a second remaining in regulation, it had six men on the floor after Jones presented the ball to Spurs guard Avery Johnson for throw-in. The Suns contended that a technical foul should have been called. None was. They protested on that basis.

"It's been a long time since we lost, but I don't care how many we won in a row, it always kills me to lose," Barkley said. "Bad things happen when you don't use your head."

The Suns felt they stood a good chance of winning the protest. It seemed a clear-cut misinterpretation of the rule. But a decision wouldn't come from Commissioner David J. Stern for at least five days.

In the meantime, the Suns had to try to save the remainder of the Texas trip. Houston went down easily the previous week in Phoenix, but the Suns anticipated that it would be a different story when playing them in the Summit.

The Rockets had lost their home fans. First, it was Owner Charlie Thomas putting the club up for sale more than a year earlier and finding no serious takers. Then came the bitter feud between All-Star center Hakeem Olajuwon and Thomas over Olajuwon's contract. The Rockets accused Olajuwon of faking an injury late the previous season and suspended him without pay. The Rockets had been through a couple of coaches in a short period of time before settling on Rudy Tomjanovich. Meanwhile, they had plummeted in the standings, failing to make the playoffs the previous season when they needed a season-finale win over the Suns.

It added up to a lot of apathy toward the Rockets.

So desperate were the Rockets, who were on a four-game skid, that for this Suns visit—Barkley's first with his new team—the Rockets were offering a two-for-one promotion: buy as many as four $12 tickets and get up to four free. Cash only.

Westphal decided it was time to move Richard Dumas into the lineup.

"Let's see what I can do," Dumas said. "I'm ready."

Westphal denied that the setting was any kind of psychological ploy in giving the rookie his first NBA start in the city where he had gone through his after-care in the substance-abuse facility run by Lucas.

Westphal did feel it was necessary to deliver a state-of-the- team address, though, to specifically discuss the "deferring" and "discombobulation" the Suns experienced in that fateful fourth quarter in the HemisFair Arena.

"It's not like we're not playing hard," Westphal said. "It's not like we're not playing good defense. We don't have anyone who is trying to mess up. But we needed to reinforce our responsibilities.

"I've said I thought we'd take a small step backward when we got Kevin back. He plays differently than our other point guards. The confusion stems from Kevin knowing when he needs to take advantage of opportunities and when he needs to take care of everybody else. I think he's trying too much to take care of everybody else. It's a fine line."

Johnson had missed 18 of the Suns' 26 games. He was about to miss some more. With the Suns putting their "real" starting lineup of KJ, Majerle, West, Barkley, and Dumas on the floor for the first time — in their 27th game — the Suns rolled to a 20-point lead in the second quarter.

Good as they had been, this was a new level for them. They looked at each other with wide eyes as if to say, "Wow, I knew we were good, but I didn't know we were this good."

And then, it happened. "I felt it coming in the first quarter," KJ said. "I came out, it got tight, I went back in, and I felt a 'tweak.'" Another hamstring injury.

It sidelined him for the rest of the game, and it offered the world quite a barometer of what the Suns are with KJ, and what they are without him.

The Rockets quickly erased the deficit against the shell-shocked Suns. It was down to five points by halftime and to two going into the fourth quarter. The Rockets led by a point going into the final 36 seconds. This was December all over again. Another bumpy-air, hard-fought game.

Barkley, drawing double-team attention, found Miller open under the basket and fed him for a go-ahead dunk. Then, with the Suns swarming Olajuwon, point guard Kenny Smith found an alley open to the basket and appeared to be driving for a layup that would give the Rockets the lead and probably the game.

Barkley sprang from the weak side and blocked it with 3.5 seconds to go.

"It was real close to goaltending," Barkley said. "But he wasn't going to get a layup. Either I was going to block it or foul him. It was real close."

"Chuck's attitude and his toughness have been key to our record and our success," Westphal said. "He comes ready to play and he makes sure his teammates do, too."

The Suns had to execute an inbounds play with 2.5 seconds to go, a situation not dissimilar to the finish of the San Antonio game.

"I begged Paul to let me throw it in this time," Majerle said. "I figured I was the right man because I knew exactly what not to do." This time, Majerle got it in, the Suns ran out the clock, and were thrilled to escape with the 106-104 decision.

"We were kind of pissed off we blew that game at San Antonio," Barkley said after his 29-point, 10-assist, eight-rebound performance.

Ainge, who came off the bench to score 21 and help the Suns pick up the pieces, admitted that "it was kind of scary. I was more concerned about Kevin than what was going on in the game."

The Suns felt they should have been 2-0 in the Texas Triangle and going for the sweep against 2-24 Dallas.

Even without KJ, this one should be a lock for the Suns, or so they thought.

"Where's this team I've been hearing about that gets killed by everybody?" Westphal asked after the Suns had to scramble in the final 90 seconds to emerge with a 111-107 win. "We had a hard time scoring on them, a hard time stopping them, and we couldn't grind them down with our bench. If they'd made a few more free throws, we'd be going home with a loss."

The Mavs, illustrating that they truly are a team that finds a way to lose, missed 14 free throws, including six during a 33-second tear in the fourth quarter. That offset the Suns' loss of 30 points to turnovers.

The Suns actually trailed by seven points in the fourth quarter and were well on their way to one of the most humiliating losses in their 25-year history before Frank Johnson stepped up — again — to replace the ineffective Knight. Johnson quickly swished four straight shots and two free throws to bail them out.

"That's why we're a good team and not a great team," Barkley said. "It was tough to get up for this game." Barkley had another MVP-type performance with his 32 points (including 12-for-12 at the line), 14 rebounds, six assists, three steals, and two blocks.

But he was knocked silly in the final minute of the first half by an elbow from Dallas forward Terry 'The Terminator'' Davis. It took three stitches to close the cut over Barkley's left eye. "Paul sat me down to get my equilibrium back. I was out of it. It's tough out there when you can't see.''

Later, Majerle took an elbow above his left eye from a guy named Brian Howard. He topped Barkley: it took four stitches to close Majerle's cut. "I guess if they can't beat us, they're going to beat us up,'' Barkley said.

The Suns had four days to get KJ ready and let Barkley and Majerle heal before hitting the road for games at Seattle and Sacramento.

In between, the Suns planned festivities at the Purple Palace to celebrate the 25th anniversary of their being awarded an NBA franchise. Among the attractions was another practice that was open to the public, their third of the season. At the previous one in December, 21,000 showed up.

The SuperSonics definitely were a hot commodity in the Seattle Center Coliseum. They had won all 12 of their home games and 17 straight regular-season games going back a season. Were it not for the Suns' two early wins over the Sonics at America West Arena, the two teams would have been tied for the league lead.

"They're for real,'' Westphal said.

For the first time in a week, KJ was on the practice floor. Medical personnel had determined that this injury wasn't a pull or a tear but an irritation of scar tissue from a previous injury.

"Is there a question in my mind? Of course. I'd be stupid if I didn't think the guy gets hamstring injuries,'' Westphal said.

KJ logged 40 minutes against the Sonics, scoring 20 points and passing out eight assists. He showed no ill effects.

But the Sonics' big guys took Barkley out of the game in the fourth quarter, although he was cantankerous when the subject was broached following the 122-113 loss.

"Don't talk to me about their defense,'' Barkley said. "Because nobody in the world can cover me one-on-one.'' Barkley scored 27 points, but he got off only three shots in the fourth quarter when Seattle stretched it out. "We had the best record in the NBA when we walked in here, and we still have the best record when we walk out,'' Barkley said.

The Sonics hurt the Suns where they are most vulnerable: trapping them and forcing them to lose 25 points to turnovers, and using their superior height on the offensive boards for 22 second-chance points. The problem was up front, as it almost always is when the Suns get into trouble. Center Mark West had two fouls two minutes into the game and had to come out. Then, West picked up two more in the first 3 1/2 minutes of the second half and came out for good.

"We've been almost step-for-step with Phoenix this year and nobody has noticed," said Eddie Johnson, the Sonics sixth man who used to play for the Suns. "This was the biggest game of the year for us."

The next day, upon arrival at Sacramento, Westphal had another closed practice. He had done that two other times on the road following losses. In those, the Suns followed up with wins at Utah and Houston.

"It wasn't any big secret," Westphal said afterward. "We talked about reducing our turnovers, and how our defense is not forcing enough of them. We talked about why we're not getting the ball to Charles in the fourth quarter."

Defense, though, was the main issue. "That is a problem," he said. "Certainly defense was the difference in the Seattle game. We weren't on the same page. We were trying to trap when we weren't supposed to, not trapping when we were supposed to. We're getting that straightened out."

Among the Suns' few weaknesses over the previous four seasons was losing to teams with sub-.500 records. So far, that had been the primary difference in this season. They were winning games they were supposed to win. They often made them closer than they should have, but they were winning them.

With Seattle now hot on their trail, the Suns couldn't afford to blow this one. If they caved in for the remainder of the month, they would undo everything they had done in December and be just another team.

"There has been hesitation and a bit of confusion, they go hand-in-hand," Ainge said. "It doesn't show up so much against a bad team, but against a good team like Seattle, it really stands out.

"Right now, we're not certain of what we want to do and how we want to do it. Seattle had absolutely no hesitation."

It appeared that things were going South for the Suns. They trailed Sacramento by 13 points with 10 minutes to go in the third quarter. Nothing was working until KJ, Dumas, and Majerle kicked them into gear with an unbelievable turnaround: 19 unanswered points in a 32-5 spurt that brought them the 114-104 verdict. It could only happen to a team like the Kings, time-honored losers.

Of course, Westphal said the Suns' defense had something to do with that. Dumas made four steals and scored 11 points in the third period. KJ tied his career best with six steals.

"People think our defense is our weakness," Westphal said. "They haven't been watching our fourth quarters, or anytime we've had our backs against the wall. We've responded. But we've probably got the type of players who'd rather do it with offense."

In the third-quarter turnaround, the Kings made four of 17 shots. "We made a stand," Westphal said. "Our defense was unbeliev- able. It was fun to see it. I think it's human nature to rely on offense. Offense is easier than defense. Defense is work. A lot of times, you win with offense. You cover your guy, hope he misses, a lot of times he does, then you get running. That's an easy game to play.

"We have a good feel for when we have to make our stand. Usually, it's in the fourth quarter. We couldn't wait that long this time or we would have gotten blown out."

They made it two in a row with a 107-99 thrashing of Miami at home on January 15, a night in which Barkley passed the 15,000-point mark for his career. He would have had to wait one more game to do it but the Suns' reserves did such a poor job after being given a 25-point lead that Westphal sent the starters back in after the Heat cut it to five.

As Ainge put it, "It was kind of typical of the way we've been playing lately; really good in stretches, and really bad in stretches."

For the third straight game, Knight didn't get off the bench.

"I don't know if there is anything I can do," Knight said. "I keep a smile on my face and try to make this into a positive. Whether I play again here or get traded, I'll be prepared so that it doesn't turn into a lost opportunity for me."

The day after they got home from their trip, the Suns were informed by the commissioner that their protest of the loss at San Antonio was denied. Stern applied an unusual interpretation of a rule that is stated clearly in the rulebook.

"As chairman of the Competition and Rules Committee for 10 years, I think I know a little about the rules," Colangelo said. "There is a reason why rules are put in. Eddie Gotlieb, one of the founders of the game, really, always told me to look at the spirit of the rules. The commissioner's decision, I believe, is based on an incorrect application of the rules. The perception is the interpretation is based on a ruling he wished to make."

The perception is the commissioner didn't want to open a Pandora's Box of upheld protests. There hasn't been one since November 30, 1982.

"I didn't expect to win it," Barkley said. "The commissioner didn't have the balls to give it to us. The bottom line is we should have won, and I don't like being jerked around."

The rulebook states clearly that the ball is in play when it is placed at the disposal of a player for throw-in. At that time, any team that has any number of players other than five on the floor receives a technical foul.

The Spurs had six players on the floor when the ball was placed in the hands of Avery Johnson by official Lee Jones with the score tied at 107 and four-10ths of a second left. Majerle began hollering to referee Joe Forte, "They have six! They have six!"

Forte then ran onto the floor, blowing his whistle and waving his arms. The Suns assumed Forte was going to assess the technical. Instead, Forte stopped the inbounds play, allowed Spurs forward J.R. Reid to leave the floor, then indicated that play was to resume without a technical.

Stern, in his interpretation of the rule, said it is not a technical foul unless the ball actually is thrown in. That is not what the rulebook states.

"The rule states in black and white what should have taken place," Colangelo said.

Majerle, whose errant inbounds pass led to the Spurs' basket that tied the game seconds before the protested play took place, said ruefully, " I guess I screwed up twice: First I threw the ball away, then I opened my mouth. I guess I should have waited until they threw it in."

Westphal was livid  at the commissioner.

"It was a New Age decision — it just felt right, so go with it," he said. "They just changed the rules. I know a lot of coaches who lost games because they got technicals for having six men on the floor when the ball was about to be thrown in — before it was thrown in, not after."

At 25-6, the suns were  heading East for six games in 10 days, their longest trip of the season.

# Chapter Sixteen

# HOPPING MAD

By now, even Westphal had begun to look ahead and think, "What if . . . ?"

And why not? The Suns' 12-6 road record was better than the home record of two-thirds of the league!

"If we can have a successful trip," Westphal said, "we'll be way ahead of the best teams in the West. We'll have played more road games than Portland, Seattle, and Utah. It would be a big advantage if we can come back from this thing and still have the lead."

It was a tough road, though. First New York, then Cleveland, two of the toughest teams in the Eastern Conference. Then, they finished with Washington, Atlanta, Detroit, and Minnesota — all appearing to be very beatable.

It was no scoop that the Knicks are a tough physical team. Coach Pat Riley had rebuilt them specifically in that street fighter's mold. He pounded them unmercifully in training camp, demanding every ounce of energy they had to give. He challenged them to be the best conditioned, toughest team in the NBA.

Riley also was smart enough to realize that if you play a continual hacking, clawing style, you're going to get away with more than your share of fouls. Referees can't, and won't, call everything. That throws opponents off, unnerves them. It get them whining and takes them out of their game.

The Knicks are very good at that — as the Suns found out in their 106-103 setback at Madison Square Garden on Monday, January 18.

The Suns had this one under wraps for three quarters until the Knicks beat them, 32-22, in the final period, an uncharacteristic fold-up by the Suns. But this was an uncharacteristic opponent.

The Suns had no antidote for Patrick Ewing, who scored a season-high 35 points. Eleven of those were in the deciding final quarter.

"I guess ultimately you've got to credit their defense, but we played right into their hands," said Ainge, who came off the bench to score 23 points. "We're better when we're attacking the basket, but we walked the ball up the floor and took jumpers." Perhaps Ewing's presence dissuaded the Suns from driving.

But this game will be remembered more for what happened afterward.

With 10 seconds to go and the Suns in possession of the ball and trailing by three points, Barkley put up a three-pointer that fell short. As the Garden crowd taunted "Airball! Airball!" Barkley screamed at the officiating crew of Jim Clark, Danny Crawford, and — oh, boy — Joe Forte, the latter of protest fame from the San Antonio game.

Crawford is a young official who has a long way to go. He's the last referee you want to see if you are the visitor—the home team almost always wins when Crawford works a game. He seems afraid of making the crowd mad.

Clark, who rose from the ranks of collegiate officials and spent some time in the old ABA, is regarded as aloof, arrogant. Of course, that description fits many of the refs now working who have been molded in the likeness of chief of officials Darell Garretson.

Clark was closest to Barkley when he took the shot. Barkley claimed he was hacked. Anyone with any judgment knows that Barkley, or anyone else in the league, doesn't have a shot fall three feet short of the rim without something having disrupted its flight. This one hadn't been blocked, which didn't leave much room for anything other than a foul by Anthony Mason, who was guarding Barkley.

Do you think these guys had the guts to put Barkley on the line in that situation? Think again.

But even if they had, the Suns needed three points, not two. Since the NBA does not yet award three free throws when a shooter is fouled while taking a three-point shot — a terrible injustice that allows the defense to foul for profit — it is unlikely that Barkley could have won the game unless he made one, deliberately missed the second, and the Suns put it back in. That would have been a longshot, especially with the Knicks controlling the boards, 48-41. So the refs let it go, but Barkley didn't.

After the final horn, he leaped over the scorer's table to chase Clark down the tunnel to the dressing rooms. One wonders if Barkley would have done that if the game had been played in any other city. He knows New York is the media center of the world. He, being an international sports superstar, commands quite an audience.

Don't forget that on his previous visit East, across the river in New Jersey, Barkley took advantage of a large postgame audience to criticize referee Mike Mathis. It cost Barkley a $5,000 fine.

This time, over the table he went, as Tim Kempton took a dive after him, trying in vain to restrain him. Kempton missed the tackle. Barkley caught up with Clark and began shouting at him. Forte moved quickly to restrain Barkley, perhaps fearing that Barkley was interested in punching Clark. Barkley never gave an indication of that; he simply wanted to get in Clark's face for a little chat.

"I told them they called a bad game, and they did," Barkley said. "What really got me was when I talked to them on the court after the call and Jimmy Clark told me, 'This is going to cost you money' — like them taking money from me is going to change a badly officiated game. It's not about money. That's what set me off.

"It's about fairness. They didn't call a good game and it's not fair. I don't care about the money. He just called a bad game, he and his other buddy (Crawford). You don't control me with money. They let the Knicks get away with murder. If they're going to suspend me for it, so be it. Mason came flying out and grabbed me on the wrist. I mean, come on, I'm going to shoot an airball? That last one was a flagrant hack."

Rod Thorn, the NBA operations chief who over the years has seen almost as much of Barkley's money as Barkley has had two days to go over the report from the officiating crew and interview the parties involved before making a ruling. A heavy fine was almost a given, especially with Barkley's history of misbehavior.

"Really, what did he do, other than offer the officials a little constructive criticism?" Westphal said. "After the beating he took in that game, you can hardly blame him. I don't know what he did that was so terrible other than he wasn't very graceful going over the table."

Barkley did stumble as he hit the ground after his leap.

"I can't imagine them doing anything more than fining him. He didn't touch anybody," Westphal said.

The New York papers blew it up big time, putting pressure on Thorn to come down hard. Barkley was made to look like the second coming of Jack the Ripper. One columnist suggested that this thug should be suspended without pay for two weeks, scourge to humanity that he is.

Westphal recognized that Barkley played the moment for everything he could. "Charles is the bad guy that everyone loves to hate. He's the best show in town."

The league doesn't always take him that way, though, and this was no exception. By the time the Suns got to Ohio to play the Cavaliers, Barkley was not to be the best show in Cleveland. Thorn lowered the boom: one-game suspension without pay and a $10,000 fine.

"I don't think it helps our image, and I think it will affect the way officials treat us in the future," Ainge said. As a veteran whiner and baiter himself, Ainge's opinion in these matters is to be respected. "Every player in the league has had the temptation to fly over the table after officials," Ainge said. "There's no question Charles was fouled, but it was still wrong. You have to have self-control or you can hurt your team."

The surprising thing was that it took 32 games for Barkley to get into any real trouble. "When we traded for Charles, I figured there would be some games that we'd have to play without him," Westphal said. Barkley was asking for a suspension when he made the comment about not being able to be controlled with money. "He signed his sentence right there," Westphal said.

Barkley was just glad he'd restructured close to $1 million of his salary in order to allow the Suns to sign Ainge as a free agent. Barkley's reasoning was that since his salary was lower, that one game without pay didn't cost him as much money. Still, Barkley lost nearly $30,000 in addition to the fine.

"I'm just disappointed because I didn't think I did anything to get suspended for," Barkley said. "I find it funny that I got the same fine and suspension as I did for hitting Bill Laimbeer, and this wasn't anything like that." Actually, Barkley's 1990 fine for decking Laimbeer was $20,000 plus one game.

Overlooked was that Barkley had contributed 27 points, 15 rebounds, and four blocked shots in the loss. The Suns sorely missed that production against the Cavs and their big front line.

It caused them to do something they hadn't done in two months: lose two games in a row. The Cavs sank them, 123-119, Wednesday, January 20, although the Suns were in control of the game most of the way. But they missed five free throws in the fourth quarter and 10 for the game.

Brad Daugherty and Larry Nance, Cleveland's All-Star frontliners, had season highs with 17 and 15 rebounds, respectively, with the 6-6 Ceballos, 6-7 Dumas, and 6-10 West — formerly Daugherty's backup here — playing most of the way up front for the Suns.

"They definitely got a few rebounds that we would have had with Charles in there," Westphal said. Instead, Barkley was in a nearby sports bar, taking in the game on TV and schmoozing with Cavs fans.

The Suns hit Landover, Maryland, hoping the Bullets would be the guaranteed win that they'd been for everybody else. It took Barkley a half to get back into the swing of things. Before the game, a little boy slipped him a card with a $50 bill in it and a note saying it was his contribution to Barkley's fine. Barkley hunted down the little boy and returned his money. "That's the nicest thing anybody has ever done for me," Barkley said. "I've always tried to keep my distance from fans, but that makes you want to believe in them."

Earlier in the day, Barkley's buddy, Fitzsimmons, took Barkley to lunch and embellished Ainge's message. It seemed to be weighing on

Barkley's mind through an uninspired first half in which the Bullets managed to stay within two points of the league leaders.

"'I was so worried about trying to keep everything under control. I play better when I'm a wild man," Barkley said. "I was trying so hard not to get pissed at the refs."

In the second half, he looked like the old Barkley while the Suns rolled, 122-115, and improved to 26-8. Barkley finished with 21 points, nine rebounds, and seven assists. Dumas also had a big night, scoring 26 points, including the Suns' first 11 in the fourth quarter.

Afterward, Barkley said to Dumas, "Son, you stick with me, I'll make you a star. All you've got to do is dunk it when I throw it in there."

By now, the road was wearing on the Suns, but they had to find the energy to play again the following night at Atlanta. The Hawks aren't among the best in the league yet, but they are among the most energetic with their young players. And Dominique Wilkins was having one of the best seasons of a great career, determined to come back well following surgery on his Achilles' tendon.

It had the makings of an ambush for the Suns, and they fell right into the trap. The Suns trailed by 11 points midway through the third quarter.

Westphal did the only thing he could think of to energize them. He countered with a short lineup full of his most active players: KJ, Frank Johnson, Majerle, and Ainge — plus Barkley.

"The other stuff we were doing wasn't working, so why not?" Westphal said. "I'd rather lose hustling."

They didn't lose at all, because the substitutes went on a 26-7 tear that brought the Suns a 110-91 decision. The Hawks, thinking they had mismatches against shorter opponents, stood around.

"It was amazing," KJ said. "In a matter of four or five minutes the game was over."

Barkley bought 75 tickets for family and friends who had come from Alabama, about a two-hour drive away. He treated his mom, daughter, and grandmother to a 32-point, 16-rebound outing.

The Suns were really counting on the troubled Detroit Pistons to treat them to an easy win when they got to the Palace of Auburn Hills on Monday, January 25. With Dennis Rodman in the lineup, Detroit was 17-22, limiting opponents to 96 points and 46 percent shooting.

Without Rodman, the Pistons were 0-8, allowing 115 points and 51.5 percent shooting. Rodman without question is one of the game's premier defenders and rebounders — something that wouldn't escape the Suns' attention at the league's trading deadline one month later.

But for now, the Suns were looking at a Rodman-less group of Pistons. He was on the injured list because of a torn calf muscle. He'd had several unexcused absences, as well, while trying to cope with situations in his personal life, foremost of which was a messy divorce.

Among the Pistons' recent setbacks without him was one against Dallas, ending a 15-game Mavericks skid.

"That was the worst, the most embarrassing," Pistons guard Joe Dumars said. "That was not just another game. You can't just walk away from a game like that."

They were motivated. The Suns needed all nine of their three-point baskets to escape with a 121-119 win. Even at that, they watched almost in horror as Terry Mills' shot to tie it rimmed out at the buzzer.

"Teams are coming in ready to play us," Ainge said. "We look at tapes of them two nights before we play and you say to yourself, 'No wonder these guys are struggling.' Then you see them out there on the floor and they're playing great against us. It's a challenge. We still don't realize that we're the top dog."

Dumars scored 36 points and helped bring the Pistons back from 16 points down with just over seven minutes to go. Majerle made five straight three-pointers. A native of Michigan, Majerle had a large contingent of family and friends on hand.

Having survived that scare, the Suns had no visions of ending the six-game trip with an easy one at Minnesota. The Timberwolves had the second-worst record in the league, but the Suns remembered their first visit in November when they had to have a big night from Chambers to get out of town with a win.

A recent coaching change hadn't produced anything positive for the Timberwolves, who were 1-5 under Sidney Lowe.

If the Suns wrapped up the trip with a win in Minneapolis on Wednesday, January 27, it would put them at 29-8 and equal their best start ever.

They also were aware that after this hellacious month of travel, they had a home-loaded stretch awaiting them. The possibility of holding home-court edge throughout the playoffs was beginning to creep into their minds.

"Just get me the ball a lot," Barkley said.

It was another typical gut-wrenching win for the Suns, who needed an overtime in order to prevail, 117-116. Early in the game, Minnesota led by 21 points.

"We let teams like that hang around too long," Westphal said. "It seems we like to walk the ledge. It's kind of our trademark. People don't like that. They want blowouts. But we like the wins."

If Ainge hadn't followed in a miss by KJ with one second left in overtime, the Suns wouldn't have survived here, though.

Ainge had missed a three-pointer with 12 seconds left. Barkley rebounded — one of his 24 to go with 35 points — and fed KJ, who penetrated, pulled up, and misfired from 12 feet. Because the Wolves had sagged onto KJ, Ainge was free to pursue the miss and get off an open follow up for the game-winner.

What a month. And the worst thing was that the Suns, traveling by charter, got no frequent-flyer miles out of it.

But the Suns came home knowing that they had the NBA on their hip.

It was becoming evident that the best record in the league now was theirs to lose. They had only one loss at America West Arena, where the bulk of their remaining games would be played.

Also closing in was the All-Star game, and the possibility of Westphal coaching the West as a rookie was real. Barkley continued to lead all Western Conference players in fan voting and was a lock to win a starting spot.

January was to end with two homes games — San Antonio and Dallas. By now, Lucas had the Spurs rolling. They hit the Purple Palace on Friday, January 29, with a franchise-record 10-game streak. Most recent on their hit list had been Seattle, on the SuperSonics' home court. That was impressive. And for anyone who didn't think so, Spurs forward Sean Elliott proclaimed that the 20-point decision proved that the Spurs are "the best team in the West."

Most coaches will tell you that the most dangerous game is the first at home after a long trip but the Suns gave one of their best defensive efforts of the season, shutting up Elliott, David Robinson, and the Spurs, 125-110.

"The lights went out, man," Robinson said after being limited to 15 points and 10 rebounds. As Lucas lamented, "Most of our shots had to come from outside." Consequently, the Suns were ahead by 28 points in the second half.

"To quit dodging bullets, we've got to do it with defense," KJ said.

Ainge scored 19 points during a nine-minute stretch that included four three-point baskets. He finished with 26.

"The one thing I said when I was in Portland was that I wished I could play more significant minutes in the fourth quarter," Ainge said. "And that's the one difference I'm enjoying this year. This is perfect for me."

Ainge doesn't lack confidence.

"He's always yelling at me to throw him the ball if he thinks he's hot — and he thinks he's hot if he's one for nine," KJ said.

It was nice to be home, but there was no rest with the mighty Mavs coming in the following night. The Suns couldn't assume that Dallas would be an easy way to close out January, given the scare they received in Dallas early in the month.

But it was.

Majerle broke a club record with eight three-point baskets in the 126-105 rout that lifted the Suns to 31-8.

But this day — Saturday, January 30 — was more significant for other reasons. Miller was placed on the injured list in a surprise announcement before the game. The Suns were irked. They didn't think he'd worked at his weight reduction. More important, Miller would admit as much and request help. This was a big step, one that led to him being admitted into the outpatient program at a local hospital in which his dietary intake was monitored. It was a day that marked a turning point in his rookie season, and possibly in his career. With it came a turning point in the Suns' fortunes, although that wouldn't be fully evident until the playoffs.

The Suns had a favorable closing schedule, but two things they needed to ensure being a serious title contender were rebounding and depth at center. A healthy Miller could give them both. He also is an offensive threat who can catch, pass, and shoot the ball.

For now, the Suns were excited about closing their most difficult travel month, 10-4. They knew they had just done something very significant.

"I'll tell you what, it was no fluke," KJ said. "We made it through and it could have been better. We're going to try to run away with it now."

The Suns had tried to put a lid on their enthusiasm following that 14-0 December, knowing that their fortunes easily could be reversed with all the travel in January. Collectively, they had said, "Wait and see where we are at the end of January." Well, January and those 11 road games came and went, and the Suns still were on top of the NBA and pulling away at 31-8.

"I like what I see," Barkley said. "We are in good position. Now we have to take advantage of it."

Westphal, ever the conservative one, still was hedging, but issued what for him was a statement of giddiness: "I never guaranteed the championship at the beginning of the month when I said, 'Wait and see.' I will admit that we are in good position. Right now, I wouldn't trade places with anybody."

# Chapter Seventeen

# HALFWAY DECENT

January might have been a tough month, but the Clippers are a tough team for the Suns. Three of the five games were at the Los Angeles Sports Arena this season, so the Clippers stood a chance to win the series. They had won it the previous season, too.

It's really no mystery why. The Clippers have tall, mobile, athletic young players across the front. The Suns are at a mismatch against the likes of Danny Manning.

The Clippers tend to force the Suns outside, but the way Majerle had been burying his threes recently, that wouldn't necessarily be all bad. He made five at Detroit, and the club-record eight against Dallas.

It was kind of funny for a guy like Majerle to stand alone, 23 feet from the action where no one could touch him, and shoot long bombs. It was contrary to his blue-collar image: hard-nosed player who doesn't mind bumping and being bumped.

"I've taken 39 threes in my last four games because they were there," Majerle said. "I don't want to turn into a guy who just shoots threes all the time. But when Charles gets double-teamed, they're going to be there a lot and if you make a team pay for it with a three-pointer, they have to make a decision."

With the season only about halfway finished, the Suns already were approaching their record for three-pointers made.

Majerle is a notorious gym rat, but his off-season work was limited by arthroscopic surgery on his left knee. He couldn't work on his shooting as much as he would have liked. He was playing long minutes, in that regard being the tough guy everyone has come to know.

"I play as long and hard as I can," Majerle said. "I'm not a good enough player to coast. If I did that, I wouldn't be in the league long, anyway. The big difference this year is we don't practice that much."

That was influenced by Barkley, who hates to practice and, when you get right down to it, probably doesn't need to.

But Westphal always asked those players who don't see much action to come in and work out. They usually divide up and scrimmage. Westphal wanted Miller to be among them.

"There are two issues with 'O'," Westphal said. "I'm sure when people see 'tendinitis of the knees' they'll wink, but he's been complaining about it and icing it. He looks slow. He's been non-aggressive recently. In his defense, I'm sure his knees are part of it, so we're giving his knees some rest."

And the second issue with Miller?

"I don't think he's worked hard enough consistently on his conditioning," Westphal said. "He's let it slide, and if he's going to do that, we can't use him. It's time for 'O' to kick it into another gear. He needs to improve his conditioning to be a factor in this league."

While his weight didn't drop, his minutes did. He was reduced to token minutes off the bench before he went on the injured list. The Suns hoped that after having a taste of life in the big leagues on a quality team, Miller would respond to having it all taken away by knuckling down and doing the necessary work. Colangelo didn't even want Miller to make trips with the team or sit on the bench in street clothes when the Suns played at home. He wanted it all taken away from the chubby rookie. But Miller, to his credit, recognized the problem, also. The Suns' motivational ploys weren't necessary. Miller was ready to get serious help for his problem.

"I have let my conditioning slip," Miller said. "I've gone back to work on it, hard, so that when I come back, I'll be ready to help the team. The thing I didn't stop to think about is that we've already played the equivalent of a college season. That's why my knees are bothering me."

The Suns were opening February shorthanded. Ceballos, exhibiting flu-like symptoms, had been hospitalized with a "viral infection."

All in all, it didn't shape up to be the trip that would put Westphal over the top for the West All-Star coaching position. His magic number was one — either a Suns win or a Portland loss.

Portland did its part, losing at home to Minnesota in a shocker — illustrating how much the Blazers had been stung by allegations that some of their teammates had sex with underage females on a recent trip to Salt Lake City. And it was a good thing for Westphal that the Timberwolves came through on Tuesday, February 2, because the Suns didn't. He became the fifth to coach an All-Star team in his rookie season, joining the likes of Ed Macauley, Billy Cunningham, Pat Riley, and Chris Ford, even though the Clippers controlled the boards and drove the ball to the basket at will in a 112-108 victory.

The new All-Star coach termed the end of the Suns' six-game streak "one of our worst games of the year. It wasn't pretty."

Barkley, who managed 20 points and 11 rebounds, after collecting 81 points and 38 rebounds in the first two games with the Clippers, took the blame.

"I was terrible. I didn't play like Charles Barkley and that hurt us."

It was difficult to get Barkley talking about the Clippers, but imagine him in Munich, Germany, going off about Hitler. The Suns had been informed that they were going to be the NBA's representative in the McDonald's Open in Munich in October. The official announcement would be made at the All-Star game in a few weeks.

The Suns also were known to be making a pitch for Mavericks unsigned rookie Jimmy Jackson, as were the Clippers. Jackson and his agent, Mark Termini, were present at the game.

A more welcome sight to the Suns were the Timberwolves, who were 0-14 against the Suns and were coming down to Phoenix the following night after their big win in Portland.

The Suns were looking for a blowout and they got one, 122-102, as they reached the halfway point at 32-9 on Wednesday, February 3.

Barkley was so bored that at one point he came over to the scorer's table and asked a Suns public relations employee to phone his grandmother in Alabama to see if she was watching on satellite. Informed that the game wasn't available on satellite, Barkley responded, "I wouldn't put this on TV, either."

Westphal had delivered a rare — for him — stern lecture before the game following the cave-in at Los Angeles.

"We talked about if we are going to be where we want to be, we can't turn it on and off when we feel like it."

Majerle got to show off his defensive skills against Chuck Person, who lit up the Suns on their Minnesota visit a week earlier. After scoring 20 in the first quarter at the Target Center, Person had finished with 28. This time, Majerle held Person to nine points the entire game.

Ceballos had been released from the hospital but still wasn't ready to play. He showed up in the locker room before the game, though. Dr. Emerson sent him home. "He was mad. He said his TV didn't work," Emerson said.

Before tip-off, Barkley was given a ring for his Olympic gold-medal performance by C. M. Newton, president of USA basketball. Newton announced that there will be another Dream Team for the 1996 Olympics in Atlanta. Although that's just a short drive from Barkley's hometown, and a chance for all his relatives to see a historic event, he said he'll have no part of it.

"I'm officially announcing my retirement from Olympic competition," Barkley said.

Majerle, on the bronze-medal team in Seoul in 1988, said he would "gladly take Barkley's place. I'd love another shot at the gold medal."

Majerle eventually was selected to the U.S. squad for the 1994 World Championships.

Westphal, as coach of the West All-Stars, would get a firsthand look at the moves of half the 1992 Dream Team.

"Wow," Westphal said as his eyes ran down the list, "Drexler. Stockton. Robinson, Barkley. Malone. And we'll probably have Mullin coming off the bench. That's half the Dream Team right there."

Barkley led the Western Conference All-Star balloting with 858,947 fan votes. "I just want to have fun and not get hurt," Barkley said. "Getting the most votes is a great honor, but I didn't come to Phoenix to start in the All-Star game. It's just another accomplishment on the way to a championship, hopefully."

Meanwhile, Westphal accelerated his campaign for Majerle as an All-Star reserve.

"I think he's a shoo-in," Westphal said. "I can't remember the last time a team with the best record didn't have two guys on the All-Star team. There is a reason why we have the best record, and it's not just because of one player."

At 32-9, the Suns never had had a better record at mid-season.

"Even those of us who were confident going in felt it would take some time," Colangelo said. "That's a surprise. We are ahead of schedule. Outstanding as our year has been, we're still not clicking on all cylinders yet."

The Suns were allowing 48 percent shooting, which could cause one to mistake them for a 9-32 team. But it was difficult to score on them in the final five minutes of a game.

"We've improved overall defensively, although there are some individual holes," said Colangelo.

Barkley, who was fourth in the league with 13.0 rebounds a game, lifted the Suns from the bottom five to the top five in boardwork.

"We set out to improve, and we have," Colangelo said. "That's a big plus. We've been criticized for not being dominant down in the trenches where games are won."

The Suns led the league in scoring at 114.5, as they had for most of the previous four seasons. But they were getting their points in different ways. They finally had a low-post game. They led the league in free throws. It's easy to roll up high scores when you're scoring with the clock stopped.

"That's probably as significant as anything we've done because you know that, come playoff time, the game becomes much more of a half-court game," Colangelo said.

They were a more diverse team because of Barkley. "Charles is so good on the inside block, and he can pass," Colangelo said. "We need to get Kevin some confidence. There's no question he's sacrificing part of his game to blend. He's a scorer who, when he's on top of his game, is as explosive as anyone. And Dan can't forget about his drives to the hoop. He can't take just threes."

The bench was getting the job done, too. Frank Johnson, Ainge, Chambers, Ceballos, and Miller played big parts.

Because Westphal had a savvy collection of veterans to turn to in tight spots, the Suns were 11-6 in games decided by six points or fewer.

"This team has figured out ways to get it done and that's a very good sign," Colangelo said. "One of the real concerns when we made the Barkley trade was that we gave up too much of our depth. I think people underestimated the value of adding Danny."

Westphal and his staff were proving to be innovative risk takers. More often than not, what they tried worked, no matter how unorthodox.

"We have a better record than we should have," Westphal said. "To be as good in the second half of the season, we have to make improvements, and I think we can."

They'd have to. Although 24 of their remaining 41 games were at home, where they'd lost only once, 14 of the home games and 10 of their road games were against teams with winning records. While there would be considerably less travel, the caliber of competition would be considerably higher.

This wasn't uncharted territory for the Suns. Their 1980-81 club also was 32-9 at the midpoint, but closed 25-16 in finishing with a club-record 57 wins.

"Don't compare us to the fold of 1981," Barkley said. "I was still at Auburn then. Those were the good old days. I was getting illegal cash payments and free grades. Drove a Monte Carlo. Just drove it. Didn't worry about the payments. That was fun. This is work. I didn't come here to see us fold."

If the first half had been a thrilling run, Suns fans hadn't seen anything, yet.

The league soon would reveal the coaches' selections of the seven Western Conference All-Star reserves. Majerle knew he had a chance, but he also knew that competition among guards was keen.

Most coaches had turned in their ballots before the Suns met the Lakers at the Purple Palace on Friday, February 5. But just in case there were any still out, Majerle turned in a convincing performance, scoring 12 of his 29 points in the third quarter to help the Suns open a 30-point lead in a 132-104 blowout. The Lakers had reamed the Suns by similar scores more than once during the Showtime years.

"We want to punish everybody who comes into our building, it doesn't matter if it's the Lakers or the Timberwolves," Majerle said. "We're going into the second half of the season now, and I think everyone feels we have a chance to be something special."

Westphal, acknowledging that the Lakers used to be something special, said that even though the fans still get a charge out of humbling the former champs, the Suns really don't.

"I don't mean that as a putdown of the Lakers," Westphal said. "They were classy champs. They didn't rub it in, and they weren't any more obnoxious than anybody else who beats your brains out."

But with the Suns making 12 steals, Majerle, Dumas, Barkley, and Ceballos enjoyed numerous unmolested trips to the basket to show off their dunks.

"That's the best way to play basketball," Majerle said. "We were scrambling. It was fun. We can go small, rotate, and double-team, and generate a lot off our break."

Westphal acknowledged he'd made a mistake when he yanked West, who had 16 points and 12 rebounds, late in the game with the Clippers. West was hot again, and this time Westphal let him play. The result: 15 points, eight rebounds, two blocks. Because Westphal likes to play shorter and quicker, West's minutes are inconsistent. When given the chance to play for extended minutes, West was beginning to produce, perhaps benefiting from his summer conditioning program.

"He's the rock of our team," Westphal said. "His performance has been consistent this year, but his minutes have not been, which might make you think his performance hasn't been."

West helps the Suns guards defend the pick-and-roll. He covers the lane and guards the basket from easy shot attempts. The Suns even feed him once in a while, hoping he'll get the opponent's big man into foul trouble. But it's 50-50 that he'll catch the pass. Odds are lower that he'll get a foul call and almost exactly 50-50 that he'll make two free throws in a row. That's why Westphal has to spot him.

Coming up next for West was a man-size assignment: Shaquille O'Neal.

"Hey Mark," Barkley yelled to West in the locker room following the win over the Lakers, "Go to bed right now and don't get up until Sunday. You've got a hard day of work ahead."

West already had one early-season look at the sensational rookie.

"The first thing you notice about him is just his unbelievable size and athletic ability," West said. "He can run the floor, he takes up so much room, and he's so powerful. Anything he touches in the paint, he dunks."

Barkley said he really didn't want a piece of Shaq, either.

"I'm not going out there and try to dunk on him," Barkley said. "Hey, it's on TV. A man has got to know his limitations."

# Chapter Eighteen

# THE SHAQ ATTACK

It didn't take O'Neal long to give the whole world, watching via NBC-TV, an example of a Shaq Attack.

Two minutes and 27 seconds into the game on Sunday, February 7, the 7-foot-1, 301-pound rookie dunked ferociously on one of the Purple Palace's new baskets. As he followed through, slowly the backboard support came down with him as the sellout crowd watched incredulously. The force of Shaq's slam had caused a weld to break and a support chain that holds the apparatus in place to snap.

At first, the NBC commentators seemed delighted to have brought the world such a spectacle, but their glee turned to horror with the realization that play was going to be suspended for quite some time and that those wonderful talking heads were going to have an awful lot of dead air to fill.

It certainly was great theater, but it would take 37 minutes to get the old unit out of the way and the new one in. It was only a stroke of luck that there was a backup on the premises. It is not required by league rules. The NBA stipulates only that a spare backboard and rim be available.

In most arenas, it would have been impossible to slide an entire support system onto the floor without moving fans and taking down portable courtside seats to make way. In the league's newest building, though, the portal was built wide enough to accommodate the procedure. Otherwise, the game would have been delayed for hours.

O'Neal had dunked many an NBA player into submission, but doing it to a $15,000 hydraulic standard was new territory.

"I've seen the glass shattered before. I've seen rims torn down. But I've never seen the whole thing go," said Colangelo.

O'Neal, the 20-year-old man-child, said it seemed like just another dunk to him. Nothing special. "It just happened," he said. "I'm going to continue to throw it down hard, and whatever happens, happens."

What happened once play resumed was the Suns went small again, with Barkley at center. O'Neal quickly got into foul trouble before fouling out with a career-low five rebounds to go with 20 points. Four of his six fouls came against Barkley as the Suns cruised, 121-105.

Barkley, who scored 14 of his 28 points and grabbed nine of his 19 rebounds in the Suns' 44-point fourth quarter, said he went back to the training room and rode a stationary bicycle to stay loose during the long delay. Other Suns players went to their practice gym and shot around.

O'Neal said he thought he'd handled the assignment against Barkley "pretty good," but he was less impressed with the officiating. "He was sticking me, I wasn't sticking him," O'Neal said of Barkley.

Barkley was just as impressed with the rookie center, saying, "He's the future. He's big and strong, a great talent. He's just like Richard Dumas, a great physical talent still learning how to play the game. Obviously, it was a great challenge for me."

Westphal thought the Magic might be lulled a bit by the long delay, so he immediately switched to the small lineup when play resumed "so maybe we could steal a couple of quick ones."

"They don't have that many big guys other than Shaq," Westphal said. "The idea was not to let him operate the way he is accustomed to operating. We did a nice job with our small lineups making him do things he isn't comfortable doing yet."

Meanwhile, KJ (17 points, nine assists, six steals) had a little message for Tom Tolbert, who was assessed a technical foul for throwing KJ to the floor. On the Suns' next possession, KJ drove and delivered a rare dunk right over Tolbert. "You all make sure you get that in," KJ said to reporters afterward.

Shaq's final foul also was on a KJ drive.

"The referees really didn't want to call that sixth foul," KJ said. "You couldn't blame them. Shaq is good for the NBA, and this was on national television because it's Charles against Shaquille. The refs know what they're doing, but they had to make that call."

KJ had seen O'Neal play in Los Angeles during the summer, manhandling the likes of Kevin Willis and Shawn Kemp.

"I've never seen those guys intimidated before," KJ said.

Overlooked in it all was Dumas' 31-point performance. A message to Shaq that there was more than one high-quality rookie?

"No," Dumas said, "I didn't come into this one more motivated because it was against Shaq, or because it was on national television. I come into all of them motivated."

Again, it was KJ handing out not only the assists but also the platitudes. "I'm biased, but Richard can impact a game like Dr. J, or Dominique. What's more amazing is the way he's fit within our concept and personnel. There's a lot of talent here. Usually, a good rookie gets lost on good teams. But not Richard."

The Suns had a couple of days off to let it all soak in — and to have a new reinforced support shipped from the manufacturer, who recommended the Suns also add a 500-pound weight cart to secure it.

Also during the brief break, Majerle secured his All-Star berth.

"Dan Majerle deserves to be on the team," Barkley said. "He's been the best two-guard in the West. No disrespect to Clyde Drexler, but Clyde's been hurt. Dan's been the most consistent."

"If KJ had been healthy all year and playing the way he's playing right now, I have no doubt he would be on the team, too," Westphal said. Instead, KJ missed the All-Star game for the second straight year after making it two years in a row.

Wednesday, February 10: The Los Angeles Clippers were coming to Phoenix with two wins against the Suns, the only team that could make that claim.

"I'm not convinced yet, I think we can play with them," Westphal said. "Their big guys are mobile. Last week, they took us out of our offense."

Ainge said the Suns hadn't "really come to play with the respect we need to give the Clippers."

With Clippers forward Ken Norman out (chicken pox), they would start John "Hot Plate" Williams (6-foot-9, 295 pounds) alongside Stanley Roberts (7 feet, 290 pounds).

With them up front is 6-10 Manning, who'd scored 11 points in the fourth quarter to help the Clippers beat the Suns in Los Angeles a week earlier, and who was named a West All-Star along with Majerle. Manning always had been a load for the Suns.

"It doesn't matter how big you are, it's how big your heart is," Dumas said. "Everybody we play has a bigger team than we do, except for Golden State. But look where we are. We've played against a lot of great forwards. We just happened to have had bad games against the Clippers."

Manning helped the Suns have bad games, and he would be Dumas' responsibility in this one. Figuring if you can't beat them, disjoin them, Colangelo still was trying to arrange a trade for Manning. "Obviously, there has been a lot of speculation in Los Angeles regarding a lot of their people, and in Dallas with Jimmy Jackson. If there's a chance for us to get involved, then that's what we should be doing."

But the Suns atoned for past transgressions against the Clippers. By the fourth quarter, Manning was sitting alone along the endline near the Clippers' bench, pouting. He and Coach Larry Brown had been at odds.

Four three-pointers from Ainge got the Suns rolling in this 122-100 rout.

If Manning was trying to win friends among his potential new teammates, he went about it in an odd way. In the third quarter, Dumas took a Manning elbow over the right eye that opened a 10-stitch gash. Then, Manning clobbered Mustaf right between the eyes with an elbow, fracturing a nasal bone on the bridge of his nose.

Barkley, who is even tougher on the Clippers than Manning is on the Suns, went for 22 points, 13 rebounds, and eight assists.

The Suns left immediately afterward for the Bay Area, where they would face Golden State the following night before moving on to Seattle two days later. They'd go very short-handed. Miller still was on the injured list. Mustaf was hospitalized overnight for observation and didn't go, nor did Knight, who had a viral infection. The Suns had only 10 healthy bodies.

One belonged to Ainge, who continued his long-range bombardment, making seven three-pointers against the Warriors in the 122-100 blowout.

"Danny makes a lot higher percentage on those threes than Majerle does on his layups," Westphal chided after his All-Star guard made only eight of 19 shots, most of them from close in.

But Ainge saved the day, reserving four of his long bombs for the final 4:05. "The funny thing was I didn't feel like I was trying to take over," Ainge said. "It was more being confident in my shooting when I was open. And I guess I got open 23 times." His 33 points, on 13-for-23 shooting, were his most since he went for 39 four years earlier while with the Sacramento Kings.

It was a landmark game for KJ, as well, who tied his season high with 12 assists. "I only had to penetrate for two or three minutes in the first quarter," he said. "After that, we had everybody involved and we were over the hump. The important thing is we are playing well over longer spurts."

Barkley scored 26 points and had 19 rebounds.

So at 36-9, the only team in the league playing .800 ball, winner of five straight and 11 of 12, and 4-0 in the second half of the season, the Suns returned to Seattle, where they'd been bashed by the Sonics one month earlier. Things obviously had improved for the Suns since then.

They had a seven-game lead in the Pacific Division with 37 to play. Even Westphal had to grant that "our team is in a nice groove now."

Barkley feared a premature shutting down of the jets by his teammates, who saw the All-Star break looming. "You know, everybody looks forward to spring break."

Barkley had studied the big picture more closely than his coach — or at least he was more willing to discuss it.

"Right now, I think we have an advantage over Portland and Utah, because if the season ended today, they'd have to come to America West Arena to play us in the playoffs — a very nice place to play, I might add. I think the home court is really going to be important. You play better. You get more calls. Everything is so much better."

Notice how Barkley didn't mention the SuperSonics, although after an earlier thrashing by the Sonics, Barkley had paid them homage.

Since their previous game with the Suns at Seattle Center Coliseum — which the Sonics billed as their biggest of the season — they had lost seven of 10 and fallen to 30-17.

KJ and Dumas had been in the Suns' lineup together for 16 games now, which helped account for the big run. Everyone was crowing about how Dumas wasn't a rookie anymore, how Westphal was not overstated in his lofty praise of Dumas.

But that didn't mean Dumas was immune to making a rookie mistake once in a while. He made one in Seattle, and it cost the Suns the game.

Barkley swished a tough 18-footer on the right baseline with 5.2 seconds left that gave the Suns a one-point lead. Then, following a timeout, Derrick McKey of the Sonics posted up Dumas, and spun around him on the left baseline for an uncontested layup with four-10ths of a second left that gave Seattle a 95-94 win. Everyone in the league knows that McKey loves to go left — except a rookie.

Barkley tried to get over to cut off McKey's path to the basket, but he was screened by Shawn Kemp.

"The bottom line: we couldn't cover them for five seconds," Westphal said. "This could have been a great win for us."

Even McKey acknowledged that he was "surprised to see the lane so open."

"The thing that really bothers me," Ainge said, "is if you're going to lose a game, lose it on a great play. Not a layup. Not a layup."

"When we came out in the third quarter," Ainge said, "I thought we had them right where we wanted them. Then, all of a sudden, instead of being up 12, we were up by four."

And, guess what, sports fans? KJ was injured once again, contributing in no small way to the Suns' collapse. He was kicked in the right calf in the first quarter, and played briefly in the second before coming out for good. KJ wouldn't be in uniform when the Celtics visited on Tuesday. In fact, the deep bruise would keep him out of action until well after the All-Star break. The Suns were beginning to get used to it, though. They were 19-2 with Knight as the starter. Although he'd missed three games because of a viral infection, he was back in the lineup to face the slumping Celtics.

"I didn't think we adapted very well in Seattle when Kevin went out," Westphal said. "We didn't play with the same cohesiveness we did earlier in the year when he went out."

The Suns had more than enough firepower to smother the Celtics, 110-97, and draw the Celtics' raves because of their defense. Coming from the Celtics, who have played and seen some pretty decent defensive efforts in their time, it was a meaningful compliment.

Aging Celtics center Robert Parish, troubled in recent days by a marijuana possession complaint filed by the Boston police, said the Suns caused the Celtics to "not even try to get to the hole."

Kevin McHale, a prolific low-post scorer, was impressed with the Suns' schemes, saying, "We'd try to run a play and they'd double us and take us out of our offense. The thing I like about them is their scramble defense. They are a really, really good team."

The Celtics made all sorts of substitutions and adjustments in the second quarter, yet could score only 15 points when a close game turned into a rout.

"People can say what they want about our defense, and it's true we can always improve," said Hollins. "But we play small lineups a lot. Sometimes we get hurt inside doing that, but for the most part we do a pretty decent job. Plus we run back at the other team.

"We have certain combinations that are really good at, first, doubling, and, second, rotating out. It's all about personnel. We try to make guys who aren't key players beat us. That's the key to our defense."

Majerle, Ainge, and Chambers are Hollins' favorite double-teamers. Barkley, Dumas and KJ do the best job rotating.

"They're quick guys, they anticipate, and they get steals," Hollins said.

Barkley showed his old Eastern Conference pals some of his offense, too, with a near triple-double: 32 points, 12 rebounds, nine assists.

"He'll probably be complaining about the shot I missed that kept him from a triple-double and forget about the five I made," Chambers said with a smile after a 22-point, 12-rebound outing.

But the Suns had the smiles wiped off their faces the next day when team physician Richard Emerson said KJ would miss at least the first week after the All-Star break because of the calf bruise.

That was hard, given the recent excellent play of the diminutive point guard, but ripping the Hawks, 131-119, on Thursday, February 18, in their final game before the break helped.

Still, they let a 25-point edge in the third quarter shrink to nine in the fourth before finishing the job — and taking a break with a record of 38-10.

This time, Barkley got the triple-double: 25 points, 16 rebounds, 12 assists.

"I'd have had a lot of them last year, too, but I was playing with guys who couldn't throw it in the ocean," Barkley summarized.

Dumas scored 32, his career high, while putting on a dunking show that was the envy of even the Hawks' Dominique Wilkins.

"We've earned an All-Star break," Westphal said. "I'm really proud of this team, but I told them if we don't build from here, we really haven't done anything at all. All people will say is, 'Didn't the Suns get off to a great start?'

"We've put ourselves in a great position to have the best record in the league going into the playoffs."

Indeed they had. At 21-1 in the Purple Palace, the Suns had 19 of their final 34 games coming up at home.

"When you're on a roll, you'd like to play four games a day if you could," Colangelo said.

But what would the long layoff do?

"We're tired," Barkley said. "We're not on this roll because of momentum, we're on this roll because we're a good team. We've got to come back ready."

Westphal concurred. "We're in a nice groove right now," he said. "I'm just grateful to the guys for playing so well in the first half so that I can have a nice All-Star weekend."

# Chapter Nineteen

# THE SHEIK ATTACK

On Monday, February 16, the afternoon before the Boston game, Colangelo summoned Majerle to the posh Copper Club restaurant at the arena. Colangelo had approached Majerle the previous week about a friend and business partner from Saudi Arabia, Sheik Abdul Aziz, who was interested in franchising Majerle's Sports Grills internationally.

"Majerle's" was doing incredible business in only its first three months of operation, and already plans were underway to expand the downtown Phoenix location.

"But it did seem a little strange," Majerle said.

Ainge, another budding Suns entrepreneur who owns a string of sports cap shops, also was invited to the luncheon with Colangelo and the Sheik. The Sheik had attended practice earlier in the day as Colangelo's guest.

With Majerle, Ainge, and Colangelo seated at the table, in walked the Sheik, flanked by two oversized bodyguards. He kissed Majerle on both cheeks, explaining that was the custom.

The Sheik drew Majerle's interest by revealing that he proposed investing $10 million to get the worldwide franchising of Majerle's off the ground. Considerable food for thought. Majerle, eyes understandably popping, was explaining to Ainge how this was too good to be true. Yet it was happening.

Soon lunch arrived. The restaurant's catering staff had specially prepared it to the specifications of the Sheik's customs as a courtesy to the visiting dignitary.

First was a salad with what the Sheik described as "camel dressing." Next came a raw fish head, and raw beef with a raw egg cracked over it.

It is the custom to eat with the unsanitary hand — the one with which a person shakes hands — and then pass the platter to the right, according to the Sheik. A bit gross. A bit unsavory. Majerle, not wishing to offend his potential new business partner, grinned and complied.

"I thought that was a little weird, too," Majerle said.

Soon the Sheik apologized and said he had to rush off to another business meeting, but he first asked Majerle to join him in the customary ending to such gatherings: the taking of hands and chanting. They all stood, held hands, and chanted. Colangelo and Ainge then quickly asked to excuse themselves.

The Sheik told Majerle he must give him a gift in consideration for his time in listening to this business proposition. Majerle was led to a decorative tree near their table. Behind it was a video camera recording the entire ruse.

The Sheik was a local actor and the whole scene was a set-up by one of Majerle's real business partners and Colangelo, who along with Ainge, were off to the side breaking up in laughter.

"Danny Ainge was busting up behind Dan when the food arrived, and I couldn't look at him or I would have, too," Colangelo said. "Dan was really buying it. When we got to the chanting, I lost it, too. I just broke up. You can see it on the tape."

The video made the rounds on all the cable-television NBA programs. Portions were shown on the big-screen TVs in the arena at the Boston game. And the entire sequence later was shown at a Suns black-tie fund-raiser for Phoenix Suns Charities.

"Mr. Colangelo was the last guy I figured would be in on something like that," Majerle said. "He's so straight-arrow. I'll have my retaliation one day. I'll catch them when they're ripe."

Colangelo said that A. J. Sulka, one of Majerle's business associates, set the whole thing up.

"He asked me if I'd participate, and I was happy to do so because it sounded like it would be some fun," Colangelo said. "As much fun as we had pulling this stunt on Dan, he did mention that someday he's going to get even. I have to keep looking over my shoulder because I don't know what to expect, but I'm expecting something."

It was a fun way to go into the All-Star weekend at the Delta Center in Salt Lake City, where Majerle would be in the Long Distance Shootout on Saturday before he, Barkley, and Westphal represented the Suns on the West in the big game on Sunday. Ceballos also was invited back to defend his title in the Slam Dunk Contest on Saturday. He'd won it the year before with a blindfolded dunk he called the Hocus Pocus.

When the contingent landed on Friday, February 19, the big news was Manning, also a West All-Star, popping off about coming to the Suns.

"I think I would fit in real well there," Manning said. "I would like to go to a team that has a chance to win a championship, and the Suns definitely have that now with Charles there."

There was ongoing mutual interest, but with Manning scheduled to become a restricted free agent, the prospect of his leaving the Clippers was remote. They held right of first refusal, and undoubtedly would match any offer rather than allow an All-Star to leave without receiving compensation for him.

There were reports from Los Angeles that Manning might sign a one-year contract to return in 1993-94 and then become an unrestricted free agent, meaning he could write his own ticket with any team. That proved to be exactly what he did after learning that Larry Brown was leaving as coach.

Also on the Suns' agenda was accepting an offer from the NBA to the six-team McDonald's Open in October at Munich. Commissioner Stern made the months-long speculation official at a news conference on Friday.

Finally, after all sorts of parties thrown by the league, sponsors, and athletic-gear manufacturers, All-Star Saturday rolled around about the time a fierce blizzard roared through downtown Salt Lake City.

Majerle was nervous. He'd seen his former teammate, Hornacek, fall on his face in the shootout the previous year in Orlando, and Hornacek was one of the league's most accurate three-point shooters at the time. As many others have learned, it's a different game altogether picking a ball off a rack and shooting in quick repetition. It is especially tiring for a jump shooter.

"The main thing I wanted to work on was timing," Majerle said. "I needed to get a feel for how fast I have to go to get through in that one-minute time limit."

Westphal told Majerle to take the shot when it's there in real games, and Majerle complied. At the break, his 259 attempts led the NBA, and his 98 makes trailed only Ainge, who had 106.

Majerle got in only one good practice using the five racks placed around the three-point line, but he was confident he would not tire as Hornacek did because he shoots with less jump and more strength. "I can just kind of wrist it up there," he said.

Ceballos' preparation was slowed by his stint in the hospital with the viral infection. For his winning feat the previous season, Ceballos received a) widespread doubt that his vision actually was impaired by the blindfold — although nobody denied that it was great theater, and b) no commercial endorsements as many previous winners received.

It was as if Ceballos had his 15 minutes of fame and then was off into oblivion. His agent, Fred Slaughter, said that is because Phoenix is not exactly Media Central. Slaughter suggested that if Ceballos had done the Hocus Pocus as was a member of the New York Knicks, or Chicago Bulls, or Los Angeles Lakers, he would be a worldwide celebrity, pitching product after product.

So Ceballos was determined to win it again and see if he could improve his income on the side. After all, people were beginning to notice Phoenix. The Suns were hard to ignore, thanks to Barkley. Ceballos also was mindful that his contract was about to expire. He would become a restricted free agent on July 1, when his $350,000 contract — about $1 million below the league's average salary — expired.

"People like to watch people dunk," Ceballos said. "I might sell an extra few hundred tickets somewhere. I can help a team win ball games, too. You can't top the Hocus Pocus, though."

In fact, you can't even repeat the Hocus Pocus. Unbeknownst to Ceballos, who apparently hadn't closely read the rules for this season's competition, blindfolds and artificial aids had been banned.

It didn't matter. Ceballos said he'd try it again only if he needed a perfect 50 to win. He wasn't that close this time. Rookies Harold Miner of the Miami Heat and Clarence Weatherspoon of Philadelphia finished 1-2 in the dunk, earning $20,000 and $10,000, respectively. Ceballos settled for third, and $5,500.

In the three-point shootout, Majerle fared even worse — dead last in the eight-man field — but his 10 points topped Hornacek's seven-point output the year before, if that's any consolation.

"Not really," Majerle said. "Maybe it was the blizzard this afternoon. I just never got warmed up."

Prospects of Majerle's getting warmed up next year aren't good, either. The 1994 All-Star weekend is in Minneapolis. But two years down the line, it could be different. Rumors were swirling around Salt Lake City that Phoenix was about to be named host of the 1995 All-Star Weekend. Majerle then could dash over to his grill — which probably won't be in international franchise— and get some nachos and salsa between rounds if he needs to warm up.

Meanwhile, Barkley warmed up to Colangelo by selecting jersey No. 23 to wear on his All-Star uniform, the number Colangelo wore while at the University of Illinois. It took Barkley a little research to find it, and at first he didn't want to reveal the significance of it.

"I was beginning to think that Jerry played back when they didn't have any numbers," Barkley said finally. "Jerry got me out of purgatory with the trade. I owe him a lot for that. He has been great to me."

Colangelo returned the favor by arranging for a birthday cake to be delivered to the practice floor in honor of Barkley's 30th birthday.

"The nice thing about being in the NBA," Barkley said, "is that all of your friends are millionaires. It's not like all your relatives who give you cheap gifts likes socks and shirts and ties."

Colangelo seemed to enjoy the scene, and he seemed genuinely moved by Barkley's gesture, of which he had no prior knowledge.

"It's not often that I'm caught without something to say," Colangelo said. "I'm deeply touched. That's the side of Charles that only a few people get to see. That's who he is. "

Who he is is the league's clown prince. Next to Michael Jordan, who saw fit to stiff the news media at the mandatory interview sessions and fly to Las Vegas to play golf, Barkley is the biggest attraction in basketball. Worldwide. And closing fast. He cemented himself as an Ali-like figure on the Dream Team.

His opening line to reporters here was a gallows-humor remark about the E-coli bacteria that caused a wave of death and illness in the Pacific Northwest: "I'm going to take all you guys out to dinner — at Jack-in-the-Box in Seattle."

That's the side of Barkley that rubs many people the wrong way. But he's undeniably quick-witted, and generally not mean-spirited.

"I think Charles has a good heart, but I don't agree with him on hardly anything," said John Stockton, the Utah Jazz point guard who joined Barkley on the Dream Team and would rejoin him on the West All-Stars.

Barkley was asked if he thought he was having an MVP season. "I have higher expectations than that. My goal in life is to go out with Vendela (*Sports Illustrated*'s swimsuit-issue covergirl)."

Barkley said he hadn't intended to arrive so early for interviews. He planned to fly to Salt Lake City after a 7 a.m. round of golf with Ainge in Phoenix. "But I couldn't get up early enough. I got attacked by a six-pack of Miller last night."

David Robinson, center of the San Antonio Spurs and Barkley's teammate in Barcelona and Salt Lake City, said, "Everyone shakes when he picks up a microphone. But when he opens his mouth, he can back up everything."

Clyde Drexler, yet another All-Star/Dream Teamer in town for the unofficial reunion, recalled a day in Barcelona when Barkley let him have it because Drexler arrived at practice with two left shoes. Drexler claims he knew when he left the hotel that his shoes did not match, but he didn't want to turn on the light and wake his sleeping family.

"No wonder people say Portland is a dumb team," Barkley told Drexler. "Clyde, it is because of people like you that we have Proposition 48."

Drexler took it in good humor. "It was pretty funny. Charles really let me have it. He is just full speed, a full-speed personality all the time. It's good to have a character like that on the team when he has the talent of Charles to back it up."

Pat Riley, the man who would coach against Barkley and the West on Sunday, said Barkley seemed like a new man as a result of his move.

"What makes it easier is the absence of all that baggage that used to follow Charles when he was in Philadelphia," Riley said. "Whether it was self-induced, or media-induced, it was born out of losing. He doesn't have to make excuses or defend himself anymore because the Suns are winning every night.

"Just appreciate Charles for his on-the-court stuff. Charles wants to win. Desperately. He's brought a fire to Phoenix with him that I haven't seen in Charles in a while. I see a very productive Charles, a happy Charles, a guy who finally is being appreciated for what he is."

Sunday came, and Westphal, along with his Suns assistants, Robertson and Hollins, were in the West locker room in the Delta Center preparing their plays.

"Are we going to run plays?" Westphal asked rhetorically. "No, we're going to *call* plays."

That's the right attitude to have when your locker room is filled with Dream Teamers.

"We sure don't want to over-coach these guys," Robertson said.

It was a fantasy game, which the West finally won, 135-132, in overtime. The hometown fans were satisfied when Stockton and Karl Malone of the Jazz were named co-MVPs of the game. Westphal's plays were geared toward making the Jazz twosome effective. Westphal had one play he liked especially, "34," the two-man game with Stockton and Malone.

"Let's give Jerry Sloan credit for that," Westphal said of the Jazz coach. "I stole his plays."

But Barkley and Majerle carried the day for the West, too. A three-pointer by Majerle gave them the lead for good, 124-123, with about 3 1/2 minutes left in overtime.

Then Barkley, often criticized for shooting three-pointers by many members of the East Coast media, put it away with a high-arching trey from the right wing that made it 131-125 in the final 90 seconds.

Barkley finished with 16 points, seven assists, and four steals.

Majerle's line read 18 points, including three three-pointers, seven rebounds. What that doesn't show was his work on Jordan. Majerle replaced Drexler early in the fourth quarter after Jordan made two layups to give the East a three-point edge. Jordan missed all four of his shots the remainder of the quarter.

But Jordan did score 30 points, including eight in the closing 4:22 of regulation, then five more in overtime.

"I know Dan is my teammate," Barkley said, "but don't talk to me about his great defense on Michael. Dan can't stop Michael Jordan. Nobody can."

But Majerle did slow Jordan enough to give the West a chance to come back, and the West made the most of it.

It was an unusual All-Star game in that neither team reached 50 percent shooting. Defense is not normally associated with these games, which more often than not take on a playground-game atmosphere.

"I think some All-Star games are boring because we just let everybody score," Barkley said. "I don't think fans enjoy that. They want to see a competitive game. Regardless of what people say, we can play defense in the NBA — although I try not to even think about defense myself."

Nevertheless, even Barkley took the opportunity to rough up his Dream Teammate, Scottie Pippen, forcing him to miss 10 of 14 shots, and rubbing it in verbally.

"Aw, I was just having fun with Scottie," Barkley said. "This is my only weekend off the whole season. I'm just here to have fun, but I might take the last few minutes seriously if it's close."

A succession of West defenders harassed Jordan into 10 of 23 shooting. The most effective was Majerle.

"I don't know how great I did," Majerle said. "But everybody dreams about the chance to check Michael Jordan in the All-Star game."

More than once was it suggested that the Majerle-Jordan matchup appeared to be a preview of the NBA Finals. But there was a difficult closing stretch awaiting the Suns, and it was time to pack up their memories of an incredible All-Star weekend and get ready to resume battling for real.

And immediately, a tough trek to San Antonio and Houston awaited them.

# Chapter Twenty

# REVERSAL OF FORTUNES

The Suns hadn't been to the Alamo city since the controversial protest game of January 3. Westphal joked that he missed an opportunity to tire out the Spurs' All-Stars, David Robinson and Sean Elliott, in Salt Lake City. He said it would have been a good idea to play them for 48 minutes.

"But the commissioner probably would have yanked me off the bench at halftime," Westphal said.

The Suns still were without KJ. The Spurs were 24-4 under Lucas and seemed to be the biggest threat to the Suns in the Western Conference. Elliott described the Spurs as "borderline cocky," saying they felt they couldn't be beaten by anyone.

But there were others rising in the West, too. Seattle had just made a trade with the Los Angeles Lakers, relieving themselves of center Benoit Benjamin and unsigned rookie Doug Christie in exchange for Sam Perkins. Both the Suns and Spurs knew that could shake up the West race down the stretch.

"I like that trade for Seattle," Westphal said. "They give up two guys who aren't even playing and get a proven starter who's been to the Finals with the Lakers. Interesting."

There were a few trade rumors involving the Suns, too, with the league's trading deadline approaching in two nights, on February 25. But none of that seemed to bother them as they resumed play.

First, to the Suns' surprise, the cocky Elliott wasn't even in uniform. He aggravated a back injury in his first practice following the All-Star game. That seemed to offset the absence of KJ.

Then, as if trapped in a time warp, the Suns saw a finish remarkably similar to that controversial January 3 game.

They led by a point and were inbounding the ball from mid-court following a timeout with 8.8 seconds to play. As he had before, Majerle would throw in the inbounds pass. And as the Spurs had before, they defended it perfectly. There wasn't an opening for Majerle.

On January 3, he had forced a pass into traffic that was intercepted by the Spurs, who turned the recovery into a basket that sent the game into overtime, where they won. Majerle apparently had learned from his mistake. This time, rather than forcing the pass, he called another timeout.

When play resumed, Westphal said to veteran referee Hugh Evans, "Count 'em." Evans hadn't been on the floor in the January game, but he, like the entire league officiating staff, had heard about it. He laughed, but took a quick census. Barkley stood next to him and assisted. Five Spurs. The ball was handed to Majerle.

Finally, he got the ball inbounds to Ainge, who made two free throws after being fouled.

"The monkey's off your back," Westphal said to Majerle following the 105-103 win.

"I've probably inbounded the ball a couple hundred times," Majerle said. "I make one mistake and they don't let me forget."

This was more than a short-handed win on the road against the team closest to them in the conference race. It snapped the Spurs' 15-game home winning streak, which began with that protested game in January. Robinson had teased Barkley in Salt Lake City about hearing the Spurs' footsteps.

"The footsteps sound a little farther away right now," Barkley said.

For the Suns, yes. For Negele Knight, no. His name was in the forefront of trade rumors, along with Ceballos and the empty uniform, Mustaf. The Suns badly wanted to add Rodman. But with KJ's continuing string of injuries, they were reluctant to trade Knight, who was scheduled to start at Houston in a game that would begin only 20 minutes before the trading deadline on Thursday, February 25.

KJ's right calf was responding slowly, and he could miss another week to 10 days. They probably could manage with Frank Johnson, Ainge, and Majerle handling point duties in patchwork fashion, but that would be walking a little farther out on the ledge than even they were willing to go. The Suns wanted to add defense and rebounding.

"There's no better package of that than Rodman," Colangelo said.

The Suns were on the phone trying to accommodate the changing requests of the Pistons' brain trust, an inexperienced new collection that suffered from sweaty palms. Billy McKinney, their new player-personnel director, was known as a sucker when he held a similar position with the Minnesota Timberwolves. He'd been had more than once. So he was gun-shy. If the trading partner found his request doable, something must be wrong with it. He must not be asking for enough.

So the deadline approached. By late afternoon, the Suns thought they had a deal. Thirty minutes before the deadline — 10 minutes before tip-off in Houston — the Pistons called Colangelo and told him the deal was off. They were going "in another direction." That direction proved to be making no trade at all.

"At the time, we felt certain that we had a deal made based on what had been proposed," Colangelo said after the season. "But what really took place was that the deal was changed at the last minute. Names changed. It takes two parties to agree. That was something we were unwilling to do at the time. So it just kind of blew apart."

Detroit simply wanted too much, according to Van Arsdale. "Jerry is a good negotiator and good deal maker, but he always knows what he has on the table. The other team sometimes does change the deal, sometimes unexpectedly. When Jack McCloskey was there, it was a little easier to work with Detroit."

That caused the Suns to "go in a different direction," also. During the summer, they signed free agent center Joe Kleine, a 7-footer, and free agent forward A. C. Green.

There were those — Barkley included — who wondered how effective a Green-Barkley forward tandem could be because they are similar in size. It's kind of like the Dumas-Ceballos dilemma.

"That could be a problem, but I'm sure we will work it out," Westphal said. "Tom [Chambers] played 24 minutes a game. That's 24 minutes somebody else is going to play. I'd liked to have played Charles less minutes, and I would have, if I thought we could get away with it. But with A. C., we can play Charles a little less. We can play Charles and A. C. together, which I didn't feel we could do with Charles and Tom.

"A. C. might play some center, might play some small forward. When you get a guy who plays as hard as he does, is such a versatile player, there's always time for him."

Meanwhile, with the trading deadline moments away, Knight wondered where he'd be going, and whether anyone really had confidence in him anymore.

"You feel kind of bad if you worry about getting traded, then you don't get traded and you play horrible in the games you need to play well in," Knight said. "Then you go back and sit on the bench and you know you had the opportunity to play and play well, but didn't do it. That's what you have to deal with.

"It's tough, especially with a winning team like this when you think of nothing but the championship. That's all we've been talking about since Charles Barkley's name first came up last year. You go out there in my situation as a point guard and you don't want to make mistakes. More than anything, my confidence is what is directing me instead of me just letting my talent go."

First, the Pistons asked the Suns to toss Miller into the trade. They complied. Then, in a late move, the Pistons wanted Dumas instead of Ceballos. The Suns refused.

Tip-off came. Knight was in the starting lineup. The trading deadline passed. And Knight still was in a Suns uniform.

The Suns tried to make the best humor of those trade rumors. Bogus messages from other NBA teams were delivered to Ceballos in the locker room — courtesy of his teammates. Ceballos got into the act himself, wearing a wristwatch onto the floor at the Summit for pregame warmups.

"It's 7:39," he said to reporters nearby. "I'm hanging in there."

Westphal, before sending the troops out, tried to boost Knight's sagging confidence by designing the first play for him.

"Better make it," Ainge told Knight, "You've only got 20 more minutes."

Even before all of that, Barkley entertained about 200 fans who took advantage of a Barkley-lookalike promotion sponsored by the Rockets in which those with shaved heads were admitted free. Barbers were on duty in the lobby for those who — like the Pistons — took their decision making to the limit.

"Everybody wants to look like me," Barkley said.

Knight, properly ignited, made six of 10 shots, one of his better efforts of the season. Unfortunately, trading deadline comes only once a season to spur him on.

Obviously, it wasn't the tension that was to blame for their worst loss in more than two years, 131-104, to the Rockets.

"Maybe we're taking our success for granted a little bit," Westphal said. "They basically knocked us over the head."

That's the way it is on Westphal's loose ship: Sometimes it works, sometimes you get reamed. But, as Barkley said, it didn't matter if the Suns were up or down, sharp or flat. They caught the Rockets on a night when "there wasn't a team in the world that could have beaten them."

What a day: The Suns got walloped, came up empty in trades, and KJ still was on the shelf. The good news was that Phoenix officially was granted the 1995 NBA All-Star game, another in a series of honors during its silver anniversary season.

Commissioner Stern flew to Phoenix to make the announcement on Friday, February 26. It was an indication of how far the state and the Suns have come since the dark days of 1987: the drug scandal, the league pulling its annual meetings out of Scottsdale because Arizona did not have a paid holiday honoring slain civil rights leader Dr. Martin Luther King, Jr. — something that no longer was true.

"That was 1987," Stern said. "The Suns have been a proud part of the NBA for 25 years, and I think it is terrific that we are able to bring the All-Star game here. I've known Jerry for 27 years. I've seen what this franchise has done, and what it has become, culminating in building a first-class team and also a first-class arena. They stepped up. Just before he broke ground, Jerry walked me past the arena site and asked, 'When can we get the All-Star game?' Jerry kept selling and selling. At one point, I told him, 'Stop selling, we're buying.' "

The Phoenix & Valley of the Sun Visitors' and Convention Bureau estimates the economic impact of landing the gala weekend to be $22 million to the community, which will be the basketball capital of the world for four days.

But if it does for the Suns what it did to the Jazz, it might not all be rosy. The Jazz lost their first two games after the break and they were headed for another one in the torture chamber for visiting teams, the Purple Palace.

"I hesitate to speculate on what other teams' problems are," Westphal said, "but it must be the after-effects of the emotional All-Star weekend. I don't know what else could have happened to them. You have to wonder."

The Suns were going for their 19th straight home win, which would tie a franchise record set at Veterans Memorial Coliseum. And the Suns, anxious to get the Houston game out of their minds, were thankful they had another one the night after. It was a bad situation for the Jazz, who were beaten, 113-106.

"We've won 40 and that's no accident," Majerle said. "We're awful good at coming back and stopping the bleeding."

Westphal chose a three-forward, two-guard lineup as his band-aid. It worked against the Jazz, a slow-footed group. Barkley posted his fourth triple-double of the season (29 points, 11 rebounds, 11 assists).

"All these guys got to do is make wide-open jumpers," Barkley said. "I wish I had their job sometimes."

Westphal knew that Stockton was tired and frustrated in his post-All-Star funk. So, he assigned Majerle to guard Stockton most of the second half.

"It seemed like a good idea," Westphal said. "I thought with Dan being a big guy, he could make it tough for John — so he limited him to 15 assists.

" But Majerle got the better of the matchup overall, scoring 28 points, including 12 in the final quarter when the game was secured.

But with Cleveland and their mobile big guys coming on Sunday, the Suns seemed to be playing with fire. While KJ was out, the Suns had gotten by against most teams by throwing the ball to Barkley, letting him read the defense like an option quarterback. He either passed out of a double-team to an open teammate, or took the ball to the basket with his powerful low-post move.

If the Suns were to break their homecourt successive-win record, they'd have to do it against the hottest team in the NBA. Cleveland was coming in with six straight wins, and 11 of 12.

The Suns were overwhelmed by the Cavs and their big front line, 101-94, on Sunday, February 28. It was humiliating. And it was revealing.

Cavs coach Lenny Wilkens was forced to start 6-foot-11 John "Hot Rod" Williams because 6-6 Gerald Wilkins had the flu. When teamed with 6-10 Larry Nance and 7-foot Brad Daugherty — both All-Stars — the Cavs have one of the game's tallest and most nimble front walls. For the Suns, and their collection of 6-foot-6 lineups, it was impenetrable.

"They exposed our major weakness, which is height," said Barkley, who nevertheless posted yet another triple-double (27 points, 19 rebounds, 11 assists).

The crusher for the Suns was that their 15-point halftime lead was erased by an incredible Cleveland run in the third quarter. In nine minutes, the Cavs turned a 17-point deficit into a two-point lead.

"It's tough to score on them," Barkley said. "Williams worked me real good. Then Nance worked me good. Then Brad finished me off at the end. That's a big team. Height was a problem for us when the game slowed."

Ainge went on about how the Cavs have no offensive weaknesses, making it hard for the Suns to play a taller foe man-to-man with no double-team help.

But Westphal wasn't buying the short-guy angle at all.

"We didn't play any defense in the third quarter," he said. "I was excited about our defense in the first half, and that was against Cleveland's tall guys. In fact, we made them adjust to us and go short for a while. I thought we had the game in hand, but I guess our players thought so, too."

Daugherty nicked the Suns for 16 points, nine rebounds; Williams for 10 points, nine rebounds, and three blocked shots; Nance, the former Suns captain, added 21 points, 17 rebounds, and five blocked shots.

They might have let Barkley get his triple-double, but the Cavs' front line was murder on Dumas, who made only six of 15 shots in the second half.

The next day, the Suns would understand why. Dumas suffered a strained back in the second quarter but didn't notify medical personnel. He began experiencing severe spasms when he got home after the game.

"You're not going to win every game," Barkley said after only the second loss by the Suns in the new Purple Palace. "I'm not the kind to mope. We started the day with the best record in the NBA. We ended the day with the best record in the NBA. That's the big picture."

But a chink had been revealed in their armor. The Suns were only 2-2 in their first week after the All-Star break, but they completed February 9-4. Ahead were 10 home games in March.

"I'm human," Barkley said. "I'm tired. Hopefully, with us coming home and playing a few teams we should beat, we'll recharge ourselves. This is our month. We'll either win or lose the Pacific Division this month."

There was a good test to open March: a trip to Portland. Things weren't going well at all for the Blazers. Drexler had been hurt, and they had the much publicized incident in Salt Lake City. Even though authorities in Utah brought no charges against any of the Blazers, it had taken a toll. And they simply seemed to be getting old. Portland had come so close to winning it all. They had been to two of the past three Finals. The year they missed, they had the best record in the West. The popular theory was that the Blazers had allowed a window of opportunity to close. They'd lost six of their previous 10 games, and Coach Rick Adelman had benched Kevin Duckworth and Jerome Kersey.

The Suns, SuperSonics, Spurs, and suddenly the Rockets were the rising stars in the West. The Blazers were in danger of opening the playoffs on the road.

The Suns weren't in the best shape, either. Neither Dumas nor KJ was on the trip, although Johnson was beginning to jog lightly. Still absent, and mysteriously quiet, was Miller.

Westphal expected to be booed by the Portland Memorial Coliseum crowd because he took Drexler out of the All-Star game in the third quarter in favor of Majerle. Drexler, voted a starter by fans, played only 11 minutes. Even Geoff Petrie, Blazers senior vice president, criticized Westphal.

But the Suns coach claimed that Drexler asked to be taken out. He was being embarrassed time after time by Jordan. Drexler's lack of mobility was caused by a knee injury. Blazermaniacs weren't buying Westphal's explanation. "I'm sure they'll be foaming at the mouth," Westphal said. And they were.

The Suns could score only 97 points and suffered a five-point loss. After the Suns held a four-point edge going into the final six minutes, Barkley didn't get off a shot the rest of the way, and Majerle took only two more as the Blazers turned it around with a 13-2 spurt. It was a rare example of the Suns failing to find a way to win down the stretch.

"Portland had to have it. I think they knew that," Barkley said. "We didn't need it as bad as them."

Despite not getting the ball in the fourth quarter, Barkley provided 20 points and 12 rebounds. But Buck Williams, the Blazers' aging power forward, kept him in check at the end when it counted.

The Blazers let Barkley shoot his jumpers, but didn't allow him to get anything inside. It was a strategy that more and more opponents were trying because too many of them had been stung when Barkley was allowed to catch the ball inside. Barkley was becoming adept at passing out of the low post. That's why the Suns were leading the league in three-pointers. Barkley found Majerle and Ainge alone for the long ones. Or Barkley picked his spots to split through a double-team to the basket, the result frequently being a three-point play.

But that was not the case here. By keeping Barkley outside, where Williams could handle him with single coverage, the Blazers, in turn, could pay more attention to the Suns' three-point shooters. This would have been an ideal defense for KJ to attack.

Barkley made only eight of 19 shots, leading Westphal to say, "It would have been nice for him to have one of those awesome nights, but he's human."

Playing back-to-back games against one of the Pacific Northwest teams is a pain for the Suns. It's a 2 1/2-hour flight from Portland, 3 hours from Seattle. The NBA schedule maker often doesn't take into account how spread out the Western Conference is. It's easy to play back-to-back in the East, where most cities are accessible in 90 minutes by air. Many of the cities are so close that teams bus to games. But that isn't the case out West.

Nevertheless, the Suns were anxious to return to action the following night to wash away the Portland experience. And they had an emotional task at hand with Philadelphia visiting.

It was the return of Jeff Hornacek. It would be an emotional night, too, for Barkley.

Philadelphia brought a miserable 19-34 record to the Purple Palace, and first-year coach Doug Moe already was rumored to be in deep trouble (he would be fired within a week).

"It probably would be emotional coming back if they were still playing in the Coliseum, where I have so many memories," Hornacek said. "But now they're in the new building, and I've never played there before. They don't look like the same team. They don't even wear the same uniforms. That will probably make it less emotional."

Hornacek and his wife, Stacy, kept their Phoenix home and continue to live there in the off-season.

"It actually became kind of funny," Hornacek said. "I had heard during last season that Jerry was interested in getting Charles, and I'd been saying all along that I thought it was a pretty good idea. I just didn't think it was a good idea for Jerry to trade me to get him."

The Sixers were struggling, but Hornacek was rolling along with the 20-point scoring average that he'd had in Phoenix the year before.

"It was tough. When I first got here, I saw some people projecting us to win a lot of games. I kind of wondered how they thought that was going to happen. We've got all these new players, and a new coach who wanted to run the motion offense. It's a good offense, but it's kind of hard to learn it in a short time, and you really have to have a certain kind of player to make it work."

Was KJ going to sit and watch this one? No way. He was activated. Both KJ and Dumas were in the starting lineup, but Dumas didn't last long. Nonetheless, it was an easy win for the Suns, 125-115, on Wednesday, March 3, with all sorts of side shows and sub-plots.

KJ played only 28 minutes but produced 16 points, six rebounds, and six assists. Before the game, West saw the often-injured KJ putting on his uniform unexpectedly and couldn't resist jabbing his close friend: "What is it, picture day?" Even KJ, known for his serious demeanor, got a smile out of that. He made seven of 11 shots and showed no signs of having missed the previous seven games — the Suns had lost three of the past four — except for the protective padding he wore on his sore right calf.

"When it happens later in the season, it makes you a little more antsy to get back," KJ said.

So do numbers like these: The Suns won nine of 10 games before KJ was injured this time, averaging 122 points. While he was out, they averaged 106 points, including three games in which they failed to reach triple figures. They also lost four times.

He wasn't due back until the Suns played Sacramento two nights later, but he said after watching the loss to the Blazers on TV that he felt compelled to help the Suns stop their skidding.

Dumas, in 10 minutes, was off and running, making four quick baskets. His back didn't seem to be bothering him. Then, he stepped on the side of somebody's foot on a power drive to the basket and severely sprained his left ankle. He was immediately taken for X-rays and missed the remainder of the game. The Suns' injury parade rolled on. Dumas had a Class 3 sprain, which is serious.

"We can't get a break," Barkley said. "It's a good thing we got Kevin back. I was glad to see him. With Richard maybe missing a month, we're lucky we've got a guy like Cedric Ceballos, too."

Then there was 7-foot-7 center Manute Bol, an old friend of Barkley's, standing 25 feet in front of the basket tossing up his unorthodox three-pointers with his shooting motion initiated by holding the ball with both hands to the side of his head. Bol had made only one three-pointer all season.

He made six here as the sellout crowd hooted and howled in amusement. Meanwhile, Ainge, the league leader in made three-pointers, missed all seven of his long-range tries.

Then there were the principals in the big trade taking on their old teams for the first time: Hornacek, predictably, was nervous. Barkley, unpredictably, was angry. Hornacek received a lengthy standing ovation when he was introduced. It seemed to get to him. Barkley said he received the first cortisone injection of his career to reduce the pain in his sprained left big toe.

"If I was breathing, I was playing," Barkley said. He certainly did, coming up one assist short of yet another triple-double, with 36 points and 17 rebounds. In fact, Barkley's point total was seven more than that of Hornacek, Perry, and Lang combined. In 31 minutes, Hornacek missed seven of 12 shots and scored only 15 points.

"It was tough to keep focused on the game," Hornacek said, agreeing that it had the feel of an exhibition game. "Our records are so different. I wouldn't say it was a joke, but it was a lot looser than it would have been if the records were similar."

Barkley was full of remorse afterward, though. He'd had his share of fun, joking with Bol after each of his long bombs. He'd toyed with his old foil, Armon Gilliam.

In their first head-to-head play, Barkley caught the ball, turned toward the basket and drew Gilliam to him by initiating his shooting motion. Then Barkley ducked under Gilliam and drove for a dunk. Later, with Gilliam having been burned by the drive, he relaxed his pressure. Barkley feigned a drive, then stepped back behind the three-point line and swished a trey. Normally, that kind of folly would bring a smile to Barkley's face — it brought one to just about everybody else's in the building.

"To tell you the truth, I'm a little disappointed in myself because I was so angry going in," Barkley said. "That's not me. I don't like playing in anger. Basketball is not life and death. It's not something to be angry about, yet I was. Finally, Manute came along and made me enjoy basketball again."

Barkley said this game probably wouldn't be as difficult for him as his first trip back to Philadelphia's Spectrum. That was scheduled in 25 days, and NBC-TV had picked up the Sunday morning battle for national telecast.

"I'm not going to be satisfied until we go to Philly, " Barkley said. "That's the one that's going to be hard on me. I've been dreading that one all season."

Somehow, despite the revolving door to the training room, the Suns still led the league at 41-13. Dumas, who had become their second-leading scorer at just under 18 points a game, was, indeed, scheduled to miss at least four weeks. Most of the games during that span were at home against teams the Suns should beat.

Among those was Sacramento, a welcome sight to the Suns. The Kings had lost seven of eight games since their All-Star guard, Mitch Richmond, underwent thumb surgery. They'd never had much luck in Phoenix when healthy. It was a game in which Barkley normally would have rested, but with Dumas going on the injured list, with Miller still on the list, and KJ still tender, Barkley had to suck it up and play despite having the pain in his toe.

The driving force in Barkley's basketball career — winning it all — pulled him through the exhaustion following the long summer with the Dream Team, of getting little rest during All-Star Weekend. It had been a long run, and he was showing the signs.

He knew the Suns could pile up some easy victories that would take them one giant step closer to securing home-court edge throughout the playoffs. Since the Suns had suffered only two losses in their brief occupancy of America West Arena, home-court edge seemed to be a powerful weapon for them. So on he went, carrying the Suns to a 130-122 win by making a season-high five three-pointers.

Barkley's five-for-six long-range shooting display moved Westphal to say he was going to take off the "Bolivian green light."

"That's where the light is really red, but there isn't a cop around, so you go through it, anyway," Westphal said.

Johnson, meanwhile, harassed Kings ballhandlers. "They were happy sometimes just to get the ball past mid-court against him," Westphal said.

The Suns let a 24-point lead slip to four in the final 10 seconds, so it wound up being a little tougher than was necessary. Ceballos, stepping into Dumas' spot, scored 23 points and had eight rebounds.

"Cedric has shown that he will perform when he gets the minutes," Westphal said. "Some games, he hasn't gotten the minutes, and I'll take the rap for that. I wasn't down on Ced; I just thought Richard was playing really well."

Ceballos no longer was just a specialist who could slash and dunk. His defense was better. His outside shooting was better. "I really appreciate Cedric and how he has reacted," said Westphal, who would grow to appreciate Ceballos even more in the coming weeks.

The following night — Saturday, March 6 — the Suns would visit Dallas, where the Mavericks had made two major announcements in recent days. First, they signed NBC-TV commentator Quinn Buckner as their coach for the following season. Second, they finally came to terms with holdout rookie Jimmy Jackson. He would be in uniform.

At 4-51 — that's right, 4-51 — the Mavs needed all the help they could get. Dallas would have to win six of its final 27 games to keep from beating Philadelphia's league record for futility (9-73) set 20 seasons earlier.

The Suns nearly stumbled against the Mavs without Jackson in a January visit, and they nearly stumbled again this time before saving a 109-102 win. More correctly, KJ saved it with his season-high 28 points, seven assists, and continued newfound success with pressure defense.

Jackson put a scare into the Suns when his heave from just beyond mid-court swished through the net for three points at the buzzer that gave Dallas a 51-50 lead at the half.

Barkley did little to help the cause before or after he was ejected with seven minutes to play. He'd made only five of 14 shots and scored 13 points. "I don't know who was worse, me or the officials," Barkley said afterward.

Johnson's two free throws put the Suns ahead by three points with just over a minute to play, and then his behind-the-back feed to Ainge for a three-pointer with 50 seconds left finished the job.

"It was the least I could do," KJ said. "Chuck has been playing so well all season. He's been carrying the load by himself a lot of nights. When he went out, I was just trying to return the favor."

Westphal has taken notice. "In my opinion, KJ is playing better than any point guard in the league right now. His statistics don't always reflect that because his role has changed. But he's doing exactly what we want him to do." Barkley added to the compliments, saying, "Kevin dominated the game tonight. He was the difference."

Finally, the Suns were going to get two days of rest before they had a return engagement with the Kings in Sacramento. West, who'd played in 392 consecutive games — the second longest active streak in the NBA — was in danger of missing the Sacramento game after he slipped in practice and suffered a strained lower back. The Suns' ironman had averaged 11 points, 11 rebounds, and three blocked shots in his three previous games. Miller, returning to practice and appearing to be much lighter, suffered a strained hamstring. West went to Sacramento; Miller did not.

"Even with this, we're headed toward the last lap with Oliver, it would appear," Emerson, the team physician, said.

West's resurgence coincided with the return of KJ, who in three games was averaging just over 20 points, six assists, and two steals.

"It's nice to have KJ come back so strong," Westphal said. "We were having a tough time scoring. We were in a lull. He's been the antidote."

The Suns had missed 90 player-games to injuries, 26 of those by Johnson.

"It's been pleasant to keep on rolling through all the injuries," Westphal said. "We just keep plugging guys in who can do the job."

The Suns were beginning a stretch in which they would play four games in five nights.

"If I can just make it through this week," Barkley said. "Paul is doing everything he can to get me some rest. The injuries definitely are a disruption, but I really feel that as long as I don't get hurt, as long as I'm out there, we have a chance to win every night."

They went to Arco Arena and walloped the Kings, 128-108, to make it 31 games above .500. It's not unusual for the Suns to get 40 points from a forward, but this time, it was from Ceballos, who made 14 of 15 shots and went 12-for-12 from the free-throw line in scoring his career high. His 12 rebounds were only one off his career high, coincidentally against Sacramento in November.

Richard who? Ceballos was beginning to thrive.

"I'm hopeful that if I do a good job while Richard is out, I'll get to play more when he comes back," Ceballos said.

Westphal said there was a pretty good chance of that. "He's a legitimate NBA starter and he shows it every time he has a chance."

By Ceballos' count, 14 of his shots were layups. He said he can't remember the shot he missed. "I just like to move and cut," he said. "Most guys don't like to play defense on a guy who is moving all the time. That's the secret: Keep moving and keep the defensive man busy. The whole game, I was just finishing plays. They just handed me the ball and I finished them after everybody else created them."

West was able to start and keep his longevity streak alive. He had nine rebounds to show for it.

The following night, the Suns would return home to begin a seven-game homestand, their longest of the season, against Golden State. Their 24-2 mark was the league's best home record.

That they smashed the Warriors, 111-100, was no surprise. The injury-decimated Warriors were skidding toward the NBA draft lottery.

What *was* a surprise was the return of Miller after 19 games on the injured list.

## Chapter Twenty-one

# A MILLER LIGHT

On Wednesday, March 10, following the Golden State game, Miller made one of the most startling revelations of the season. For most of the previous five weeks, he had been spending his nights at Healthwest Regional Medical Center, where his diet was closely monitored by a nutritionist.

Miller reduced his weight by approximately 40 pounds to 285. It is approximate because Miller said even he didn't know for sure how much he weighed when he entered the program. He'd found a way to trick the scale the Suns had been using to weigh him.

"I cried out for help, and they got me some," Miller said. "I want to make it clear that this was voluntary, it was not punishment. I agreed to do it. I feel better about myself as a person and as a player. It was time for me to do something for myself. I love to play ball, but there was no way I could run the court in the NBA with the weight I had."

However much that was, it contributed to Miller suffering a stress reaction in his right foot in December and tendinitis in his knees.

After he went on the injured list on January 30, Miller said he'd do three workouts a day, come back the next day and find that he'd gained "maybe three more pounds."

"Nothing was working for me," Miller said. "I was to the point where I had to have help."

The Suns had lost patience with him. Westphal called the day Miller went to the hospital to begin his 1,500-calorie-a-day outpatient program, and the waiving of Rambis, the low points of the season. Westphal said it also was the turning point of the Suns' season. They would need a healthy Miller to get through of the playoffs.

"I don't know the answer to why I was an obese person," Miller said. "I'm just glad everybody kept their faith in me. I don't want to let anybody down. I want to show everybody in the NBA who didn't pick me that I do have a heart, that I do have pride, and that I do have what it takes to play in the NBA."

Miller said 285 pounds was his lowest since his sophomore season at Arkansas. It was only a starting point. He vowed to be at 275 by the beginning of informal workouts in September and down to 265 by the time the Suns end preseason training camp in October.

"I've been through that situation myself," Barkley said. "Losing weight is the hardest thing I've ever been through. I'm very proud of him. But it's important for him to know that he should lose weight to make him healthy, not lose it to come back on the team."

Miller gave the Suns one point and three rebounds in his 11 minutes. He was noticeably lighter on his feet, but also seemed to have suffered some loss of strength.

The Warriors had only nine players in uniform. One of them, someone named Barry Stevens, was from the Continental Basketball Association and had been signed by the Warriors to a 10-day contract— sight unseen— so they'd have enough bodies for practice.

West continued his rebounding tear, yanking down 13. Barkley went for 30 points and 10 rebounds, Ceballos for 20 and nine.

Next up on the Purple Palace Hit Parade was Dallas. The Mavs successfully rotated their defense to double-cover Barkley while running defenders at Majerle and Ainge before they could get a clean look at the basket.

"We're not shooting many wide-open threes anymore," said Majerle.

After shooting nearly 38 percent from three-point land before the All-Star break, Majerle was shooting only 28 percent out there since. Ainge, a 47 percent three-point shooter and the league leader before the All-Star break, was making only 32 percent since. That's not all bad, but it pales by comparison. Most coaches find 33 percent shooting acceptable, the same return on points per shot as when shooting 50 percent from inside the arc. Overall, the Suns were on a pace to break NBA records with their 37 percent three-point shooting. They'd cooled to 31 percent since.

Opponents were beginning to be more selective in who came over to help Barkley's man in double coverage. They were now using the man assigned to West, who was not much of an offensive threat, instead of dropping a guard. When a guard doubled Barkley, he had little difficulty getting the ball outside to the wide-open three-point shooters. Now West was taking advantage of being unguarded and was rolling up numbers that are big for him.

Westphal was ill and missed practice the day before the Mavs arrived, but Robertson said the Suns can beat those defensive ploys if West stays active and if Majerle and KJ drive.

"Majerle has started taking it to the basket again, and I've even seen Ainge putting it on the floor and driving," Robertson said. "And the guy who's really benefiting is Kevin. When teams stay home on Majerle and Ainge, it's pretty hard to keep KJ from penetrating. I don't think there's one person who can keep him from penetrating. And nobody in this league is going to stop Charles one-on-one."

The Mavs were an ideal team on which to try out those theories in the 116-98 rout, the Suns' sixth straight win. Westphal didn't belabor the point. Of his starters, only Ceballos played more than 33 minutes. That gave Miller a great opportunity to show off his rebuilt body, and he made the most of it in his 25 minutes: 10 points, six rebounds, seven assists, four steals, and two blocked shots.

"I ran the floor better," Miller said. "I had more steals than I've ever had in my career. I'm just now getting comfortable again. It's been a month and a half since I played with them in a game situation."

Miller had continued spending his evenings at the hospital even after being activated. But he said he'd hired a cook to prepare the special meals in his diet. Miller planned to make this night his last under supervision. That didn't preclude him from accepting a free meal at a local steakhouse as compensation for doing a post-game television interview to explain how he lost so much weight. "I can still eat, I just have to watch it," Miller said.

Miller was fitting in nicely. "He's quicker, and it's really nice to see that," Westphal said. "He can give us so many dimensions beyond blocking shots and rebounding, like his passing. Plus he can catch and score."

Miller didn't provide the only entertainment for the sellout crowd. Late in the first half, KJ lost his left shoe while maneuvering at the top of the key as Barkley held the ball on the right side. When KJ tried to pick up his shoe, Barkley, grinning from ear to ear, lobbed a pass KJ's way. KJ put down the shoe, caught the ball and quickly jacked up an errant three-point try to beat the shot clock.

"It was a pretty funny play," Barkley said.

KJ wasn't so sure.

Barkley tried to engage him in a battle of shoe companies, suggesting that KJ would benefit by switching from Converse to the Nike Air Max that Barkley endorses for several million dollars a year.

"We call them Air Max instead of Air Chuck so that people who hate me will still buy them," Barkley said. "It might help indirectly if my name isn't on them."

It's a good thing the Suns could enjoy the fun while it lasted, because the New Jersey Nets visited next, on Saturday, March 13. The Nets came in 4-1 on the road against the Pacific Division, better than the Suns' 4-7 road mark against the Pacific. The Nets were 10 games above .500 for the first time in nine seasons.

The difference seemed to be Chuck Daly, the master of crisis management. In Detroit and with the Nets, he had the opportunity to put those skills to good use. They're also big and active, a deadly combination against the Suns, who were humiliated on their home floor, 124-93, on Saturday, March 13. At one point, the Suns trailed by 40 points in their largest loss ever to the Nets, their worst home loss in eight seasons, and their worst overall loss since their all-time biggie, 151-107, at Seattle in 1988.

"Obviously, we're ashamed," Barkley said.

"We've got to make sure nothing like this ever happens again," Majerle said.

It only rekindled what the Cavaliers had shown two weeks earlier, that big Eastern teams can handle the Suns.

"It was our ugliest game of the year," Westphal said. "I wish I could blame somebody. I can't even blame the refs. They weren't bad."

Derrick Coleman (6-foot-10) set screens for shooting guard Drazen Petrovic, who made seven of his first nine shots against Majerle and finished with 29 points.

"Derrick is a big guy to be setting screens," Majerle said. "All 'Petro' needs is a little room anyway because he's a great shooter."

Coleman didn't just give himself up. He also had 23 points and 12 rebounds. Surprisingly, he made three of four three-point tries. And Rumeal Robinson, forced to play point guard after Kenny Anderson suffered a broken wrist, had 23 points and 10 assists, showing doubters that he can play the point.

"It's just embarrassing," Barkley said. "My job is to get us motivated and into the game, so I'll take the blame for this one."

How bad was it? For the first time, the Suns failed to make a three-pointer in a game.

"It's a little feather in our cap, but it's like that joke about the mirror over the bed that says, 'Objects may appear larger than they actually are,' " Daly said. "It's not that big. They're the best team in the league. We know that."

The Suns needed the rare four-day break that awaited them. Everyone was tired and frustrated. And, of course, there were all those nagging injuries to heal before Portland came to town on March 17.

Westphal gave them only a day off before they hit the practice court — and hit was the word. KJ and Kempton duked it out.

"New Jersey gave us a jolt, and that was reflected in this practice," Westphal said. "I was hoping we wouldn't have to practice, but we had to roll up our sleeves and get back to work."

The Suns might have become lax after playing a long list of lightweights before New Jersey clubbed them.

"I think that directly contributed to our not playing with any intensity," KJ said. "It's been a long time since we lost to a team we shouldn't have. If we have just one game like that out of 82, that's not bad. But lately we've played to the level of our competition, and our competition hasn't been that strong."

The Suns had played six straight against teams that were at least 11 games under .500 and had a combined winning percentage of .286.

"The wins were coming too easily, too automatically," Westphal concurred.

Some good did come during the brief break: the Suns clinched their fifth straight playoff berth on Tuesday, March 16, when Denver lost to Minnesota, and Golden State lost to Boston.

The Portland game the following night also marked the end of the third quarter of the season for the Suns, who were 46-14.

"Going into the fourth, at least we know the game is going into overtime," Westphal said.

The Suns were encouraged to learn that Dumas was off crutches and progressing a bit more rapidly than medical personnel anticipated.

"I want Richard back as soon as possible," Westphal said. "He and 'O' are guys who know the game, but we need to have them working with us. They're rookies. We want to go into the playoffs with all our bullets in the chamber."

And after the Suns gained some redemption by thumping the Trail Blazers, 129-111, on Wednesday, March 17, Westphal said, "That's more like it. It was a long wait to get the taste of that New Jersey game out of our mouths, but we needed a day of rest and two hard days of practice. I think that refreshed us."

Improved rebounding was high on the agenda during the break. The Suns came back and outrebounded one of the league's best at it by 30. Leading the way was Ceballos, who had a career-high 14 of the Suns' season-high 64. He and Tom Chambers scored 24 points each. KJ had a season-high 14 assists.

"You can't ever expect to outrebound somebody by that much, especially a great rebounding team like Portland," Westphal said.

But, according to Ceballos, "We had to make a statement." The heat was on the Suns. It seemed everyone in the national media was lining up to take a shot at the Western Conference leaders.

As Barkley often said, they now were a marked team. It's one thing to come from nowhere, surprise the league for a while, and compile a nice record. It's another to be the favorite night after night and still win when every opponent is taking its best shot. Even though they'd lost four games since the All-Star break, they weren't doubting themselves as much as those outside the locker room.

Looking ahead, the Suns saw Detroit visiting on Friday, March 19, Indiana on Sunday, and Eastern Conference leader New York on Tuesday. This was their chance to show that they could, indeed, handle anything East of the Mississippi.

So in came the Pistons in a state of disarray. They were a long way away from their Bad Boys days. Many of the old familiar names still were there: Dumars, Thomas, Laimbeer, Rodman. But it wasn't the same without Daly at the helm, without Jack McCloskey in the front office calling the shots. The Pistons basically were going through the motions under Coach Ron Rothstein, a man the players despised. They had a 28-34 record to show for it. The unthinkable only a few seasons back appeared to await them: a trip to the draft lottery. And, undoubtedly, a coaching change as well. They outrebounded the Pistons by 24 and won by 30 points, 127-97. Sixteen of those rebounds went to Barkley, who also scored 22 points.

Rodman arrived on the scene five minutes before tip-off with the words "Bite the Melon" carved into his hair. In 39 minutes, he got 13 rebounds, mostly against his buddy Barkley.

A more welcome sight to the Suns was the return of Ainge's three-point shot. He made five of 10 as he scored 23 points in 27 minutes.

"Damn, Danny, is your arm all right?" Barkley asked in mock concern in the locker room. "You need some ice on that elbow? You fired that thing every time you touched it."

Ainge, one of the few Suns who is not overmatched by Barkley in a battle of wits, shot back, "Had to. When I'm open, I'm our best option." And off to the shower Ainge strode.

As he was toweling off later, he said, "There for a stretch I wasn't getting very good looks. I'd be 0-for-1, 1-for-2, 0-for-2. I just didn't get many shots from out there because my man was staying on me. But the Pistons left me alone."

Majerle also got a couple of treys to fall. "It's a shot that will come and go, but it went a little too much for me. We really hadn't been hitting them lately, so maybe Detroit figured they'd lay off."

Indiana is among the tallest teams in the league with 6-11 Dale Davis, 6-11 Detlef Schrempf, and 7-4 Rik Smits across the front. Even shooting guard Reggie Miller (6-7) has good size for his position. That's the kind of team that often picks the Suns apart.

Pounding Portland and Detroit helped to wash away the taste of the New Jersey embarrassment. The Suns looked at Indiana's 9-21 road record and assumed this would be nothing more than the final tuneup before the New York Knicks came to town.

Not so fast. The Suns led by 14 at the half, but couldn't handle the Pacers on the boards and couldn't execute a play at crunch time in a 109-108 loss.

"They beat us up good," Barkley said. "That team has bodies, lots of bodies. They just kept rotating, rotating, and rotating people in and out on us. I think from now on, teams are going to use that against us whenever possible. When we play against these teams that are a lot bigger than us, it is going to wear us down. It'll take its toll."

So did peeking ahead at the showdown with the Knicks, which promised to be one of the premier games of the season.

"You know if their attention is a game ahead, you're in town at a good time," Pacers coach Bob Hill said.

Only once before, on a November 28 visit to Golden State, had the Suns lost to a nonwinning team. Majerle, who made only three of 11 shots, put on his practice clothes and immediately went to the Suns' practice gym to shoot. His parents were in town from Michigan. They had planned to go out to dinner after the game. Majerle sent them back to his house instead.

KJ, with only his third 20-10 game of the season (21 points, 11 assists), recalled a training-camp chat he'd had with Barkley.

"I told Charles that when we're in the game at the same time that we should never lose, or even let the other team lead, or even for one moment let them think that they have a chance," KJ said. "Maybe we're not as mature a team as we think we are. I'll give Indiana credit: this is going to get us ready for the remainder of the season.

"We are a team that is always being hunted now. Teams play their best against us, especially if we let them hang around and get confidence. We've got to tighten the grip and stop toying with them like this. We've got to beat them, and beat them bad."

It takes a lot to get KJ riled like that, and he clearly would hold those thoughts for the Knicks, who arrived on the Suns' doorstep with the combative motto, "Tough town, tough team."

# Chapter Twenty-two

# PUT UP OR SHUT UP

No one had more flagrant fouls than the New York Knicks. No one held opponents to fewer points or to a lower shooting percentage.

That was the personality that Coach Pat Riley bred into the Eastern Conference leaders.

It was working. The Knicks (45-18) were only three games behind the Suns (48-15) for best record in the NBA. If the Knicks were to win this one, they'd take the season series and thus have a playoff tie-breaker on the Suns if the team were to finish with identical records.

More than that, the game seemed simply a matter of pride for the Suns. As much as they wanted to downplay their troubles against the East, the fact remained that the Suns were 1-5 against the Knicks, Bulls, Cavs, and Nets — the teams with the best records in the East. All four of the Suns' losses in the Purple Palace were to Eastern Conference teams.

"We have the best record, but we haven't proven that we're the best team yet," Majerle said.

"It's about time we rise to the occasion and beat some Eastern teams," Ainge said. "It will be nice to get that squared."

Westphal insisted it was not a "statement game," although the Suns coach, who is in the habit of giving his players time off for good behavior, took the unusual step of working them hard for more than two hours the day before the game.

"A 'statement' is when you beat somebody in the playoffs," Westphal said. "We do put a little more emphasis on this because it's against the team that's closest to us for best record in the NBA, so we'd like to knock them down a notch. It's bigger than just one of 82, but it doesn't mean anything in the event you meet them in the Finals."

West seemed to put it into perspective best. "It doesn't matter what you are against the East, it's what you are all-around, and we've lost fewer than anybody else so far," West said.

And as Barkley put it, "If we can have home edge through the playoffs, that would be big. We just have to out-work them. We've done that and beaten a lot of big teams."

The stage was set. It was the class of the East against the class of the West, but it was anything but a classy, or classic, game. It was as ugly as a New York ghetto. The Knicks' trash-talking, street-thug style of play backfired. The Suns busted them. A bench-clearing brawl just before halftime caused six players to be ejected and would lead to the largest mass fines ever handed down by the NBA. When order was restored, the Suns punished the Knicks, 121-92, on Tuesday, March 23.

Afterward, the Knicks refused to open their locker room door to reporters, in violation of NBA rules. No comments from players or coaches. Not even a statement was released through the Knicks' media flak, who was traveling with the team.

The Suns, however, had plenty to say.

"For all of you who wondered if we could play Eastern ball, was that Eastern enough for you?" Westphal said.

As Barkley was dressing, he said to reporters, "You guys are going to have to hurry. I've got to get home and see SportsCenter. There should be some good highlights."

With 24 seconds left in the opening half, Knicks guard Doc Rivers was called for an offensive foul against KJ. Rivers elbowed the Suns guard to push off. They had a brief, heated chest-to-chest exchange of words. A crowd gathered to separate them. Ainge and John Starks of the Knicks shouted at each other, and then Riley came off the bench toward the crowd. He and Ainge, former rivals when Ainge was with the Celtics and Riley with the Lakers, exchanged words. KJ, Rivers, Ainge, and Starks all were given technicals.

With five seconds left in the half, KJ was called for an offensive foul. He didn't like it, and Rivers taunted him a bit.

Then, on the Knicks' inbounds play, KJ stepped up to Rivers and delivered a forearm high to Rivers' chest that sent the Knicks guard sprawling to the floor, directly in front of referee Nolan Fine, who made no call as time expired.

Rivers then got up, took a swipe at KJ, and missed. Rivers tried to chase the Suns guard, but Barkley grabbed Rivers. Too late. As KJ was being restrained by Knicks assistant coach Dick Harter, Greg Anthony, who was on the Knicks' bench in street clothes because of an ankle injury, came onto the floor and belted KJ on the forehead. KJ shook loose and went after Anthony. Riley dove onto KJ and they went to the floor. Riley ripped the trousers of his expensive Italian suit.

Chambers then caught up with Anthony, grabbed him, and threw him back into a chair on the Knicks bench, ripping Anthony's dress shirt.

"He should be suspended for the rest of the year," KJ said of Anthony. "It was a cheap shot. How can a scrub in street clothes come off the bench and do something like that?"

That was the scariest part of the incident. Many in the sell-out crowd did not know who Anthony was. Some Suns fans thought that Anthony, because he was on the floor in street clothes, was just some combative Knicks fan. Several rose and stepped to the edge of the floor. Authorities knew conditions were ripe for a riot, but arena security personnel and Phoenix police got it under control, and the teams safely reached their locker rooms at halftime, with the Suns holding a six-point lead.

"The Knicks came in very, very tough," KJ said. "We had to respond. You can't let somebody come into your house, move furniture and other stuff. The house owner has to take some kind of stand."

As the teams came back onto the floor for the second half, the officiating crew headed by competent veteran Ed T. Rush informed Rivers, Starks, Anthony Mason, and Greg Anthony of the Knicks, as well as KJ and Ainge, that they were ejected.

By then, KJ and Anthony already had exchanged more words. The ejection notices started another scuffle, this time between KJ and his own teammates. KJ started after the officials and had to be restrained by Miller and Mustaf. KJ battled to escape their grasp, all the time arguing vehemently with Westphal, who was trying to calm him.

"Hey," Miller yelled at KJ, "we're teammates, bitch!"

KJ could have injured one of them. Mustaf already had suffered a deep thigh bruise in the main melee that would put him out of commission briefly.

A fair question was why the officiating crew would allow the ejected players to return to the floor in the first place. Rush said that league rules preclude officials from going into the locker rooms. Their only other means of communicating with the coaches would have been through a written note. Rush said he preferred to explain the situation to the coaches personally, so the only recourse was to allow the players to return to the floor before giving them and their coaches the news. Even that wasn't the end of it.

The ejected players had to be separated in the hallway outside their locker rooms once again by Phoenix police and arena security officers.

With the Knicks down to rookie Hubert Davis at point guard and seldom-used Tony Campbell at shooting guard, and with the Knicks' big people playing very passively in the wake of the brawl, the Suns had little trouble opening a huge lead during the final two quarters.

Just about everyone was hoping that they had not witnessed a preview of the NBA Finals.

"If we play the Knicks in the Finals, it will be World War III," said Majerle, who scored 22 points. "If enough people tell you you're soft, and a team with a hard-nosed reputation comes in here and expects to physically beat you up and do exactly what they want to do to you on the court, it's going to make you stand up to them."

Overlooked in it all was a 31-point, 11-rebound effort by Barkley, and a 20-point, 12-rebound effort by Ceballos.

Before he could dress and get out of the locker room, KJ already had been contacted by NBA security director Horace Balmer for his account of the brawl. It is the league's policy to assess fines and suspensions before a team plays its next game. The Suns were due to visit the Lakers the following evening, so the NBA had to act fast. There was no shortage of evidence. All the major cable television networks had highlights on the air moments after it occurred.

The Suns anticipated that KJ would be fined. They weren't braced for what the league handed down: KJ suspended without pay for two games — costing him $45,121 — and fined an additional $15,000. His total hit: just over $60,000. Johnson received word at his hotel room in Los Angeles a few hours before the game with the Lakers. He flew home immediately and initially wouldn't talk to reporters.

In all, 21 players received fines and suspensions totaling $292,512.20, a league record.

Westphal termed the sanctions against KJ, whom the league said precipitated the incident , a "horrible miscarriage of justice."

The  greatest irony  is that in the biggest mass punishment ever administered by the NBA, Charles Barkley was among the four players on either side who was not fined.

Anthony received a five-game suspension without pay, costing him $65,060, plus a $20,000 fine. The fine equalled the largest individual punishment ever handed down. He stepped to the top of the list alongside Barkley and Bill Laimbeer, each of whom was nicked for $20,000 following an incident between the Pistons and 76ers April 20, 1990.

Rivers also was suspended without pay for two games, a $21,829 punishment, and given a $10,000 fine.

The league took the unusual step of fining the Knicks organization $50,000 and the Suns $25,000 for failing to control their players. In all, 10 Suns players lost $106,621.95 in fines and suspensions, and 11 Knicks players lost $185,890.25 in fines and suspensions.

The number of players punished, 21, also set a league record for one incident.

The Knicks had moved on to Salt Lake City for their next game against the Utah Jazz. Riley, finally ready to talk, accused the Suns, and KJ in particular, of using the game "to prove their manhood." Riley further accused the news media of backing the Suns into a corner.

"The whole thing was precipitated by a week-long barrage of media coverage on the Phoenix Suns, about how soft they were and about how Eastern Conference teams had beaten them in five out of six games, and that they weren't physical," Riley said. "It's almost like they had to prove their manhood, and they decided to do it against us. Obviously, the Suns came with the premeditated thought about a statement they had to make for their manhood."

The Suns were livid that KJ was suspended for an incident in which he did not receive as much as a personal foul call by Fine, much less a flagrant foul or a technical foul.

"You can build a case that if the officials had taken control earlier, it might have been avoided," Colangelo said. "As a side play, Rivers told KJ early that he was going to take him down. A big part of the game should not be intimidation, yet in reality, it is a big part. Things did get out of hand.

"I see a team building a particular image and gloating over that image. That's a problem. This is not the first one the Knicks have had with the league this year. 'Tough town, tough team' is the style being instilled in how they play, and that's not right."

Conversely, Riley said the league was going out of its way to come down on the Knicks.

"If Anthony Mason had done to Dan Majerle what Kevin Johnson did to Doc Rivers, Anthony would have been thrown out of the game of basketball," Riley said. "That's the double-standard that's being created right now. If anybody tries to lay this all on us, Kevin Johnson instigated the whole thing. Period. That's where it started. We made the mistake of retaliating."

Once again, that was coming from Pat Riley. The same Pat Riley, who only three weeks earlier, when New York writers noted that the Knicks had become too physical, reminded them that when he took the job, people were saying they were too soft.

"People wrote that you could go to the basket on the Knicks, go to lunch, and have your car washed before one of them would step up and defend," Riley had said. "The same people who wrote that we were too soft then are saying we're too physical now. Well, we're not going back. We're not going to change. It's not going to happen."

That sounds suspiciously as if the Knicks' new style is an attempt to prove their manhood, spurred by the media. Either that, or the Knicks are a gang of thugs who refuse to take responsibility for their actions, led by a man looking for the first scapegoat he can find. Lest anyone think this is just a Suns' thing toward the Knicks, contempt for the Knicks has grown league-wide.

"I think the league was waiting for this," Charlotte coach Allan Bristow said. "Hopefully, they sent a strong message to the whole

Knicks organization from top to bottom. Personally, I'm disgusted with the image they like to project and their style of play. As a coach and a fan, I was completely turned off by it, but they seem to get enjoyment from it."

George Karl, coach of Seattle, said the Knicks' philosophy is to "try to use the foul on every play so the refs get tired of calling it and let them go. They've cheated all year."

The most insightful comments came from Houston coach Rudy Tomjanovich, whose face was Kermit Washington's personal punching bag in one of the game's ugliest incidents 16 years earlier.

"The NBA has a wonderful product full of great athletes. They've got to protect that," Tomjanovich said. "It would be a shame if one of these athletes was seriously hurt because of something like that. Any time things get out of hand, they've got to take a quick, hard stand. I was happy to see the league come down not only on the players, but also on the organization."

Michael Jordan, asked whether he thought the Knicks were dirty or just physical, responded, "You can't have one without the other. Now they're going to be without their point guards for a few games on a long trip. That could throw them out of rhythm when everything was going so well for them."

As for the Knicks, Greg Anthony released a statement in Salt Lake City that read, "It was really an immature act on my part. I got involved emotionally. It was really unfortunate. I want to give apologies to the Phoenix Suns organization and fans, and to Kevin Johnson. I just got caught up in it, but that's no excuse for my actions."

Rivers said he was "embarrassed by it, to be honest."

"I'm not a fighter," Rivers said. "But I don't know if I'm a lover, either."

Riley said he kept the locker room closed to reporters because he and his players had not cooled off, and he did not want to risk having anyone escalate the incident after the game "like they did."

"The Suns laid it off on us," Riley said. "They can thump their chests, but I think our actions in not talking showed a hell of a lot more integrity and dignity about this."

As the months went by and the Suns reflected on the incident, time did little to change their assessment of its cause and effect.

"It appears that Kevin was aware maybe of some of the rap on him, that maybe he wasn't tough enough," Colangelo said. "I think he responded. He was going to be kind of a different guy, take on a different personality, with maybe an edge on his personality. That's a difficult thing for anyone to do. You are who you are, and it's important to be who you are. You can't be someone you're not."

Westphal said he tried to keep the incident in historical perspective.

"I've seen a lot worse fights than that," he said. "As it relates to Kevin, I can understand exactly why he did what he did. I've had players threaten me before on the floor. When that happens, there are two things you can do: back down and let them win by threatening you with their mouth, or knock them on their butt first chance you get. Then whatever happens, happens after that."

Westphal believes that when a team takes its identity from physical and verbal intimidation, as the Knicks do, they often can't handle it when it is returned in kind. The Knicks certainly were timid in the second half.

"When they come out from the start of the game telling KJ that if he drives, he's going down and going down hard, how is he going to respond?" Westphal said. "And every time he runs by somebody he gets an elbow, whether it's Doc Rivers, or Oakley, or Ewing — everybody on the team, every time you come near them, they elbow you? Every time you go up for a shot somebody hits you hard and tries to put you down, and then they're telling you about it, and telling you how they're going to hurt you?

"Maybe they intend to hurt you and maybe they don't, but the fact is they're telling you that at the time. How are you going to respond? I think Kevin responded the only way an athlete should respond. He said, 'All right, you're talking about it, I can play that way, too.'"

Westphal recalled how Paul Silas, now an assistant coach with the Nets, once handled Darryl Dawkins in the playoffs.

"Silas had the greatest line I ever heard about that. In his heyday, everybody was afraid of Dawkins. He was intimidating Seattle in the playoffs, telling everybody he was going to knock their heads off. So Silas got right in his face and said to Dawkins, 'Let me tell you something, you've got a head, too.' The young Sonics looked up to Silas, and said, 'Hey that's right.' We ended up winning that series, and it was directly related to Silas stepping forward and reminding Mr. Dawkins that his head was vulnerable.

"So to me, Kevin had a chance to collide with Doc, and didn't avoid it, and made sure it was a good collision. Then I don't blame him for getting up and chasing Kevin, either. I don't necessarily think you have to have a bench-clearing brawl in order to straighten it out. Even for a bench-clearing brawl, there weren't many punches thrown. It was pretty much Greg Anthony coming off the bench, which was totally out of line. Most of it was just pushing, and talking, and pointing fingers.

"It was magnified because of the Knicks' stance as that kind of team, and because of the perception — whether right or wrong — about us being soft, and because the game's on TV and it was built up as a big clash. So it took on more significance than the average incident would take on. To me, I didn't think it was that big a deal. People asked me what I thought would happen if we met the Knicks in the Finals. I said it would be a good series, it'd be basketball."

Van Arsdale, a fiery sort in his playing days, said he resented the outcome of the fines and suspensions, agreeing with Westphal that the Knicks' style brings out aggressive responses from opponents.

"You know going in that you're going to have to play physically and risk having a fight to compete with them," said Van Arsdale, who like Westphal was a teammate of Riley's on the 1976 Suns team that played in the Finals. "I resent the way the game is played right now by the Knicks. I don't think that's the way basketball was meant to be played. That's not to say it's not supposed to be aggressive with a lot of clean contact. I just think there were too many incidents this year where the Knicks incited that kind of play. They've hurt some people. As a former player, I don't appreciate that, but that's the way they're coached to play. I like Riley, but it doesn't surprise me. I think he's gotten to the point where he feels he doesn't have to answer to anybody."

Fitzsimmons thought Barkley should have paid KJ's fine.

"The reason Kevin gets riled up is because of Charles," Fitzsimmons said. "Have you ever seen, until Charles got here, Kevin be that way?

"So I'm telling you that Charles had a lot to do with Kevin playing the way he played, changing his personality on the court. So I say Charles ought to pay the fine."

Further, the former coach and current Vice President of Nothing believes KJ may have brought the whole thing on himself, indirectly. He rarely gets calls, and there is a reason for that.

"I think he complains too much," Fitzsimmons said. "Certain guys know how to do certain things. Tiny Archibald got calls all the time. He'd holler before he ever got hit. But Kevin, he'll make a face and complain. Officials don't like that. The way a driver to the basket has to get calls is to only complain when he gets hit hard. Don't complain when you make contact with somebody and you don't get hit hard and you miss the shot. You're frustrated because you missed, but Kevin has the tendency to make faces, get emotional about it.

"If you really feel somebody's putting his hands on you, then during a dead ball,  you be close to that official, not up in his face, looking away somewhere else but telling the official, 'The guy's holding me down. He's pushing down under.' You don't get up in their face in front of the crowd, you don't show emotion. I've told Kevin that's why he doesn't get the call."

# Chapter Twenty-three

# HERE COME THE SUNS

If the Suns found the Knicks pugnacious, they found the Lakers anything but. It was more like "give peace a chance."

"If a fight broke out while we were on the floor, I'm wondering if any of our guys would stay," Lakers coach Randy Pfund said after the Suns cut them open, 120-105, at the Forum.

It was the beginning of a critical eight-game segment for the Suns. If they could win five or six of them, they would be in strong position to ride out the season with the league's best record. But if they stumbled, they'd open the door for the Knicks or Bulls in the East, and perhaps the Sonics in the West, to catch up. Six of the eight were on the road, four on an Eastern trip that included Barkley's return to Philadelphia and a visit to the Chicago Bulls.

While the Suns left Pfund contemplating his future, they also left Los Angeles with their fifth straight 50-win season, an unprecedented streak in club history.

Barkley was good for 33 points and 12 rebounds. Ainge came back by making 12 of 16 shots and scoring 27 points and then saying he felt he "owed everybody something" following his ejection in the second half against New York.

Everyone was wondering how the Suns would respond to their distractions, but they were well-focused. That was the case again when they came home on Friday, March 26, to face Milwaukee, another team that was reeling. The Bucks had won only 15 games since the Suns met them in Milwaukee on December 6. The Suns just wanted to get it over with and get on with their long trip East, where they would get KJ and perhaps Dumas back.

After coming back from 13 points down in the third quarter with small lineups again, the Suns prevailed, 109-103. It took 31 points and 15 rebounds from Barkley to offset a hot shooting display by Brad

Lohaus, who played his high school ball in Phoenix and always makes a point of being a menace when he returns to the Valley. Lohaus, at 6-foot-11, has a nice outside touch, as he showed with four-for-four three-point shooting and 20 points.

Just before halftime, Chambers suffered a quadricep injury while diving to catch an errant pass from Miller. That knocked him out for the long trip, and it unmasked one of the few strategic errors the club made.

Just before the game, the Suns had placed Mustaf on the injured list in anticipation of activating Dumas in Philadelphia. Why they didn't hold off on making the move is a mystery, but it proved to be a mistake. Had they waited, they could have placed Chambers on the list after the game. Now, they would be without both big men on the road. Even though Mustaf had done little, it's always nice to have a 6-foot-10 body sitting on the bench with six fouls to give when you're going against Chicago, Boston, and Indiana.

Further clouding the big-man picture was the recurring back problems experienced by West. He'd been sore for several months, and his back was flaring up again. He lasted only 10 minutes against the Bucks. So Westphal's move to small people wasn't necessarily born out of some strategic genius. It was really the only thing he could do under the circumstances. It worked.

Milwaukee isn't known as a force on the boards, but the Suns' lineup of midgets outrebounded them, 31-9, in the second half.

Barkley pulled them out of their funk, scoring 10 of the Suns' first 12 points in the second half. Seven of his rebounds came during the fourth quarter, including a big one with 22 seconds to go and the Suns leading by only three points. Twelve of his points came during a 27-9 run that reversed the game. It was the fourth straight game in which he surpassed 30 points.

Yet he was steaming. Barkley is in the habit of kicking the scorers' table on his way to the bench during a timeout if he is not pleased with the proceedings. This time, he put one of his new Air Max Nikes through an expensive sign on the front of the table near the bench.

"I think we were already on the plane to Philly," Barkley said of the Suns' lapses. "I know I've definitely thought about it. It's going to be emotional for me, and probably very difficult. I'm glad it's finally here so I can get it over with and stop thinking about it. "

On Saturday, March 27, all of Barkley's old media buddies were waiting for him. He wasn't his usual loose, carefree self. He was serious, subdued, and melancholy. Reflecting on his eight years in Philadelphia, Barkley said, "It was tough being a 76er."

He directed most of his venom at Katz, who tore apart the 1983 world-championship team and bungled the rebuilding with terrible trade and draft decisions.

"It was tough for me, even when things were going well," Barkley said. "It's a tough organization to play for.

"I just think they do things incorrectly. Like Maurice Cheeks found out he got traded from a reporter. And calling Rick Mahorn on the phone to tell him he was waived. And I think they could have called me and told me, or said something to me, about my trade. I felt like Harold could have called and said 'thanks,' or 'hello,' or even 'good-bye.' I think Harold could have taken the time to call me or say something. I haven't heard from him since."

That's in sharp contrast to what it's like in Phoenix, Barkley continued.

"Look at the Suns players who still work for the organization, or are still involved. The former players have no relationship with the Sixers. Look at Moses, look at Doc, look at Maurice, look at Andrew and Bobby. No player who was any good is still involved. It's just not that type of organization. But when you look at the Suns, Celtics, or Lakers, they are. I'll always be a 76er. I just wish the situation I'm in now could have happened here."

Barkley cited Colangelo's commitment to winning, regardless of the cost.

This homecoming was an emotional experience for Barkley, who also was reunited with his wife, Maureen, and his daughter, Christiana, during the weekend.

"Obviously, there's going to be hype. It's my first time back, and it's on NBC for the whole world to see," Barkley said. "The thing I have to do is just relax and play, not try to play too well. When we played the Sixers in Phoenix, I played angry because of my resentment toward the organization. I don't want to play that way again. I was mad. That's over now. This time, I expect to feel a little more relaxed."

Westphal, who was traded a few times himself, doubted that Barkley needed his insight to help him through.

"But me being traded was like a blip on the radar screen. Charles being traded was high on the Richter scale," Westphal said. "Charles is used to hype everywhere he goes. He'll be ready."

Ainge felt similarly, but talk of the homecoming caused him to reflect on his first trip back to Boston Garden after being traded to Sacramento.

"They gave me a 10-minute standing ovation and that made me feel that what I did was appreciated and worthwhile," Ainge said. "Man, it was difficult. There were so many distractions. I knew the Celtics didn't want me anymore, so there was incentive to have a good game. But they trapped me hard. I had a terrible time even getting shots off. But the first time Boston came to Sacramento, I scored 39 points and we took them to overtime."

The difference, Ainge said, is Barkley is an international superstar and the Suns had the best record in the league.

"So I don't think Charles needs any advice from me or anyone else about how to handle this," Ainge said. "Plus I know the fans here really appreciate him. I expect them to really help Charles."

No one envisioned exactly how much. As the Suns ran onto the floor, the Spectrum crowd rose and greeted them with a lengthy and deafening cheer. It was quite a moving moment when Barkley's shining head finally popped into view at the end of the line and the crowd's roar seemed to climb several decibels.

What an embarrassment that had to be for Katz. This wasn't going to be a road game for the Suns, it seemed. Barkley was appreciated. This was the guy who used to rip his laggard teammates to their faces in the locker room, who once was fined $3,000 by Katz for saying, "We've just got a bad team. The whole damn team is bad." He took on Katz without fear of reprisal. Asked about his brazen attitude, Barkley once bristled and responded, "I'm a '90s nigger. I do whatever I want."

He never hid his perception of the City of Brotherly Love as racist. He's cited the treatment of sports luminaries who played for the city's other major league franchises, particularly the NFL Eagles. Most of those sports' great players happened to be black. A recent example was the Eagles allowing free agent defensive end Reggie White to get away. It took some doing, but the Eagles now are held in almost as low esteem as the Sixers.

As it stood and roared its approval of Barkley, the sellout crowd seemed to be saying that not only did they miss him, but that he was right. Interestingly, the Philadelphia news media wouldn't admit it. That morning, *The Philadelphia Inquirer* ran a story on Barkley suggesting that he was the same boorish troublemaker he'd always been, that Phoenix fans and news media view him through rose-colored glasses, and that Barkley "was keeping away as many fans during the regular season as he was attracting" before he was sent to Phoenix.

Given the size of *this* crowd, it was an interesting theory. If true, that meant that on this rainy Sunday morning, Barkley had kept away 18,168 — with travel treacherous, when every one of them could have watched it at home on NBC. Yet they were there. Eighteen, one-sixty-eight. Only the Sixers' third sellout of the season, and the other two were for Jordan and the Bulls. They didn't come to see Barkley fall on his face, and he didn't.

The Suns had come out first. When the Sixers finally came onto the floor, they were booed. At 21-45, they were on a pace to have their worst record in 20 years.

As Ainge had predicted, they were there to applaud Barkley's every move, and jab the Sixers at every chance. Katz sat slack-jawed. Even in his closed little world, he had never anticipated this.

"You would expect to have the fans' support at home," said Sixers guard Johnny Dawkins. "We had nothing to do with Charles leaving. This is the most disappointing thing I have experienced in basketball."

Did Barkley revel in it? Of course. As the boos grew louder as the Sixers were introduced in the darkened arena, Barkley sat at the end of the Suns bench wearing a huge grin.

"I'm not an evil person, and I have nothing against the Sixers players," Barkley said. "I really don't wish anyone ill."

But he was enjoying the moment.

There were signs everywhere. "It's a Katz-astrophe." "Trade Katz for Barkley." Behind the Sixers bench, someone had stationed a life-size cardboard cutout of Barkley in a Sixers uniform.

Later, when the Suns had their 110-100 victory well in hand, after Barkley scored 15 of his 35 points in the fourth quarter, the Spectrum crowd broke into chants of, "MVP! MVP!" That's something even the crowds at America West Arena hadn't gotten around to doing yet.

When Barkley went to the free-throw line with 51 seconds left, ready to ensure the Sixers' 23rd loss in 27 games, something scary happened. A fan eluded security and ran onto the court, grabbed the stunned Barkley, and hugged him.

"He told me, 'I'm probably going to get arrested, but I'm happy to meet you,'" Barkley said later. "I thought it was really funny. I just hope he doesn't get into trouble over it."

Barkley missed three of his first four shots and admitted that he was nervous. He also was covered by the 6-11 Lang. New Sixers coach Fred Carter noted that taller players had given Barkley and the Suns trouble recently, and Carter figured that Lang would be motivated to show a national TV audience that the Suns were wrong in including him in that trade package.

But Barkley's teammates stepped up until he fell into his comfort zone. Ceballos had a career-high 15 rebounds to go with 26 points.

"We wanted Charles to have a big game," said Ceballos, who in 13 starts in place of Dumas was averaging 20.5 points and 9.8 rebounds. "We were going to do everything we could to put him into a situation where he could succeed."

West grabbed 12 rebounds and shut down the only real Sixers nemesis, rookie Clarence Weatherspoon — who has been called the next Barkley and might have felt that he had something to prove as well.

Overlooked was the return of KJ from his suspension. He responded with 19 points and eight assists.

"I've had a lot of time this season to reflect on what I mean to this team," KJ said. "If Chuck didn't warrant it and Paul asked me to do it, I might have a problem with changing my role. I knew when he came here that mine probably would be the most important one in terms of me accepting it and executing it. I have had to change my game a bit, let go of things for the betterment of the team.

"The common goal is winning. I'm sure that if we weren't winning, that Charles and I would be banging heads. We've all had to make adjustments, but it wasn't as difficult maybe for some guys who are accustomed to being complementary players."

KJ, whose only public comment on the fight and suspension had been a terse, "Sometimes referees make the wrong decisions," broke his silence. He said he had written a "strong letter" to NBA operations chief Rod Thorn

"I just told him I thought what they did to me was wrong," KJ said. "As far as any appeals go, I'll wait until I hear back from Rod to see what his response is."

But the day belonged unquestionably to Barkley. He avoided any confrontations with the old teammates he'd ripped, particularly Armon Gilliam and Charles Shackleford, although Barkley did break into a wide grin when Gilliam was called for traveling when he tried to score inside on Barkley.

"It was an interesting experience," Colangelo said. "And it couldn't have happened any better than it did, with one exception: The fact that that fan got on the floor. That was a little bit scary. That shouldn't have happened."

"I'm just glad it's over," Barkley said. So were the Suns.

"Paul has said all along that the more distractions we have before the playoffs, the better off we'll be because that's going to be a media circus, too," KJ said. "I was glad for Charles, coming back and having a big game and having the fans respond to him like they did. And I was glad for us. It was a challenge for all of us."

But it was only the beginning. The next stop was Chicago where the two-time champion Bulls were anxious to prove that the Suns, while having the best record, weren't necessarily the best team.

Chambers was placed on the injured list and Dumas activated, although Dumas was not ready to play significant minutes. The way Ceballos was going, the Suns didn't need huge contributions from Dumas. It was unclear whether Chambers would make it back before the season ended. He'd suffered multiple muscle tears in his left quadricep, and only four weeks remained.

"It looks pretty bad for him," Westphal said.

Meanwhile, it was starting to look good for the Suns. They arrived in Chicago five games ahead of both the Bulls and Knicks in the loss column. That meant that a finish of at least 11-4 would assure the Suns of the home-court edge throughout the playoffs.

That was beginning to appear to be a realistic goal.

"I felt in my mind we were not going to lose 20 this year," KJ said. "I really believe that. Every other team already has lost 20."

Westphal figured that if the Suns could sweep the trip — what a lofty goal that was! — he could begin to rest players and prepare for the playoffs.

"We do have a nice big lead," he said. "If we can come off this trip and not be hurt too badly, I think we'll be real close to locking up the best record. That's why the Philadelphia win was so important. We wanted to make sure we got one on this trip. Now, if we can get one more, we'll be OK. But if we can get two or three more, we'll about have it locked up."

With a road record of 22-11 — tied for the league best with Chicago — that seemed reasonable for the Suns.

"I don't think we're striving for some level of perfection that isn't attainable," KJ said. "But if we want to win, we can't afford to play at only a fraction of our ability as we sometimes do. This is a great challenge. The Bulls beat us in Phoenix. We've had a few letdowns against the Eastern Conference, and they could be representing the East in the championships."

But in Chicago, the reporters and fans — and probably even the Bulls — weren't convinced the Suns were legit until they increased a quick 6-0 lead to 29-15, and then held on for a 113-109 win at Chicago Stadium on Tuesday, March 30.

"It was a rough day reading the newspapers here," Barkley said. "One called us 'Pretenders, not Contenders.' Another said we were too small.

"It's frustrating having to prove yourself all the time. It's like we're playing a different schedule, like we're playing the Little Sisters of the Poor and everybody else is playing real NBA teams. It's unnecessary. It's uncalled for. We have a fantastic team. We've proved 53 times this season what we really are."

No other team had proven it as many as 50 times yet. The Suns hadn't relinquished the best record since the day they achieved it back in Charlotte on December 9.

Now, in a span of seven days, the Suns had beaten the Knicks and Bulls, the two strongest teams in the East, quieting some of the critics who said they couldn't beat anybody to the right of the Mississippi.

"If we'd lost to the Knicks, maybe we'd have some serious questions ourselves as to whether we can win," Westphal said. "They'd have been creeping up on us. Now, we have a nice cushion."

Mathematically, this wasn't a game that secured anything for the Suns. Psychologically, it was. This was the rallying point of the closing drive.

KJ cut loose for 16 assists, his most of the season, to go with 23 points. "I really believed that if I ever got out there for any length of time, that good things would happen."

Ceballos continued his tear, making Scottie Pippen look like a stick figure. Ceballos went for 27 points, 21 of those in the first half, and many of them slam dunks in Pippen's face as Ceballos slashed to the basket without much resistance.

"That was not something we had expected," Bulls coach Jackson admitted.

Westphal said he wasn't surprised, though. "I think the Bulls found out that you can't guard Kevin or Charles with one man, and that if you double them, Ced will slash to the basket for easy ones, or Dan and Danny will bury a three. I've been saying that KJ adds so much when he's healthy, and I think people are seeing that now."

The Suns showed their mettle down the stretch and, typically, they did it the hard way. They lost the lead when Jordan drove for a basket that put the Bulls ahead by two points with just over five minutes to play.

"You knew they were going to make a run sometime," KJ said. "But I honestly never felt there was a doubt because we dictated the game from start to finish."

As Barkley said, "It was just two points. That's nothing. We came right back at them and answered every challenge they threw at us." With 26 points and four steals, Barkley always had an answer for Chicago.

Jordan, who scored 44, said he thought Barkley got the Suns motivated after the Bulls handed them that 17-point loss in November at America West Arena, when Barkley said they couldn't be puppies if they wanted to play with the big dogs.

"You know it doesn't take much to get him started," Jordan said. "He's got them strong now."

The one thing the Suns really needed was rest. That's something that normally is hard to come by on a long trip, but through a quirk in scheduling, the Suns had two off nights coming up in Boston before taking on the Celtics in the Garden on Friday, April 2.

"Even without Richard and Tom—and they're two vital parts—we're showing our true colors," KJ said.

And the Suns, who tied franchise records with their 23rd road win and their 13-3 run through March, got good news concerning both players. Dumas returned to action in Chicago. Although it was for only two uneventful minutes, he was on the road back. And Chambers, according to Suns medical personnel, wasn't injured as seriously as first thought. He might return in two weeks instead of four.

First things first. In the Garden, the Suns ended the Celtics' nine-game winning streak as Barkley scored 37 points and grabbed 11 rebounds in the 118-114 win. Reggie Lewis scored 32 points as the Celtics kept coming back on the Suns. Three tough, emotional, hard-fought road wins in tough places.

They took out the Pacers, 110-100, to extend their club record for road wins to 25, their overall win streak to seven, and finish 12-2 on the road against the Eastern Conference. Twelve and two. The only losses were the controversial one in Madison Square Garden where Barkley chased Jimmy Clark, and the following game in Cleveland when Barkley was suspended.

They were that close to sweeping the Eastern Conference ON THE ROAD. Overall, they finished with a franchise-record 22-6 mark against the East. For those who bashed the Suns as a gang of softies from the sunbelt, that's a higher winning percentage than any other team had against the East. There was a lot of emotion in the Suns' locker room. They'd suspected all along that they were on the verge of greatness. While these accomplishments didn't necessarily put them there, they certainly gave them tangible evidence that they were within arm's reach.

It wasn't a done deal by any means, but none of them doubted now that they would have home-court edge through the playoffs. This really was a special moment in their season.

"Don't anyone tell me we can't play with the East; that's bogus," said Barkley, borrowing one of KJ's favorite words. "We've lost more games against the West."

The Suns were at 55 wins— two short of the club record— and staring 60 in the face.

"We don't care about that," Barkley said. "We just want to have the best record, whatever it takes."

Barkley and KJ know what it takes. On this trip, Barkley averaged 32.7 points and 8.3 rebounds. He would be named NBA player of the week. Over nine games, KJ was averaging 17.1 points and 9.3 assists.

"Sometimes the legitimate knock on us is that we get ahead and relax," Westphal said. "We have gotten better at attacking pressure defense. When we get smooth on that, nobody will even be able to think about pressing us.

"We've kind of turned into a defensive team. That showed on this trip. That starts with Kevin, who has been phenomenal since he came off the injured list. And I don't think there's any debate that Charles is the MVP."

What also emerged on this trip was the Suns' maturity. They were challenged at each stop, but they didn't buckle. And they were getting help from new sources.

Miller, for instance, was the hero in the Indiana game with his career-high 16 rebounds, nine of those in the first quarter.

"I know we've got a great record when we outrebound the opponent (41-2)," Miller said. "That's an easy way to win, and I can help us do that."

Westphal had been playing Miller at power forward alongside West in certain situations, but this time Miller got the call at center after West picked up two quick fouls.

They rode a huge wave back to Phoenix. Their magic number for locking up the home-court edge in the playoffs was eight with 12 games remaining.

Westphal planned to rest worn out warriors Barkley, Majerle, and Ainge. KJ would play only in the first of back-to-back games to avoid fatigue and hopefully reduce the risk of injury. And, Westphal still wanted to tinker with certain looks. He was growing fond of playing West and Miller together, perhaps sensing that he'd need the size against troublesome big teams in the playoffs.

"The key is to have both healthy and neither in foul trouble, or we can't use them together," Westphal said.

He also wanted to get Dumas more minutes to work him back into the rotation.

Going into the playoffs, Westphal expected to have something that, he rarely had all season: his top 12 players together healthy.

"It's unimaginable what it would be like," Westphal said. "We haven't experienced that yet. You can get by with eight or nine guys like we've been doing as long as they're versatile enough to play a couple of positions."

# Chapter Twenty-four

# BOMBS AWAY!

In the first game at home after a long trip, players' defenses are down. They want to unwind and catch their breath. They tend to assume that playing at home is an automatic win.

That is especially true when the team that is paying the call is one that you've thrashed all season. Like the Lakers.

It had been five years since they'd won a championship, but it still seems strange viewing the Lakers as a guaranteed win. The Lakers had lost eight out of nine and were two games below .500 going into the closing three weeks of the season. A playoff berth was anything but certain for them.

So conditions were favorable for trouble.

This game, perhaps more than any other, epitomized the Suns' season. It was going a little too well. The Suns opened with 44 first-quarter points and were up by 20 early in the fourth quarter. Westphal began sending in bench players.

KJ had scored a season-high 32 points, 21 in that first-half bombardment. Then, in the fourth quarter, the Suns went almost 8 1/2 minutes without making a field goal. The Lakers roared back.

With 1:27 remaining, Byron Scott swished a three-point basket that gave the Lakers a 110-109 lead, and then Scott's two free throws with 24 seconds remaining made it a three-point deficit.

It was a stunning turnaround. Not to worry, though. Majerle answered with a three-pointer that tied it with 11 seconds left.

Lakers' turn. As the clock ticked down to 1.6 seconds, rookie guard Anthony Peeler turned and fired a 17-footer over KJ that hit nothing but net. Lakers by two.

This time, the Suns had played with fire and been burned. Or had they?

As the Suns trudged over to the bench for their timeout strategy session, Westphal tried to hearten them by saying, "OK, baby, it's not over." Sure, sure.

The Suns had their play and they were inbounding from mid-court with just a tick more than a second left. Wisely, the Lakers took a delay-of-game warning before Miller could fire the inbound pass, their way of surveying the Suns' alignment without using a timeout.

A. C. Green correctly diagnosed what Westphal had cooked up: Majerle was going to come off a Barkley screen and launch another three-pointer. Green advised his teammates.

Could that really be? The Suns must have anticipated the delay-of-game warning. This had to be a decoy. Two points would send it to overtime. The Suns acquired one of the game's best low-post players expressly for situations like this. Surely, if he didn't score, he'd get fouled, or both. They had to go to Barkley. Why put it all on the line with a risky three-point shot?

Green knew the Suns a little too well — and before long would get to know them a lot better. Majerle moved a few steps back, more than 30 feet in front of the basket. That appeared to be too far for even Majerle to get off a makeable shot in the time remaining.

But in it came to Majerle. Green ran at him, but Majerle's 33-footer was in the air.

It seemed to hang for minutes. Majerle had been directly in front of the basket , an easy spot, squared up, with a good look.

When it ripped through the cords for a 115-114 win, the arena erupted in a deafening roar that lasted for minutes. It was as if the Suns had won the world championship. Even the normally cool and collected Majerle jumped on the scorer's table and danced as the cheers rained down.

"I'd been telling our guys that I have crazy range," Majerle said. "But that's the first time I've hit one like that, especially that far, to win a game. I had to celebrate.

"We let the Lakers hang around, and they hit some big shots. But no matter how you do it, it's exciting to win like that. I don't know if we get overconfident or what, but we've had so much success this year, we just have the feeling that we're going to win no matter what."

That's the Suns for you. Most coaches would have been looking for the two-pointer. Not these guys. Not this collection of oddballs.

"I'm just glad it went in, because it kind of saved me for the night," said Barkley, who struggled through eight-for-19 shooting, including two-for-nine in the second half. "They were getting me the ball but I couldn't make anything happen. It's like I was point-shaving. It's a bad feeling when you're out there hurting your team."

But, as Barkley has said so many times, this is a team on which he doesn't have to be Charles Barkley every night.

"All those plays have two or three options," Westphal said. "I'd have been happy to go to Charles, but I thought that Majerle would be the open man just based on where we had our guys. And it turned out that he was. With so little time we really don't have the luxury of deciding who's going to take the shot. All you can do is hope that things work right and somebody gets a good shot."

There seemed to be some force working for the Suns this night on many fronts. In addition to their miracle finish, New York lost to Atlanta, Chicago to Milwaukee, and Seattle to Dallas — of all teams — at home. They'd gained a game on their three closest competitors on Tuesday, April 6, and it marked the first time ever that the Suns swept the season series from the Lakers.

The Suns seemed to be toying with them as they let that big lead slip away. Miller was shooting jumpers. Ceballos was going behind the back on his way to the basket and turning it over. They'd play just well enough in spurts to keep the Lakers at bay.

"It was a miracle answered," said Green, who as a lay minister, knows a miracle when he sees one. "You always remember your last impression, and this obviously is ours. It will stay with us. But we should use this as a positive and build on it instead of letting it be devastating and thinking that we can't possibly find a way to win against this team if we meet them in the playoffs."

Again, prophetic words from a man who seemed to know.

Ahead for the Suns: a visit to Sacramento on Thursday, April 8; a home game with Denver on Friday; and a visit by the Utah Jazz on Sunday.

Spirits were high. They were loose and confident. It was their version of spring fever. The Suns had won eight straight, and 16 of their past 18. They were a win away from tying their all-time best, 57.

It's a great sign that his players find these unorthodox ways to win, Westphal said, "but I wish we didn't have to do it that way. It'd be all right with me if we blew somebody out once in a while."

"It's made for some interesting finishes and we've probably allowed our opponents to shoot a higher percentage than we should have," Westphal said. "There are times when Charles gets bored, and I don't think that's going to happen in the playoffs. I'm not putting it all on him by any means. But when there's a challenge, that's when Charles is at his best. When we're up 20 in the fourth quarter, he's not going to be the same as when the game is on the line. I think when we get to the playoffs, you're going to really see Charles turn it on."

Should it be any surprise, then, that when the Suns were down by three in the fourth quarter at Arco Arena that Barkley turned it on and pulled them to their 57th win, 123-114?

Ceballos, who has his best games against the Kings, had a 28-point, eight-rebound outing before suffering a stress fracture on the final play of the game. It would prove to be a significant event.

Neither Ceballos nor KJ, who scored 21 points and had seven assists, was expected to play the following night back home against the Nuggets.

"Let's not joke ourselves, it's hard to get motivated for a game like this," said Barkley, who scored 20 points in Sacramento. But Majerle, who scored 22, said that "we all know this is a special year for us. We've got to take advantage of it. It would be a shame to blow a game like this against a team we know we should beat."

And, predictably, the Suns had to hang on for a cliff-hanging 98-97 win against the Nuggets, who had lost nine straight and 13 of its past 14 games in Phoenix, and whose 7-30 road record was among the worst in the league. It was victory No. 58, a club record.

With 2.9 seconds remaining, Ainge swished a 20-foot game-winner after Majerle's offensive rebound of a Barkley miss gave the Suns a second chance to save the game.

The Nuggets had one last chance, but guard Robert Pack slipped on a drive while guarded by Frank Johnson, who made seven of 11 shots playing in place of the resting KJ.

"We'd have been in trouble this year without Frankie," Westphal said. "I don't know how many games he's helped us pull out."

Barkley had helped them pull out a few, too, and this was no exception. He posted his league-leading sixth triple-double — 26 points, 19 rebounds, 12 assists. Westphal joked that Barkley actually had a quadruple-double, once his 16 missed shots were factored in.

"All in all," Westphal said, "we were fortunate to score 98 points. We could not make a basket."

The Suns shot 40 percent. Only their opening-night 38.2 against the Clippers was worse. Dumas, back for the injured Ceballos, missed 10 of his 11 shots. Frank Johnson scored 14 points, inspired by Barkley's eavesdropping on the Denver huddle.

"Charles told me he heard them saying, 'Don't leave Danny, leave Frank' when they double-teamed," Johnson said. "It's like they basically challenged me to step up."

Four of his baskets came during the final eight minutes.

"He should," Barkley said. "His man is sitting in my lap. All he's got to do is hit wide-open jumpers."

That they had broken their all-time win record was hardly even discussed by the Suns, who assumed they'd surpass the old mark set in 1980-81.

Those Suns were upset in their opening round, after having a first-round bye, by the Kansas City Kings — coached by Cotton Fitzsimmons.

Fitzsimmons said that 57-game winner "was a really good team, but it can't compare with this team. The Suns have so many weapons today. But let's give the '81 team its due. It was the only team to win a Pacific Division title in the '80s except the Los Angeles Lakers."

According to Fitzsimmons, "What really got them in the playoffs was expectations, which we hope doesn't happen again to this team. There were a lot of similarities, but the 57-game winner had nobody as dominating as Charles Barkley. I think you'd have to call DJ [Dennis Johnson] against Majerle a tossup. The '81 team didn't have the quickness and penetration of Kevin Johnson. It did have an outstanding center in Alvan Adams, who did it with outside shooting, passing, and finesse. And Truck Robinson was very good, but he certainly was no Barkley."

Robinson concurred, saying, "This team has a much better chance than my team had. They've got all the pieces. Oliver Miller and Mark West are going to be the keys to this team getting to the Finals. We sure didn't have the fun these guys are having now. It was all work, work, work for us. Paul gives these guys a day off once in a while."

It was Easter Sunday, April 11. And a win over the Jazz would give the Suns their second Pacific Division title and home-court edge through at least the Western Conference playoffs.

"These are the dog days," Barkley said. "We just want to get them over with, sew up the best record, and get on to the playoffs."

This one was easier for the Suns than some of their battles against the likes of Sacramento and Denver. With 29 points and nine assists from KJ, the Suns walloped the Jazz, 112-99. The Suns blew it open in the fourth period when they held Stockton and Karl Malone to a combined six points.

Majerle played 41 minutes, KJ 40, and Barkley 37. Westphal said no longer would that be the case, effective the following night in Los Angeles against the troublesome Clippers.

"I don't want to wear anybody out," Westphal said, "but at the same time, I don't want to disappoint the fans who've paid to see these guys play. This will be our fourth game in five nights, and we still have a lot of big games coming up."

When Ainge swished a three-pointer that gave the Suns a nine-point edge over the Jazz with just under three minutes to play, Barkley leaned over the scorer's table to Fitzsimmons, who was doing radio color commentary, and said, "Well, that's one banner out of the way."

It was a reminder to Cotton that, months earlier, Fitzsimmons pointed out that Barkley had played no part in erecting or selling out the Purple Palace. Instead, Barkley's charge was to hang banners from the rafters of the new structure.

But during a battle for a rebound with Karl Malone, Barkley suffered a strained muscle in his right shoulder. That meant that he'd pass on the trip to Los Angeles — as did KJ, Ceballos, and Chambers.

"You just don't want to sit out too much and lose timing," KJ said. "But Paul hasn't made too many mistakes this year."

"Man," Barkley said, "the worst thing about this is I won't be able to play golf. I just want to be healthy. I came here with one goal. If we lose, let's lose because some team outplayed us. Let's not lose because of freak injuries. That would be cruel."

Barkley was placed on the injured list. By league rules, he would have to miss a minimum of five games. Dr. Emerson said Barkley was looking at "at least a week."

The Sports Arena didn't appear to be the ideal venue to go for their 60th win, not under these conditions — perhaps not even under the best conditions. The Suns lost both previous games there. Sounded like the ingredients for a bus wreck.

And, as if things weren't suddenly looking down enough, they actually had one on their way to a 111-104 loss that ended an 11-game winning streak.

The crash came at the intersection of Crenshaw and Slauson in South-Central Los Angeles on the afternoon that a verdict in the Rodney King civil rights trial was expected. Police were braced for another riot. South-Central LA was the last place to be if a not-guilty verdict was returned against the police officers who were on trial. It turned out the King verdict did not come down, none of the Suns were injured in the crash, and they got in and out of town without further mishap.

However, Ainge joked after his four-for-19 shooting that he was suffering from whiplash. "My performance should help me with my lawsuit against the bus company."

The Suns normally arrive 90 minutes before a game. They lost about 35 minutes because of the incident.

"We had to sit there and wait while the police filled out the proper forms," an irked Westphal said.

They had only nine players in uniform, and among those who suited up were West, who was limited by his sore back; Frank Johnson, who almost didn't make it after suffering food poisoning; Mustaf, who'd been on the injured list for two weeks; and Kempton.

"Still," Majerle said, "we expected to win. We didn't come looking for moral victories. We have enough guys on this team who can step up and win a game like this. And we would have, if we'd got a few shots to drop at the end."

But as they had in nearly every other game against the Clippers, the Suns shot miserably. This time: 41 percent.

The only bright spot was Dumas, who showed the first signs of returning to form with 28 points and a career-high 12 rebounds. With Ceballos out indefinitely, having Dumas back was a necessity.

The Suns' 60th win would have to wait at least one more game, at home against Minnesota, a team that never had beaten them. Barkley was concerned that the Suns' chemistry, great during the 11-game streak, would be disrupted while he was out.

"It's so good right now, and things are going so well," he said. "It would be better if I had to miss only two or three games."

Westphal planned to start Dumas and Ceballos together at the forwards, and to take a longer look at West and Miller together — score permitting. Chambers also was activated. Westphal tried them all, and none was particularly effective. Still, the Suns glided to a 98-84 victory and their 60th win.

"It's just a number," Majerle said. "If we win 65 and then lose in the first round of the playoffs, it wouldn't mean anything."

As Ainge pointed out, "It's not our real team out there."

And as Barkley said, after sitting on the bench in street clothes, "Are the games this boring when I'm playing?"

And finally, KJ said, "We went after each other harder in practice than we did against Minnesota in the game. And we probably had more fun in practice, too."

Only nine other franchises have reached the 60-win milestone. Of greater importance to the players, though, was that the victory reduced the Suns' magic number to one for clinching home-court edge throughout the playoffs. Another Suns win or another Knicks loss would do it.

The Suns' rookies — Dumas and Miller — each felt he had a point to make against the Timberwolves' highly touted rookie, Christian Laettner. Laettner, the only college player on the Dream Team, was the third pick in the 1992 draft. But in this game, he was only the third-best rookie on the floor. Dumas and Miller felt that, absent a few warts, they would have been draft lottery picks like Laettner and they were eager to show him.

Miller had a career-high six blocked shots. Dumas was good for 22 points, seven rebounds, and four assists.

"I really believe Richard matches up with anyone who was in the lottery except Shaq," Westphal said. "And 'O' is contributing to the winningest team in the league. There aren't many rookies I'd trade them for."

Laettner had four shots blocked and committed 10 turnovers.

"I know if things had been right, I'd have been up there, too," said Miller, who was bumped down to the Suns at No. 22 because of his weight.

And, added Dumas, "Deep down, I'd like to prove to people that I would have been a lottery pick. I put the team first, but you can have personal goals, too, if you know how to handle them."

Dumas also seemed to be learning how to handle his life, something that cost him a high first-round selection.

It was Friday, April 16, when the Sonics came to town. They'd split their past 10 games, and Coach George Karl was shaking up his lineup again.

The Indiana-New York game was beginning two hours ahead of the Suns-Sonics. If the Pacers won, the race was over. The Suns' record would be unsurpassed.

During the break between the first and second quarters, the news came over the public-address system at 8:03 p.m.: Indiana 100, New York 94.

The road to the NBA championship now officially ran directly through the Purple Palace, where the Suns would enjoy home-court edge throughout the playoffs. The news was greeted with a long standing ovation, which the Suns acknowledged with nods.

They lost to the Sonics, 108-102, but they wouldn't have to pick up the newspaper any longer to read what their magic number was for clinching.

"Since I've been on this team, we've been building for this day," West said. "But now that it's here, it's just another stop on a long road to our ultimate goal."

West and KJ have been with the Suns the longest, coming from Cleveland in a trade in February, 1988.

"I don't know that this is an unbelievable feeling," KJ said, "but it is a great accomplishment. We have a great record at home, now we have to do something positive with it."

Chambers, who came to the Suns in July, 1988, when Fitzsimmons was taking over as coach, called it "a proud moment."

"It means a lot to have played for this franchise, to be part of about 300 wins over five years, to play for the best team, really, over that span," Chambers said.

And then, Westphal would utter the most controversial words of the season.

"The last five games are exhibitions," Westphal said. Exhibition season. While true, it set a tone that would characterize the Suns' play. What Westphal said was correct. The games no longer meant anything. The Suns had what they wanted. It was all wrapped up. But the Suns also didn't want to lose the competitive edge that had carried them so far.

"You can't lie to the players, they know these games are exhibitions now," Westphal said. "This game became one as soon as the Indiana score was announced. But I don't want us to get in the habit of losing. This is nice. I wouldn't want anybody else to have home-court through the playoffs. Everybody wanted it, we got it."

There was trouble ahead, though. The Suns had not lost more than two in a row all season, but coming up were games the following night at Utah, then Houston at home, a visit to Portland — when Barkley would be eligible to return from the injured list— and then a home game with San Antonio before a season-ending visit to Denver.

In keeping with the late-season, no back-to-back rule for KJ, he didn't make the trip to Salt Lake City. They all might as well have stayed home. Westphal started Mustaf who, along with his teammates, did little in a 110-101 loss. It was exhibition basketball at its finest, although Ceballos came through with 25 points and 10 rebounds to make it close at the end.

It didn't get any better for the Suns when, two nights later, they became the Rockets' 10th straight victim, 111-97. For the first time this season, the Suns had dropped three straight games. This was worse than "exhibition season" for the Suns. It was more like "expansion." In the opening quarter, they shot 23 percent and scored only 13 points.

Hakeem Olajuwon, building late-season steam as a challenger to Barkley for MVP, showed why with his 30 points, 14 rebounds, and five blocked shots.

"We were embarrassed, I was embarrassed," said Westphal, whose team was booed by the home fans after falling 20 points in arrears in that awful first period. There were suggestions that the streaking Rockets had become the team to beat in the West.

"Well, we're not saying that," said Rockets guard Kenny Smith, whose 18 points and 12 assists were too much for the Suns. "Hey, they've got Charles Barkley sitting down there on their bench right now in his pinstriped suit. He'll come back and change the complexion of a lot of things. No one in here is thinking the Suns are in a slump. I doubt if they're thinking they are. They're just having fun now. Heck, they're probably even playing golf on game days."

Probably.

Since a seven-game skid put the Rockets two games under .500 in mid-January, they'd won a whopping 40 of 49 games.

Majerle played a season-low 21 minutes, none in long spurts. "I hate playing like this.

Westphal hastened to say that this game doesn't mean the Suns won't be ready for the playoffs. "It means we still have some work to do. We'll get it back. We still have three exhibition games left, and I'm not going to panic. Whether we finish with 63 wins or 60, when the playoffs start, we'll be ready."

Ainge predicted more of an effort against the Trail Blazers on Thursday, April 22. "Heck, we can't come out with any less."

The Suns lost three in a row and four of the five while Barkley was on the injured list.

As he normally does following an effortless loss, Westphal worked the lads hard in the practice gym. Two hours and 10 minutes worth. He doesn't normally close the workouts to reporters, though.

"We just wanted to get our focus back," Westphal said.

Afterward, Barkley said his shoulder felt fine, but his conditioning was shot. Strength and conditioning coach Robin Pound confirmed that with a little after-practice drill with Barkley that had him huffing and puffing. During a scrimmage, his sore shoulder "got hit pretty good a couple of times. I didn't do anything crazy, I just wanted to see if I could bang a little."

Despite his conditioning loss, Barkley's shoulder seemed healed enough for him to play, so he would be activated for the final three "exhibition" games.

"I'm sure I'll come back a little rusty," Barkley said. "I want to be 100 percent and at my best for the playoffs. I think that will be about a week-long process to get there."

While saying there was no excuse for the Suns' lack of effort against the Rockets, Barkley said he's not shocked that his teammates lost while he was out.

"I am a vital part of our team," he said. "It's tough to win without me. Kevin hasn't played every game and obviously I haven't played for a week and a half. We've got to get back on the same page. I don't want us to develop any bad habits."

Meanwhile, Westphal was trying to straighten everyone out on exactly what he meant by "exhibitions." He said that was the idea behind the closed workout, to "get back to basics, find intensity, refocus on what we want to do offensively and defensively.

"I don't know if people got the wrong idea when I said the rest of these games are exhibitions for us," Westphal said. "What I meant by that is we can't go up or down in the standings, so the games don't mean anything in that regard. But we always try to play combinations that we want to see that might benefit us down the road. I think the players understand that.

"I won't back off on what I said. We will be ready for the playoffs."

# Chapter Twenty-five

# FOLLOW THE BOUNCING BALL

Over an 11-game stretch, Ainge was shooting only 32.1 percent. In that skid was a four-for-19 outing against the Clippers and one-for-12 against the Rockets. Ainge said it wasn't his age, or playing more minutes. He was just shooting the ball a little too flat. That was good enough for Westphal, who added, "I'd still put my money on him for the last shot."

There was another reason for Ainge's skid, but it took a couple more days before he grudgingly admitted that he'd been hiding a wrist injury for some time. The admission came following an April 22 visit to Portland.

This one was anything but easy for the Suns, even though Barkley made six of his first eight shots. He showed no lingering effects of his shoulder injury.

The Blazers had won seven straight at home and nine out of 11 overall. For the first time, they were showing signs of not giving up their Western Conference crown easily.

In the third quarter, Portland sprang 12 points in front after the score was tied. Just as quickly, the Suns came back to take a one-point lead. Back and forth it went to the finish, until a three-pointer by Chambers tied the game with 1:24 remaining.

A dramatic three-point play by Chambers with 3.7 seconds left gave the Suns a one-point edge, and, seemingly, the game. But with 0.5 second showing, Cliff Robinson of the Blazers broke the Suns' hearts by swishing a 20-footer that caused the sellout crowd to erupt. The Suns called a timeout and had the ball at mid-court. A half-second left.

It would take nothing short of another miracle fling like Majerle's that beat the Lakers' hearts 16 days earlier. There was less time remaining, though, in this situation.

The Blazers expected a lob to Ceballos, who stationed himself under the basket. Miller would throw the inbounds pass. According to the rules, the clock does not start until the ball is touched by a player inbounds. The Suns reminded the officiating crew of that during the timeout, and it soon became apparent why.

Miller fired the ball from mid-court off the backboard. The Blazers didn't react, assuming there was no way the Suns had enough time left to grab the loose ball and get off a shot. They obviously were not students of Suns history.

The clock had yet to begin ticking when Barkley grabbed the loose ball on the ricochet, flung it toward the basket, and it ripped through the cords as the horn sounded.

Portland Memorial Coliseum was like a morgue. Final score: Suns 115, Blazers 114.

If the Blazers fans were frozen silent by what they had just witnessed — which was another creative piece of coaching from the fertile mind of Westphal — the Suns were delirious. The skid was over. Barkley was back. And they'd finally pulled out a close one on the floor where they had lost so many.

"That was a very well-conceived play, and that's very typical of Paul's coaching," Robertson said. "He considers himself an offensive-minded coach and he enjoys coming up with plays that have some frills to them. He also enjoys doing the unexpected as this play.

"So that type play, while it was the most dramatic of the year, was only one of many that you might call out of the ordinary that Paul employed during the course of the season — like having Charles Barkley out at the top in an open set playing one-on-one to take the final shot of a quarter or game."

After the season, Westphal recalled that his ricochet play-call "just came spur of the moment."

"It was such a longshot," he said. "It just seemed like a good idea. Actually, it didn't come quite spur of the moment. I was kicking myself for not having done it earlier. There was a game that we lost earlier in the year that we were in a similar situation and I didn't think of that. In rehashing that game in my mind, I kept thinking, 'I wonder if we'd thrown the ball off the backboard . . .' So if the situation came up again, I was ready with it.

"I've seen teams throw a pass off the backboard as a play. In fact, we did it in exhibition, and Houston used to do it with Billy Paultz catching in the high post, and they'd have Moses Malone flashing to the low post. If the defense fronted Moses, Paultz would throw the ball off the backboard, and Moses just turned and rebounded the ball. So it wasn't a play that's never been run before in basketball. But inbounding from half-court I've never seen run. The advantage is the clock doesn't start when it hits the backboard, so it's like an inbound pass from underneath. You can't count on it working very often, but there was a good element of surprise there in Portland."

How ironic that it was Barkley who pierced the Blazers' hearts just a few feet from where Hollins had suggested that the Suns needed to "get a Barkley."

For Barkley: 25 points, eight rebounds, five assists, two steals. Not a bad way to come back. For KJ: 14 assists. For Chambers: 16 clutch bench points. He was back from his quadricep injury just in time for the playoffs. For the Suns: six more three-pointers, which gave them 387 for the season, breaking the NBA record of 386 previously held by the 1988-89 New York Knicks.

Once again, this team of oddities had walked the ledge and not fallen off.

"That's what I'm supposed to do, right?" Barkley said. "The pass really was supposed to come off the glass to Ced. I didn't realize he didn't touch it, but with that little time you just react, you just have to go to the ball and throw it up there and hope everything works out."

For Westphal, it was his 61st win, the most ever by a first-year NBA coach. He was more excited about prospects for the near future.

"Charles has these last two games, and KJ will play with him in two of them, plus almost a week of practice leading up to the playoffs," Westphal said. "That should be enough time for them to get back in sync with each other.

"I got a chance to take a look at our top 10 guys in various combinations. It's important to get them minutes with each other so they feel comfortable in their role because those are the guys we'll use in the playoffs, if we avoid injuries."

The next day, back in Phoenix, the Suns got the horrifying, out-of-the-blue news: during the postgame celebration in Portland, KJ suffered a sprained medial collateral ligament in his left knee.

He would be out approximately two weeks, meaning he would miss most, if not all, of the Suns' first-round playoff series against the Los Angeles Lakers. The ligament was stretched, but not torn. It is common among football players, who routinely collide with incredible force, but rare in basketball, according to Dr. Emerson.

"I knew it right away, too," KJ said. But no one else did. He did not appear to limp getting on or off the charter jet after the game.

"I've had a lot of injuries, but I've never had a knee injury. I knew it was serious because I lost my balance and hyperextended it," KJ said. "I just laughed. I could not believe it. I mean, what a freak thing. You know, for me it might have been better if Charles had missed that shot and we'd lost the game. But I am glad we won it. I'm glad it was me and not anybody else. I'm more equipped to deal with it. It's amazing. I started the season injured, and I finished it injured. I figure I've got to get a break somewhere.

Johnson would wind up missing 33 regular-season games, yet the

Suns still posted the best record in the NBA. Twenty-seven times they won when KJ was not in the starting lineup.

"To have any kind of fluke thing like this happen is more than ironic," Colangelo said. "We've been resting Kevin late in the season in the second game of back-to-backs specifically to reduce the risk of injury."

It was KJ's second injury suffered during a celebration — and during the course of this season, he suffered one almost every way imaginable. Remember when he tried to lift Miller during a preseason celebration and nearly suffered a hernia? And that was before Miller went on his weight-reduction regimen.

Henceforth, KJ promised, he would remain on the bench and be calm during any postgame celebrations. Until the end of the season.

"And then," KJ said, "I'm going bungee jumping."

With the Spurs coming in on Saturday, April 24, the short-handed Suns would be tested once again. They felt good knowing one of those in uniform would be Barkley, but he wouldn't be with them long.

With one minute left in the first half, Barkley was fouled twice by David Robinson directly in front of referee Joe Borgia. There was no call on either. Barkley was irate.

But Borgia, who not only is a weak official but also has a hair-trigger temper — a deadly combination — gave Barkley two quick technicals and he was gone. Borgia got his 15 seconds of glory on NBC-TV, but there must have been a lot of dials suddenly clicking.

"I hope people didn't turn it off when Charles got kicked out, because it turned into a heck of a game," Westphal said.

The Suns found a way to win without KJ and Barkley. They limited the Spurs to 44 second-half points, and the struggling Ainge got an 18-foot jumper to fall with 12.6 seconds left that gave them a 99-97 win.

"We've been doing this all season," Westphal said. "It's become a habit."

The sprained wrist on Ainge's shooting hand had been bothering him for about a month. "I didn't say anything, because I thought it would get better with time."

With Barkley long gone, his teammates couldn't resist the opportunity to jab him.

"Note what a great defensive team we became once Charles was out of there?" Chambers said.

"He must have had a 2:45 tee time," Ainge said.

But Ainge said that if they had to play without Barkley in the playoffs, surely it would be because he was injured or had fouled out.

"I've never seen Michael Jordan, or Larry Bird, or Magic Johnson get kicked out of a big playoff series and I don't think you'll see that from Charles, either," Ainge said. "I think Charles understands his value to this team. You never know what it takes to get a technical or an ejection. Some refs call it quick, some let it go a long way. The bottom line is you can't take the chance."

So at 62-19, the Suns flew to Denver to wrap up their most successful regular season.

Upon arrival in the Mile High City, Majerle was amused to read that Nuggets guard Reggie Williams, a career vagabond, was quoted about Majerle, "There ain't nothin' to his game. He just sits there like Jeff Hornacek and shoots, and lets Kevin Johnson and Charles Barkley do the work. I don't know what would happen if he played on another team. He's in the right place at the right time."

Williams is in a position to know what it is like to be in possession of no game. Williams had been waived by the Spurs and Cavaliers after the Clippers realized the mistake they'd made taking him fourth overall in the 1987 draft. Soon, he was traded.

Then, in yet another act of bravery, Williams would not suit up for the season finale to prove his point in a head-to-head battle with Majerle because of an injury.

"It doesn't bother me," Majerle said. "I notice he hasn't done a whole lot in his career. I'm a two-time All-Star and an Olympian, and I've improved every year. I'm happy with where I am."

So are the Suns, who weren't particularly motivated to wrap it up against a 35-46 foe looking to go on summer vacation with a win over the league leaders.

Chris Jackson did to the Suns what they'd been doing to the rest of the NBA all season. At the final horn, he swished a three-pointer that sent the Nuggets out 120-118 winners. Barkley missed an 18-footer with 11 seconds left and the Suns leading by a point.

"I was glad to see a last-second shot go in against us after all of them that we've made," Westphal said. "Let's get that out of the way now, instead of in the playoffs. We played it as a fun game. We did try to win it down the stretch, but for the most part, it was loose."

Like the first 81 weren't?

The only bright spot was Ceballos locking up the NBA field-goal shooting title. By making four of five shots, Ceballos finished the season at 57.55 percent, just ahead of runner-up Brad Daugherty of Cleveland at 57.08.

"Ced didn't have a pocket calculator out there, but I did," Westphal said. "I was going to make sure he stayed on top."

What a ride it had been.

The Suns' current mindset was quite a departure from the high they were on coming home in early April from that Eastern sweep. It was going to be a struggle to regain that .

But they would have the home-court edge in every playoff series.

"It's kind of precarious, but it's what we worked all season for," Westphal said. "The totality of it means something because we have the home-court edge. But as soon as we lose one playoff game on our home court, those first 82 games don't mean anything."

That was a sobering thought after all those hard-fought, down-to-the-wire victories.

So was opening against the Lakers without Kevin Johnson, even though the Suns swept them, 5-0, during the regular season as the Lakers went 39-43, their worst record in 18 years. Like the Suns, they had suffered a number of significant injuries and had done a great deal of experimenting. In the playoffs, the Lakers would be healthy and they would be playing their best combinations, some of whom remained from the Showtime Era. People like Green, Worthy, and Scott know what it takes to win.

Westphal loaded up the Suns and took them to Prescott, Arizona, for a mini-camp. It's about a two-hour drive north of Phoenix. The beautiful mountain community is at an elevation of about 5,600 feet. It would be cool and, Westphal hoped, calm.

He envisioned it as a chance to isolate the Suns and try to refocus them on the task of winning their first NBA championship. But wherever the Suns went, there were mobs waiting for them, whether it was the lobby of the hotel, or the parking lot outside the gymnasium at Yavapai College, where they  worked out for three days.

Hundreds of fans tailed them armed with pennants, hats, t-shirts. One man had an athletic supporter he hoped one of the Suns would sign. The Suns were caught unprepared for this reception.

"It's kind of surprising," Westphal said. "On the one hand, it's gratifying. On the other, that's not what we're here for."

By the end of the first day, the players had requested security escorts to their cars at the hotel and the gym. Prescott police finally arranged for the players' rental cars to be backed onto the sidewalk just outside the doors leading to their closed practices. The police then cordoned off the area to keep fans back long enough for the players to get in and drive off.

"It's not like we're trying to throw a veil of secrecy over what we're doing," Westphal said. "We just want to focus with as few distractions as possible. We really didn't want a circus."

Barkley, asked how he was going to get through the mob, responded, "I'm going to walk right through the crowd to my car. I'm pretty good at getting fans off me, you know."

Otherwise, Barkley said he was having a fine time. "It's fun to be with your teammates. This builds camaraderie. The first night, we stayed up all night playing cards. You have to go to war with these 12 guys, so you want to be close friends. We have the most difficult situation of anybody. Everybody expects us to beat the Lakers, but you know the Lakers will be the Lakers in the playoffs. So we have fun, but when we lock down that gym, we've got total concentration on one thing, and that's being the first to win 15 games in the playoffs."

When they unlocked that gym, look out. Among the attractions in Prescott is a small casino. Several players found their way.

"This ain't Monte Carlo," Barkley said, in comparison with the Dream Team's pre-Olympic mini-camp. "Beer is a lot cheaper here, though. Over there, it was $25. "They just have slot machines here. That doesn't do much for me. I'm a real gambler. If you're going to gamble, gamble. Paul should have taken us to Las Vegas instead."

No matter how much lip service the Suns were giving the Lakers, it was a good question whether deep down inside they really took them seriously. Of course, the way the Suns wound up the season, they needed to take everybody seriously.

Even though it was a hassle going anywhere in Prescott, Westphal said the mini-camp was not a bust. "We got done everything that we intended to get done. We had good, intense practices and we went over everything to make sure that we're all on the same page."

# Chapter Twenty-six

# SATISFACTION GUARANTEED

The Lakers were hearing how they were the equivalent of sacrificial lambs. The mighty Lakers of the 1980s handed the undermanned Suns a number of horrible thrashings in postseason play, and this time, the fortunes would be reversed — or so it was written on the left coast.

At the same time, rumors of Coach Randy Pfund's demise were rampant. In some ways, he was being set up as a sacrificial lamb himself. It was hardly his fault, the un-Laker-like record.

First, he assumed that Magic Johnson had un-retired when he planned his team. On the eve of the season, Magic re-retired, scuttling all the plans. Then, Scott suffered an early-season injury.

Worthy, one of the Showtime era warriors, got off to a forgettable start. Remember his line following an early-season loss to the Suns about going to K-Mart to get himself a new jumper?

Next came the mid-season trade of Sam Perkins. In return, the Lakers got a promising newcomer, Doug Christie, who might pay them dividends down the line, but he was hardly a seasoned playoff veteran who could do them much good this year.

Finally, Pfund was asked by management to experiment with his young players, including rookie guard Anthony Peeler, and younger big men like Elden Campbell. That meant sending Worthy to the bench for a while, but Pfund complied. He got his players some experience at the expense of several games — exhibition games, to borrow a phrase.

But all of that is why the Lakers would be different now. Now, they were playing for real with their best players.

"We had a great run for eight or nine years, but I understand now how other teams felt when we were beating them all those years," Scott said.

But, Pfund said, "We're going over to Phoenix loose, with nothing to lose."

That's dangerous.

Another thing the Lakers had going for them was height. Across the front line, they had 6-foot-9 A. C. Green, 6-11 Elden Campbell, and 7-0 Vlade Divac. The Suns' front wall of 6-6 Barkley, 6-6 Ceballos, and 6-10 West was the shortest of the 16 playoff teams. But it hadn't held them back so far.

"I don't think of us as short," Westphal said, "because we have been such a good rebounding team."

Another factor was Knight opening the playoffs as the starting point guard, just as he had opened the regular season.

"I've had so many personal ups and downs," he said. "I've been ticked to the point where I wish I could say, 'Forget it,' and wait to be traded. There were games where I'd be sitting and I'd see a situation where I thought I could fit in and be productive. We'd win the game without me, which is good, but I'd want to be part of it.

"Everybody would be celebrating and I'd think, 'Man, did I really help the team by sitting there?' I'm definitely ready for this challenge, and I'm definitely going to make the best of it."

Never had the No. 8 seed won on the floor of the No. 1 seed in the playoffs.

But with the Suns sputtering badly in the second quarter and scoring only 13 points, and Lakers guard Sedale Threatt a constant menace, the Lakers pulled a 107-103 upset in the opener.

Seven times the Suns had the ball in the final 2:41 of the game. Seven times they failed to score after leading by five points.

"It's simple," Westphal said. "They played playoff basketball, and we didn't."

Not even 34 points, 15 rebounds, and one halftime lecture from Barkley could save the Suns. Majerle missed 11 of 15 shots, Ainge 9 of 13.

But Threatt, working primarily against the embattled Knight, made 17 of his 24 tries, few from closer than 15 feet, leading Barkley to say, "I think it was obvious that Sedale Threatt was the best player in the world tonight. Sedale is a good player, but, come on, he's not as good as we made him look."

As Worthy put it, "When a player gets in a zone like that, it's beautiful to watch. Sedale is a very spirited player, and when he gets it going like that, you just let him go."

Although Barkley's numbers appear impressive, Campbell kept him from getting the ball on those late possessions.

"The shot clock kept running down," Ainge said, "and they kept rotating fresh guys on him."

Worthy suggested that the pressure of being the favorite might have worked against the Suns. "We've been where they are. You're supposed to win. They're talking about you all day on the radio, and the town is going bonkers. You start to feel it."

It was only one game, but the Suns, indeed, could feel the heat — and it wasn't just because summer was approaching in the desert.

They knew they now had to win at least one game in the Forum to save the series. As Westphal had discussed on the eve of the playoffs, those 62 wins that brought them home-court advantage now were wasted. Already there was some finger-pointing at the young coach over the exhibition-season issue, and the trip to Prescott. The Suns certainly showed no signs of being ready for the playoffs, and those two issues were perceived as liabilities to the cause.

But there was a chance the Suns would get KJ back for the second game. His healing was a bit ahead of schedule. For the Suns, it was a good thing.

But he hadn't practiced. That would come on the day between the first two games on Saturday, May 1. May Day. That wasn't yet the Suns' cry, but another game like the last one and perhaps it would be.

"It's like that old John Wayne movie," Westphal told encircled reporters. "Somebody told this guy if you get gut-shot, you don't ever survive. He believes it. So the guy gets gut-shot and instead of going to the doctor, who probably could save him, he puts the gun to his head. Well, we're gut-shot, but we're not putting the gun to our head."

This comparison was understandable. While a student at USC, Westphal no doubt was required to view the entire collection of movies by the Duke, an old SC man himself.

So which flick was this example from?

"I don't know. Take your pick. They're all about the same."

The Suns knew that if the remainder of their games against the Lakers were "all about the same," they'd be taking up residence in Boot Hill. They were going to have to shoot their way out of this old west situation.

They assumed the return of KJ would be a suitable answer to Threatt.

In the opener, the Lakers didn't regard Knight as much of a penetrating threat, and they set their defense accordingly. But KJ had the tools to break them down and create for himself or Barkley.

"I've worked out on it for two days now, and there's been no pain or swelling in my knee," KJ said. "Every time I've come back this season I've played better. My athletic ability is my greatest strength but I need to downshift. I don't need to be in fifth gear all the time, or try to be creative all the time. With the personnel we have, I don't need to."

KJ knew what he had to do. "I'm not in the glamor position anymore," he said. "I'm not the guy who scores all the points and looks into the crowd. I have to do the grunt work. It's the unsung position, but my teammates appreciate what I do."

His assignment against Threatt in Game 2: "You have to wear him down."

But the Lakers used a similar ploy effectively against Barkley, first with Campbell, and then with Green.

"The idea is to make him fight like a dog for everything," Green said. "We wanted to do everything we could to put him in a position where he might not want to catch the ball. It worked for one night, but you're playing Russian roulette.

"In the playoffs, you have so much time to focus and prepare. It's not like the regular season, where you might spend only a few hours going over a scouting report for one game. This is totally different. You can get inside each other's heads. You can somehow trick them and camouflage what you do. It's not about X's and O's anymore. It's about who wants it the most."

And the Lakers were getting greedy.

The Suns knew that never had a team won an NBA playoff series after losing the first two at home.

As Barkley put it, "This is a must-win."

But they didn't: Lakers 86, Suns 81.

The Suns seemed to have things under control until they were limited to 11 fourth-quarter points. Four points from Divac in the final minute sealed it. Afterward, Westphal made a speech that approached his "exhibition season" proclamation for controversy:

"The next game is over there Tuesday. We're going to win that. Then the next one is Thursday. We'll win there, too. Then we're going to come home next Sunday and win that one, and everyone will say what a great series it was."

Well what else was he going to say? We have no chance? We're staring one of the greatest upsets in the history of sports in the face?

Westphal said the words, and he later said he truly believed them. But few Suns fans really believed they were going to win three straight and salvage the series. That, in itself, would be one of the greatest comebacks in sports history. It would be unprecedented.

"We made up our minds that if we were going to go down," Barkley said, "we were going to go down with our best shot, which we did not do back in Phoenix."

The Suns made a discovery in Game 3 that would swing the series: Oliver Miller.

Miller helped the Suns build a 15-point lead with his rebounding and inside scoring, then helped hold the lead at seven points going into the closing two minutes.

No one who follows the Suns had this one counted in the books just yet. Successive three-pointers by Divac and Threatt showed why.

The Lakers made a game of it right to the wire. In fact, Los Angeles had possession with a chance to take the lead going into the final minute.

Colangelo sat behind the Suns bench, ashen-faced, cupping his chin in his hands. Was he watching the greatest Suns team he'd ever assembled go down in flames in an unthinkable first-round sweep?

But Worthy missed a shot that Miller rebounded, and then Miller's two free throws with 46 seconds left put the Suns up by three. The other rookie, Dumas, later had to make two free throws with 18 seconds left to save a 107-102 win on Tuesday, May 4, and extend the Suns' incredible season at least two more days.

Barkley's 27 points and 11 rebounds helped give the Suns the cushion, but clearly, contributions from the two rookies at crunch time carried them through.

Ainge and Majerle, who were a combined two-for-18 from three-point range through the first two games, shot a combined five-for-eight here. Majerle also limited Scott to six points.

"If we don't come out of this thing," Colangelo said, "this is all people will be writing about and talking about all summer. Maybe after all the good things that have happened for us this year, maybe this can happen, too."

Majerle said he got a longer look at the basket, crediting the return of the penetrating KJ. He gets a defender's attention.

"I could tell right from the beginning that there was a difference," Majerle said. "The reason for that is that when KJ is penetrating like that, the Lakers have to collapse on him."

KJ also helps the Suns play faster, a style the Lakers don't enjoy.

"I'm still breathing," Colangelo said.

Westphal was criticized after the two losses in Phoenix for not playing the rookies late in the game. He had chosen to go with experienced players at crunch time. This time, they rewarded him.

Miller responded with 11 points, eight rebounds, four assists, two steals, and two blocked shots — plus those two big free throws.

"Oliver Miller was the player of the game," Barkley said.

That's what Pfund was afraid of. He knew Miller was the one player who might be able to counter the Lakers' height advantage.

"Paul told me when we left Phoenix that he was going to play me more in the third game, and I was going to be a big factor," Miller said. "I couldn't let him down."

Westphal changed up the Suns' defense in the third game, using more traps.

"I probably should have done that sooner in the series," he said. "But I thought that Kevin coming back would be enough to get us running in the second game. I was reluctant to trap then because I didn't know how Kevin would play in his first game back."

Meanwhile, Barkley was trying to figure out how to score against Campbell and his menacingly long arms.

"There isn't another power forward who can do what he's done," Barkley said. "Elden has long arms, and he can jump, plus he's strong. He has definitely made me make small adjustments on my shot. I changed the arc just enough to throw it off. Not many players have ever made me do that."

On Thursday, May 6, the Suns came out loose, relaxed, and confident that they finally were going to do to the Lakers what everyone anticipated from the beginning. And they did.

Game 4 went to the Suns, 101-86, forcing the deciding fifth game on Sunday at America West Arena.

"We're finally playing like the Suns now," Ainge observed. Why?

Westphal led the players in the telling of a few jokes at halftime.

"None of them were very good, either," Ainge said. "I think that's what did it. They were so bad, they were funny."

After the score was tied early in the third quarter, the Suns shut down the Lakers on nine out of 10 possessions to build a big lead. That is the most effective way to push up the tempo of a game. The Suns knew that speed would be their greatest ally .

Another would be Barkley's shooting touch.

After making eight of 24 in Game 2 and nine of 23 in Game 3, Barkley came back with 13 of 21 shooting, propelling him to 28 points. He also grabbed 11 rebounds.

"You can't keep Charles under 50 percent for long, no matter how good the defense is," Westphal said.

After scoring 43 points in the first half, the Suns scored 58 in the second.

"They slowed it down in the first two games," Barkley said. "The last two, we were able to speed it up. I don't think we lost any confidence, we were just playing into their hands in the half-court game the way we were playing."

By midway through the fourth quarter, the Suns were ahead by 20.

"I said the other day I thought we had exposed some of their weaknesses," Pfund said. "Tonight, I think they exposed some of ours. Our biggest weakness seems to be the home floor. They showed that their quickness also can be a real problem. Now we're facing a near impossible task to go back over there and win again."

Miller grabbed five fourth-quarter rebounds. For the game, he had 16 points, eight rebounds, and two blocks. Just as Pfund had feared. The Suns definitely had a new weapon that changed the series.

"I could never do the things I'm doing now at the weight I was carrying," Miller said. "I feel quicker. I'm jumping so much better."

Limiting the Lakers to 37 percent shooting gave Miller and team-mates plenty of opportunities to hit the boards and trigger breaks.

The Suns left Los Angeles immediately after the game, hoping to get two nights' sleep in their own beds before Sunday's series-deciding showdown. When their chartered jet pulled up at a remote gate at Sky Harbor International Airport in Phoenix just before 1 a.m., the Suns were startled to find about 4,000 fans waiting to greet them. The faithful were in a mood to celebrate.

The Suns appreciated their growing adulation, but they were not comfortable with this. In fact, Westphal was downright testy. So was Barkley. The series was only tied, not over. But local television stations cut into late-night programming live to cover the Suns' return.

"It takes three to win, not two," Barkley said. "We haven't done anything yet. Our fans are the greatest, though. Even when we were down 0-2, they were sending us faxes by the thousands in Los Angeles. We won't forget that. But the airport made out like bandits. The parking garage was crammed and cars were lined up to get in. I think our fans were just showing us respect for not packing it in. I told them, 'Go home, so I can go home.'"

Westphal didn't blame the fans for coming out.

"But if they would have told me they were planning a celebration, I would have told them not to do it," he said. "They turned it into a party against my wishes. I don't want to be a jerk or anything, but we've got a job to do, and we haven't finished it yet."

To get it done, Westphal said they'd continue to seek the counsel of Magic Johnson, the retired Lakers great who was doing color commentary for NBC-TV — seek it and then do just the opposite of what Magic suggests. Johnson was critical of the Suns for trying to run. He said the formula for playoff success is deliberate, crisply executed half-court basketball.

"We learned a lot by listening to Magic tell us what not to do," Westphal said. "We did the exact opposite and won."

Westphal actually was criticized by Phoenix-area reporters, who were more familiar with the Suns' personality than Johnson, for slowing down the first two games, both of which the Suns lost. The rookie coach also took some heat for playing the vets instead of using Miller and Dumas in the fourth quarter, which he eventually did in wins in the third and fourth games.

"I don't think that in the first two games we were following quote-unquote conventional playoff wisdom," Westphal said. "I think it was because we didn't have our penetrator. Kevin didn't play in Game 1, and in Game 2 he wasn't able to push it yet. As Kevin got healthier, we pushed it more in Game 3, and a lot more in Game 4."

As Pfund lamented, "Danny Ainge and Dan Majerle and Oliver Miller are all playing well for them now. For a while, we had them tentative. Now, it looks like they're warmed up. It looks like they're back to where they were at the best point of the season."

Either the Suns would become the first to win a best-of-five series after dropping the first two at home, or the Lakers would become the first bottom seed to win three on the road and advance through a first-round matchup.

"Let's face it," Pfund said, "it's a terrific scenario. Either the Suns are a team of destiny, or we're going to be the greatest underdog of all time."

The Suns had begun spouting off about this "team of destiny" notion, especially Barkley, who at every chance said he believed this group was destined to unseat Chicago as the world champ.

One week after delivering his infamous guarantee, Westphal said he was sticking with it, but was no prophet.

"My predicting days are over," he said on the eve of the clash. "The only prophets are in the Bible."

Instead, Westphal was playing superstitions. This showdown would come on Mother's Day, just as a 1979 Western Conference Finals battle had with Seattle. The Suns led that series, 3-2, and were going for their second trip to the NBA Finals with the game at their old home, Veterans Memorial Coliseum. Westphal was a Suns starting guard. His mother, Ruth, sang the national anthem.

The Sonics pulled a 106-105 upset to tie the series, and then eliminated the Suns in the seventh game in Seattle and went on to win the championship against Washington.

This time, Westphal said his mom "definitely will not" sing the anthem.

"Mom is going to stay home and watch the game on TV," Westphal said. "She might sing the anthem, but she'll be singing along with whomever is singing it in the arena. We're going to keep her out of range."

The co-star with her son in a series of commercials for a hamburger chain in which they routinely exchange lighthearted jabs, Ruth Westphal denied that her singing had cost the Suns that Seattle game 14 seasons earlier.

"It was the refs," she said.

Early in the fourth quarter this time, the Suns enjoyed a 10-point lead. The Purple Palace was rocking. The fans were certain that the Suns had fought back valiantly and taken the series. But by the one-minute mark, following a furious 22-8 run, the Lakers had stormed to a four-point bulge and the place was quiet. Bam, bam. Just like that the Suns' fortunes had taken yet another gigantic reversal. They were 60 seconds away from elimination by the only losing team in the playoffs.

Barkley and Majerle—the latter of whom was so stricken with the flu that he had to be given nourishment through an IV needle before the game— went to work.

A baseline basket by Barkley trimmed it to two points as the clock ticked inside one minute. Then, after Barkley rebounded a miss by Threatt, Majerle got an off-balance 15-footer to fall with 13.6 seconds left that tied it. But the Lakers apparently would have the last shot to win it, and thirteen seconds is plenty of time.

As it turned out, it was too much time. Threatt sensed that he needed to run the clock a bit to avoid scoring too early and giving the Suns a last try. A post-up seemed likely, against the shorter Suns.

But by the time Threatt realized that only a few ticks remained, there wasn't time to power the ball inside. His only option was a hurried pass to Scott, who was unguarded behind the three-point line. If there had been even a fraction of a second more, Scott might have gotten the shot off in rhythm. Even though he wasn't having a great series, he is the last man you want to give an open shot with a series on the line.

Considering what Majerle had done to the Lakers with his three-pointer in April, it would have been a fitting ending for the Suns to be burned by a heart-breaking three themselves.

Instead, Scott had to catch and shoot to beat the clock. His hurried attempt was a bit short. Off to overtime they went.

The crowd was at once relieved and uneasy. How far out on the ledge can these guys go? They wouldn't be the Suns if they didn't make it difficult for themselves.

What would the extra period bring? Were the Lakers crushed after missing their chance in the last minute to complete the great upset?

Were the Suns puckered after having lost the double-digit lead in the closing 10 minutes? Who would prevail under pressure? Coming up were five minutes to validate a season.

Onto the court strode Oliver Miller.

Miller scored six quick points in overtime, including a slam dunk that gave them a five-point edge with just over a minute to go. When it was over, Miller had nine points and five rebounds in overtime. For the game, he scored 17 points, grabbed 14 rebounds, and blocked a Suns playoff record seven shots in the 112-104 win.

"I didn't go through all that for nothing," Miller said of his winter nights at the hospital. "It helped me a lot. I wish I would have done that earlier. If I was like I was then, I don't think I could have played like this."

And, as Westphal predicted, everyone said what a great series it was.

"I'm not gloating," Westphal said. "I'm very humble. It didn't come easily — but I never predicted that it would come easily."

"I know a lot of teams wish they had me now, especially guys who talked about how I have no heart, I have no pride, I'm a loser," Miller said. "I went out and proved them all wrong. Look at me now, that's what I've got to say to them. I'm helping the best team in the NBA go further in the playoffs.

"Jerry West told my agent that I'm a disgrace to the NBA, so I especially wanted to kick the Lakers' butts."

Maybe Pfund knew that, and maybe that's what he based his concern upon. Don't let the guy have the chance to make his point, because he just might make it.

Majerle told reporters that his early-morning flu-bug had him "praying to the porcelain God." Majerle emphasized that it "was a virus, not anything I ate at my restaurant—and if it was something I ate there, I wouldn't tell you."

Besides the heroics of Miller and a 31-point, 14-rebound game from Barkley, there were plenty of others to share the glory for the Suns. KJ, in his best game of the series, turned in 24 points, 13 assists, and four steals. Majerle wasn't too weak to swish three three-pointers among his 19 points.

The Lakers had given it their best. Worthy, once known as "Big Game James" for his playoff proficiency, made six baskets in the fourth-quarter comeback. He finished with 24 coming off the bench. When it was over, Worthy seemed to sense that it was really over for the remnants of those glorious teams of the 1980s. First came the retirement of Kareem Abdul-Jabbar in 1989; then Johnson's after he discovered that he has the virus that causes AIDS.

Worthy, Scott, and Green are all that's left of the dynasty. Scott said publicly that he didn't expect to be back, and he was right. The Lakers announced in July that they would not re-sign him. Green also was an unrestricted free agent who would make the Purple Palace his new home.

Worthy, whose days in the league are shortening, sensed that when the Lakers go to training camp in 1993 that he might well stand alone as the sole survivor of those wonderful days.

"We went out right," Worthy said. "We wanted to come into the playoffs and conjure up something. We came close to doing something that we've never done before, more special than all the things in the past. We were expected to do those things. No one anticipated that we would be in this series. That's why winning it would have made it so special for us."

For the Suns, a Western Conference best-of-seven semifinal against the San Antonio Spurs awaited.

"One of the hardest things in sports is to come back after a high like this," Westphal said. "It's something we have to overcome."

But the Suns were proving adept at overcoming obstacles.

"To go over there down 0-2 and win both games, come home, and be down four with a minute to go, get it into overtime and then win, that shows the kind of toughness and pride we have," Barkley said.

In some ways, having gone through a season walking the ledge served them well here. How many other teams would have had the composure to pull through in a short series? That, in a nutshell, is what these Suns are about. Westphal knew it. That's why he made the "guarantee."

"I really believed it when I said it, I really did," he said. "I had been around this team long enough to know what they were made of. And I really believed we were a better team than the Lakers, even though they played a fantastic series. I wouldn't have said that if Kevin was still hurt. I knew Kevin was getting better. I don't like to use injuries as an excuse for losing, but when we look back, I think it's fair to say that if Kevin was 100 percent, we would not have lost those first two games. I could see that he was getting better and that we would have something more like the real Kevin Johnson for the rest of the series. That made it a lot easier for me to say those words."

# Chapter Twenty-seven

# IT'S NEVER TOO LATE
# FOR A SNOW

The Spurs might be inclined to run with the Suns. Their style of play is more similar and the matchups generally were better than the Suns faced against the Lakers. San Antonio's forwards weren't as tall, which was good news for Barkley and Dumas.

"It will be nice to play somebody my own size, finally," said the 6-7 Dumas, who would be taking on 6-8 Sean Elliott.

Of course, the Spurs had the great equalizer in the middle, 7-1 David Robinson. In four regular-season games, Robinson nicked the Suns for 25.8 points, 12.8 rebounds, and 4.0 blocks. The Spurs won only one of the four, and that was the controversial protested game.

Robinson hadn't been able to put the Spurs on his back and take them to great heights. In fact, they'd been embarrassed in the opening round two years earlier by the mighty midgets from Golden State. So Robinson saw this as a chance to prove that his name deserves to be mentioned among the other greats by beating the team most expected to advance to the Finals.

"I talked to Charles Barkley and Scottie Pippen at the Olympics this summer, and they told me my team is immature," Robinson said. "I got defensive, but it really is true. I needed to do more to really be strong and take control when needed. Playing on the Dream Team really opened my eyes to that. I took a look around at Charles, Magic, Michael, Larry. Some of the things they do, just the way they play, the way they look at the game, is on a different level. It takes a special team to be a champion, and I don't know if we've had that."

Barkley respected Robinson, whom he assumed would guard him occasionally. The Lakers had success using a tall player, Campbell.

"All tall left-handers give me trouble because when I go to my right, I'm going right into their left hand," Barkley said. "But I can go outside and get some open jumpers. I might even get a few of them to fall in this series."

Barkley had no idea that he had just joined the list of basketball prophets with that statement.

In the opener, on Tuesday, May 11, Barkley missed 16 of 21 shots playing primarily against Antoine Carr. No matter. Dumas made nine of 12 against Elliott. KJ did likewise to his counterpart, Avery Johnson, the difference being that Avery Johnson never has been an All-Star.

With 25 points, seven assists, and five steals from KJ, and seven rebounds and five blocks from Miller, the Suns handled the Spurs, 98-89, at the Purple Palace.

They won, despite an absolutely monster game from Robinson: 32 points, 10 rebounds, seven blocks, four assists, three steals. The rest of the Spurs were nowhere to be seen.

"Earlier in the year, people were saying we traded the wrong guy in the Barkley deal," Westphal said. "And then Kevin got hurt. I just don't think he got the respect he deserved."

The most touching scene of the evening came in the Spurs' locker room when Lucas, who operates the Houston after-care center where Dumas spent most of the previous year, paid tribute to his recovering protégé. Lucas coached Dumas on the Miami Tropics of the U.S. Basketball League the previous summer. It was there that Lucas first described Dumas as "Dr. J with a jump shot."

"He's one of my children," Lucas said. "It's great to see him having a great year. And that's not for basketball, but for his life. Richard and I go way beyond basketball. It's about his life and my life. It's a double-edged sword. I'm cheering for him, but at the same time, I'm mad because he hurt the Spurs."

Dumas repaid that respect. "He has helped me a lot. I appreciate everything he's done for me. We're just trying to take everything — everything — in stride."

So was Ceballos, who was playing only 12 minutes a game in the playoffs after averaging 20 during the regular season.

"It's a shock," Ceballos said. "I'm asking myself, 'What did I do wrong? Why didn't I take care of things so I could be in the rotation?'"

Elliott made three of 13 shots and scored eight points against Dumas, much to Lucas' disgust. There were rumors in San Antonio that Lucas and Elliott didn't see eye-to-eye. Elliott's name continued to pop up in trade rumors.

"I think that was one of my best defensive games," Dumas said. "Everybody says I don't play defense. I was up for this game."

Another strong defensive job was done by Majerle on Dale Ellis, who had two points to show for 24 minutes of work. Earlier in the day, Majerle was named to the NBA's second all-defensive team.

But everyone was mystified by Barkley's shooting slump, including Barkley. He came into postseason action No. 2 on the all-time list in field-goal percentage at 56.9. Through six games, he was at 43.8.

"I've never been through anything like this," Barkley said. "You're lying if you say you don't think about a slump. It weighs on your mind."

Especially when 2 million people in your community expect you to take a team to the championship. Everyone had a theory: Barkley still didn't have his timing from the late-season layoff; his shoulder was bothering him more than he was letting on (he had surgery on the same shoulder three years earlier); his hamstrings were sore and perhaps preventing him from getting his legs into his shots; the burden of carrying a team on his back was getting to him.

Maybe even the great Charles Barkley was succumbing to pressure.

"This is very frustrating," said Barkley, who went to the Suns' practice gym and shot for 20 minutes after the game. "It can drive you crazy. But I don't think I'm going to stop firing it, that's for sure."

In typical Suns fashion, they watched an 18-point lead midway through the third quarter dwindle to four with 4 1/2 minutes to play. But a win is a win, and after having lost the first two at home in the previous round, the Suns were elated to have it.

In Game 2, on Thursday, May 13, the Suns anticipated that Elliott and Ellis would be greater factors. They hoped that Robinson wouldn't be. And everyone was wondering when Barkley would be himself.

Barkley responded emphatically, making 12 of 18 shots and scoring 35 points in a 109-103 win.

"There is a God," he said. "If I'm making my short jump shot like that, then I've got pump-fakes, I've got layups, I've got a lot off of that. It also opens so much for everybody else."

Barkley made a Suns playoff-record seven steals and had an incredible block on Robinson as he went for a dunk.

"See, the guy who voted for me for All-Defensive team knew what he was doing," Barkley said.

All of that helped the Suns put the Spurs 16 points in arrears in the fourth quarter. But you know the Suns. With 90 seconds to go, the Spurs were down by only five.

"I thought we were not too bright with our shot selection at the end," Westphal said.

The Suns often didn't pay attention to the clock or the situation.

But the Spurs weren't being particularly aggressive, either. Elliott and Ellis continued their slump, combining to make seven of 19 shots and score 22 points. Robinson came through with 27 points, but West and Miller made him work hard for every one of them.

Lucas, whose team was going home for games Saturday and Sunday, wondered whether the Spurs had what it takes.

"We're not bringing enough toughness to the party," Lucas said. "We're the bigger team and we're being pushed around. That has to change."

That stung his players, just as it was intended to do.

Believe it or not, the Suns never had led a best-of-seven playoff series, 2-0. This was new ground.

So was staying on the outer limits of the sprawling Alamo City. The Suns couldn't get a hotel room downtown on the famed Riverwalk where they normally stay. They were displaced by a national convention of urologists. Imagine, 6,500 urologists selecting a city whose biggest attraction is a gently flowing waterway winding through its downtown.

The Suns also were not happy about the games being played on back-to-back days. They were a bit older than the Spurs, and they didn't figure to recover as quickly. Ironically, a Saturday-Sunday format helped the Suns eliminate the Lakers in the final series that Pat Riley coached in 1990. Then, the Suns were the younger team playing at home. They routed the Lakers in both games of the West semifinals en route to a 4-1 series win. Here, conditions were reversed all the way around.

For good measure, Lucas still was goosing his team with inflammatory public comments.

"These games down here are going to be much more physical because of that." Barkley said. "They're going to try to rough us up a bit. They've got to win. I don't think anybody can come back from 0-3 against us. They're going to play their asses off."

The Suns didn't plan to change their style as some teams do on the road. They still wanted to force turnovers and run.

"Maybe I'm naive, but I don't think there's any difference playing at home or on the road — at least I don't like to acknowledge any difference," Westphal said.

Ainge, who has a reputation for playing well on the road, agreed.

"I've heard some coaches say they have to maybe play more controlled on the road, but I think that's the worst thing in the world that you can do," Ainge said. "You might change your game based on who you play, but not based on where you play. To me, there's no greater feeling in sports than hitting a big shot on the road when the opposing crowd is on its feet screaming."

The Suns had few chances to experience that in Game 3, on Saturday, May 15. They looked like a tired old team, and the Spurs like young pups out for a run in the 111-96 shellacking. Lucas turned them loose to take advantage of all that wonderful athletic talent.

"We wanted aggressiveness," Lucas said. "We weren't getting any skinned knees diving for loose balls. We were different than we were in the first two games in Phoenix. When you slow down like that, you become a different team. We had to show who we are."

Ellis scored 20 points, Elliott 17.

"We're going to be more wide open now," Elliott said. "We're going to make them play defense instead of just standing around."

Robinson was in foul trouble most of the way and scored only 13.

"I guess one of the keys for me is to not score a lot of points," Robinson said.

The Suns, inexplicably, didn't capitalize on The Admiral's long absences. He played only 28 minutes.

"When you can't make a basket, it's pretty hard to get going," Westphal said of the Suns' 41 percent shooting.

KJ led them with 26 points and was somewhat irked at Westphal for taking him out in the third quarter when the Suns showed signs of making a run. Barkley had 22 points — but shot only nine for 21 against Carr and "Mr. Mean," Larry Smith.

Majerle couldn't throw it in the ocean (two-for-10), nor could the Suns' bench (combined nine-for-36).

Ainge now was in a slump to equal that of Barkley. By missing all five of his tries, he was three-for-19 in the series. His frustration never was more evident than at the end of the first half, when the Suns ran a three-point play for him. His shot appeared to be dead-center in the hoop, then it rattled out. All he could do was look at Westphal, grin, and shrug. Barkley raced over to hug him.

"He just told me to keep shooting," Ainge said. "And I will keep shooting them. I came out here early this morning before the game and I couldn't miss. Then, clank."

The Suns became so rattled that even the mild-mannered Majerle received a technical foul — he thought it had been about two years since he last had one — after throwing a forearm at Ellis. Majerle said it was in retaliation for Ellis' cheap shots that had gone unpunished.

"If he wants to play that way, fine, we'll play as physical as he wants, just don't call fouls on me," Majerle said. "Every time down he hit me someplace and they didn't call it."

The Spurs successfully had gotten into the Suns' heads the way Green said in the first series that it is possible to do in the playoffs.

Barkley, drawing on the odds, thought it would be hard for the Spurs to come back the next day and do it again. "It's awfully tough to beat a good team twice in two days. It's not automatic, but I like our chances."

But, another day, another loss for the Suns, who saw the series deadlocked after four games following a 117-103 reaming. Worse, the Suns had shown no signs of being able to handle the Spurs.

"We're not in a panic state," KJ said. "We're not going to go home and lose and put ourselves in a hole like we did in the Lakers series."

Barkley correctly pointed out that the Suns needed only to win two more, and that two of the final three games would be played in the Purple Palace.

"The main thing in the playoffs is to protect the homecourt," Barkley said. "Everybody is tougher at home. They were, we are." Of course, Barkley also was playing the odds for a Suns win in the second of the back-to-back games at the HemisFair Arena.

Late in the first half, it appeared as if Barkley was right. The Suns were up by nine, and could easily have made it 12, had they not missed three quick free throws.

But by halftime, thanks to some inside work by Robinson, the Spurs cut it to four. Then, in the third quarter, Barkley was held scoreless as San Antonio pulled away.

A chance to break through on the road and take a commanding lead in the series was wasted. The Suns, essentially, caved in.

"I would like to get the ball in my hands a little more," Barkley said.

Robinson couldn't share that complaint. The Spurs knew they were going only as far as "The Admiral" carried them, so they fed him continuously. The Suns fouled him, unable to prevent him from getting off a shot any other way. He shot a Spurs playoff-record 23 free throws, making 18.

"It's hard to defend free throws," Westphal said.

As the frustrated West put it, "Every time he got near the basket, he got the whistle. It was just one of those days. You have to live with it." West has been living with it his entire career.

In all, Robinson scored 36 points, more than any San Antonio player ever had in a playoff game. But through the work of West and Miller, Robinson made only nine of 20 shots.

Carr, who contributed to Barkley's shooting woes, suffered a series-ending ankle injury in the first quarter. Barkley still could manage only 18 points, making seven of 20 shots against Larry Smith.

"I don't think Larry can guard me," Barkley said. "This really pisses me off. But you've got to have the ball to shoot it."

And Dumas, after his splendid start, had not been heard from in two games. He scored seven points. To underscore his futility, the high-leaping Dumas missed a dunk — said he jumped too high — and slammed the ball off the heel of the rim.

"That's how life is," Dumas said. "Some days the garbage is good, some days, it isn't."

This one stung the Suns.

On Monday, May 17, the league announced its coach of the year award, as voted by a nationwide panel of reporters. Ballots are turned in during the final week of the season, so Westphal could neither lose votes because his team sputtered against the Lakers, nor gain any in tribute to his prophecy. But a lot of people in Phoenix thought the rookie coach was deserving, even if he is a little unorthodox. He found a way to win more games than anyone, despite having his point guard out more than one-third of the season and having five new players in significant roles. But the Red Auerbach Trophy went to Riley, whose Knicks were despised from coast to coast, by fans and basketball people alike. Westphal was a distant fourth.

"That's the last thing in the world I would want to complain about," Westphal said.

In fact, Westphal said he'd be pleased if his career paralleled that of Riley, whose Lakers rolled to all those championships, while Riley went unrewarded until his final season.

"It's wrong," Barkley said. "Paul IS the coach of the year. I think the thing Paul does is he lets you be yourself. He's not a yeller or a screamer, but he's always in control. He treats you like a person."

"It's not easy to go from 53 wins to 62," Majerle said. "Paul elevated all our games. A lot of teams that win 50 can't get to the next level like we have."

Westphal's perceived snub took the focus temporarily off the task at hand, which was dealing with two serious thumpings.

"We're a team that's very competitive, very talented, and has shown the ability to rise to the occasion," Westphal said. "We've also shown the ability to be distracted when we think things are easy. But we have found a way to get the job done. This team is what it is. You can't artificially force it to go against its nature. It's a dangerous game to play and it's not one that I prefer. If we have to keep making it difficult on ourselves, keep scraping our fingernails across the blackboard, so be it. I certainly don't like being 2-2, but it's better than 0-2 like we were against the Lakers."

Being down 3-2 wouldn't be any delight, either, but the Suns were speeding along that course through three quarters in Game 5 on Tuesday, May 18. They were listless. A perfect example: In the closing seconds of the third period, with the Spurs leading by three points, Avery Johnson, who at 5-foot-11 was the shortest player on the court, chased down a Spurs' miss and swished an uncontested shot at the buzzer.

Calling Charles Barkley! If the Suns were going to get anything going, Barkley had to be the man to initiate it.

"Our team, as much as I hate them for it, waits until it gets its back against the wall before giving us its best," Westphal said.

And that's just what Barkley gave. In just over 2 1/2 minutes, Barkley scored 13 straight points in the fourth quarter. Meanwhile, the Suns held the Spurs to six points over a nine-minute stretch.

Barkley seemed to will the comeback with his 19 fourth-quarter points and six fourth-quarter rebounds with Robinson guarding him.

"I didn't want to say two weeks from now that I didn't do everything I could," Barkley said after the 109-97 win that put the Suns a victory away from the Western Conference finals. "They were doing a lot of things to take the ball out of my hands, but they couldn't take it out of my hands and keep me off the offensive boards both."

Barkley made three three-point plays in the fourth quarter, all after he'd grabbed an offensive rebound. He finished with 36 points, making 11 of 16 shots, and 12 rebounds.

"This is the guy we've been reading and hearing about who can take over a game," the dejected Avery Johnson said.

Yet another Johnson, Frank, had almost as much to do with it. He hounded Avery in traps, forcing the Spurs to make an extra pass to get into their offense. That, in turn, caused them to use more of the shot clock. As time ran down, they panicked.

But the Suns didn't.

"I just couldn't believe what was happening to us," Majerle said. "I was upset and irritated. I couldn't believe that we were letting an opportunity slip away from us. We said in the huddle going into the fourth quarter that it was time to give everything we had. That first play set the tone defensively."

The Spurs suffered a 24-second shot-clock violation to open the fourth. The tide began to turn.

"Our defensive pressure had been there all along; it just finally began to wear them down," Westphal said. "The bottom line is not X's and O's, it's who's in the uniforms. Charles' uniform isn't big enough to hold his heart. Same for Frank."

The seldom-used Johnson said he tries to stay sharp at age 34 by playing Ceballos one-on-one before practices.

"And I've been killing him, too," Johnson said. "But if I really need an easy win, I take on 'Moose.'"

This time, the Spurs were stung.

"We had this game won," Elliott said. "We had them against the ropes at home in the fourth quarter."

Lucas was highly incensed; first, because his players squandered that beautiful situation, and second, because the Suns' reserves were waving towels from the bench as the Spurs shot in front of them. Lucas, who'd been glaring at the Suns, went to Westphal and had words after the game. Knight, who did little else, was singled out as the culprit.

"Every time Dale or Sean came in front of our bench, I told them that this is our zone," Knight said. "I said, 'Don't you come over here and try to hit a three-pointer. If you're going to hit one, you're going to have to do it from the other side.'"

Frank Johnson said Lucas was only firing up his troops for Game 6 in San Antonio.

"Luke knows what he is doing," said Frank Johnson, who played briefly with Lucas in Houston. "It was the end of the game and he knew it was a loss. He was looking for a way to motivate his guys for the next one. He's the master of that."

But that couldn't take the luster off Barkley's incredible performance. Even more incredible was that Barkley got off no shots in the first quarter, only two in the first half, and nine through three quarters.

"If anybody wants to watch a game about how to play basketball, they ought to watch a tape of that," Westphal said of Barkley's fourth-quarter clinic. "Save that tape and show it to the kids. That's what a man does with a game on the line. It was like he was the only player out there on the court. It didn't matter what San Antonio did, he was going to find a way to get the job done. There have been guys like Charles who have risen to the occasion, but very few."

Ceballos said he "just wanted to pass him the ball because I knew that this was something one day I could tell my kids about."

Colangelo, with the color having returned to his face following the Lakers series, sensed that this one had just swung to his team. "It wasn't just that we won the game, but how we won it. Charles was in the pack, and all of a sudden he just jumped out in front of everybody."

The Suns felt pretty good about having two games remaining to win one, and knowing that if it went seven, the last one would be at home.

"I'll take on any team in the world here," Barkley said.

"The Admiral" was convinced.

"Charles is the MVP," Robinson said. "He brought the Suns to another level. People think the Suns were already a great team. They were very very good with Dan and Kevin, but Charles put them at that next step."

Being at that next level means having the ability to win a big playoff series on the road, something the Suns had an opportunity to do on Thursday, May 20.

It wasn't going well at all. Early in the fourth quarter, the Suns were in arrears by 10 points.

"I hate those guys," Westphal said. "They just had to put me through the wringer one more time."

As always, doing things the hard way and — Westphal's protestation aside — loving it, the Suns rallied to win the series.

The Suns went up by four when KJ made a free throw with 31 seconds left. Then, Ellis swished a three-pointer to wipe out most of the lead with 15 seconds to go. With 12 seconds left, Ainge, one of the best clutch free- throw shooters in the game, stepped to the line for two, but made only the first. Barkley fouled Robinson on the rebound of the second.

"I figure Charles must have fouled the guy on purpose just so he could make a heroic shot at the end," KJ said.

Robinson made both free throws with 11 seconds showing, tying the score at 100.

The Suns would inbound from mid-court following a timeout. What would Westphal cook up? KJ on a penetration? Barkley posting up? Majerle for a three-pointer? A ricochet pass off the Spurs' mascot coyote?

Westphal snowed the Spurs.

Probably the last thing they expected to see was Barkley handling the ball alone at the top of the key as a point guard in an open set. This was a typical Westphal coaching decision. Normally, KJ, who was having a big game, would be out there with the ball with his four teammates spread across the baseline in the "1-4" set. Instead, the Suns' coach wanted it in the hands of his MVP candidate, even though he was out on the floor, beyond his usual effective scoring range. In case the Spurs played Barkley a little too tightly to deny him the ball, Westphal also had KJ, Majerle, and Ainge on the floor — all capable ball handlers and shooters.

"All I was concerned about was that we'd shoot too soon," Westphal said. "We wanted Charles to take it right to the buzzer, either win or go to overtime, but not leave them enough time to make it scary."

Barkley had the ball out on top as the clock ticked down. Inside 10 seconds, then five. Robinson waited for the anticipated drive. Barkley got Robinson backpedaling, then stopped and popped a 20-footer.

"I knew David wasn't going to let me go to the basket," Barkley said.

Swish.

The Spurs had 1.8 seconds to work with. Barkley had shot a little too soon. Anyone want to wager that the ball would come in low to Robinson following the timeout? The Suns expected it, but Robinson stationed himself on the right wing, about 18 feet from the basket, to accept the inbounds pass. He caught the ball, but as he tried to put up his last-gasp shot, Miller blocked it.

The Suns were in the Western Conference Finals for the third time in five seasons, and the sixth time overall. What a way to end it, All-Star against All-Star, Olympian against Olympian.

"I thought about trying to run up on him and make him hit a running jumper," Robinson said of Barkley's series-winner. "But by the time I started to move toward Charles, he had already taken a couple of steps inside the three-point line. I wasn't going to let him drive. He hit it, that's why he's my choice for MVP."

"It was a great thing to behold if you are a basketball fan," Westphal said.

Robinson wasn't so sure. "I felt like a train that hit the wall."

For another year Robinson would have to live with criticism that he can't lift the Spurs the way Barkley lifted the Suns, or Michael Jordan lifted the Chicago Bulls. The series-winner capped a 28-point performance by Barkley, half of those coming in the dramatic fourth-quarter. He also took 21 rebounds and made four steals.

For Miller, it was a bit of redemption when he swatted away Robinson's last shot. Earlier, Miller missed two free throws and also allowed Robinson to get an offensive rebound that led to Ellis' three-point basket. But Miller scored 12 points, grabbed five rebounds, and blocked five shots.

Chambers also made some big plays — three baskets — late in the game. He scored 10 points in 13 minutes.

But Barkley, once again, came up huge. "If you want to be successful in life you have to make yourself successful. I want Charles Barkley to be a great basketball player."

He was, and so was KJ, who scored seven straight points after the score was tied at 92.

"In a lot of ways, Kevin's been our most consistent player in the playoffs, maybe our MVP of the first 11 playoff games — although No. 34 deserves some consideration, too," Westphal said.

KJ finished with 18 points and eight assists.

"Everybody questioned at the beginning of the year whether Charles and I could get along," KJ said. "Well, I always felt that if you put me on a team with a great post-up player like Charles, I'd be even better."

The Spurs, who recovered from a terrible beginning under Coach Jerry Tarkanian, were gone, and so was the HemisFair Arena. Barkley closed it with a flair. The Spurs move into the new Alamodome.

Barkley said going into the series he might have to take David Robinson outside and that, hopefully, he could get a few shots to fall. In the end, that's exactly what it took.

"I'm glad we won so we can get a few days of rest," he said.

The Suns needed it. Houston won in the Summit to tie its semifinal series with the SuperSonics at 3-3. The Rockets would have to go back to Seattle for the deciding seventh game. The Suns would get at least three days of rest before the Western Conference Finals opened at the Purple Palace.

The popular theory was that the Rockets would be the tougher opponent, what with Hakeem Olajuwon on a season-long tear and the Rockets having picked it up late in the season.

But through a quirk, a missed call, the Rockets yielded the home-court edge to Seattle in their series, which put the Sonics in position to wrap it up. That would be better for the Suns, many thought.

The fate of the Rockets, and perhaps the Suns, swung on the final day of the regular season. Houston needed to beat San Antonio in order to earn the home-court edge on Seattle. Robinson was credited with a tip-in that sent the game to overtime, where the Spurs eventually prevailed. Replays showed that Robinson's tip clearly came after the final horn had sounded. Houston should have won the game and should have had the home edge on the Sonics.

Instead, it turned into a seven-game marathon that featured an overtime finale before Seattle won on its home court.

"They're very different than anybody else in the league because of the wildly different styles they can play," Westphal said of the Sonics. "They can go big. They can go small. And their traps are unlike any others. They make a game crazy with all their trapping."

The Suns proved they can make a game crazy, too, with their last-second heroics. They'd done it all year.

"It was never too late," Westphal said. "Hopefully that will always be a personality of our team."

# Chapter Twenty-eight

# A MOST VALUABLE PLAYER

In the opener on Monday, May 24, the Sonics played like a team that had just arrived in town following a grueling seven-game series. The Suns blocked 16 shots, forced 17 turnovers, and limited Seattle to 41 percent shooting in an easy 105-91 decision.

"Shhhh," Westphal said. "We don't play good defense around here."

Scouting the Suns is quite a chore. Westphal often keeps his own players guessing. For example, he started Ceballos in Game 1 in place of Dumas, who did not score in 14 minutes in the sixth game against San Antonio. Ceballos is more experienced in slashing to the basket.

The Sonics made the mistake of doubling Barkley with Ceballos' man. It slowed Barkley, who was limited to 12 points with six-of-14 shooting. But it left Ceballos open for dunk after dunk and 21 points. He made eight of 12 shots.

"They were confused," Barkley said. "They thought we were Philly, where they could double me all they want. They must have decided that they weren't going to let me beat them, and that's exactly what happened. Our other players beat them."

On his surprise start, Ceballos had the line of the playoffs: "I think Paul's dog decides who starts. When Paul gets up in the morning, if his dog licks his left hand, he goes with Richard. If his dog licks his right hand, he starts me. So every time I shake Paul's hand, I make sure there's a piece of steak in mine."

KJ thinks there's another reason: "Ced is the best-kept secret in the NBA. Every time he's called upon, he gives you 20 points and about seven or eight rebounds, and doesn't make many mistakes."

But chances appeared good Dumas would be in the lineup in the second game. Ceballos aggravated that stress reaction in his left foot.

"If we put Richard back in there, he's liable to have the same kind of night Ced had," Westphal said. "It was like Richard and Ced took turns having great years. I thought going into the season that small forward was going to be a problem, but it actually has turned into a strength for us. It's such a strength that I can't give them both the minutes they deserve."

Miller was stepping out of the darkness of obscurity, as well, with games like this — 15 points, 10 rebounds, five blocked shots.

"It makes you mad," Seattle coach George Karl said, "when a team finds a player we didn't think they had. But since the third game of the Laker series, it was obvious Miller was going to be a contributor."

Seattle does not have a superstar. The Sonics' scoring leader is Ricky Pierce, who was limited to six points in the opener. Sam Perkins, who came from the Lakers in a mid-season trade, is a star, but not a superstar. Shawn Kemp is headed in that direction. He's already big in Seattle, where Kemp is known as the "Reign Man."

"He's got this city fired up again," Karl said. "It's scary, too, because he isn't even close to reaching his full potential yet."

The Sonics might not have a Barkley, or a Jordan, or an Olajuwon, but they have many very good players, any of whom can beat you. Their frenetic trapping defenses force opponents to use time off the shot clock, taking them out of their comfort zone as they try to execute.

But in the opener, the fatigued Sonics couldn't make anything happen. The Suns, on the other hand, do have a superstar. Everyone knew the league's MVP award was coming the next day. Barkley swore he hadn't been tipped off because "I can't keep a secret. When I was in Philadelphia, the 76ers were trying to keep it a secret that the team was terrible, but I was already out telling people."

Stern was on his way to Phoenix on the day of the announcement. If that wasn't clue enough, Majerle stopped the action in his grill after the game and made the announcement , buying a round for the house.

Barkley was the first Suns player to receive the award.

"Obviously the greatest thing Chuck brought to the Suns was his will to win," Ainge said. "That was never more evident than the last two games of the San Antonio series where he picked us up and put us on his back.

"There were so many times that Chuck got the big rebound or made the big shot when there were two, three, maybe even four guys around him. That's been contagious to the rest of us."

It wasn't close. Barkley's 835 total points in the balloting outdistanced runner-up Olajuwon's 647. Jordan, the two-time MVP, was third with 565.

"I can't explain the last year of my life," Barkley said. "Nobody gets it this good. I go from the Dream Team, to the best regular-season record, to the Western Conference Finals, to the MVP. Nobody's ever experienced what I've experienced in the last year before. I'm just disappointed I wasn't on a better team sooner. I should have gotten traded sooner."

And then, Barkley shook everyone up by saying that if the Suns won the title, he'd probably retire. You never quite know how seriously to take him. The inclination was to take it with a grain of salt. But knowing Barkley, who marches to his own drummer, he was liable to do it. He already has more money than he knows what to do with. Outside endorsements, primarily with Nike, are worth about $10 million to him. He has three years left on his contract with the Suns, worth $13 million more.

"It is a possibility, it could happen," Barkley said. "I don't think my life could get any better than it's been the past year. It would be ideal to leave while I'm on top. There would be nothing left to accomplish."

But his attorney, Tom Sullivan, shed the most light when he said, "It would be normal to have a letdown after winning a championship, especially if it comes on top of everything else Charles has accomplished over the past year. But Charles is a racehorse. If you open the gate, he's going to run. I don't believe he would retire."

Sullivan also said that Barkley did not have an MVP incentive in his contract. "I don't think he gives a hoot about any additional monetary gain," Sullivan said. Just the ring.

The Suns were convinced they were on course.

"All it takes is seven more wins," Barkley said. "I've been playing my whole life, since I was 9 years old, and it's down to seven wins. What an incredible feeling that everything you've worked in life to accomplish is right there. There's a light at the end of the tunnel, and it's not a train."

Or it wasn't until Game 2.

"I always felt the further you go in the playoffs, the home court only becomes valuable in seventh games," Karl said. "I don't think it's that much of a factor up until then."

Right you are, George. On Wednesday, May 26, the Suns missed 15 free throws and Perkins swished two critical three-pointers late to pull the Sonics to a 103-99 upset win at the Purple Palace. Now they had to go to Seattle, where they lost both regular-season visits, with the series tied.

As Majerle put it, "They just kept hanging around. That's what you do on the road. You hang around until the end and then you find a way to steal it."

No one was more excited than Eddie Johnson, the Sonics' sixth man, who'd performed a similar role for the Suns three seasons earlier. "If this doesn't pump us up, I don't know what will," EJ said. "Now, we get to go home and take care of business."

Pierce put his horrible first game behind and scored 34 points.

"Dan Majerle is a great defender," Karl said, "but we did a better job of setting picks for Ricky, and he hit some huge shots."

And Perkins was left alone behind the three-point line while the Suns were desperately trying to cling to a small lead.

It's the old familiar story: the Suns led by 10 points with 11 minutes left. Gradually, they let it slip away. In the final 2:52, Seattle outscored the Suns, 12-2. At the 1:58 mark, Perkins cut the Suns' lead to 97-96 with a trey. After Majerle threw away a pass with 18 seconds remaining, the Sonics fully intended to work the ball inside to 6-10 Derrick McKey, who had broken free. Miller spotted him. Figuring it's better to concede a three-pointer than a dunk, he dropped off Perkins and covered McKey. The ball swung to Perkins. Steady and cool as ever, Perkins made another three-pointer at 9.8 seconds that put the Sonics ahead by two.

"I've always felt good with the three," the 6-foot-9 Perkins said.

He made one while with the Lakers that beat the Bulls in Game 1 of the 1991 NBA Finals at Chicago Stadium.

There still would have been plenty of time against most teams, but not Seattle, with its smothering defense. KJ found nothing available as he drove. He kicked the ball out to Ainge in the corner, whose hurried shot missed badly. Barkley grabbed it and put it in, seemingly the game-winner, but the play was nullified when Barkley's old menace, referee Mike Mathis, called him for an elbowing foul. The Suns were doomed.

"If I'm playing checkers and I'm losing, I'll accidentally knock the board over," Barkley said. "There's not a worse feeling than seeing somebody else having fun at your expense. You can't leave guys wide open for threes in a tight game, and you can't miss free throws."

Imagine if something like that were to happen to them with the NBA championship on the line.

Barkley shot nine-for-19, scoring 24 points. KJ was a horrendous three-for-eight from the floor, six-for-11 at the line for 12 points. Worse, he had only four assists.

Majerle's numbers were the Suns' best: 29 points, 10 rebounds. But he had that critical turnover, missed four free throws, and watched Pierce have the big night.

"We have to punish the trap," Majerle said. "We more or less gave that game to them. We have to realize who is being trapped, who is open, and get the open man to dive to the basket to take the pass."

Ceballos is the Suns' best at spotting those openings. He played sparingly in Game 2 on his sore left foot. The Suns needed quicker decision making with the ball and better reads by players without the ball. The open player has to make the defense pay for its gambling.

That's not easy against Seattle because they play zone defense with the three players who are not involved in the trap, which helps them continue the trapping process once the ball is passed. The three not involved in the trap front their men, making it difficult for the trapped player to deliver a pass.

"I think that stuff you all are talking about is bull," Barkley said. "If we make our free throws and box out on the boards, we win. Personally, I don't think their defense had all that much to do with it."

But KJ consistently walked the ball up the floor, was trapped, and had the shot-clock go inside five seconds with the ball still 20 feet from the basket.

"The Sonics have a different style of defense than anybody," Ainge said.

But EJ, who maintains his off-season home in the Valley and often works out with Suns players, knew they'd be confident they could break through in Seattle. "That's why I think this game is the most important in the series. If we win, our confidence goes right up."

Interestingly, Seattle had yet to use what the Suns considered its greatest advantage — height in the low post. The Sonics were using their big guys primarily as pickers to free Pierce and EJ.

"If we had won playing the way we played, we would have gone to Seattle, played like that again, and lost by 20 points in Game 3," Ainge said. "Now, maybe we'll go up and play like we should, and win. Then we'll be in the same position everyone expected us to be in after three games. We'll still be up, 2-1."

On the eve of that third game, Barkley for the fifth time was selected first-team all-NBA. He and Jordan were the only unanimous selections.

"It's a nice honor," he said, "but I've got more important things on my mind. First, I was MVP, and now this. I'm sure when I step on the court, Seattle isn't going to give a damn about it."

True enough. The league's MVP and all-NBA first-teamer managed seven-for-20 shooting and only 16 points. But he did take 16 rebounds and make four steals.

The real hero, though, was Barkley's little buddy, Frank Johnson, who scored seven points in a 12-0 blitz to open the fourth quarter that carried the Suns to a 104-97 victory and a 2-1 lead. Among Johnson's shots was a rare three-pointer.

"If you ask me, that was the back-breaker right there," Seattle guard Gary Payton said. "We never expected that from Frank. It just killed us."

That's why the Suns call him "Fourth-Quarter Frank." In that final period, Seattle was limited to 38 percent shooting and 17 points. In the third quarter, KJ was kneed in the thigh and had to come out briefly. He hobbled back late in the fourth, but he couldn't penetrate. Frank got them through several crucial minutes while KJ was treated.

"I was fortunate Frank stepped up," KJ said. "During the season, we had seven guys who averaged double-figure scoring. During the playoffs, we've had only four. Notice that we had seven again tonight. I think our bench took Seattle's depth as a challenge."

Frank said he couldn't help but think how close he was to being out of the game as a player: "I probably should be scouting this game."

KJ's wasn't the only injury. Westphal put Dumas back in the lineup because Ceballos' foot was sore, but Dumas turned his left ankle in the second quarter and had to come out. Dumas was on his way to a big game: five-of-eight shooting and 11 points in 18 minutes.

As Ainge suggested, the Suns now were right back where they were supposed to be. "We went out and played fearless, I think that's the best word to describe it. We turn it off and on. It's human nature, but we can't afford it at this point."

Having said that, Ainge knew full well that the Suns undoubtedly would turn it off and on again. Speaking of flipping the on-off switch, Barkley hadn't scored a point in the second half until he put back a missed free throw by KJ with 1:50 to go. Seattle had — guess what? — trimmed a 10-point deficit to two before KJ made the first and missed the second. Barkley's score on the offensive rebound restored the lead to five.

"I never get concerned as long as I am breathing," Barkley said.

Evidently. The sellout crowd frequently broke into chants of "Barkley sucks! Barkley sucks!" He responded by scratching the side of his head — with the middle finger of his right hand.

"I'm not here to win friends," he said. "I'm here to win games. Some fans are just idiots."

Barkley wasn't finished having fun.

In response to signs throughout the arena proclaiming, "Not in Our House," Barkley said, "This is OUR home. When is the lease up on this house? We'll move in here."

That, of course, made all the Seattle papers in a big way, and Barkley expected even more venom from the crowd in Game 4 on Sunday.

"I wanted them to concentrate on me and not the game."

Barkley offered that if the crowd was irked by his antics in Game 3, "they're going to hate me tonight. It's going to be fun. We're going to kick their butts."

The Sonics were trying to figure out how to get EJ going against his old team. He'd made only four of 19 in the series. The Suns were just about applauding whenever he took a shot.

Seattle writers were after him, too. EJ was writing a daily column for a Seattle newspaper. The competing paper observed that EJ was "shooting like a sportswriter." The fallacy in that statement is that many sportswriters are better than 20 percent shooters. And so is EJ. Having endured a few of his streaks — good and bad — themselves, the Suns knew full well that EJ could pop out of it and make 18 out of 20 the next time out. So they weren't gloating. In fact, they were uneasy.

"I'm due," EJ said. "I think this is the longest lull I've been in this year."

When Karl sent him to the scorer's table to check into Game 4 on Sunday, May 30, the crowd was with him. "Ed-die! Ed-die!" they chanted, that after he went 0-for-6 in the previous game. This time, he made five of nine shots as Seattle shot 54 percent and reamed the Suns, 120-101. The series was even after four games. There was little defensive effort from the Suns. That was noted by Westphal after the game.

According to KJ, "Paul couldn't even talk to us. He talked to us for about a minute and walked out. We can't even look ourselves in the mirror."

The Sonics did shift the focus of their attack inside to Kemp, Perkins, and McKey to complement EJ's outside work. The three Seattle big guys roughed up the Suns' front line.

"This was the first time all year I've felt that we just quit," Ainge said. "It just wasn't important enough to us."

Suns fans look at it only from the Suns' perspective. They forget that Seattle is a good team, perfectly capable of winning big games. By getting the split, the Suns put themselves back into position to win the series simply by winning home games.

"Lots of guys talk, but most of them don't know their ass from a hole in the wall," said Barkley, who led the Suns with 27 points. "Nobody wants to give anybody else any credit. Seattle outplayed us today. That's it."

Barkley was right. While the Suns' lapses didn't seem reflective of a team seriously in pursuit of the Larry O'Brien Trophy, who says that every series has to be a sweep? It takes only four wins to advance.

The Suns were letting an underdog build confidence. Kemp, McKey and Perkins combined for 59 points and 21 rebounds. Seattle had chosen to play a different way. That is why they are dangerous.

"I've heard people say that we don't have a superstar on our team, a go-to guy," Karl said. "Well, we have a lot of All-Star players on our team. Tonight, Derrick McKey was our Charles Barkley. The other night, it was Ricky Pierce. And the next time, it might be Shawn Kemp or Sam Perkins. I think it's a lot of fun this way. We're much better when we play wild and crazy. Now, it looks like we'll go inside a little more. The Lakers did that in the first round successfully. I think in many ways that the war has just begun."

Westphal didn't share Karl's enthusiasm. He was so incensed that he pulled his starters midway through the fourth quarter, essentially sending up the white flag. KJ, denying that his bruised thigh was bothering him, made only two of 11 shots, scored six points, had seven assists.

"I don't know if anybody consciously laid down," Westphal said, "but we can play a whole lot better. Whatever the reason, it is not acceptable."

The Suns were down by only three at the half, but Seattle buried them with a 21-7 spurt to open the third quarter. The Suns were questioning their effort, their dedication, their professionalism. Was it the beginning of divisiveness? Were the wheels falling off?

"I see just the opposite," Westphal said. "I don't see finger pointing, I see guys taking responsibility. You can only get to the truth when you identify a problem. It's important to do that. It's not that we weren't trying. And it's not that we didn't want it. We just weren't trying intelligently."

Although Westphal yelled at his players during their closed practice, he did not show them any video of the previous game. "I wouldn't do that to them. I still like these guys. That's how TVs and VCRs get damaged."

At least the Suns still had their sense of humor, if not their lead.

According to KJ, "Paul normally doesn't overdo it as a coach, but there are times when a team doesn't respond to that and has to be put back on track. Maybe slapping our heads a couple of times is what we needed. Paul really got into us. You could see his disappointment. More importantly, we were disappointed in ourselves.

"Paul really challenged our small forwards in a big way. Paul has a good way of issuing a challenge in his own sly way in trying to bring out the best in players."

When the semifinal series with San Antonio reached 2-2, Barkley put the Suns on his shoulders and carried them to two more wins.

"I'm not going to put it on Charles, or anybody else, to carry us like that," Westphal said. "It's going to take better play from everybody."

Barkley, still mystified about the uproar over the Suns losing a game in Seattle, said, "If you ask the SuperSonics if they'd rather be in their shoes or ours, I bet they'd rather be in ours."

Nerves were wearing thin on both sides. Ceballos was talking trash to McKey, and Barkley to Kemp. Karl was whining about KJ's incessant whining.

"Kevin has learned to cry," Karl said. "What are we supposed to do, get out of his way? Treat him like a queen? Like a little princess?"

Shot back KJ: "Treated like a queen, huh? He could have at least used the word 'king,' or 'prince.' Or maybe he doesn't have a preference. Guess that says it. We'll give him something to whine about ."

Miller was hospitalized briefly the day before Game 5 because of intestinal flu. KJ reported that his thigh bruise was feeling much better.

Before the game, Colangelo received his unprecedented fourth NBA Executive of the Year award, sponsored by *The Sporting News.*

"Anytime you win an individual award like this, the real credit goes to the people who work with you and around you," he said. "We've been very fortunate in that regard because we've had great people. But the respect of your peers is probably more important than anything, and I thank ownership and management throughout the NBA for their support."

*The Sporting News* also honored Barkley as its player of the year. Unlike the MVP award sanctioned by the NBA, *The Sporting News* award is voted on by players. And unlike his flop the night he received his MVP trophy, Barkley was a demon on this night, Tuesday, June 1.

With Barkley going for 43 points — his playoff career high— 15 rebounds, and 10 assists, and Majerle swishing an NBA playoff-record eight three-pointers, the Suns closed in on the Finals with a 120-114 win at the Purple Palace.

It wasn't an unusual script. In fact, most Suns games, like those old John Wayne movies Westphal talked about back when the Suns were down 0-2 to the Lakers, have a sameness about them: Suns take lead, Suns lose lead, Suns pull out dramatic win after all.

This time, the Suns led by seven at the two-minute mark, then failed to score on four straight possessions as the Sonics closed to one.

With 20 seconds to go, Majerle launched his final trey. If he missed and the Sonics rebounded, they'd have the ball and the chance to take the last shot to win the game. But Majerle's shot swished cleanly through the net, giving the Suns a four-point edge.

"If Majerle misses, it's probably a different ball game," the disappointed Karl said. "But I don't think anybody can be unhappy with this game. You don't like to get beat by threes, but Majerle was making them in a zone I'm not sure we can defend. You'd think if a guy plays 47 minutes like he did that fatigue might set in. I was wrong."

EJ, no stranger to three-point shooting himself, just shook his head in admiration. "You know, it looked like the middle was wide open on his last one. He probably could have put the ball on the floor and taken it to the basket. But he pulls up and shoots another three, a long three. To do that in that situation, man, that's confidence."

Majerle said he thought about driving, "but I was hitting threes all night, so why not? That was one of the biggest shots of my career. I didn't think about it at the time, but if I had missed and they rebounded, they'd have been in excellent position to go down and win the game. But I wasn't going to turn it down. I was left open. I'm going to shoot it."

Majerle was heaving them from that "crazy range" he told his teammates he had after he made the 33-footer to beat the Lakers. Most of his 10 attempts were from a step or two behind the line.

"Derrick McKey is 6-foot-10 and has those real long arms," Majerle said. "I could see him running at me. I figured the way I was going, I had just as good a chance of making it if I backed up another step."

Chambers also disrupted the Sonics' defensive plan by making four baskets in the fourth quarter when he scored nine of his 11 points. With Ceballos and Dumas hurting, Chambers loomed as a key.

The Sonics were caught in a deadly dilemma. They had to double Barkley, or this might have been the night he really did go for 100. They knew someone had to help on KJ when he drove, or he'd take it all the way to the basket. That often left Majerle alone from long distance.

"You still have to make them," Westphal said. "And almost nobody can make eight out of 10 from that far in a gym by themselves."

The Sonics could only hope they'd respond in kind on their home court and force a deciding seventh game.

Miffed because he wasn't getting the ball in the second half in this series, Barkley went to Westphal for a closed-door chat before the fifth game. At halftime, Barkley reiterated his request to his teammates.

"There might have been some cussing," Frank Johnson said. "Then again, I don't listen to Charles a lot. Every other word out of his mouth is cussing."

In his defense, Barkley said, "Sometimes, we try to get others involved instead of getting me involved. But once I become aggressive, their defense scrambles, and I can get the ball to other guys. Then, when those guys make their shots, it makes my life a whole lot easier."

The Suns' small forwards took Westphal's challenge and limited McKey to nine points, but Kemp kept the Sonics in the game by scoring 20 of his playoff career-high 33 points in the fourth quarter.

Now, could they put the Sonics away on the road, or would they have to endure a seventh game? Knowing the Suns, they weren't going to do it the easy way.

"Facts are facts: We have two chances to win one game," Westphal said.

Karl also was facing the facts: "We don't have the luxury of making a mistake and having a down game."

Like the Suns, the Sonics were accustomed to doing things the hard way. In their best-of-five opening-round series against Utah, Seattle trailed, 2-1, going to Salt Lake City. Then came the harrowing and exhausting marathon with Houston that wasn't decided until the Sonics pulled out an overtime decision in the seventh game.

"But we're on our deathbed," Karl said.

The Suns didn't want to risk having it turn into a one-game series in which a bad day can end a season.

"In a seventh game, a guy can get hurt, a guy can get in foul trouble, somebody can hit a big shot," KJ said. "You don't want it to come down to that."

The Suns didn't have to be reminded of what their next victory would mean. Barkley certainly could taste it. That's why he was continuing his campaign to receive the ball in the second half.

"We should never go down the court four or five times in a row and me never touch the ball," he said. "Just because it comes to me doesn't mean it's going to end with me. I can create things for other guys. We had a five-point lead. I scored the first basket of the second half, and I didn't touch it again. The next thing I know, we're down five."

That's as critical as Barkley had been publicly about his new team, but the stakes never had been higher. Everyone among the Suns knew that he was right.

"I've got to say, 'Give me the fucking ball, and give it to me now,'" Barkley said. "I always want the last shot. Somebody's got to be the hero, and it might as well be me."

But for the Suns, there would be few heroes in Game 6 on Thursday, June 3. Seattle set up a dramatic seventh-game showdown with a 118-102 rout. There wasn't a member of the Seattle starting five who didn't score at least 16 points. Pierce led with 27. There were several near-altercations, lots of words, dirty looks, and shoves. One involved Sonics backup center Michael Cage and Ainge.

"Besides Bill Laimbeer, Danny is probably who you want to punch most in the league," Cage said. " But that's not going to solve anything. We laughed about it later."

After Barkley and Majerle combined for 77 points in the fifth game, Barkley made four of 14 shots, Majerle four of 11.

Of one sequence in which Barkley missed, rebounded, missed again, rebounded, and missed again, Ainge said, "The way he was hopping up and down with his arms over his head, I thought he was doing the 'Nutcracker Suite.'"

Kemp made good on his word with 22 points and 15 rebounds. The Suns really had no answer to him. He was a load for Barkley, who is six inches shorter. Still, Barkley, following his 13-point, 11-rebound outing, said, "I was just tired from the other night, they didn't work me over. I like our chances Saturday."

The Suns were out of the game from the second quarter on. They trailed by as many as 20 points. The thrashing wasn't the end of their woes. Ceballos was carried off in the second quarter. Dr. Emerson said the "stress reaction" had deteriorated into a "stress fracture." Ceballos was out of the playoffs. He would require surgery and a lengthy rehabilitation to get ready for fall training camp.

"I've never felt anything like it before," Ceballos said after hearing the telltale snap. "I couldn't put any pressure on my foot."

What a way to end a remarkable season for a young man who had come so far as a player and as a person. He handled his situation with

Dumas with grace and humility. Ceballos had been on the floor for only four minutes, but he'd made three of four shots and scored eight points.

"Who knows?" Ceballos said. "If I hadn't gotten hurt, we might have won, and I might have been the star of the game."

But if the Suns did prevail in Game 7 on Saturday, they'd have to play the Finals with only 11 men. Under NBA playoff rules, rosters are frozen. Replacements are not permissible.

"There's one more game, and it's in the Valley of the Sun," Barkley said, trying to put the best spin on it all. "People wonder why we play 82 games during the regular season. This is why."

In some ways, the Suns were exactly where they wanted to be. . They thrived on the types of situations they would face in the series climax at America West Arena.

The Sonics were confident that, having played six games evenly with the 62-game winners, they could pull the upset and move on to the Finals.

While the Suns and Sonics were traveling back to Phoenix on Friday, June 4, the Chicago Bulls were hosting the New York Knicks in Game 6 of the Eastern Conference Finals. The Bulls, after a break-through in New York, led, three games to two. Playing at home propelled the two-time champs to a 96-88 win and another trip to the Finals with a chance to three-peat. The Bulls would come to the Purple Palace to open the championship round if it played the Suns. Chicago would open at home if they played the Sonics. They didn't seem intimidated by either possibility. There hadn't been a three-time defending champ since Boston's run of eight in a row ended in 1966. Only the Celtics and the old Minneapolis Lakers ever won as many as three straight. The Bulls were hungry to take their place in history.

As Riley said after his Knicks were eliminated, "I don't see anybody beating them. The Bulls are back on top of their game now."

Meanwhile, the wheels were spinning in Westphal's head. Who starts at small forward with Ceballos out? Dumas? Move Majerle down to forward and start Ainge in Majerle's guard spot? Or how about Tom Chambers?

Although the veteran had helped the Suns throughout the play-offs, including the deciding game in the San Antonio series, it appeared doubtful the Suns would exercise their option to bring Chambers back for another season. A loss to Seattle and Chambers' career in a Suns' uniform probably was over. He knew it, Westphal knew it.

"I've known that all season long," Chambers said. "Now, it's finally coming to a head."

Starting Chambers might be just the emotional edge the Suns need to get through the big game.

"Young guys have a tendency not to realize the position they're in, the opportunity awaiting them," Ainge said. "They're thinking this is going to happen all the time. Us older guys know better and have a greater appreciation of this situation."

While Westphal was mulling what to do, the Sonics were gearing up their psychological warfare. Kemp said he couldn't wait for his final shot at Barkley.

"I want him," Kemp said. "Home court or no home court, this is what dreams are all about."

There's a line between youthful enthusiasm and foolishness. Kemp seemed to have crossed it.

"I don't believe I'm going to let us lose," Barkley responded.

"We've got Chuck," Ainge said of the Suns' success record in critical games. "He has been huge in these kinds of games."

Karl said if he could be granted one wish, it's that his team would come out "free and loose" — or that Mark West would wind up with the ball on each Suns' possession instead of Barkley or KJ.

"I think everyone knows that when a team starts playing well, it snowballs," Karl said. "And I can't deny that we're playing awfully well right now."

But the Suns sensed that they were about to take a giant step toward their perceived destiny of winning it all.

"The hardest thing is the waiting," Ainge said. "It's almost like you're a kid sleeping in your uniform the night before your first Little League game. It's probably the biggest game most of the guys on our team have ever played in. You can't imagine anything more fun unless it's the seventh game of the NBA Finals. This is second best."

Barkley concurred, calling it "an emotional game, an emotional day. It's no place for weak sisters."

Westphal said his message would be simple: "The last thing you have to do is jack a team up to play in the seventh game of a playoff. I'll just tell them to remember what they do well, don't be afraid, and go do it."

Twelve-thirty p.m., Saturday, June 5. The arena had been rocking for an hour. The crowd arrived early, fully expecting that it would be part of something special.

Arizonans were tired of hearing their state bashed. If it wasn't the impeachment of former Gov. Evan Mecham, then it was the failure to have a state holiday honoring slain civil rights leader Dr. Martin Luther King, Jr., or the fact that convicted savings and loan swindler Charles Keating lived here, or that the state's two U.S. senators were among those accused of giving favor to Keating, or — you name it.

Arizonans were hungry for the world to see that where they live really isn't such a bad place. The success of the Suns had gripped the state as nothing within memory had. People embraced the Suns. People who at the start of the season might not have been able to name a member of the team — there actually WERE people who didn't know who Barkley was — suddenly were sitting up and taking notice.

They knew the game was being telecast internationally. This seemed a wonderful forum not only for the Suns to advance to the Finals, but also to vindicate the state with the whole world watching.

"There was so much at stake today," Colangelo said. "It meant so much to so many. That's why this is so emotional."

From the start it was emotional. Jeff Munn, the arena public address announcer, delivered the first charge to the crowd as he introduced the Suns' starters:

"At forward, from Utah, No. 24, Tom Chambers."

Westphal had decided to give Chambers the starting assignment in the biggest game he'd ever played. The move obviously was recognized and appreciated by the crowd who greeted Chambers with a thunderous roar. He hadn't been the most effective player over the past three seasons, but the loyal Suns fans hadn't forgotten Chambers' first two years in Phoenix, after he left Seattle as an unrestricted agent on July 5, 1988.

In each of his first two seasons, Chambers broke the Suns' scoring record. He once tossed in 60 points, his career high, against his old teammates, the Sonics, the team he would face again this day, with his first trip to the Finals riding on the outcome. What a moment this was for the crowd, and what an opportunity it was for Chambers.

The key word for the Suns was "attack." Don't get caught in a Sonics' trap. Time after time, KJ sliced to the basket, and in this game he got the calls. He made 14 of 16 free throws as he scored 22 points, had nine assists, four steals, and two blocks.

The Suns also accommodated Barkley's request for the ball, especially in the fourth quarter. He made 19 of 22 free throws for the game. In the fourth quarter, Barkley scored 15 points and grabbed 12 rebounds.

And Chambers came through with 17 points, six rebounds and two blocked shots. More important to the Suns, and undoubtedly satisfying to the 6-foot-10 Chambers, he helped limit McKey to six points. He was a better physical match for McKey than Dumas or Ceballos. When Chambers left Seattle, he did so because the Sonics were replacing him in the lineup with the younger McKey.

The Suns looked up at the scoreboard and saw a six-point lead at halftime that grew to 11 in the third quarter.

In the fourth, it reached 18 points as the Sonics continued to hack. The Suns just stepped to the line and blazed away. They tied an NBA playoff record with 57 free throws made in 64 attempts. Even with EJ netting 18 of his 34 points in the third quarter, the Sonics couldn't gain ground.

By the time Munn announced, "Two minutes!" the crowd was on its feet. There was no stopping the inevitable. The Suns weren't going to let this one get away. One by one the starters came out to thunderous ovations.

Finally, the horn sounded, purple and orange streamers exploded from the rafters, and the Suns were in the NBA Finals with a 123-110 win.

Colangelo wiped tears from his eyes. Barkley covered his head with a towel and wept.

Chambers, normally the stoic old warrior, was skipping around like a young pup, grinning, and repeating, "We're going to the Finals! We're going to the Finals!"

KJ said it was "like I've dipped my hand in a honeycomb and tasted something sweet."

Finally, Barkley said, "I'm going to have a six-pack of beer, sit in my Jacuzzi, and have some fun."

That would probably be without the rubber duck that Barkley normally shares his soaks with in the Suns' clubhouse Jacuzzi. He had just scored 44 points and snared 24 rebounds — both his playoff career highs.

Westphal actually had told Chambers in the closing seconds of the Game 6 loss in Seattle that he would start in this one but he had to keep it a secret. Westphal loves to spring surprises.

"I was so happy, I wanted to call everybody I know and tell them," Chambers said. "I was really nervous. I had butterflies for the first time in a long time. I've never been the kind of guy who screams and hollers, but I wanted to jump for joy. It's like any job that you've worked at for 12 years to get to that ultimate opportunity, that big promotion, or whatever it is that you've worked for."

Westphal later would say that the highlight of the season for him was seeing the look of satisfaction on Chambers' face and hearing the roar of the crowd when Chambers, two weeks short of his 34th birthday, came out in the closing minutes.

But the man behind it all, Colangelo, probably also was the man who was most emotional when it was over. He'd been through so much for so long with this team. Now, he was four wins away from being on top of the world.

"When all the speculation began this year that we might get to the Finals, I was hoping it would be the Bulls who would be there, too," he said. "This is special."

The Suns had stunned the basketball world in 1976 when they dumped defending NBA champion Golden State in the Western Conference Finals. They met Boston. It was a hard-fought series, that included the famous triple-overtime game in Boston Garden, and Gar Heard's clutch moon-shot.

"I remember in 1976 standing on the floor of the Boston Garden before the first game looking at all their banners and thinking that we would be back to the Finals several times, and soon," Colangelo said, smiling. "It took 17 years, but it means a great deal to me.

"Forget the financial ramifications. We've far exceeded anything anyone could dream of. This is about trying to get our first banner in our new building. Look how excited everyone is right now. Look at all that has happened just in the past year. We had a fabulous season followed by a rollercoaster ride through the playoffs. Now imagine how excited everyone would be if we got our first championship."

It wasn't hard to gauge. The excitement really picked up when the Suns got off the hook in the first round. By now, all of the area newspapers were bannering the Suns' game on Page A-1, followed by daily special sections wrapped around the regular sports section. Local television newscasts led off their daily reports with the Suns. Never had anything swept the area so dramatically. Most people couldn't get enough of Sunsmania.

Not only were tickets being scalped for unbelievable prices, even seats at tables in Majerle's Sports Grill were being bartered for a good price. Patrons were turning down offers of $100 during and immediately after the games. Also, fans were lined up well into the night to get into the Suns' souvenir store in the arena. Some waited for three hours until nearly midnight. It was madness!

Cars and trucks all across the Valley were decorated in purple and orange. Windows of businesses had supportive slogans painted on the glass, or posters or banners displayed.

Barkley, the man who generated the excitement, had delivered in a Herculean way once again in the Suns' biggest game. This was what the Suns had acquired him to do, and this was why Barkley was the league's Most Valuable Player. When Barkley finally made his way to the locker room after an interview with NBC-TV and was hanging around on the floor for a while to soak it all in, he removed his game jersey and handed it to a little boy.

"Tell your dad I said, 'Good luck,' " Barkley said to little Coby Karl.

"This has been the most gratifying experience of my life because there has been so much pressure put upon me and my team. And for us to get to this point shows what kind of men we are. I mean, from Day 1, here and around the league, everybody said, 'Well, the Suns put him there to win a championship.' They don't understand what kind of pressure that puts on me and the team. I know we're here to win a championship. It could be a one-shot deal. We want it. I'm proud of the way I've handled it to this point."

As the emotion wore off and the reality set in, Barkley actually began to get a bit testy.

"You know," he said, "all year long people have been bashing our team. We're not tough enough. We're not tall enough. We don't play good enough defense. We can't beat the Eastern Conference teams.

"We've made a lot of people look like fools. Call us whatever you want, but call us Western Conference champions."

# Chapter Twenty-nine

# "A TEAM OF ODDITIES"

By now, stories about Jordan's alleged late-night trip to an Atlantic City casino and an allegation in a recently published book that he was a big-time compulsive gambler had the Bulls superstar burning — as if he needed anything to motivate him.

He stopped talking to reporters, which didn't prevent those covering the championships from billing it as Barkley vs. Jordan even though they rarely, if ever, would compete head-to-head.

Since the cat had Jordan's tongue, reporters simply went to the human quote machine, Mr. Western Conference Champ, who was anything but Like Mike, to fill the void.

"He's not used to getting beat up by the press like I am," Barkley said. "People don't understand what it's like having everyone voicing their opinions about your life — which is none of their damn business. I'd like to stop talking, too."

But he just wouldn't, thank God. As always, Barkley did a masterful job of filling reporters' notebooks.

"There's no way you can know your friends won't write a book about you. Most of my friends are people I grew up with. I have very few friends I have met since I became 'Charles Barkley,'" he said.

While growing up in Leeds, Alabama, he was known by his middle name, Wade.

"I would rather be hated for what I am than loved for what I am not. That's why I'd rather do my own thing. Everybody's your friend when things are going well. The first time things go bad, they're against you."

Then, directing a barb toward NBC-TV insiders Bill Walton and Peter Vecsey, who said the Suns had no chance of getting past Seattle in the conference finals, Barkley said, "'No matter what happens in the Finals, we still get the last laugh. I'm their worst nightmare. I'm a black guy who won't be quiet.''

He was miffed at the Eastern media that billed the Eastern Conference finals as the championship round. The Suns weren't given much of a prayer against the Bulls by anyone east of the Superstition Mountains. One Chicago columnist took the liberty of describing the Suns as "short, soft, and spastic."

"You get tired of getting bashed all the time," Barkley said. "Me, I knew all year we were going to get here. I gave the Sixers a list of five teams I wanted to be traded to. I didn't know who I was going to take to the Finals, but I knew somebody was going with me. Phoenix, no question, has the greatest fans in the world, but that's because they're bored and ain't got nothing else to do. It is a ghost town after 11 o'clock. But it's a great place to raise a family.

"Personally, I believe in my heart we're going to win the championship. I've believed it from Day 1. I felt if we had good players around me, we would win."

Westphal was proud that his team had handled everything that had been thrown its way: "Everyone has been dwelling on our weaknesses all year, but there are only two teams left."

Even the Suns acknowledge that they do things a little differently. Bulls coach Phil Jackson picked up on that, too, and uttered these words: "They are a team of oddities."

Jackson noted that their post-up player is 6-foot-5 : Barkley; that they have a versatile backup forward who is nearly 7-feet: Chambers; their shooting guard is a muscular 6-6, yet a deadly three-point shooter: Majerle; and they have a wily veteran guard off the bench: Ainge.

"A lot of teams get to the Finals being unconventional," Jackson said. "They are very unconventional."

Jackson also seemed to appreciate the fact that the Suns weren't a gang of thugs, as the Knicks are. "We'll see people met in the lanes and there will be collisions, but we're not going to see the same kind of physical play. I think this could be a little bit liberating. Our guys have had bodies strapped to them the past two weeks."

Critics and believers alike agreed that the Suns would win if they could engage the Bulls in a running game. The Bulls recalled the thrashing the Suns handed them in Chicago Stadium on March 30, when none of them could handle KJ in the open court.

"That's where they overwhelm us," Jackson said. "In March, we put Michael and Scottie on Kevin, then we also used Paxson and B. J. Armstrong. We tried a lot of people. We'll do that again. Kevin's got a great will, a stubbornness that he's going to beat you. It can get him in trouble. It can make him great. The key for us is slowing their engine, and that's Kevin. We've got to put a Volkswagen engine in that Corvette."

The Bulls were mystified why Dumas had not gotten off the bench in the seventh game against Seattle. They suspected that Chambers would remain in the lineup, but wondered what Westphal was cooking up with his "team of oddities." Dumas had not been a factor in either regular-season game against the Bulls. He was not back from his drug suspension for the first, and he played only two minutes in the second while coming back from his ankle injury. So he was an unknown.

The loss of Ceballos, who had the monster 27-point game against the Bulls in Chicago, undoubtedly would be a factor.

"He came up with shots in clutch situations," Pippen recalled — as he should because most were in his face.

Most agreed the series would swing on matchups beyond the glare of the limelight on Chuck and Mike. How about the Suns' inexperience in the Finals, Chuck?

"That's the biggest crock of shit I ever heard," Barkley said. "The Bulls won it all the first time they went to the Finals. I guess their lack of experience didn't hurt them any."

Despite Barkley's protestations, the Suns' lack of experience did seem to hurt them in the opener on Wednesday, June 9, at the Purple Palace, where scalpers were getting as much as $1,000 for a ticket.

KJ played as if it was his first game in the NBA. Even Barkley later confirmed that he had a bad case of the nerves. None among the Suns really approached his best as the Bulls swamped them early and cruised to a 100-92 triumph.

"I think the edge was psychological," Jackson said. "Our experience in the Finals probably won us this game."

Jordan was neither silent on the court — scoring 31 points, 14 in the fourth quarter to prevent a Suns comeback — nor in the postgame interview room. League officials persuaded him to break his silence: "I had the feeling that you guys missed talking to me. It's all about making history now. We maintained our poise. That's part of the maturity of our team, especially on the road."

Pippen outscored Dumas, whom Westphal started, 27-20, but Dumas gathered 12 rebounds.

"The main thing was the excitement of being here," said Dumas, who despite being a rookie appeared to be the Suns most composed player. "We were just going, 'Wow.' They're used to this."

With viewers in 109 countries watching, Barkley missed 16 of 25 shots. KJ missed nine of 13, had only two assists but five turnovers. The Suns were down by 14 in the first quarter and by 20 midway through the second.

Even Barkley had to admit, "We got off to a bad start — nerves, or whatever you want to call it. That's why they're the two-time defending NBA champions. But if my memory serves me correctly, they lost a home game in each of those Finals series. So let's not go crazy. If we lose Game 2, then we can go crazy."

B. J. Armstrong supposedly was the most overmatched player on the floor going against KJ. But not only did the Bulls point guard limit KJ, Armstrong scored 16 points, including three three-point baskets.

"We just mixed up defenses on them," said forward Horace Grant, who was successful against Barkley. "I think they were confused a little bit. I don't expect us to keep them down like that again. Either one of them can take over a game any time."

The community was stunned. Geez, were all these Eastern reporters right after all? Maybe the Suns do play in a weak conference. Maybe they are in over their heads. One convincing home loss turned many of the enthusiastic purple-and-orange streamer wavers into doubters.

The day after, KJ wasn't amused by his play, but he was amused by the media frenzy it generated. "I got more attention than Charles Barkley today, that's a first. I played terribly. I was an ally of the Bulls. I made a lot of boneheaded turnovers. We were playing six-on-four. I had my whole family in town. They went out to eat without me. They couldn't find me. I went into kind of a retreat. I just kind of went into hiding to get my faculties together, reflect, and get things into perspective."

Barkley didn't go into hiding, but he had things in perspective. "It's not a life-and-death thing," he said. "I've got a life. Basketball is my job." Barkley was subdued, humorless, not himself.

Nor was KJ, who chucked — pun intended — his usual serious demeanor and loosened up. He was glib.

"We didn't just get our feet wet in the Finals, we got soaked," KJ said. "I came in early to watch the films. I had to dodge the coaches. I didn't want them to get their fangs into me so early. I had to look at the films first so I'd have some answers for them. Once you've done that, you can face anybody and deal with it."

Armstrong, with help from his frontline friends, hadn't allowed KJ to penetrate.

"I couldn't play any worse," KJ said. "This is a time for our organization to get some credit we deserve. If you don't win ball games at this level, you're not going to get that. If I do my part, people will see what Kevin Johnson means to this team."

The bottom line was that the Bulls shot 53 percent, the Suns 44. The Bulls swept to the basket for layups, the Suns couldn't get near the basket. The Bulls didn't have to double-team Barkley. Their defenders stayed home on everybody. There weren't many open Suns shooters.

The Suns needed to force up the speed of the game. To do that, they first had to stop the Bulls.

It all sounded good. Doing it was another matter.

Game 2 rolled around on Friday, June 11.

KJ still couldn't get going. He scored only four points and had only six assists. He also had four turnovers and fouled out. Barkley followed a bad game with a good one, as he normally does, but it wasn't enough.

With their 111-108 setback, the Suns became the first ever to lose the opening pair of the Finals at home.

"Well," the exasperated Barkley said following his 42-point, 13-rebound performance, "we're in the right state for holes. Right now, we fit right in with the Grand Canyon."

Jordan matched Barkley's 42 points. Pippen and Grant, the Bulls' forwards, came up bigger than Barkley's supporting cast, and that was the real difference. Pippen was good for a triple-double — 15 points, 12 rebounds, 12 assists — while Grant scored 24 points.

Ainge came off the bench to score 20 for the Suns, but as he tried to launch a three-pointer that could have tied the game with 28 seconds to go, Pippen ran at him and blocked it. Ainge castigated himself for not pump-faking Pippen. There was plenty of time.

Ainge took time away from Dumas, who played only two minutes in the second half and only 17 in the game. Dumas, irked, dressed quickly and left. Westphal said Majerle and Ainge were producing, so he let them play.

"I know it looks very, very bad," Westphal said, "but I don't feel that we're dead."

To add injury to insult, Barkley suffered a hard fall in the second half that bruised his right elbow. And KJ actually was booed by the America West Arena crowd.

"I know you can't hide," KJ said. "I played 30 minutes, and I wasn't even a factor. Obviously, I have to play much better for our team to be effective."

When Frank Johnson came to the scorer's table to check in for KJ, the building erupted in cheers. That set Barkley off. The fans were frustrated, but that's no way to treat one of the pillars of the franchise. People have short memories.

"First of all, to the Phoenix fans who booed Kevin Johnson, we could not have gotten here without him," Barkley said. "And if you're going to boo Kevin Johnson and give him a hard time if he's struggling, please don't come to the fucking games because we don't need you. And I'm not concerned if they don't like it. They know where to find me."

Barkley was steaming. "But I really do think the sun will come up tomorrow. And I think I'll still be up watching it. It's definitely one of those nights where I won't be able to sleep."

He was tired enough to sleep, though. Barkley had to carry the Suns by himself.

"I kept telling Horace to go at him, because it seemed like he was doing all the scoring, but he seemed like he got tired in the fourth quarter," Jordan said. "I thought that would really put a strain on their other guys to score. If we can keep Charles from getting help, and if B. J. keeps KJ under control, we can put ourselves in a very good position. Actually, we're already in a very good position. Now we go home for three. They're going to have to play better than they've played."

Few believed that even the Suns, who prevailed so many times after situations appeared hopeless, could get out of this one.

"When we lost the first two games to the Lakers, everybody was saying it was the biggest upset in the history of the NBA and that the Suns were choking," Majerle said. "But if any team can go down 0-2 at home in a series and come back to win it, it's our team. I know they're not the Lakers, but we can do it."

By reading the Chicago newspapers upon arriving the following day, the Suns never would have guessed they had a chance. The headlines were big, black, and convincing. A sweep awaited them. The mighty Bulls were going to end this thing quickly in four games so that all concerned could get on with their lives.

After all, the Grateful Dead was scheduled to give a concert in Chicago the following weekend and Jackson, quite the Dead-head, had every intention of being there and not on a plane back to Phoenix for Game 6. The greater concern in the Windy City was in gearing up for the victory celebration. It had been violent and bloody the year before.

The Suns, on the other hand, weren't quite ready to think about the end.

"We'll see if we quit, or see if we play," Ainge said. "I've got a feeling this team is going to play. And I think we have a chance to win. We know that if we play a good game, we can beat the Bulls. But we haven't played a good game yet. Their execution has been better than ours. They know where guys are going to be on the floor. They know how to space when Michael has the ball so that it is difficult to trap. We can do that same thing. We don't adjust to defenses as well as Chicago, but then, they've seen it all."

The Suns normally don't talk much about defense — except Majerle, and that's what he does.

"I was in Michael's face the whole night and he still hit big shots," Majerle said. "Obviously, we have to do something a little bit different. Maybe I can be more physical with him. I only had one foul. Maybe I can deny him the ball more and not give him so many free looks at the basket."

Yet the biggest adjustment the Suns made was in their defense when they took on the Bulls in Chicago Stadium in Game 3 on Sunday, June 13.

Dumas would guard Armstrong. KJ would cover Jordan. Majerle would take Pippen. Barkley had Bill Cartwright. Mark West checked Grant.

Westphal shook up the assignments, and it shook up the basketball world. With 6:19 to go in the fourth quarter the Suns had an 11-point lead. What an incredible turnaround. But, true to script, it didn't last.

Among the plays in the Bulls' comeback was Pippen, inbounding from under his basket, throwing his pass off the seat of Ainge's shorts, retrieving the ball and laying it in. It was a creative piece of playground basketball — the kind of thing that Westphal might concoct — that cut the Suns' lead to three.

"Lionel even reminded me about that possibility in the huddle during the timeout," Ainge said. "I was expecting it, just not so soon. I only turned my back on him for a second."

Just as quickly, the Bulls tied it up.

On to the first overtime, where the Suns trailed by two points going into the closing minute before getting off the hook.

In the second overtime, with 32.6 seconds showing, the Suns were down by four. A Barkley jumper, then an 18-footer by Majerle with 3.2 seconds left, and finally strong defense on Jordan that forced him to give it up to Pippen, who rushed and missed a desperation shot, pulled them out of this hole. How many lives do the Suns have?

In the third overtime, the Suns had had enough. After trailing by two points, they scored nine straight and pulled out a 129-121 win that revived their spirits and stunned the Bulls in one of the most memorable games ever played in the Finals.

Majerle's sixth three-pointer, which tied a Finals record, got the rally going, taking the Suns from two points down to one up with just over three minutes left. Then Majerle made a steal, and Barkley finished the play off a KJ assist for a three-point edge. Then Barkley swiped the ball from Bulls backup Stacey King and layed one up.

It conjured memories of the only other triple-overtime in the Finals, which the Suns lost to Boston in 1976.

"That was the greatest game I ever played in," said Barkley, who was questionable until he had fluid drained from his badly swollen right elbow less than an hour before game time. "It's not about winning and losing. It's about doing the best you can. We gave it everything we had, and so did the Bulls. But we had to have this one. You can't go down, 3-0, to the Bulls."

There were so many subplots.

First KJ. Villain of the games in Phoenix in the eyes of many Suns fans, KJ played all but the final 20 seconds of this marathon, setting an NBA playoff record with 62 minutes of work. In it, he produced a near-triple-double with 25 points, nine assists, and seven rebounds. This time, he was the hero, picking up the slack for the sore-armed Barkley.

"When I got off the bus at the hotel yesterday, I couldn't figure out why people were cheering," KJ said. "Then it dawned on me. They were cheering me because they thought I'd helped the Bulls."

"When Charles talked about the Phoenix fans turning on me, I took strength from his comments. As long as I have the support of my teammates, I'm fine. The fans are going to say whatever they want, and so is the media. Charles and I are in the trenches together. "

There was Barkley, giving it his best. He made nine of 20 shots for 24 points and snagged 19 rebounds.

"The best thing is now I have three days to rest my elbow," he said.

Finally, there was the ghost of 1976 and the first triple-overtime game. Westphal was wearing a Suns uniform in that one.

"I liked this one better," he said. "I think this one will go down in history as one of the greatest basketball games ever. This was a better game from start to finish."

Jordan scored 44 points, but made only 19 of 43 shots with KJ pestering him. While not as strong as Majerle, KJ is quicker with his hands and feet. He disrupted Jordan's rhythm.

Pippen came within an assist of another triple-double with 26 points, 10 rebounds but, like Jordan, he couldn't find the bucket as the game wore on. Pippen made 12 of 35 from the floor.

The length of the game seemed to have more of an effect on the Bulls than the Suns. With the Bulls missing so many, the Suns could rebound and run. That led Pippen to observe, "It was like a playground game. We never could control the tempo."

Barkley couldn't resist needling his buddy, Jordan. "I know I'm the best one-armed player in the world. But, damn, I see Michael shot the ball 43 times. He'll be icing his elbow, too."

Jordan denied that KJ wore him out, but Jordan did acknowledge that as the game wore on, all of his shots seemed to be off the front of the rim.

"It was my legs," Jordan said. "I didn't have my legs."

Westphal gave KJ the news about his new defensive assignment on the plane ride from Phoenix.

"I thought this is what I don't need right now," KJ recalled.

KJ tried to find peace in reading the Bible. He likened his situation to that of Job.

"But after rereading the story, I realized that Job never had to guard Jordan," KJ said.

Because the NBA has sold out to NBC -TV, there would be two days off in Chicago before the fourth game — that after having only Saturday off for cross-country travel to Chicago for Game 3. It's like hurry up and wait. If the league is going to bow to television's demand that the Finals be played only on Wednesday, Friday and Sunday, then why not mandate that the series open on Friday?

Play Friday-Sunday at the opening site, take Monday and Tuesday off for travel before resuming Game 3 on Wednesday at the next site. Play Games 3-4-5 on Wednesday-Friday-Sunday.

The travel format would be repeated if a series went six games.

The present schedule is inconsiderate of the needs of newspapers. The Sunday paper is the largest of the week, the most read. Most newspapers try to produce big Sunday packages during the Finals. It is extremely difficult to do that when there is no media availability with coaches or players on the only day between games while the teams travel.

Advance material for Sunday packages this year had to be obtained hurriedly following Friday's late game. Then, because reporters were bucking deadlines to file their stories on Game 2 late Friday, there wasn't sufficient time to collect material for the Sunday paper. There would be no access to anyone on Saturday.

Also, the last thing players want to talk about immediately after one tiring game is the next one. They're usually more insightful after they've had a day of rest.

This schedule is a slap in the face to the print medium, which is there every day of the season covering these teams! While newspapers pay no rights fees to cover the league as television networks do, newspapers do provide free exposure nationwide every day of the season that is worth billions of dollars to the NBA, its teams, and its players. Newspapers do devote huge sums of money for the necessary travel to follow an 82-game season. Television covers only a few select games. The print medium is there every day of the season and has earned the right to better treatment!

It's a disservice to the fans and the players. This is supposed to be the league's showcase event, but the league treated Game 3 this year — and each year since NBC got the TV contract in 1991 — as if it's just another whistle-stop during the regular season.

Would the Bulls have been as fatigued in the third overtime if they'd had that additional day of rest? The NBA has gotten a little too big for its britches while catering to television.

Be that as it may, the Suns now would have two days to address their psychological condition. What a high it was to come back and win a game of that magnitude.

One person who hadn't forgotten about newspaper reporters was Barkley, who the following morning told a group of them that he plans to embellish the story of the 3-hour, 20-minute test of will and nerves when he retells it to his daughter in 25 years.

"I'll be telling her, 'Darling, they said my career was over. What happened was I had my arm ripped off in a tractor-trailer accident the night before the game. I had to have major surgery. They reattached my arm just before game time. The doctor said, 'Charles, you can't go out there. You could die.' I said, 'Doc, I gotta go out there. We're down 0-2, and they need me.' The doctor said, 'Please, Charles, please don't do it.' 'Doc, I'm playing. That's all there is to it.' "

In a somewhat grumpier frame of mind was Jackson, who obviously was irked about the free-throw shooting disparity but was trying to be careful what he said about it. The Bulls were mystified how in 63 minutes, they could shoot only nine free throws, and the Suns shot 31 free throws.

"It wasn't a great game," Jackson said. "It didn't feel historic to me."

Perhaps beauty is in the eye of the beholder.

As Game 3 wore on, Jackson assigned Jordan to KJ since KJ was guarding him, an attempt to save Jordan's legs. He wouldn't have to run and find Majerle every time down the floor. That left Majerle open to make his record-tying string of three-pointers, though.

"I think the other guys forgot that Majerle has range that is unlimited," Jackson said. "When he gets to half-court, you'd better start picking him up."

Jordan tried to take over the game despite being fatigued. The Bulls' superstar was criticized for trying to do too much.

"You can say I'm playing too hard, or trying too hard, but that's the only way I know how to play," Jordan said. "I'm very capable of carrying the load, but I try to get everyone going early. When my teammates don't shoot well, or are not willing to take the big shot, I step up. Then sometimes they wait to see if I can carry it. The next thing you know, we're totally outside our system. It's a Catch-22 from my standpoint."

KJ, with his assignment on Jordan, was in a "Catch 23" situation. He wanted to make it clear that he had not asked Westphal to guard No. 23 of the Bulls after the Suns fell behind 0-2, as was being reported in Chicago. He said he did suggest before the series began that he might be given a crack at Jordan at times, "figuring he's going to score 40 to 60 anyway, so it might be a different look worth exploring."

"But after we were down 0-2 and I was playing poorly, that was the last thing I wanted to hear, that I was guarding Michael," KJ said. "I don't want Michael to get mad because he read that I said I wanted to guard him. The last thing I need is for him to go out there thinking he has something to prove."

KJ, with his quick hands and feet, did seem to prevent Jordan from getting that first step to the basket that Jordan got against Majerle.

And KJ's penetrations collapsed the Bulls' defense, leaving Majerle and Ainge open for their three-pointers. The Suns were shooting 51 percent from beyond the arc in the series.

"I think everybody should appreciate Ainge because he brought that shot to the NBA a long time ago," Bulls assistant coach John Bach said. "He shoots with abandon. Now he's made Majerle his compatriot. They have the conscience of a rattlesnake. We've told our guys you've got to get on Ainge as soon as he leaves the scorer's table. And Majerle is not just shooting them from behind the line. Sometimes he goes back to the logos. Those are pretty damn far out. Sometimes you need a golf cart to get back to him."

Their hopes for a sweep were dead, but the Bulls insisted they still planned to finish the job at home. Win the next two and be done with it. That would be bucking the trend in this unusual series. Through three games, the home team had yet to win.

"We're going to talk to the commissioner and get the rest of the games scheduled here," Barkley said.

Never before had the Finals reached the fourth game with the home team having failed to win.

"On the road, you weather a storm, but at home, you have to create one," Jackson said. "That's difficult to do, because when you get to this juncture both teams are great road teams."

As Westphal observed, "The travel now is the same for both teams, which certainly isn't true in the regular season. So I think a lot of the home advantage is negated."

With both teams well rested and well analyzed, Game 4 finally was upon them on Wednesday, June 16. Not only was Chicago Stadium sold out, but 12,800 showed up at America West Arena back in Phoenix to watch on the big-screen TVs. In the Valley, the triple-overtime thriller had drawn a bigger audience than even the Super Bowl. The Phoenix NBC affiliate reported a 50 Nielsen rating and a 77 percent share. The Super Bowl had pulled a 45 rating and 67 share.

There were reports that even the people of Tucson were getting behind the Suns — unusual considering the rivalry that exists between the cities, especially in sports. Tucson is primarily a college-sports market, given the success of the University of Arizona athletic teams. Before the season, the Suns couldn't find a Tucson station willing to be part of their television network.

All of the spectators and viewers were rewarded with another classic battle in Game 4, although it didn't take three overtimes, or even one, to settle it.

Jordan went for 55 points, as if telling his critics that he can NEVER do too much.

Barkley, who again had fluid drained from his swollen elbow, posted a triple-double with 32 points, 12 rebounds, and 10 assists.

The Suns made another stirring comeback, from 13 points down in the third quarter to two down and in possession of the ball in the final 33 seconds.

Then hard luck hit KJ again.

He appeared to be surveying the court as an inbounds pass was thrown to him. He bobbled it. Armstrong gathered it in. The Bulls came down and Jordan made a soft jumper in the lane despite being banged by Barkley, who went to the floor and stayed on all fours after the shot fell and the whistle sounded. Barkley knew this one was over. Jordan left no doubters when he added the free throw to finish the three-point play with 14 seconds left.

Final score: Bulls 111, Suns 105.

With a 3-1 lead, the Bulls appeared now to have the series well in hand, with the fifth game in the Stadium on Friday night.

"Keep the faith," Barkley said. "Anybody who knows anything about our team knows that we will be ready Friday night. Every time there has been a challenge this year, we have risen to it. But I do have to say that I like their chances."

Everyone did. Imagine beating the Bulls three straight. That's what the Suns were facing. And no team ever had rallied from a 3-1 deficit to win the Finals.

"That is a lot to ask," Westphal said.

Only once, when Elgin Baylor of the Los Angeles Lakers rolled up 61 points against Boston in 1962, had anyone scored more points in the Finals than Jordan had against the Suns.

"We thought we had a chance to steal this game," Westphal said. "The biggest difference was they had Michael Jordan and we didn't."

The crowd at the Stadium was just short of horrified as the Suns reduced the lead to six with 3:36 left, and to two with 1:01 remaining. By now, they'd seen enough of the Suns to know they were dangerous.

"I didn't look up, it wasn't like I was distracted," KJ said. "The pass was a bit behind me. It just slipped out of my hands. You hate to see an accident like that swing a big game but there still was no excuse for letting Jordan get a three-point play at the other end."

Jordan, who scored 22 of his points in the second quarter, including 16 in a row, said this was a pretty good game, but not his best. "My best game is always my last." That wasn't exactly comforting to the Suns.

"We had plenty of opportunities," said KJ, who scored 15 of his 19 points in the second-half comeback.

He was in position, once again, to be the Suns' hero and erase the memory of those first two games.

"People are going to remember that one play," he said. "Hey, we were down two points and there was enough time left. If we'd gone back and got the defensive stop, we'd have been right back down there with the ball, trailing by two, with seven or eight seconds left to make a play.

"I think we had a valiant performance," KJ said. "I don't think our confidence is gone. In fact, it might be even higher because Michael Jordan scores 55 and we still have an opportunity to win the game."

Confidence was higher in Chicago, where windows now were being boarded up in expectation of a victory riot on Friday.

# Chapter Thirty

# FINALS JEOPARDY

June 17, 1993. The one-year anniversary of the Barkley trade. In many ways, the Suns were exactly where they expected to be. Everyone had envisioned the hard-charging Barkley slipping his mouthpiece in, rubbing his palms together, and digging in to lead the Suns to the Finals.

Yet there was a sense of unfulfillment among the Suns. They had stage fright in the opener and really weren't in the game. They played so poorly in the second, yet had a chance to tie when Ainge's shot was blocked.

They were right there in the fourth game until the ball slipped away from KJ, and then the Suns let Jordan make that killer three-point play. The Suns were convinced they could be leading this series, 3-1, just as surely as they were trailing it by that margin.

How many times does this opportunity come along? The Bulls were in the big show for the third year in a row. They expect it. The Suns were hardened by the knowledge that this was their first appearance in 17 years. While they didn't expect another 17 years to pass before they returned, they saw that it could.

So you don't let these things slip through your fingers. The symbolism of KJ's play was unmistakable. As Jordan put it, "We don't want to let this slip through OUR fingers." He went so far as to say that if the Bulls didn't wrap it up on Friday, they'd be going back to the desert without him.

Everybody was digging in for the fifth game on Friday, June 18. The Suns were determined to prove that they belonged. The Bulls were determined to take their place in history.

And the Chicago police were busy making their riot preparedness speeches as employees of fancy shops along Michigan Avenue were removing merchandise from their display windows and boarding them up.

The locals were heartened by news that a severe thunderstorm was due to pass through the area at about the time the game would end. They figured a good downpour might keep would-be rioters off the streets.

"I don't know all the answers," Barkley said. "I do know that we've been in every game in this series. We are for real. I believe in us. But if I were up, 3-1, I'd be getting ready for a party, too."

The Bulls didn't anticipate a Suns' cave-in. Not with the Suns conceding Jordan his points, knowing that few of the other Bulls were willing to step up and take a big shot. Not with the Suns capable of reeling off a quick spurt, thanks to their three-point shooting, or fast breaks triggered by the long outlet passes of Miller or Barkley, or by KJ's lightning penetrations. The Bulls were happy to have the upper hand, but even they realized that it easily could be turned around.

The Suns talked about taking the lane away from Jordan so that his points weren't quite as easy to come by, but Pippen doubted that they actually could do it. "Phoenix is not an aggressive-type team," he said. "They like the wide-open game. I don't know if they're aggressive enough to stop him."

The ominous clouds did, indeed, begin building up by late afternoon. It was, well, windy in the city — and not entirely the making of all those blustery Bulls fans.

It rained hard on their riot. Suns 108, Bulls 98.

"You can take the boards off the windows," Barkley said.

Suddenly, the dancing in the streets was in downtown Phoenix, where traffic came to a halt after their team lived to see another game, a home game. It was peaceful, though.

"We're civilized in Phoenix" Barkley said.

The Suns couldn't help but jab Chicago in that regard.

"We saved the city," Westphal only half-joked in his postgame interview.

Mayor Richard Daley didn't care for the Suns' lighthearted attitude toward what he said was a serious situation. He took it up with the league. The Suns didn't seem to care what the mayor thought, though.

"All we heard about was the security for the riots after the win they expected, so when we got to the Stadium we talked about how we could save the city," said Majerle, whose salvation effort included 11 points, 12 rebounds, and seven assists.

Westphal didn't relent, either. "We had a nice week here. We wanted to step forward and pay Chicago back for its hospitality. We didn't want to see the city burn today."

Barkley reminded everyone that he'd been saying all along that a championship season was the Suns' destiny. "I reminded Michael of that when we had dinner at his restaurant the other night. He said I was reading from a different Bible than he was. He said this was our last dinner."

Ainge was hopeful that Jordan would make good on his promise not to accompany his team back to Phoenix. "I think Michael will lose all of his credibility if he shows up in Phoenix. We've caught him in a lie. Hopefully, he'll show some integrity and keep his word."

KJ was good for 25 points and eight assists (Bulls fans no longer were cheering him at the Suns' hotel), Barkley for 24 points and six rebounds.

But the rookie Dumas stood up and played the biggest game of his career. He made 12 of 14 shots and scored 25 points. If he wasn't surprising Pippen with his 15-footers along the baselines, Dumas was turning Pippen around and dunking on him — much as Ceballos had in the regular-season game in the Stadium. Dumas had scored more points, but never more important points.

"The defenses are always focusing on Kevin, Dan, and Charles," Dumas said. "For me, it was just a matter of slipping into the open spots. There were a lot of them. I just had one of those days. It still happens, you know."

Jordan made 16 of 29 for 41 points. The rest of the Bulls made 21 of 50 and scored 57 points. The Suns kept them outside. The Suns also dominated the boards.

The Bulls began to take a cue from the Suns and launched a Finals-record 18 three-point shots. Eight of them landed. They discovered a new weapon, courtesy of their adversaries. The Suns would regret it.

"We clogged the middle and didn't let their guys get straight paths to the basket like they did in the last game," KJ said. "That took a lot of pressure off our defense. We also felt if we did the job on the boards and eliminated their second-shot opportunities, that we'd fare pretty well."

Grant was reduced to tears in the locker room after he missed all four of his shots, scored one point, and basically was an empty uniform.

"Any time you get an animal cornered, it will fight," said West, who with nine rebounds helped ensure that Grant came up empty.

Finally, Ainge buried a three-pointer with the Bulls down by eight that put the dagger through their hearts with 3:25 to go. Fans began beating a hasty retreat into the rain.

Meanwhile, Suns fans headed to the airport to wait for their early-morning return. There were 12,000 on hand when the jet pulled up at 2:30 a.m.

Barkley told them he'd had a talk with God, and God informed him that the Suns are, in fact, a team of destiny.

KJ, who guarded Jordan in the two wins in Chicago, was the likely choice to give it a go again.

"But Paul likes the Israeli army a lot," KJ said. "He says the one characteristic of the Israeli army is that it never does the same thing twice, even when it works. So I'm not going to jump the gun."

The Suns improved to 5-0 in the playoffs in must-win games. But to win the title, they'd have to beat the Bulls in two more must-wins. Both would be at home, but since moving into their new arena, the Suns had never beaten the Bulls there. They figured they were due.

The Suns also sensed an edginess about the Bulls, who were so sure they'd finish the job in Chicago.

"We never get overconfident, but we should have taken better care of our home court," Pippen said.

In their effort to do just that, the Suns brought in trumpeteer Jesse McGuire to toot the national anthem. With McGuire on the horn, the Suns were undefeated at the Purple Palace. He had pulled them through Game 5 against the Lakers and Game 7 against the Sonics. It wasn't clear whether it was the horn, or maybe an aura about McGuire from his day job that motivated the Suns: performing autopsies as supervisor of the forensic-science division of the Maricopa County Medical Examiner's Office.

Maybe McGuire should have checked the Suns' huddle for a pulse when he finished his rendition. Chicago scored 37 points in the first quarter and assumed a nine-point lead. It was about like the beginning of the first game of the series. Their shooting didn't bring them back. They made only 39 percent for the game, including seven of 18 by Barkley, six of 14 by KJ and seven of 17 by Majerle. But the Suns' 47-39 edge on the boards kept them in it. They chipped away.

Trailing by eight going into the fourth quarter, the Suns held Chicago scoreless for the first 6:09. Three times the Suns forced the Bulls into shot-clock violations.

By the one-minute mark, the Suns held a four-point lead and had possession of the ball. Few in the Purple Palace doubted that the series was headed for Game 7 — and they liked the crazy home team's chances of winning it.

At 45 seconds, Frank Johnson missed from the top of the key. Jordan got the rebound, took the ball the length of the floor unchecked, and finished with an easy gliding layup.

There was no excuse for that. Still they had the lead and the ball and now 38 seconds to kill.

The Suns used every second on the shot clock. Finally, after Frank Johnson declined to try another shot, he lobbed the ball to Majerle in the right corner. Majerle had to shoot quickly. He missed everything at 14 seconds. Shot-clock violation on the Suns. The Bulls took timeout.

The Suns had to make one last defensive stop. They figured at worst, they would go to overtime if the Bulls scored. The last thing they planned to do was turn an inbounds play into an open-court situation. But they did. The Suns were up, challenging the inbounds pass. In retrospect, that might have been a mistake. Maybe they should have allowed the ball to come in, then trap it to make the Bulls use the clock.

In it came to Pippen. Barkley went for the steal and missed, a critical first misstep in a chain reaction.

Pippen was alone to bring the ball up the floor behind the Suns' pressure. Ainge was covering John Paxson, a deadly shooter who made several clutch fourth-quarter baskets that gave the Bulls their first championship two years earlier.

Ainge could see that West left Grant alone inside to step up and stop Pippen's drive. Ainge quickly reacted and dropped inside to cover Grant, to whom Pippen alertly passed.

Grant's confidence was shattered. After going zero-for-four in Game 5, he was zero-for-five in this one. He didn't want to take the last shot, not even from close range against a player six inches shorter who isn't known as a leaper. Grant undoubtedly could have dunked over Ainge.

Instead, Grant, saw Ainge coming and quickly volleyballed Pippen's pass out to Paxson, now alone behind the three-point line. Nobody had gotten to him in time.

It seemed to hang in the air for hours.

Paxson said as he watched the ball in flight he recalled the thousands of times he'd taken similar shots, for far fewer stakes, in his driveway back in Kettering, Ohio, a Dayton suburb, while growing up.

As it neared the target, it appeared to be on a true line.

"We just reacted," Ainge said of the Suns' defense. "You don't want to give up a three, but you don't want to give up a dunk, either."

Closer and closer it got. There was no question that it would be long enough.

It couldn't happen to the Suns, not after all the jams they'd wriggled out of all season, not after they'd come back in this one.

They were a team of destiny, weren't they? But it dropped through the hoop with 3.9 seconds showing. More than 19,000 hearts sank with it.

Paxson put the Bulls in front, 99-98, with their 10th successful three-pointer of the day, breaking the Finals record the Suns set a week earlier in the triple-overtime game. The Bulls were determined after making a few in Game 5 to continue jacking them up. They missed only four in an incredible long-range shooting display.

"We force them to shoot from the outside, and they make 10 of 14 three-pointers," said Westphal, whose team had similarly hurt foes more than once. "Our guys did everything you could ask a team to do."

The Suns still had a chance. Three-point-nine seconds is an eternity for a team of destiny. Even a foul shot would get them to overtime.

Who knows? Westphal was just crazy enough to try the ricochet pass off the backboard again. Or Barkley out front handling it in a one-four set. Or who knows what other surprise he might have been saving for a situation like this?

"We should have saved that ricochet pass for Game 6 against Chicago," Westphal said later during the summer. "The thing that really set it up to make it work was the element of surprise. I thought about it in the Chicago game, but I really didn't think that we would catch them sleeping. So we went with a more conventional play."

As the Suns inbounded from mid-court following their timeout, Ainge and Majerle were crossing in the corners. Miller was on the floor to receive the pass in his large hands, and to set a pick for Barkley with his large body. In it came to Miller, who quickly got it out front to KJ.

The Suns guard drove, but Jordan quickly cut him off. KJ wanted to take just one more dribble, but Jordan made him pull up.

"I saw Charles posting up Scottie Pippen out of the corner of my eye, but there just was not enough time to get it to him," KJ said. "There was only time for me to shoot the ball."

From the weak side, Grant leaped and blocked the shot. He saved the win, put the Bulls into the history book, and atoned for his general malaise in the closing two games.

How ironic that the team that lived by the three-pointer, setting an NBA record with 398 of them, would die by it in this 99-98 heartbreaker.

How ironic, too, that after adding one of the game's best clutch post-up scorers, the Suns once again couldn't execute a half-court play when they most needed one, that their last gasp would be snuffed out by a blocked shot.

"I can't think of a more dramatic finish in all my years in the NBA," Jackson said.

"What a terrible way to end it," Ainge said.

"Our luck just ran out," Majerle said.

"We had a great year," KJ said. "But we lost three games on our home court in this series. We didn't deserve to win the world championship."

The words didn't come so easily for Barkley, who has been waiting all his life for this and knew full well it could be his only chance. The destiny that he spoke of all season had given him the finger.

He spent a long time in the shower before he emerged, dressed, and came to the interview room. Nearly an hour had passed.

"I think the thing that hurts more than anything," Barkley said, "is that we have been at this for eight months, and now, just like that, it's over.

"Right now, I want to say it was a great season, but the loss hurts so much. I think we're just as good as they are. We could have won any of the four we lost, or even all four. It doesn't matter how close you come, though.

"It's times like this that's it's bad to be an athlete. Fans go back to the real world tomorrow. For us, this is our real world. I put so much into this season. I don't know if I can reach that level of intensity again. I put all my eggs into this basket. I expected us to win the championship."

Earlier, a grateful Jackson tended to agree with Barkley's assessment, saying of the Suns, "We never could really get a hold of them, not tonight, not in the whole series. They always found a way to get back into games."

As the Suns came off the floor for the last time, Hollins had no player personnel recommendations like the year before in Portland.

What was he going to say — We've got to go get us a Michael Jordan?

"I didn't say anything. I was just shocked like everybody else," Hollins said. "It was a stunning ending. We thought we had the game. Up four with a minute to go. Next thing you know, the game is over and the season is over. It was just shocking.

"At that point, I thought all we needed was two more points. We had a couple of opportunities. It was like everything that could go wrong did go wrong."

Jordan was thankful the scare was over. His Finals-record 41-point scoring average certainly was the difference in a series in which the final cumulative score was 640-640.

"This means a lot because we made history," said Jordan, named MVP of the Finals for an unprecedented third straight year. "I think it sets me apart from Magic and Larry because they were never able to do this. Things certainly looked dim for us at certain points, but we did the necessary things down the stretch to win the game."

That is a trait that defines Jordan and this group of Bulls, and all true champions.

And with the off-season signing of versatile Croatian superstar Toni Kukoc, the Bulls' chances of winning four in a row seemed better than average before Jordan's shocking retirement in October.

"This was a dream," said Paxson, who lost his starting job to Armstrong after having off-season knee surgery. "Maybe we were the ones destined to win after all."

If the Bulls could do it by scoring only 12 points in the fourth quarter — an all-time Finals low — and relying on a miracle shot, maybe Paxson was right.

Jordan told reporters later that as he and Barkley exchanged hugs and words at mid-court, "I told Charles I loved him, and destiny just was not for him this time."

Colangelo said his youngsters learned a great deal as they moved along in the playoffs.

"I hope we learned that you can't afford breakdowns when you get to this level," he said. "We had them against Los Angeles, we had them against Seattle, and we had them in this series. It came down to one shot that kicked us out of the playoffs. It really hurts. It has nothing to do with heart and character. You're just allowed a certain amount of mistakes, and we used up our quota. We're still looking for our first championship. Hopefully, next year. Our players got a taste of what it's like to play for it, and they liked it."

So did the Suns' fans. They could sit back, draw a deep breath, and truly believe that the best is yet to come.

When the Bulls arrived back in Chicago, Jordan walked down the steps after the long flight home and asked, "Is our city still here?"

There had been only scattered looting this time, just lots of people drunk and disorderly. There were rocks and bottles thrown, minor vandalism, 682 arrests, two deaths, many minor injuries.

Barkley was making noises again about perhaps retiring, but few took him seriously. It seemed to be a heat-of-the-moment comment after one of the greatest disappointments in his life. Still, knowing Barkley, he certainly was capable of walking away from it.

"I'm a guy with a great personality," he said. "I'm sure I'd find something to do."

# Chapter Thirty-one

# WALKING THE LEDGE

While the days immediately after the Finals were bright and sunny in Phoenix — So what else is new? — it was as if a cloud lingered overhead. The community was in a funk. There was a mourning period of nearly a week before there were signs of normal life.

The Suns would take a couple of days off, then meet on Wednesday, June 23, to clean out their lockers and divide their playoff shares.

There would be one last hurrah, an exclamation point on an incredible silver anniversary season: a parade through downtown Phoenix. There might be as many as 100,000 people, police anticipated. Depends on how hot it is Saturday morning.

One thing was certain: more people had watched the Finals than ever before. The national rating — a percentage of the televisions in the U.S. — for the six games was 17.9, breaking the old mark of 15.9 for the 1987 Lakers-Celtics series. The national share — the percentage of TVs actually in use — was 33, breaking the old mark of 32 in that Lakers-Celtics matchup.

Jordan and Barkley and the drama of a half dozen games had captivated not only the competing cities but the entire country.

By Wednesday, Barkley saw things in a different light. After taking part in the disbursement of the Suns' $1,171,250 winnings in the league playoff pool, he confirmed that he would be back.

He said he might even hit the weights this summer to strengthen himself for another run, but that he absolutely wouldn't pick up a basketball until training camp in Flagstaff.

Barkley said his body was sore — his knees, back, shoulder, and hamstrings. He was, after all, a ripe old 30 now. And he'd never been through such a rigorous campaign. Of course, it was made even more rigorous by the Dream Team. The summer would be his first real rest from basketball in two years. His travel schedule zipping from golf tournament to golf tournament would rival that of the NBA regular season. But it was fun. It was exactly what he wanted to do.

One by one the Suns filed out of the locker room for the last time.

Absent were Mustaf, who'd already returned to the Washington, D.C., area to conduct his summer camp, and Chambers, who was already on the beach in Hawaii.

The Suns had made no official announcement about Chambers' future yet, but Colangelo said the Suns planned to pursue a free agent hard. The only way they could get a big name was to create a salary-cap exception by not exercising their option on Chambers.

The irony of the day is that it was the one in which the Suns would have played the seventh game of the Finals.

"Everybody feels in our hearts that this is not the type of day we wanted to spend in our locker room, dividing up our playoff shares," KJ said.

Barkley said the greatest thing about the Finals is that people around the league who had little respect for the Suns or the Western Conference now have a greater understanding and appreciation.

On Friday, Colangelo made it official. Chambers was gone.

"I thanked him profusely for all that he has contributed to this franchise," Colangelo said. "I thought it was important for him to know that our relationship is strong. I think our fans can look forward to the day when Tom Chambers' number is hanging in the rafters at America West Arena."

The Finals had been a new experience to all except Ainge, Westphal, and Hollins. They own championship rings. They had more than an inkling what it was all about.

"The only thing that any of us said was, 'Have fun, enjoy it,'" Hollins said. "'If there's 20 media guys you have to talk to, so what? It's the Finals. Remember that. If you weren't here you'd be at home watching the games on TV. Do the best you can, and there's a lot of people watching wishing they could be in your shoes.'

"Danny Ainge had a great quote. He said he didn't think that we really believed to a man, when the series started, that we could beat the Bulls. To a man, they'd have to be honest enough with themselves to admit it or disagree with it."

They're a grab bag of personalities and skills — and many nights it was as if Westphal reached into a grab bag to select the combination of players who were together on the floor.

"We were on thin ice all year," Robertson said. "So many games were won with last-second shots, sometimes by design, sometimes not by design.

"In my mind, that shows several things about our team. First of all, we're a very talented team. Secondly, we've got guys that are willing to make the big play to try to win a game. Some people don't want to stand up and be counted at nut-cutting time. We've got some guys that are not afraid to do that. And I am hopeful that this coming year we'll be able to continue to win, and not necessarily on shots off the backboard from out of bounds, but hopefully in a more controlled manner because, quite frankly, I think we have great talent."

But doing things the way they did them was honest. That's who the Suns are.

"We were a victim of our personality in that regard," Westphal said. "We took our cue from Charles. He's a guy who lives on the brink. We'll be close to winning, then he'll throw a few hook shots up just to miss so on the last shot everything will be riding on it. And he'll usually make it. He amuses himself that way.

"Now it drives me crazy, drives the fans crazy. I'm going to hope that he's not quite that way so much next year. I'd like to get a lead, put a team away, let him sit on the bench and enjoy the last five minutes. But that didn't seem to be what suited him the best, and the rest of our team kind of took that attitude along. But it sure made for a lot of exciting games."

Hollins thought the Suns did things the hard way because it was the only way they could do them. They had some deficiencies.

"We were a very short team," he said. "We didn't have everything you would like. It was a mix-and-match team.

"So they all complemented each other. When the combinations were just right, it all worked perfectly. But during the course of a game, you just can't have all those combinations on the court all the time. They were outmatched some nights — quickness, rebounding, shooting, whatever it may be — and they always had the ability to find some kind of chink in the opposing team's armor to win. That came because of their competitiveness."

Van Arsdale thought that was an indication of the maturity of the veteran players — Barkley, Ainge, KJ, West, Chambers, and Majerle — who'd been in so many playoff games and so many different circumstances.

"They'd get ahead — 10-, 15-, 20-point lead — then it seemed like almost on purpose give up the lead to show the other team that they could win under any circumstances," Van Arsdale said. "They'd lose those big leads and they'd almost dare teams to beat them because they knew it wasn't going to happen. They really made me feel uneasy. I like things to be steady and consistent, but they thrived on that and really enjoyed playing that way."

Those strong personalities carried them through.

"In the Laker series, they had their backs to the walls, and a lot of teams would have said, 'Let's try to win one to make it halfway respectable, and then we'll take the summer off,'" Van Arsdale said. "But they wouldn't quit."

Hollins recalled the Minnesota game that Ainge won with a last-second put-back basket in January.

"Everybody said, 'They should have put Minnesota away early.' Minnesota played out of their head and to the best of their ability, and they staggered us," Hollins said. "We took the punch and turned around and came back, tied the game at halftime. They came out in the third quarter and staggered us again. We took the punch and went ahead. We win the game on a missed-shot follow.

"I mean, that is not the way our team wanted to do it. That was the way they had to do it.

"Look at the Chicago series. There were a lot of times in all of those games where most teams would have said, 'It's over.' This team kept scratching and clawing — Michael Jordan scored 55 points, Michael Jordan scored 42 points, the Bulls shoot 65 percent. But at the end, this team was right there in all those games. Look at how they're talking about us. The Bulls supposedly wiped us out, but you can go back through every game and see that they were all close games, except probably the first one. That's just the nature of the team."

They'd developed such resiliency from winning so many games in which they supposedly were beaten. They believed they could win any game in any situation. They weren't afraid to walk the ledge.

"People don't understand that," Westphal said. "It's like when Barkley says, 'I'll play 18 holes tomorrow if we win. If we lose, I'll play 36.' That's really the exact same thing John Havlicek used to say. That's just pure Havlicek all over again. Nobody criticized John Havlicek for saying it, though, because he said it in a way that wasn't quite as colorful as Charles, and people didn't like to criticize Havlicek anyway.

"If you're in there trying, you're going to fail sometimes. But if you don't try, you're always going to fail. And you can't be afraid of failure. The worst thing that will happen, the sun will come up and you'll play golf. It just means he's not afraid of the consequences. If he gives it his all, he'll be able to look himself in the mirror and deal with it."

That, to Westphal, is what the concept of "walking the ledge" is all about.

"And what's beyond the ledge, to me, is we know we're giving it our best. A lot of people out there don't know that. It's our life they're talking about. Once you understand that they can't hurt you and you know you're doing your best, then you get to the point where Charles is at: 'Bring them on, say whatever you want, here's something back for you, quote this.' You just don't care about criticism because you know you're doing your best.

"We can walk the ledge, because we know if we fall, we'll get right back up and get on the ledge again."

When you've been around a while, you gain perspective. Westphal has been around a while, even though this was his rookie season as an NBA head coach. He knows what it means to go to the Finals.

"More than anything it was humbling," he said. "I have great respect for Cotton, to have coached as long as he did, and never really have the team to do what our team did this year. But he spent 20 years in the NBA getting the most out of what he had. Then for me to come in the first year and have the team that can do it, I don't take credit for that. I was in the right place at the right time with the right team. You can't expect to be that blessed very often. I don't take it for granted because it doesn't happen to too many people."

Westphal is just as happy for Colangelo.

"His vision was validated," Westphal said. "Jerry has been through a lot of ups and downs. For him to have left Chicago 25 years ago, start out here as an employee, and then end up owning the franchise and turning it around out of the depths, that is great. One of the best memories of the season was when he went with us back to Chicago and we beat Chicago in the regular season, and then we all went out and had a big Italian dinner in his old neighborhood.

"I was happy for Jerry as we kept advancing. That Laker series, the poor guy was dying and all he could do was sit there and watch. He really cares about basketball. He's a businessman and he wants to make money, which nobody can criticize anybody for, but he really loves basketball and he loves this team. He built this palace, sold it out for every game. Every decision he made, it was sound business-wise, or even if it wasn't sound business-wise, if he could find a way to rationalize it or justify it for his team, he did it. An owner like that is hard to come by. He really deserves this success. To see his face during the most successful times is something I'll never forget."

One of those was the club-record 14-game streak through December.

"As we look back on it, it probably could have been around 20," Hollins said. "We blew a couple of games before we started the streak, then the game in San Antonio that would have kept it going for a while. It was exciting.

"And all of those last-second games: Minnesota, down in Dallas, Majerle's three in the Los Angeles game, the ricochet pass in the Portland game, the Orlando game fouling Shaq and he couldn't make the free throws — all of those moments were great. A lot of those game-winners could have missed, and maybe we'd have been 55-27.

"Then coming back from 0-2 and beating the Lakers, beating the Sonics who just knew that they were the better team and they had the great game plan that was going to stop Kevin and stop Charles. To hear them whine about if they hadn't done this, and if Majerle hadn't made all those threes. Then to win the series and knock all the critics back, especially the Eastern media, who thought it was going to be Houston or Seattle coming out of the West.

"Those were all gratifying moments. And obviously, the Finals, having been there as a player and to get back from a coaching perspective, and having the best record, and coaching in the All-Star game were big highlights as well.

"Losing to Chicago was a downer, but even some of the losses we had aren't downers. We played. When the players walked off the court, there were very few games that we didn't leave it all out there."

# Chapter Thirty-two

# REFLECTIONS FROM ON HIGH

Saturday came.

It was a scorcher, the hottest day of the year so far. Before noon on June 26, the temperature already was at 100 degrees on its way to 113.

Phoenix police thought that would deter the crowd for the Suns' appreciation parade downtown, so they'd taken minimal security measures. A purple line was painted just past curbside along the 2.5-mile parade route. Spectators were asked to stand behind it. About 175 extra police were on duty.

Were they in for the surprise of their lives.

By the time the parade started, police estimated that 300,000 people — three times what they anticipated — were on hand. Spectators weren't all standing in neat rows behind the purple lines, either. Many were on rooftops, on parking garage ramps, some even on streetlight poles. Like the Suns, they were ready to do whatever it took.

Sunsmania had taken on a life of its own. It was as if a city was in denial. They refused to let this incredible ride through the silver anniversary season end.

"The way our city and state came together, that's what I'll remember," Colangelo said. "They fell in love with this team, and this team fell in love with them. For me, that is the legacy of this team.

"From everything I've been told, there's never been an event as significant as our parade, witnessed by the 300,000 who were downtown and the 80 percent penetration on television (all three local network affiliates covered it live). That doesn't leave very many other people who were not a part of that whole scene."

The Suns certainly did give the people of Arizona something to be proud of.

"We've been chided for a lot of things over the years — politically, MLK, real estate, all of the things that don't make you feel very good,"

Colangelo said. "Finally something came along that people felt good about. It was an absolutely astounding event that took place. I'll never forget it. It was something so special that it's very difficult to repeat. Now, in my own mind, we had a great dress rehearsal this year, because next year we're coming back for the big dance."

Westphal also was dumbfounded by the reception.

"I'm sure there's a big portion that like the Suns because they think Dan Majerle's cute," he said. "I've run into so many women at the supermarket that say, 'I never liked basketball before but I like it now.' It's something that brings families together. Others might have really felt that the eyes of the world were on them, and made them think it was a bigger deal than it had ever been. Once they all got into it, I think they liked it for the same reason I like it: because these guys are interesting.

"Personally, I never felt that because Charles Keating lives here that this is a bad place. But I'm sure some people are fighting that perception, and that's a big part of it, too."

Hollins said it is reminiscent of his early years of Blazermania.

"Portland had a lukewarm affection for the Blazers. They'd been in the league for six years, and hadn't done anything," he said. "They missed the playoffs by one game the year before we won the championship. It just exploded when we made the playoffs. By the time we got to the Finals, it was sort of like here. There were live news flashes. You'd go downtown and every window had a Go Blazers or a Blazermania sign in it. It was the same feeling that the fans here showed.

"It shows you the magnitude of sports in unifying a community. It's my belief that it's the ability to associate with people who are accomplishing the goals that they set out for. To me, that's what athletes stand for — when you see the work ethic, and the discipline and the teamwork, when you see the taking of God-given ability and accomplishing all that they can accomplish with it."

The first convertibles to roll along the parade route bore front office personnel.

"I think that Jerry and me both were lucky we had sunglasses on because we were crying, because we knew what it meant," Fitzsimmons said. "Not that the players didn't, but we started it together. It became a reality, something we had hoped for, something we had planned, our longest dreams: We were gonna have a good team, were gonna have a new building, people are gonna love this team. Now, we were riding in a parade. It was very emotional for me."

Next came the coaches.

"That was the biggest thrill of the year," Westphal said. "I'm a person that hates parades. You couldn't pay me enough to sit at the Rose Parade and watch it, and that's the greatest parade in the world. Who wants to be in a crowd, be uncomfortable, watching stuff go by? You hear people say, 'I love a parade,' well, I hate a parade. But this was moving.

"Having lost, there's a letdown for the fans as well as the team. But to have however many thousands of people show up on the hottest day of the year, making themselves uncomfortable, lining the sidewalks, and especially to see all these little kids sitting up in front on the curb, sun in their faces, big smiles on their faces, it was definitely the highlight of the year. No question.

"You can get jaded in professional sports but I don't think that that day could fail to move anybody, no matter how jaded, because of the kids and the families that never will get to go to the games. But they had fallen in love with the team and they just wanted to see these guys go by. And it was something.

"It does become show business, and I don't love that part of it. I wish they were all hard-core basketball fans who appreciate the pick-and-roll and love guys who can get down and play defense. But that's not how you draw those people. There are other things. They see this international celebrity, Charles Barkley. It's great that there's something about the whole show that excites that many people. It's fun to be a part of it."

Finally, the players were rolled out.

As the parade progressed, the crowd violated the purple line as badly as Barkley violates a defender in the low post. Slowly, the crowd advanced to nearly the middle of the street so it could actually touch the players as they passed.

They saved the best for last. And he didn't last long.

Barkley's car had traveled barely two blocks. The crowd surrounded it. The driver had to stop. Even Barkley had a terrified expression on his face. The people were peaceful and meant well, but this had the makings of a mob scene. Police quickly formed a human cordon around Barkley and escorted him out of the car, through the crowd, and back into the arena. He was out of the parade, to the disappointment of hundreds of thousands of people.

While the remainder of the parade made its way along the route, Barkley was taken to the fourth-floor balcony of Colangelo's office overlooking a courtyard. The balcony would serve as the podium for a post-parade ceremony.

Barkley quickly got on the microphone and explained that he'd been relieved of his parade duty for everybody's safety. Just seeing him and hearing him was enough to satisfy most of the fans.

"We never expected this many people to show up," Barkley said.

It was a scary moment. People just attacked the car. Everyone was excited, but there were just too many people.

It might have been the largest gathering ever in Arizona. The annual Fiesta Bowl Parade has drawn nearly 300,000 at its peak. Even a visit by Pope John Paul II in 1987 drew fewer than 100,000 spectators outside St. Mary's Church only three blocks from Colangelo's pulpit.

"I don't think the fans realize that we didn't win," Barkley said.

One police officer suffered a sprained ankle while escorting Barkley away. Other than that, the huge crowd was peaceful and appreciative.

"They can't be no more depressed than we are about losing to Chicago," Barkley said. "Sometimes it doesn't work out the way you hoped. We're one of the two best basketball teams in the world. We had a chance at it. Nobody else had a chance at it. Just look forward to next year.

"I started feeling bad on Monday. I actually could not believe that we lost. I don't think I realized it until Monday night. Nobody feels worse than I do. This is my life. I ain't got nothing to think about all summer other than we didn't win the championship."

Finally, the parade ended and many flocked to the courtyard beneath Colangelo's balcony, clinging to the final words from the people to whom they'd become so attached.

"Really, the thing I thought about as I was standing up there was how far we've come over 25 years," Van Arsdale said. "I thought about being back at the Coliseum when there were 2,500, maybe 3,000 people in there. I don't think the Bulls have gripped that city the way we gripped Phoenix this year. You can't go anyplace, and I'm not even playing anymore. That's all they want to talk about. It looked like an appearance by the Pope, didn't it?"

Hollins found it all a bit scary.

"Somebody up on the balcony raised their arms, and 300,000 people raised their arms," he said. "I was a little uncomfortable with that."

To Robertson, who'd worked so long to come up through the ranks, it was an eye-opening morning.

"That was one of the most moving experiences I've ever had," he said. "Not so much standing on the balcony, but riding in that car in the parade. I found people to be orderly, very warm. Any sign that you directed toward them was reflected back to you by hundreds of people at a time, either verbally, or physically in some manner. And you saw all ages, from little bitty children, who in many cases were not even sure what was going on, to elderly people who all felt some love for the Suns and wanted to be a part of this season in some way.

"It was a shock to everybody when the season was over. People were on a roll, they were on this ride, they were swept along in this tide, and they were not prepared for it to end. They gave lip service to the fact that it might end, but they were not prepared. None of us were. And the way it ended so abruptly, people wanted to, and still want to, hold onto this thing. There are remnants everywhere now — signs still in cars, signs in windows of houses and places of business.

"I started out in one of the smallest high schools in the state of Louisiana. We only had 35 boys in the whole high school, and for me to be able to stand up on that balcony and ride in that parade, I could never have envisioned that ever happening. And it was quite a thrill for me."

Westphal, like Hollins, is uncomfortable with the adulation. It's OK to love the Suns for who they are and what they did, but don't worship them, he said.

"It's a fine line. I hope we never cross it, but we probably have for some people," he said. "I caution about overcelebrating. I really feel strongly about that. I caution about too much fanaticism."

The players are used to it.

"Standing on the balcony seeing all those people, I have to be honest with you, I think Jerry, myself, Paul, Lionel were probably more moved by it than any of the players, and it was a great feeling," Fitzsimmons said. "I'm happy for Jerry, who is willing to put his life out there on the line, credit-wise and everything else, in order to get this done. It's happened, and it makes me feel very good. For Paul to step in and be so successful, it's a dream come true. We came up just a little short, we're not gonna give up hope because we're gonna be back there next year."

"I've been back with the Suns six years now. I've had mostly good times, some pretty traumatic times, trying to reshape the team. I traded away and gave away some of the Suns' favorite players. That wasn't a happy thing. I knew we'd take heat for it but we had to do it. I guess the best way to describe it would be an incredible six years. People keep asking me, 'Well what does the Senior Executive Vice President do?' I take Barkley's car home when he goes on vacation. I'm basically Jerry's right-hand man because he's left-handed, and he uses that pretty good. I'm proud of not just the team but the basketball operation because six years ago, we didn't have a basketball operation."

Colangelo said he could recall when the building was completed and he went out on the balcony one day and looked out over downtown Phoenix.

"I must tell you the thought crossed my mind: What would it be like to win a championship and look down from this balcony and see people wall to wall, body to body?" Colangelo said. "We didn't get a championship, but that vision was there. We have the perfect setting. This season was memorable, but my, oh my, just think how great it's going to be when we win it all."

The program was now well under way when Barkley stepped back up to the podium as the crowd roared its approval. He spared hundreds of thousands of people a blinding by wearing a baseball cap over his shiny head under the midday sun.

"We did not come here to be runners-up," Barkley said. " I think we should all do this again next year, but next time we'll have the championship."

Check out these other exciting sports titles from Sagamore Publishing.

## To order with check or money order:

Send order (book cost plus $3.50 shipping for 1st book; $.50 for each additional book) to:

Sagamore Publishing
P.O. Box 647
Champaign IL  61824-0647